Blue Pawn
Red Pawn

And the Communist Party of
Vietnam's Gambit for Legitimacy

The **ISEAS – Yusof Ishak Institute** (formerly Institute of Southeast Asian Studies) is an autonomous organization established in 1968. It is a regional centre dedicated to the study of socio-political, security, and economic trends and developments in Southeast Asia and its wider geostrategic and economic environment. The Institute's research programmes are grouped under Regional Economic Studies (RES), Regional Strategic and Political Studies (RSPS), and Regional Social and Cultural Studies (RSCS). The Institute is also home to the ASEAN Studies Centre (ASC), the Singapore APEC Study Centre, and the Temasek History Research Centre (THRC).

ISEAS Publishing, an established academic press, has issued more than 2,000 books and journals. It is the largest scholarly publisher of research about Southeast Asia from within the region. ISEAS Publishing works with many other academic and trade publishers and distributors to disseminate important research and analyses from and about Southeast Asia to the rest of the world.

Blue Pawn
Red Pawn

And the Communist Party of Vietnam's Gambit for Legitimacy

Nguyen Hoang Thanh Danh

ISEAS YUSOF ISHAK
INSTITUTE

First published in Singapore in 2025 by
ISEAS Publishing
30 Heng Mui Keng Terrace
Singapore 119614
E-mail: publish@iseas.edu.sg
Website: http://bookshop.iseas.edu.sg

The responsibility for facts and opinions in this publication rests exclusively with the author and his interpretations do not necessarily reflect the views or the policy of the publisher or its supporters.

ISEAS Library Cataloguing-in-Publication Data

Name(s): Nguyen, Hoang Thanh Danh, author.
Title: Blue pawn, red pawn and the Communist Party of Vietnam's gambit for legitimacy / by Nguyen Hoang Thanh Danh.
Description: Singapore : ISEAS – Yusof Ishak Institute, February 2025. | Series: Indochina Unit ; 24 | Includes bibliographic references and index.
Identifiers: ISBN 978-981-5203-95-0 (soft cover) | ISBN 978-981-5203-96-7 (ebook PDF) | ISBN 978-981-5203-97-4 (epub)
Subjects: LCSH: Đảng cộng sản Việt Nam. | Communism—Vietnam. | Democracy—Vietnam. | Elections—Vietnam. | Vietnam—Politics and government.
Classification: LCC JQ898 D293N574

In Vietnamese, "Blue Pawn, Red Pawn" (*quân xanh* and *quân đỏ*, respectively) refers to selections with preordained outcomes. Blue pawns represent token candidates while red pawns represent candidates with guaranteed selection. Although commonly associated with elections, this concept permeates many aspects of life in Vietnam, from contract bidding and job interviews to entrance exams.

On the cover of the book, two senior voters in red and blue traditional Vietnamese *Áo Dài Khăn Đóng* attire are seen examining the ballot before voting takes place. Voters of advanced age and high social standing are often invited by election officials to take on such roles.

Cover design by Lee Meng Hui
Index compiled by Sheryl Sin Bing Peng
Typesetting by International Typesetters Pte Ltd
Printed in Singapore by Markono Print Media Pte Ltd

To Mom, a most dedicated Party member, and a greater mother, still.

Gửi Mẹ, một Đảng viên kiên trung, và hơn thế, một người Mẹ vĩ đại.

Contents

List of tab Les

List of fi GURes

Preface

The Party is absolute.

Being born into a family steeped in communist traditions shortly after the initiation of *Doi Moi*, I, like most of the children of my generation, took certain truths for granted—one being "the Party is absolute." Our textbooks were filled with narratives of the Party's glorious victories and monumental achievements. Adults around us would scorn and even punish us for any perceived disrespect towards the Party's leaders, even if unintentional. Stepping outside, banners in bright red proclaimed, "Long live the glorious Communist Party of Vietnam." We spent numerous days each year celebrating the Party's milestones like the birth of Ho Chi Minh, the foundation of the Party, the battle of Dien Bien Phu and the liberation of the South. Children as young as nine were required to join the Ho Chi Minh Young Pioneer Organization and don the red scarf, which represents the socialist ideology and the blood of those who fought and died for the country under the leadership of the Party.

As a naturally curious and somewhat troublesome child, I often found myself in hot water for asking questions or expressing myself in ways that were not welcomed. I vividly remember my grandfather, a veteran of the First Indochina War, furiously tearing up my innocent parody poetry about Ho Chi Minh. While my friends found it humorous, it was the first time I saw my grandfather that angry. That incident quashed my aspirations of becoming a poet.

In university, I was appointed as the political commissar of my class, likely due to my academic achievements and my family's loyalty to the

Party. After graduating, I was invited to a "Party membership preparation class", a stepping stone to becoming a full-fledged Party member. In my final report, I criticized the Party's governance and economic policies. Only one person failed that class.

Moving overseas for higher education provided me with opportunities to speak with both refugees who had fled Vietnam post-1975 and foreign scholars studying the country. Their perspectives on the Communist Party of Vietnam starkly contrasted with what I had experienced back home as many among them considered the Party to be an oppressive, authoritarian regime that subjugated the Vietnamese people while yielding to China.

Even within Vietnam, support for the Party was not universal. My father, hailing from the South, would often rant about his disillusionment with communism when drunk. Whispers of high-ranking officials' misconduct circulated within my family, especially from those in law enforcement, often surfacing even before any news coverage, if that misconduct was covered by state-run media at all. Yet, despite acknowledging the systemic corruption, there was a pervasive belief in the defence of the Party's survival, summed up in the Vietnamese saying, "*còn Đảng, còn mình*"—the survival of the Party ensures our own.

I began working on this book in 2015 as part of my doctoral dissertation to find the answer to the question: Is the Party absolute? Much has changed since then, both in Vietnam's political landscape and in my personal journey as a curious child seeking answer. I have been rejected interviews and endorsement many times due to the "reactionary" nature of my research. I have even been warned that going forward with this topic could get me in trouble. On the other hand, a reviewer once criticized my book as pro-communist propaganda, accusing me of lacking the courage to critique the Party.

In this book, I wanted to present the truth as it is, and let readers decide whether it is a piece of reactionary literature, pro-communist propaganda or something else.

a cknowledgements

Although I stand as the sole author of this book, it is not solely my work. There are many people to whom I owe thanks for their contributions; without them, this book would never have been published.

Firstly, I would like to express my heartfelt gratitude to my academic mentor, Professor Shiraishi Masaya, for his tireless guidance of my research, limitless patience and immense knowledge. Without his invaluable input, my dissertation would not have become the book it is today.

The draft of my book has undergone many reviews; each time, major changes were made, adding new layers of content. Looking back, I can hardly recognize the draft it once was, and for the better. For this, I have the reviewers at Waseda University Press and the ISEAS – Yusof Ishak Institute to thank. Some of them, I believe, are more well-versed in many topics discussed in this book than I am, and their contributions have made the book much more worth reading and enjoyable to read.

The Ministry of Education, Culture, Sports, Science, and Technology of Japan and the ISEAS – Yusof Ishak Institute deserve my deepest gratitude for their financial support and the opportunity to make this book available to readers.

I would like to express my heartfelt thanks to all the brave people who accepted my requests for surveys and interviews and provided me with invaluable information about the inner workings of the Party, the electoral system and the press in Vietnam. I believe that they all sincerely wish for the betterment of their country, although in different ways. I hope to make this book available to them in Vietnamese in the future.

Lastly, I would like to convey my gratitude to my mother and my wife. My mother, a veteran Party member and former government official, despite her fears about my work, sacrificed a great deal of her influence to help me secure priceless interviews and materials on topics which are considered taboo in Vietnam. My wife, a Vietnamese citizen, shared my mother's concerns but provided me with encouragement and companionship throughout my years of struggle all the same.

Glossary

ANTD	An Ninh Thu Do, Lit. Capital Security, official mouthpiece of Hanoi Public Security.
ASEAN	Association of Southeast Asian Nations
BBC	British Broadcasting Corporation
CAND	Cong An Nhan Dan, Lit. The People's Public Security, official mouthpiece of the Ministry of Public Security
CPV	Communist Party of Vietnam
EU	European Union
Nhan Dan	Lit. The People, official mouthpiece of the Communist Party of Vietnam
PAPI	Viet Nam Provincial Governance and Public Administration Performance Index
PAV	People's Army of Vietnam
VOA	Voice of America
VOV	Voice of Vietnam
VTV	Vietnam Television

1

Introduction

On 10 June 2018, thousands of protesters flooded the streets of Hanoi, the capital of Vietnam, and other major cities during a week-long series of demonstrations that saw both widespread offline and online dissident activities. The demonstrations came two days before the final vote on the Special Economic Zone Act was scheduled to take place.[1] The Special Economic Zone Act is a law that would enable the government to lease land in three designated economic zones to foreign entities for up to ninety-nine years.[2] Protesters were met by large cordons of police officers who attempted to contain the demonstration. The demonstrations were, for the most part, peaceful; however, footage has surfaced on the internet showing police officers and individuals who appeared to be plainclothes officers dragging protesters into police cars and unmarked vans.

The protests received extensive media coverage overseas while state-controlled media inside Vietnam kept their coverage of the incident to a minimum. Domestic media outlets reported that people in many localities took to the streets, causing social disorder and that the police detained some protesters.[3] Ultimately, perhaps partly due to the pressure arising from the protests, the National Assembly of Vietnam gave in and voted to postpone the implementation of the bill indefinitely.

This was not the first time Vietnamese took to the street to express their dissatisfaction. Large scale protests erupted across Vietnam in May 2014 in response to the deployment of a Chinese oil rig in the disputed waters of the South China Sea, which was perceived as an illegal and aggressive move by the Vietnamese. The demonstrations quickly escalated into riots with as many as 20,000 protesters torching and looting foreign-owned factories. Subsequent clashes between the police and rioters resulted in at least twenty-one people killed and almost one hundred wounded.[4] In 2016, a series of demonstrations were held from May until as late as December to protest the dumping of toxic waste into the coastal waters of Ha Tinh, Quang Binh, Quang Tri and Thua Thien–Hue provinces in Central Vietnam by a Taiwanese steel plant. Prolonged exposure to toxic substances discharged from Formosa's steel plant through drainage pipes resulted in a massive number of dead fishes found washed up on shore, endangering the life of the locals whose livelihoods depend heavily on fishing.[5] Unapologetic and combative remarks from the management of the steel plant further angered the victims, and demonstrations spread nationwide.[6]

Despite those protests and demonstrations, the CPV's authority has remained unshaken. The Party, founded in 1930 and ascended to power during the final months of the Second World War, has been the sole ruling party of a unified Vietnam since 1976. The CPV emerged victorious after multiple wars and even survived the collapse of the Soviet Union, which had caused the downfall of many other communist regimes. In 1986, the Party implemented a series of economic reforms known collectively as *Doi Moi*, which transformed Vietnam's ruined economy into one of the fastest growing in the world. The CPV's ability to survive and maintain its political domination over Vietnam's politics is particularly remarkable considering Vietnam had been constantly at war and faced economic sanctions and diplomatic isolation until the 1990s.

The resilience of communist regimes has been extensively studied following the collapse of the Soviet Union when regime changes took place in dozens of countries. Regimes with adequate preparedness and adaptiveness, possessing effective state apparatus and sufficient legitimacy, and facing little pressure from the West would often find themselves resilient to the shocks and upheaval of crises. Regimes lacking these conditions would be weakened or overthrown. The elements upon which the survivability of a regime depends could be divided into external and internal factors.

External factors include the global and regional political environment, Western linkage and leverage, which favours democratization, and black knight support, such as that provided China and Russia, which generally helps to prolong the existence of the regime. If an authoritarian country is located in a democratic neighbourhood, the likelihood of democratization is higher.[7, 8] Huntington argued that the democratization of a country in a non-democratic neighbourhood would have a profound impact on its neighbouring countries by revealing the possibility and incentives for democratization and by encouraging political opposition in those countries, as well as providing an example of what kind of strategies could be used to challenge a dictatorial ruling regime.[9] Bunce and Wolchik[10] pointed out several cases in which a sufficiently strong political opposition movement could push for electoral changes, not only in their own country but also in neighbouring non-democratic regimes. Nevertheless, as shown by Way, despite successful electoral revolutions in Armenia in 2003 and 2008 and Azerbaijan in 2003 and 2005, regime change through elections failed in other countries in the same region.[11] This reveals that as much as political challengers can learn from the lessons of their neighbours, ruling regimes can also learn from the failures of other authoritarian regimes elsewhere to strengthen their grip on power.[12]

According to the Economist's Democracy Index in 2023, six of the ten Southeast Asian countries (excluding Brunei) are considered flawed democracies, while four are authoritarian regimes.[13, 14] During the Vietnam War, certain Southeast Asian countries such as Thailand

and the Philippines openly opposed the communist North Vietnam, even sending troops to fight alongside the US Army and the Army of South Vietnam. However, since Vietnam's withdrawal from Cambodia in 1989 and become a full member of ASEAN, the overall regional environment has become much more favourable to the long-term survival of the CPV. ASEAN's fundamental principles do not mention democracy, instead they emphasize values such as mutual respect for independence, sovereignty, territorial integrity, national identity and non-interference in internal affairs. ASEAN members do not concern themselves much with the political system of their neighbours, as long as the regime in question does not threaten regional stability. Therefore, diplomatic and economic pressure on Vietnam to democratize primarily originates from Western countries, such as the United States and the European Union, rather than from its neighbours. In contrast, diplomatic and economic ties with Russia and China support the continuity of the current regime. The CPV has been successful so far in balancing its foreign relations, which in turn contributes to the regime's survivability.

Internal factors can be divided into "hard" and "soft" aspects. The "hard" aspect includes the organizational power of the ruling regime and its performance, which can be evaluated through statistics such as the number of members of the ruling party, the number of police officers, GDP per capita and the like. On the other hand, the "soft" aspect, meaning the regime's legitimacy, is harder to evaluate and tends to be overlooked.

Among the "hard" and "soft" internal factors, Bellin,[15] Way,[16] and Levitsky and Way[17] argue that a regime's resilience primarily depends on its organizational power which includes institutional establishment, the organization of the ruling party, and the loyalty of the military and law enforcement apparatus. Additionally, Tuong asserts that effective economic policies for a state's industrial development is as important as the regime's cohesive structure.[18] In the case of Vietnam, Shiraishi also mentions that the flexibility of the state's structure established by the CPV's leadership and its socioeconomic policies were the main reasons for its resilience.[19]

Stable and well-connected organizational structure reduces the risk of regime change from within and the security apparatus serves as a deterrent against disobedience and can be deployed to control and suppress mass protests and riots if necessary. The primary function of this security apparatus is to maintain order for the ruling regime using intimidation and even violence. "Low-intensity" activities may include denying political opposition access to basic social services, imposing special taxes or attacking dissidents using plainclothes collaborators.[20] The threat of harassment, detainment and prosecution can discourage opposition from openly opposing the ruling regime.

The CPV has also successfully used "low-intensity" activities through its law-enforcement apparatus to intimidate and restrict opposition and dissidents, which keeps the formation of domestic political opposition in check. Thayer emphasizes the repressive role of four key state organs in bolstering Vietnam's one-party state: the Ministry of Public Security, the People's Armed Security Force, the General Directorate II (military intelligence) and the Ministry of Culture and Information,[21] which play a vital role in the survival of the regime.[22]

Abuza notes that the Politburo, which serves as the command centre of the CPV, is a select elite group that fiercely monopolizes political power and prevents the growth of civil society.[23] However, Thayer argues that the CPV, despite projecting a united front to the public, is deeply divided internally, and its organs of oppression are controlled by Politburo leaders who engage in factional infighting.[24]

Nevertheless, although factional infighting has always been a common occurrence within the Party, its highest-level members have always been in consensus regarding the CPV's political domination. This consensus has been one of the main driving forces behind the Party's ability to survive. Despite infighting and internal purges throughout the history of the CPV, such as the Nhan Van–Giai Pham affair between 1955 and 1958 or the prosecution of anti-communist revisionists between 1963 and 1967,[25] the CPV has been able to maintain a relatively stable institutional establishment, a cohesive organizational structure, and a loyal military and law enforcement apparatus. The CPV's tenacity is a testament to its organizational power.

According to Thayer, this organizational power can be compromised on three counts. Firstly, the robust centralized authority of the CPV faces potential erosion from state organs at the subnational level, which historically have demonstrated a degree of autonomy or resistance to central directives. Secondly, the Party leadership is internally divided regarding the speed and breadth of economic, political and social reforms. Thirdly, since the mid-1980s, Vietnam has implemented economic reforms aimed at establishing a market economy with socialist characteristics, leading to significant societal changes, particularly in communication technology, including the proliferation of mobile phones, satellite television and the internet. In combination with a growing number of Vietnamese students pursue education abroad annually, this has resulted in increased contestation in state-society relations.[26]

Dimitrov suggests that the lifespan of a communist regime depends on four types of adaptations that help it expand its support base beyond the electorate. These adaptations include the introduction of economic reforms, policies to promote inclusiveness of both reform winners and reform losers, institutionalization of horizontal and vertical accountability, for example, parliamentary query sessions or offices that directly receive and respond to citizens' complaints, and the modification and reinvigoration of communist ideology based on nationalism to make it more appealing to both ordinary citizens and intellectuals.[27]

There are other measures that authoritarian regimes can take to strengthen their rule, such as compromising and power-sharing with different social groups to discourage them from rebelling against the regime's rule,[28] improving elite cohesion that aims to reduce the risk of betrayal and defection within the ranks of the leadership and organizing popular movements to manage and weather political crises.[29]

Nathan,[30] Brownlee[31] and Magaloni[32] argue that creating a meritocratic system that rewards cadres for exhibiting favourable attitudes and actions while punishing disobedience can be used to encourage party members to remain loyal. However, meritocratic systems may become problematic during political or economic crises, as the Party may be forced to reduce the rewards for its members and be unable to maintain their loyalty. Bratton and van de Walle,[33] Geddes,[34] Nathan[35] and Hale[36] suggest that an authoritarian party can consolidate internal power by arranging a system of power-sharing among its most powerful members. By establishing norms and procedures for succession, the Party's leadership ensures that disagreements among its top members are kept to a minimum and that the Party's hierarchy remains undisturbed. Furthermore, the leadership would remain resistant to challenges from the public or their political opposition.

In Vietnam, the most visible example of a system of power-sharing at the top level is the Politburo, which usually includes more than a dozen of the most powerful politicians. Although from time to time, certain powerful decision-makers can dominate this collective leadership, such as the cases of Le Duan in the 1970s and 1980s and Nguyen Phu Trong from the 2010s until his death in 2024, no politician in Vietnam has been able to reach the level of power comparable to Stalin or the paramount leaders of the Chinese Communist Party.

Empirical studies conducted by Geddes,[37] Brownlee[38] and Magaloni[39] have shown that highly institutionalized authoritarian ruling parties with more effective, functional organizations tend to be more durable compared to parties lacking those qualities. In such cases, the ruling party often establishes patronage in which only those loyal to the Party can enjoy access to financial support, political positions and other privileges. In many cases, the Party goes further by officially adopting a political ideology that helps to bind its members together. This is especially true for parties that have risen to power through armed struggle and violent revolution.[40]

In Vietnam, institutional establishment takes many forms, from the pro-communist grassroots movements under the Vietnamese Fatherland Front to the myriads of state-owned enterprises. The CPV and the institutions under its umbrella are further bound by its political ideology, Marxism-Leninism and Ho Chi Minh Thought. This cohesion is bolstered by a decades-long history of armed struggles. Hai argues that the institutional establishment helped the CPV to successfully restore and maintain public trust, kept its opposition in check at home and smartly reduced external pressures. The institutional establishment under the control of the CPV has proven relatively effective in countering the formation of new social forces.[41] Although civil societies are formed, so far, they have been unable to demand significant changes from the ruling regime, nor could they meaningfully threaten its institutional establishment.

An unwritten system of cadre nomination for leadership positions exists, where young and promising government employees, referred to as *cán bộ nguồn* (potential cadres), are earmarked for leadership roles. Prospective candidates are groomed early and are usually selected to work as a political commissar. Up-and-coming cadres are expected to maintain a patron-client relationship with a higher-ranking official, which, in turn, forms a faction. Multiple factions exist within a body of government, competing for power and influence. Upon the uneventful retirement of the head of such faction, the leadership position is usually passed to the next in line. In rarer cases, the downfall of the leading senior politician may lead to the collapse of the whole faction.

In addition to a regime's organizational power and internal security apparatus, many scholars argue that its performance, which can be observed through economic growth and the distribution of wealth, is one of the most important elements that contributes to the resilience of that regime. Huntington points out that to maintain long-term popular support and enhance its political resilience during crises, an authoritarian regime would also need remarkable economic performance and firm control over natural resources. Regardless of how they rose to power, non-democratic regimes often cling to their power through violent revolutions and maintain political legitimacy not via free and fair elections, but by the values attributed to them by their subjects.[42] As a result, to remain in power, these non-democratic regimes must compensate for their lack of democratic constitutionality with economic growth and the improvement of the living standards of their citizens.

According to Przeworski and Limongi[43] and Geddes,[44] dictatorial regimes that achieve high enough GDP per capita and mitigate the negative impact of economic crises to avoid slowdowns will have a higher chance of remaining in power. Shiraishi[45] attributed the survivability of the CPV to the successful adaptation of the market economy under a socialist one-party political regime. According to Hiep, socioeconomic performance as the result of the adoption of *Doi Moi* served as the single most important source of legitimacy for the CPV in the twenty-first century.[46]

However, economic development and the betterment of living standards have not always been enough to justify the rule of authoritarian regimes in contemporary politics. As early as the late 1950s, modernization theorists like Lipset,[47] Rostow,[48] and Huntington[49] suggested that economic development could destabilize society by introducing new social forces that cannot be controlled through established institutions, especially in the case of authoritarian regimes. This issue, however, proved to be less acute with regimes that are extremely rich in natural resources, most notably in some Arab countries where despite living standards and GDP per capita being comparable to those of developed Western countries, social forces that would push for political changes have failed to form. Van de Walle[50] and Way[51] explained this phenomenon by positing that by distributing a portion of their massive wealth, which originated from their vast natural resources (e.g., oil reserves) among the population, those ruling regimes had created a dependent middle class that must rely on it for their material well-being. For less-fortunate authoritarian regimes that are not blessed with immense natural wealth, economic development could help strengthen the legitimacy of their rules, while economic downturns and recessions could negatively impact this legitimacy.

However, economic performance alone would be insufficient to make up for erosion of other sources of legitimacy. While the living standards of the Vietnamese have been increasing since the initiation of *Doi Moi*, the same could be said about social inequality and corruption. Vietnamese citizens can also compare their living standards to those of people in Western democratic countries thanks to the influx of information through the internet and cross-border movement of people, and this is a source of dissatisfaction. Furthermore, prosperity achieved through the introduction of the market economy contradicts the communist creed, which requires the CPV to redefine their version of communism.

Thayer argues that since the mid-1980s, Vietnam has undergone profound political, economic and social changes, leading to increased accessibility to information for ordinary citizens.[52] Market reforms have enabled the formalization of a private sector and spurred grassroots civil society initiatives. This surge in information dissemination and civil society activism has prompted a re-evaluation of state-society dynamics, including the applicability of the Leninist model.[53] Consequently, scepticism has arisen regarding the correlation between Vietnam's economic achievements and the socialist ideology espoused by the ruling CPV.

Economic crises, such as the 2008 financial crisis or the COVID-19 recession, not only slow down growth, which is detrimental to the CPV's performance legitimacy, but also make social inequality and corruption more evident to the public, which damages socialism as the Party's official state-building ideology. Nhu and Tuong argue that while Vietnam's economy is now integrated into the global economy, the lack of effective leadership has led to its low position in global value chains and heavy reliance on China. This has resulted in mounting challenges facing the CPV in various sectors of the society, including workers, media, universities and state-owned enterprises, decades after the initiation of *Doi Moi*.[54]

Malesky examines the political landscape of Vietnam in 2013, focusing on the constitutional drafting process and the unprecedented confidence vote in the National Assembly. These events unfolded against the backdrop of the nation's persistent economic challenges, elite political competition, growing international engagement and an increasingly informed populace, influenced by a dynamic blogosphere. He asserts that forthcoming Vietnamese leaders must prioritize performance over relying solely on patriotic sentiment for legitimacy in the contemporary context.[55]

While agreeing that performance legitimacy is important to maintain the obedient-worthiness of the CPV, Thayer maintains that traditionally, the legitimacy of the CPV has arisen from other sources such as military victories against foreign forces and the charismatic legitimacy that the Party's leadership inherited from Ho Chi Minh.[56] Thayer also argues that Vietnam has attempted to base its legitimacy on rational-legal norms through the adoption of the 1992 Constitution and legislation. The CPV has endeavoured to reinforce its rational-legal authority in territories under its control by holding elections and passing laws soon after seizing power from the occupying Japanese in August 1945. The ratification of the 1992 Constitution of the Socialist Republic of Vietnam is just one example of the CPV's continuous efforts to uphold the rule of law.[57] Thayer argues that the traditional sources of legitimacy for the CPV have been exhausted, and that attempts to adopt alternative legitimization models have been ineffective. However, he and Hiep also note that nationalism has been revived as an additional source of legitimacy due to the emergence of conflict in the South China Sea.[58]

The CPV understands clearly the vital importance of political legitimacy to its survival and has been adaptive to changes by adopting strategies suitable to its situational needs. During wartime, this had helped the Party to gain a massive popular base to support its war efforts, while during peacetime it had allowed the CPV to openly take responsibility for its failed economic policies and launch reforms.[59]

Prior to *Doi Moi*, the legitimacy of the CPV had been founded on tradition-based achievements and values, Ho Chi Minh's charismatic leadership and socialism as a state-building ideology. However, with the evident failure of communism worldwide, economic development started to become an increasingly important source of the Party's legitimacy. With rapid economic development and the betterment of people's living standards, Vietnam had experienced a great deal of political stability. Nevertheless, even though Vietnam continued to enjoy an annual GDP growth rate of more than 6 per cent even amid the 2017–18 global financial crisis, the early 2010s saw increasing social unrest. Policies and actions of the CPV were being challenged from inside the country, a phenomenon uncommon for more than two decades. This suggests that the political legitimacy that the CPV had been enjoying has become less effective in preventing people from questioning, and to some extent, challenging its rule. To reinforce its legitimacy, the CPV has resorted to a combination of tactics, from persecuting dissidents to starting anti-corruption campaigns and using propaganda to emphasize its democratic legitimacy through elections.

Scholars studying post-Soviet Vietnam often overlook the soft aspect of the CPV's rule for two reasons. Firstly, the "hard" aspects of CPV resilience, such as its well-established organization, loyal military and law enforcement apparatus, and rapid economic growth are often prioritized. Secondly, even when the significance of legitimacy is acknowledged, evaluating its impact on the resilience of an authoritarian regime poses a daunting challenge. While the "hard aspects" of regime resilience can be measured using statistics like GDP, GDP per capita and the size of the police force or military, there is no universally accepted metric to statistically evaluate legitimacy. A comprehensive understanding of the CPV's resilience against all odds requires a thorough examination of its legitimacy, as mere numbers alone cannot explain the defeat of the United States in the Vietnam War or the CPV's ability to survive after the collapse of the Eastern Bloc. This book aims to demystify this elusive aspect of CPV rule, with a specific focus on its claim on democratic legitimacy through legislative elections and the National Assembly.

This book consists of seven chapters. Chapter One is the introductory chapter. Chapter Two explores the pillars of the CPV's legitimacy, excluding its democratic claim. Chapter Three investigates the factors prompting the CPV to increasingly emphasize its democratic legitimacy. Chapter Four analyses documents and leadership statements from the CPV's inception to the present, arguing for the consistent assertion of democratic legitimacy in those. Chapter Five provides a comprehensive examination of Vietnam's National Assembly elections and the Assembly's structure, exploring its functions within contemporary Vietnamese politics. Chapter Six presents findings from two surveys conducted shortly after the 2016 and 2021 National Assembly elections, assessing Vietnamese perceptions of democracy and elections. These surveys illuminate the effectiveness of CPV propaganda efforts, revealing a generally positive view of democracy among Vietnamese voters. However, while many Vietnamese citizens are aware that the CPV has been using a rigged system called *"quân xanh, quân đỏ"* (blue pawn: a token candidate; red pawn: a candidate who is more or less guaranteed election) to select delegates for the National Assembly, with the elections serving as a façade to legitimize it, they generally exhibit indifference and tolerance towards CPV rule. The last chapter provides the conclusion of the book.

Notes

1. *VOA Vietnamese*, "Bùng nổ biểu tình chống Luật Đặc khu, nhiều người bị bắt" [Anti-Special Economic Zone Act demonstrations erupted, many arrested], 11 June 2018, https://www.voatiengviet.com/a/nổ-ra-biểu-tình-chống-luật-đặc-khu-nhiều-người-bị-bắt/4432357.html (accessed 7 July 2024).
2. *An ninh Thủ đô*, "Luật Đặc khu sẽ không còn thời hạn thuê đất 99 năm" [The Special Economic Zone Act no longer has 99-year lease], 8 June 2018, https://anninhthudo. vn/chinh-tri-xa-hoi/luat-dac-khu-se-khong-con-thoi-han-thue-dat-99-nam/770733.antd (accessed 7 July 2024).
3. *VnExpress*, "Người dân nhiều địa phương xuống đường gây náo loạn" [People in many localities pour into the streets causing disorder], 10 June 2018, https://VnExpress. net/tin-tuc/thoi-su/nguoi-dan-nhieu-dia-phuong-xuong-duong-gay-nao-loan-3761525. html (accessed 7 July 2024).
4. Kate Hodal and Jonathan Kaiman, "At Least 21 Dead in Vietnam Anti-China Protests over Oil Rig", *The Guardian*, 15 May 2014, https://www.theguardian.com/world/2014/ may/15/vietnam-anti-china-protests-oil-rig-dead-injured (accessed 7 July 2024).
5. BBC, "Biểu tình phản đối Formosa tại Hà Tĩnh" [Anti-Formosa demonstrations in Ha Tinh], 13 December 2016, https://www.bbc.com/vietnamese/vietnam-38293486 (accessed 7 July 2024).
6. BBC, "Vietnam Protests over Mystery Fish Deaths", 1 May 2016, https://www.bbc. com/news/world-asia-36181575 (accessed 7 July 2024).
7. Gleditsch Kristian Skrede and Michael D. Ward, "Diffusion and the International Context of Democratization", *International Organization* 60, no. 4 (2006): 911–33.
8. Brinks Daniel and Michael Coppedge, "Diffusion Is No Illusion: Neighbor Emulation in the Third Wave of Democracy", *Comparative Political Studies* 39, no. 4 (2006): 463–89.

9. P. Samuel Huntington, *The Third Wave: Democratization in the Late 20th Century* (Oklahoma: University of Oklahoma Press, 1991), pp. 85–95.
10. Valerie Bunce and Sharon L. Wolchik, "Favorable Conditions and Electoral Revolutions", *Journal of Democracy* 17 (2006): 5–18.
11. Lucan A. Way, "The Real Causes of the Color Revolutions", *Journal of Democracy* 19 (2008): 55–69.
12. Thomas Carothers, "The Backlash against Democracy Promotion", *Foreign Affairs* 85 (2006): 55–68.
13. The Economist Intelligence Unit, "Democracy Index 2023", 2023, https://www.eiu.com/n/campaigns/democracy-index-2023/ (accessed 7 July 2024).
14. The six flawed democracies are East Timor, Indonesia, Malaysia, the Philippines, Singapore and Thailand. The four authoritarian regimes are Cambodia, Laos, Myanmar and Vietnam.
15. Eva Bellin, "Reconsidering the Robustness of Authoritarianism in the Middle East: Lessons from the Arab Spring", *Comparative Politics* 44 (2012): 127–49.
16. Way, "The Real Causes of the Color Revolutions", pp. 59–62.
17. Steven Levitsky and Lucan A. Way, *Competitive Authoritarianism: Hybrid Regimes after the Cold War* (Cambridge: Cambridge University Press, 2010), pp. 7–8.
18. Tuong Vu, *Paths to Development in Asia: South Korea, Vietnam, China, and Indonesia* (Cambridge: Cambridge University Press, 2010).
19. Masaya Shiraishi, ベトナムの国家機構 [The Structure of the Vietnamese State] (Tokyo: Akashi Shoten, 2000), pp. 15–16.
20. Levitsky and Way, *Competitive Authoritarianism: Hybrid Regimes after the Cold War*, pp. 68–75.
21. This function of the Ministry of Culture and Information was succeeded by the Ministry of Information and Communications.
22. Carlyle A. Thayer, "The Apparatus of Authoritarian Rule in Vietnam", in *Politics in Contemporary Vietnam: Party, State, and Authority Relations*, edited by Jonanthan D. London (London: Palgrave Macmillan, 2014), pp. 135–61.
23. Zachary Abuza, *Renovating Politics in Contemporary Vietnam* (London: Lynne Rienner Publishers, 2001).
24. Carlyle A. Thayer, "Political Legitimacy of Vietnam's One Party-State: Challenges and Responses", *Journal of Current Southeast Asian Affairs* 28 (2009): 47–70.
25. Peter Zinoman, "Nhân Văn—Giai Phẩm and Vietnamese 'Reform Communism' in the 1950s: A Revisionist Interpretation", *Journal of Cold War Studies* 13 (2011): 60–100.
26. Carlyle A. Thayer, "Weak States and Strong Societies in Southeast Asia", in *Weak States, Strong Societies: Power and Authority in the New World Order*, edited by Amin Saikal (London and New York: I.B. Tauris & Co. Ltd., 2016), pp. 149–72.

27. Martin K. Dimitrov, ed., *Why Communism Did Not Collapse: Understanding Authoritarian Regime Resilience in Asia and Europe* (Cambridge: Cambridge University Press, 2013), pp. 303–12.
28. Beatriz Magaloni, "Credible Power-Sharing and the Longevity of Authoritarian Rule", *Comparative Political Studies* 41 (2008): 715–41.
29. Steven R. Levitsky and Lucan A. Way, "Beyond Patronage: Violent Struggle, Ruling Party Cohesion, and Authoritarian Durability", *Perspectives on Politics* 10 (2012): 869–89.
30. Andrew J. Nathan, "Authoritarian Resilience", *Journal of Democracy* 14 (2003): 6–17.
31. Jason Brownlee, *Authoritarianism in an Age of Democratization* (Cambridge: Cambridge University Press, 2007).
32. Magaloni, "Credible Power-Sharing and the Longevity of Authoritarian Rule".
33. Michael Bratton and Nicolas van de Walle, *Democratic Experiments in Africa: Regime Transitions in Comparative Perspective* (Cambridge: Cambridge University Press, 1997).
34. Barbara Geddes, "What Do We Know About Democratization after Twenty Years?", *Annual Review of Political Science* 2 (1999): 115–44.
35. Nathan, "Authoritarian Resilience".
36. Henry E. Hale, "Regime Cycles: Democracy, Autocracy, and Revolution in Post-Soviet Eurasia", *World Politics* 58 (2005): 133–65.
37. Geddes, "What Do We Know about Democratization after Twenty Years?".
38. Brownlee, *Authoritarianism in an Age of Democratization*.
39. Magaloni, "Credible Power-Sharing and the Longevity of Authoritarian Rule".
40. Way, "The Real Causes of the Color Revolutions".
41. Nguyen Hong Hai, *Political Dynamics of Grassroots Democracy in Vietnam* (Houndmills, Basingstoke, Hampshire; New York, NY: Palgrave Macmillan, 2016).
42. Huntington, *The Third Wave: Democratization in the Late 20th Century*, pp. 13–14.
43. Adam Przeworski and Fernando Limongi, "Modernization: Theories and Facts", *World Politics* 49 (1997): 155–83.
44. Geddes, "What Do We Know about Democratization after Twenty Years?".
45. Masaya Shiraishi, "ベトナム共産党支配体制下の市場経済化" [Market economy under the leadership of the Communist Party of Vietnam], in アジアの政治経済・入門新版, edited by Hiroshi Katayama and Hiroshi Ohnishi (Tokyo: Yuhikaku, 2010), pp. 223–309.
46. Le Hong Hiep, "Performance-Based Legitimacy: The Case of the Communist Party of Vietnam and 'Doi Moi'", *Contemporary Southeast Asia* 34 (2012): 145–72.
47. Seymour Martin Lipset, "Some Social Requisites of Democracy: Economic Development and Political Legitimacy", *American Political Science Review* 53 (1959): 69–105.

48. Walt Rostow, *The Stages of Economic Growth: A Non-Communist Manifesto* (Cambridge, UK: Cambridge University Press, 1960).

49. Samuel P. Huntington, "Political Development and Political Decay", *World Politics* 17 (1965): 386–430.

50. Bratton and van de Walle, *Democratic Experiments in Africa: Regime Transitions in Comparative Perspective*.

51. Way, "The Real Causes of the Color Revolutions".

52. Carlyle A. Thayer, "Political Dissent and Political Reform in Vietnam, 1997–2002", in *The Power of Ideas: Intellectual Input and Political Change in East and Southeast Asia*, edited by Claudia Derichs and Thomas Heberer (Copenhagen: Nordic Institute of Asian Studies Press, 2006), pp. 115–32.

53. Carlyle A. Thayer, "Mono-Organizational Socialism and the State", in *Vietnam's Rural Transformation*, edited by Benedict J. Tria Kerkvliet and Doug J. Porter (Boulder: Westview Press; Singapore: Institute of Southeast Asian Studies, 1995), pp. 39–64.

54. Tran Nhu and Vu Tuong, eds., *The Dragon's Underbelly: Dynamics and Dilemmas in Vietnam's Economy and Politics* (Singapore: ISEAS – Yusof Ishak Institute, 2023).

55. Edmund Malesky, "Vietnam in 2013: Single-Party Politics in the Internet Age", *Asian Survey* 54 (2014): 30–38.

56. Thayer, "Political Legitimacy of Vietnam's One Party-State: Challenges and Responses".

57. Carlyle A. Thayer, "Vietnam", in *Political Party Systems and Democratic Development in East and Southeast Asia*, vol. 1, *Southeast Asia*, edited by Wolfgang Sachsenröder and Ulrike E. Frings (Aldershot, Brookfield, Singapore and Sydney: Ashgate Publishing Ltd. in association with Friedrich-Naumann Stiftung, 1998), pp. 449–508.

58. Hiep, "Performance-Based Legitimacy: The Case of the Communist Party of Vietnam and '*Doi Moi*'".

59. Nguyen Hoang Thanh Danh and Casey Robinson, "A Study of Decision Making by North Korea and Vietnam When Facing Economic Upheaval", *Journal of the Graduate School of Asia-Pacific Studies Waseda University* 34 (2017): 18–36.

2

Sources of Legitimacy of the CPV

Our country is a democratic country. All benefits are for the people. All powers belong to the people.

Ho Chi Minh[1]

Definition of Political Legitimacy and the Legitimation Model of the CPV

There have been two main scholarly approaches in defining legitimacy, namely the empirical descriptive definition and the normative definition. The descriptive definition is based upon the ruled people's faith in the ruling authority, whereas the normative definition is based upon the justification of the coercive political power of the ruler.

One of the most prominent pioneers of the conception of descriptive legitimacy was Max Weber, who proposed an authoritative account of legitimacy that did not include any normative standards.[2] Weber suggested that a ruling regime can only be considered politically legitimate if its subjects feel a certain level of obedience towards it.[3] He argued that political legitimacy comes from three main sources: traditional legitimacy, which is based on the history and longevity of the political system; charismatic legitimacy, which revolves around the leaders' personal qualities and leadership; and rational-legal legitimacy, which depends on the regime's rule of law and the reinforcement of law.[4] If we look at the CPV through the descriptive lens, the authority of the CPV is tolerated by the Vietnamese people because they believe in the traditional values that the Party represents, the leadership of Ho Chi Minh and his successors, and the rule of law upheld by the Party's apparatus.

In contrast to Weber's descriptive definition, scholars who study political legitimacy from the normative approach such as Ripstein[5] and Rawls[6] believe that political legitimacy is simply the justification of coercive political power. In other words, a ruling regime can be considered to be legitimate even if it exercises coercive power over its citizens as long as such a practice can be legally justified. Based on this view, as long as the ruling regime can cling to power and ensure that its political authority does not meet with too much resistance, it can be considered the effective authority and over time this type of authority can create a sufficient right to rule.[7] The main function of political legitimacy, in this interpretation, is to differentiate between merely effective or *de facto* authority and legitimate authority. According to this view, CPV has been able to sufficiently maintain and justify their use of coercive power so that their rule is perceived as legitimate by the Vietnamese people.

Despite contradicting views on the nature of political legitimacy and its relationship with political authority, coercion and obligation as mentioned earlier, most scholars agree that the possession of legitimate authority is one of the crucial factors that contribute to the resilience of any political regime.[8, 9, 10, 11, 12, 13, 14, 15, 16, 17, 18, 19, 20]

During the tumultuous history of the CPV, there are instances that are hard to explain using the normative approach; for example, during the Second Indochina War, the Viet Cong had enjoyed popular support and could carry out military operations even within territories far behind the border, which were under the clear control of South Vietnam's army for a long time. The Viet Cong and the North Vietnamese PAV could even launch the 1968 Tet Offensive, which required massive manpower and supply effort aimed at the very heart of South Vietnam. While the Viet Cong and the PAV are not above coercion and violence, it would be logical to suggest that there are more to the justification of coercion that motivated a part of the South Vietnamese population to believe in the authority of the communists.

There have been two approaches that have been used by contemporary scholars in assessing the legitimacy of a regime: evaluation through the claims of the regime and evaluation through the perception of the people of such claims. Although claims to legitimacy made by dictatorial ruling regimes are often deemed biased and one-sided by commentators, Gerschewski[21] suggested that such claims can be considered an informative source if put under an expert's scrutiny. Easton[22] and Lipset[23] posited that although authoritarian regimes' claims to legitimacy are subject to change over time, in principle the fundamental claims remain unchanged with new legitimation strategies being employed.

In general, given the oppressive and secretive nature of most dictatorial regimes, the latter approach is notoriously challenging. The discussion of topics deemed sensitive under an authoritarian rule is usually repressed by the ruling regime's security apparatus and thus conducting public opinion surveys and qualitative interviews to evaluate the ruling regime's legitimacy is exceedingly difficult. Furthermore, Kuran[24] pointed out that people who are living under authoritarian rule tend to be influenced by preference falsification.[25] He argues that preference falsification is particularly impactful when it comes to social science in two ways: it makes finding out the true intentions of an individual much harder, and when a person avoids showing discontent about the ruling political regime and its policies, the people around them also tend to do the same thing.

A common method to overcome such difficulties is to use whichever proxy data accessible to the researcher, such as independently evaluated corruption indexes, protests, dissidence and election participation.

However, Gilley[26] pointed out that the relationship between this proxy data and a regime's legitimacy is not clear-cut, and in many cases is not reliable. In the case of Vietnam, for example, the extremely high voter turnout in legislative elections reported by the government, which has been consistently around 95 per cent since 1992, is highly unlikely to be trustworthy.

Grauvogel and von Soest combine both approaches and propose a six-point scale to evaluate legitimacy in authoritarian regimes.[27] They select regimes based on the Authoritarian Regime Dataset[28] and come up with the Regime Legitimation Expert Survey and suggest that a ruling regime's legitimacy could be classified into the following six dimensions: (1) ideology; (2) foundational myth; (3) personalism, which is based on charismatic leadership; (4) international engagement; (5) procedural legitimacy and (6) performance legitimacy. This classification is based on the differences between input-based and output-based legitimacy claims suggested by Easton,[29] incorporated with the procedural and international dimensions proposed by Burnell,[30] Scharpf[31] and Schatz.[32] Of these six dimensions, foundational myth, ideology and personalism can be classified as input-based claims, while performance is output-based; the two added dimensions of international engagement and procedural legitimacy are listed independently. These six dimensions of legitimacy are inherently different, although they are interlinked.[33] Nevertheless, legitimacy in real-world politics is usually much more complicated than it appears when theoretically divided into categories on paper.

Regarding the case of CPV, Hiep suggests that there are four traditional sources of legitimacy, namely nationalism, socialism, Ho Chi Minh's charismatic leadership and external recognition. He also argued that from the mid-1980s, performance legitimacy has emerged as the single most important source of legitimacy of the CPV as other sources had become irrelevant and obsolete.[34]

Existing scholarly literature often overlooks the CPV's democratic legitimacy, primarily because the ruling communist regime in Vietnam has never been recognized as democratic by any entities apart from itself and its allies. However, in contemporary political discourse, even the most totalitarian regimes strive to present themselves as democratic. The CPV is no exception and has consistently asserted itself as the rightful representative of the people's will. This assertion warrants serious scrutiny, particularly since the late 2000s. In this book, the legitimacy of the CPV is theorized to be derived from four potential sources: tradition-based achievements and values, Ho Chi Minh's charismatic leadership, socialism as a state-building ideology, and performance legitimacy and self-proclaimed democratic legitimacy, manifested through legislative elections and the National Assembly.

In addition to the first and second sources, which align with Weber's traditional and charismatic authority, the CPV also boasts significant rational-legal authority. After seizing power from French and Japanese colonial occupations in August 1945, the Viet Minh promptly organized a National Assembly election. The newly elected National Assembly then passed the 1946 Constitution in November of the same year. Despite continuous warfare that began shortly after the passage of this constitution, the CPV consistently made significant efforts to maintain law and order in territories under its control. Just one year after the fall of Saigon, despite the tumultuous situation in newly unified Vietnam, the CPV made the 1976 National Assembly election a priority to legitimize its rule over the country. The rational-legal aspect of the CPV's authority is subdivided and analysed as part of its socialist ideology, its performance and its democratic legitimacy. This analysis reflects both the CPV's own perception of its legitimacy and how it is perceived by its constituents.

Except for democratic legitimacy, which is the focus of this book and as such will be discussed in greater detail in later chapters, the other three sources of legitimacy of the CPV will be discussed in this chapter.

Tradition-Based Achievements and Values

Traditional legitimacy derives from the sanctity of tradition and is passed down from predecessor to successor, often taking the form of heredity. Traditional authority tends to discourage social changes and aims to maintain the status quo. Feudalism and patrimonialism are among the most typical embodiments of this type of legitimacy. Usually, traditional legitimacy is based on the relationship that is formed between the patron and the client; in a feudal context, that would be the relationship between the subject and the feudal lord.

There have been several discussions on the extent to which a regime should be considered adherent to tradition. The strictest example of traditional authority is a hereditary monarchy, where the next monarch is decided based on a statutory line of succession, usually from father to son. However, traditional authority can be passed to a ruling regime that can sufficiently assert that its rule does not stray from the traditional values of its nation. For example, in Vietnam, while dynasties changed, the feudal system persisted for over a thousand years.

It could be said that the CPV had very little traditional legitimacy during the first years of its foundation. One of the first missions that the CPV assigned to itself was to overthrow feudalism, and there had been other national liberation movements led by far more traditional leaders such as members of the royalty or mandarins. Furthermore, before the rise of the CPV, communism was an entirely unfamiliar ideology to the average Vietnamese. Nevertheless, the CPV proved to be the most successful national liberation movement in no small part thanks to the popular support it had enjoyed. This is partly due to the Party's effective justification of its rule by linking its achievements to the core values upheld by the Vietnamese as an ethnocultural group.

For more than 1,000 years, Vietnam was under the direct rule of various Chinese dynasties. This has led to two interesting and uniquely contradicting characteristics. On one hand, the mandarin ruling class of feudal Vietnam were faithful adherents of Chinese theories of statecraft and social values, which has left a profound influence. On the other hand, after thousands of years of struggle against China for national independence, fighting against foreign forces has become a defining characteristic of Vietnamese nationalism. This would later become the basis of the communists' legitimacy in their wars of resistance against the French colonial empire and later the American-backed

South Vietnam. It could be argued that the two aspects of traditional values upheld by Vietnamese people that had the most substantial impact on their concept of traditional legitimacy are the profound influence of Chinese culture and statecraft doctrine, and nationalism resulting from a long history of struggle against foreign invaders, most notably the Chinese.

Several scholars have examined the role of traditional values in reinforcing or undermining the legitimacy of Marxism to Vietnamese political elites and the public. Nguyen Khac Vien, a French-educated Vietnamese historian and member of the CPV argued that Marxism is similar to Confucianism in the sense that both ideologies "concentrated man's thoughts on political and social problems" and as such was easy for the Vietnamese intellectuals who were educated in Confucianism to grasp.[35] Duiker, the author of one of the most comprehensive and authoritative biographies of the Vietnamese revolutionary leader Ho Chi Minh, pointed out that Marxism was attractive to Vietnamese because, akin to Confucianism, Marxism incorporates its doctrine in quasi-sacred texts; contains the belief that the educated, gifted elites should take responsibility in guiding the masses; emphasizes the importance of personal morality and selflessness in society; puts the community over the individual; maintains the belief that social greater good should be prioritized over the pursuit of material wealth; and holds the conviction that human nature is pliable and can be guided to enlightenment.[36]

Echoing the above arguments, McAlister and Mus stated that the August Revolution "was not merely imposed from the top down but had local antecedents that gave it real roots in the countryside" and "because the communists have gone beyond the partial political programs of their competitors and tried determinedly, though not always successfully, to grapple with the symbols and idiom of traditionalist politics, they have had the most effective revolution movement in Vietnam".[37]

Some scholars, however, disagree with the notion that Marxist teachings were seen as rational and obedience-worthy by people who embraced traditional Vietnamese values. Young purported that

"Vietnamese invest true authority with those who possess the quality of *uy tín* (moral legitimacy), consisting of *tài* (ability), đức (virtue), and *số* (destiny)" and that "the core philosophic rationalization of the Vietnamese cultural pattern is the notion of *đức phúc*, an amalgam of Buddhist and Confucian notions, with pre-Confucian origins, stressing individualism and private economic incentive in the context of the family". As a result, Young concluded that "a Vietnamese leader who does not promote *đức phúc* inhibits the people from doing what they most want to do in that inner part of their being by which they identify themselves as Vietnamese. Such a leader has no *đức* and therefore, no *uy tín*."[38]

Vasavakul argues that those authors failed to consider three factors. First, the notion that traditional Vietnamese values are the main element of the CPV's political legitimacy is misleading, and Vasavakul proposed that modern, nontraditional ideologies are the basis of the CPV's legitimacy. Second, there is no overarching tradition set shared by the entire Vietnamese peasantry and traditional values differ between regions. The concept of "Vietnamese tradition" was perhaps created by the communists to validate their claim for political authority. Third, legitimacy is determined not only by compatibility or incompatibility between values pursued by the leadership and those followed by the masses, but also by the capability of the ruling regime to offset, facilitate and homogenize conflicting values and traditions.[39]

In the above arguments about the compatibility between the traditional values of Vietnam and the ideology proposed and the course of action followed by the CPV, there are several points that are not addressed, or addressed inadequately. While Vien's argument that both Confucianism and Marxism "concentrated man's thoughts on political and social problems" is correct and while it is true that Confucianism "recognizes political participation as an important civic virtue and encourages citizens to exercise it judiciously as a means for effective democratic control and direction of government",[40] Vien did not consider the difference in the scope of political participation between Marxism and Confucianism. Confucianism revolves around the notion of "three principles and five virtues"[41] in which the most emphasized doctrine is the relationship between the ruler and his subject.[42] Political participation in Confucianism, as such, is not encouraged to be developed beyond the scope of a nation-state and must always be accompanied by loyalty towards the monarch. In contrast, Marx theorized that an ideal society could be established through the organized actions of an international working class, empowering the entire population and unchaining humankind from the bondage of the labour market.[43] As such, according to Marx, the notion of nationhood is not the focal point in politics. Marx, in his *Critique of Hegel's Philosophy of Right* in 1843, effectively claims that democracy is superior to monarchy.

In his argument, Duiker failed to point out that the concept of leadership differs greatly between Confucianism and Marxism. While Confucius proposed that leadership should be entrusted to the few well-educated elites with gifted intelligence under a monarch; Marx and Engels suggested in the Communist Manifesto that "the first step in the revolution by the working class, is to raise the proletariat to the position of ruling class, to win the battle for democracy" and maintained in their later works that universal suffrage is "one of the first and most important tasks of the militant proletariat".

Furthermore, while both Marxism and Confucianism highlight the sacrifice of self-interest for the greater good, the definition of the greater good differs between the two doctrines. Marx examines the interaction between the individual when put against the totality of the society; whereas Confucianism emphasizes the sacrifice of the individual, not to the society as a whole but to other individuals of higher priority as regulated by the "three principles" proposed by Confucius.[44] Having said that, the CPV had successfully reinterpreted Marxism in a way that fits the traditional values held by ordinary Vietnamese people.

Young's explanation of traditional Vietnamese legitimacy falls short on several points. First, while it is true that Vietnamese held their rulers accountable to certain standards as *tài* (ability) and *đức* (morality); *số* (fate) is a rather paradoxical criterion because if one manages to seize and hold onto power, he would be in possession of *số*. By being able to rule the country for many decades, the CPV would naturally be considered to be the rightful owner of the mandate of heaven by its subjects. Furthermore, by emerging victorious in devastating wars against the most modern and powerful armies in the world at the time, it would be unfair to assert that the CPV was devoid of *tài* (ability). In addition, Ho Chi Minh is widely considered by Vietnamese to be a benevolent father figure. Consequently, one should not disregard Ho as a symbol of the CPV's virtue. Contradictory to Young's understanding of Vietnamese traditional values, *uy tín* (creditability) was not an overall standard that a ruler had to adhere to, rather, it originated from *tín* (fidelity), one of the five virtues of Confucianism. *Phúc* is a concept that basically means long-lasting happiness and is not normally linked to the qualities that a leader must have.

Vasavakul's underestimation of the role that Vietnamese tradition plays in the claim to authority by the CPV leads to incomprehensiveness in the analysis of those claims. It should be noted that Vietnamese traditions have been constantly under the influence of Confucian teachings for thousands of years and, as a result, despite being not native to Vietnam, Confucianism is an integral element in Vietnamese culture. The leaderships of Vietnam's independent movements during the early twentieth century were usually composed of people with backgrounds in Confucian education. Ho Chi Minh himself and one of his most prominent rivals, Ngo Dinh Diem, as well as many high-ranking officials in both North and South Vietnam during the Vietnam War, received Confucian education. The fact that Ho has Mandarin roots is repeated many times in history textbooks in Vietnam to make him look traditional and not out of touch. Furthermore, while regionalism has indeed posed a significant obstacle to the CPV's efforts to assert authority across the country, nearly 90 per cent of the Vietnamese population today belong to the Kinh ethnic group and speak a common language. Despite regional differences, areas predominantly inhabited by the Kinh share core values and traditions that the ruling party leverages to strengthen its authority, most prominent among them are the influence of Chinese culture and nationalism.

Profound Influence of Chinese Culture and Statecraft Doctrine

The two most important aspects of Chinese statecraft that influence people's perception of the rule of the CPV are the concept of the mandate of heaven, and the ruler-subject relationship as a part of Confucianism. The mandate of heaven was a concept used by the Chinese empires since ancient times to justify their rules. This concept is familiar to the concept of the divine right of kings in medieval Europe. According to this political and religious doctrine, a just ruler is bestowed with a mandate of heaven to rule. This mandate, however, is not permanent and can be lost if the ruler mistreats his subjects or angers heaven.[45] Any individual from any social class can be sanctioned with the mandate of heaven if said person manages to wrest the power from the previous dynasty, presumably disgraced by heaven, and hold on to it. This is well explained by the Vietnamese proverb "The winner is made king; the loser becomes an outlaw."[46] This concept of might makes right has always been familiar to Vietnamese and Chinese alike and is very similar to what is suggested by Machiavelli in his political treatise, *The Prince*.

According to Confucianism, a transition of government should occur when a ruler loses his mandate of heaven. Although Confucius did not explicitly encourage change of government through violence, he accepted violence as a legitimate means of obtaining authority.

In the history of Vietnam, in addition to rebellions against occupying foreign forces, rebellions against the Vietnamese ruling dynasties from both inside and outside of the royal court were not out of the norm. A change of regime could happen with little bloodshed, as in the case of the transition between the Dinh dynasty and the Early Le dynasty and later between the Early Le dynasty and the Ly dynasty. However, for the most part, a new dynasty would usually emerge after seizing power by force from an occupying Chinese force or the previous dynasty. The State of Au Lac, the Ngo dynasty, the Later Le dynasty, the Tay Son dynasty and the Nguyen dynasty all established their authority over Vietnam in this manner. The violent method that has been constantly employed by the CPV to fight against its enemies is also considered a legitimate method of claiming authority according to both the mandate of heaven concept and the communist doctrines.

Marx suggested that in countries with strong democratic institutional political systems, it is possible for the transition period between capitalism and communism to be peaceful; however, should the working class be denied freedom of political expression and the transition period cannot be carried out peacefully, then the "lever of our revolution must be force".[47] Ho Chi Minh, as an adherent of Marxism, wrote "in the arduous struggle against the enemy of the (working) class and the (Vietnamese) people, we must use revolutionary violence to fight against anti-revolutionary violence, to seize the government and to protect our government".[48] Ho maintained that revolutionary violence is inevitable and that the use of violence to achieve victory in class struggle is in accordance with Marxism, as he put it "Vietnamese revolutionaries were under the vigorous influence of the October Revolution and Marxism-Leninism. It was as a thirsty traveller finds fresh water to drink; a hungry person is given food to eat."[49]

Armed conflicts in Vietnam did not end with the defeat of the French at the Battle of Dien Bien Phu. Anti-communism efforts were revitalized with the establishment of the State of Vietnam in the South and the United States' interference. As the gloomy perspective of a new, bloody war was looming, in January 1959, the 15th meeting of the Central Committee of the CPV reaffirmed that the most plausible scenario for the Vietnamese revolution in the South would involve armed rebellion in collaborating with the armed forces from the North.[50]

Even until his death in September 1969, Ho Chi Minh remained convinced that revolutionary violence is the only possible way to achieve national unification. He wrote in his will "it is possible that the resistance war against America will be prolonged. Perhaps, we will lose a lot more men and resources. In any circumstance, we must uphold our determination to fight against America until our complete victory."[51]

It is sensible to conclude that the use of violence is justified in both Marxism and in accordance with Vietnamese traditional values. As a result, a significant proportion of the Vietnamese population at that time was sympathetic to, or at least tolerant of, the vision of the communists to fight for a unified Vietnam nation state under communist rule with force. As such, despite decades of devastating warfare and war-weariness, the CPV had consistently been able to maintain a formidable fighting force and gain considerable support from the population.

The main concepts of Confucianism were also reinterpreted by the CPV to be more suitable to their socialist ideology and the context of Vietnam. Ho Chi Minh explained the core virtues in Confucianism that must be upheld by a communist as follows:

Nhân (benevolence) is to wholeheartedly love and support one's comrades and fellow Vietnamese. (*Nhân* is) to determinedly fight against harmful people and actions to the Party and the Vietnamese people.

Nghĩa (righteousness) is to uphold fairness and honesty and to harbor nothing to hide from the Party. (*Nghĩa* is) to protect the interests of the Party and disregard self-interest. When assigned to a task by the Party, no matter how trivial the task is, one must devote oneself entirely to it.

Without *trí* (intellect), one will be confused and prone to corruption. With *trí*, one's mind will be clear and unclouded and can easily absorb theories and find the right direction. One can clearly understand other people and events around oneself. As such, one can do what is beneficial to the Party and avoid harmful actions to the Party.

Dũng (courage) is to be brave, fearless, and to have the courage to do the right thing. One must have the courage to correct one's mistakes and to fight against unrighteous wealth. One must have the courage to sacrifice one's life for the Party, for the Fatherland without even a moment of hesitation.

Liêm (integrity) is to refrain from coveting material wealth, social positions, and bodily pleasures. (*Liêm* is to) stay away from flatterers. As such, one must always uphold integrity and remain incorruptible. There is only one thing one must be greedy of, that is to be greedy of knowledge, of labour, of self-improvement.

The above virtues are revolutionary virtues and not outdated virtues. Those virtues are new virtues, great virtues that do not aim to gain personal fame but to serve the overall interest of the Party, of the Vietnamese people, of humanity.[52]

The five cardinal human relationships which Confucianism teaches, in particular the relationship between ruler and subject, were also reinterpreted by the CPV to be more suitable to their political doctrine. This line of propaganda has been particularly emphasized as a part of the doctrine of the PAV and the People's Public Security of Vietnam.

Confucian teachings written in the Analects indicate that subjects must be absolutely loyal to their monarch and, in turn, the monarch must provide the subjects with protection and guidance.[53] As the CPV was fighting to eliminate feudalism and all of its remnants in Vietnam, the old interpretation of Confucius' teachings could no longer be applied to justify the loyalty of the people and the army to their new communist rulers; the CPV changed Confucius' notion of loyalty and filial piety to "be loyal to the CPV and be filial to the Vietnamese people". This new adaptation of Confucian loyalty has been indoctrinated to all military personnel and police officers. The first of the ten oaths of enlistment that every prospective Vietnamese military personnel must pledge clearly indicates that a military man must "sacrifice everything for the Fatherland; under the leadership of the CPV, strive to realize a peaceful, independent, and socialist Vietnam, actively contribute to the struggles of the people all around the world for peace, national independence, democracy, and socialism". The third oath emphasizes both nationalism and socialism, calling for "restless pursuit to improve socialist patriotism, proletarian internationalism, and endeavour to strengthen the determined and enduring fighting spirit, to remain humble in victory and undaunted in defeat".[54, 55]

Likewise, any prospective police officer must take an oath to "remain absolutely loyal to the Vietnamese people and nation, to the CPV, to the Socialist Republic of Vietnam, restlessly strive and sacrifice to protect the independence, freedom, sovereignty, territorial unity and integrity for the security of the Fatherland". Police officers are supposed to "strictly follow policies, instructions, and directions issued by the Party and the government's law, Vietnam People's

Public Security's resolutions, directives, and consuetudinary; ready to go anyway and do anything should the Fatherland, the Party, and the people require it".[56]

Nationalism Stemmed from a Long History of Struggle against Foreign Invaders

According to Nielsen, nationalism is the combination of two phenomena: the mindset of the citizens of a nation who define themselves as members of that nation and the actions that those citizens are willing to take in order to claim or maintain their nation's sovereignty and interests.[57] Both of those aspects, however, possess facets that need further explanation, such as statehood or sovereignty.[58] Nevertheless, most scholars agree that nationalistic views on the definition of statehood require two conditions, namely the authority over territorial sovereignty, and the people from an ethnic-cultural group that assigned them with the mission to protect such sovereignty.

Nationalism is deeply ingrained in the Vietnamese mindset. In 2014, Gallup released a report on people's willingness to fight for their country, and Vietnam ranked fourth on the list, with 89 per cent of Vietnamese respondents saying they were willing to fight and lay down their lives for their country. As this willingness to fight for one's country can be seen as the essence of nationalism, according to the aforementioned survey, Vietnam can be considered one of the most nationalistic countries in the world.

This nationalistic tendency is evident in Vietnam through anniversaries and celebrations of events perceived to be national achievements, ranging from military victories against invading armies to football match wins. Foreigners living in Vietnam can easily observe this fervent display of nationalism in the attitudes and actions of the Vietnamese people. Celebrations of a football victory in Vietnam were described by surprised foreigners as wild, amazing or even crazy.[59]

Several foreign scholars have discussed the topic of Vietnamese nationalism. Johnston argued that Vietnamese nationalism emerged during the late nineteenth and early twentieth centuries because of cultural contact between Vietnam and the West, particularly France. Based on Kohn's definition of nationalism, Johnston opined that although Vietnam was a homogeneous society, it had not yet reached the stage of social, economic and political development that leads to nationalism. However, the arrival of the French shattered the village-based traditional Vietnamese society and united the Vietnamese people against a common enemy: the French colonial empire.[60]

Sharing this view, Ball mentioned that the French's effort to educate the people of Indochina only ignited their Indochinese subjects' resentment and hatred, with the intellectuals at the helm.[61] Giran, based on his observation of the Annamite people, argued that nationalism is absent in Vietnamese society and that as long as their culture and customs are respected, Vietnamese are willing to accept any ruler, even foreign ones. He also maintained that tribalism and regionalism are the most notable traits of Vietnamese society.[62]

Young recognized the importance of nationalism as a source of legitimacy for any ruling regime in Vietnam. Nevertheless, he argued that due to the perceived incompatibility between communism and nationalism, the real people who represented nationalism in Vietnam were the leaders of South Vietnam.[63]

Among Vietnamese scholars, there is a general consensus that Vietnamese nationalism is much more deeply rooted than what is proposed by their Western counterparts. The 1980 Constitution of the Socialist Republic of Vietnam establishes that a sovereign Vietnamese state was formed four thousand years ago, and along with it, Vietnamese nationalism. Even though the Vietnamese public widely believes that Vietnam as a nation is four thousand years old, this number is unfounded. Later constitutions of Vietnam also mention the long history of Vietnamese statehood in their preambles; however, they are more cautious in their wording, usually only stating that Vietnam's history traces back thousands of years.

There are unresolved issues in both Western and Vietnamese approaches to the conception of Vietnamese statehood and nationalism. Western scholars tend to overemphasize the importance of Western influence in creating or reinterpreting Vietnamese nationalism. While it is true that Western influence, especially from France, greatly transformed the Vietnamese society and therefore Vietnamese nationalism, the history of Vietnam before the arrival of French colonialists and the Chinese factor in the establishment of Vietnamese statehood and identity have been overlooked by Western scholars.

On the other hand, Vietnamese scholars' view that Vietnamese nationalism is a continuous and unbroken line fails to explain the changes in Vietnamese nationalism before, during and after the French colonial period. Moreover, the impact of tribalism and regionalism, prominent traits of Vietnamese society, is also more or less ignored in their view. The narrative that Vietnam is a homogenous society and nationalism is a virtue shared by all those who live within Vietnam's borders is questionable, at best.

Combining both approaches, it could be argued that the creation of modern Vietnamese identity and nationalism has been greatly influenced by the Chinese and French. While the French colonial period shaped Vietnamese nationalism, it is considered by many Vietnamese to be just a continuation of thousands of years of struggle against foreign forces.

The CPV has been consistently drawing upon the history of Vietnam to strengthen the public's sense of nationalism. Throughout its history, the Party has been constantly fighting against foreign forces or enemies who were foreign backed. Victories in those conflicts enabled the Party to assert its role as the guardian of sovereignty and independence and thus allowed it to gather a vast number of people under their banner, regardless of their allegiance to communism. Apart from the 1946 Constitution of the Democratic Republic of Vietnam, the first words of the preamble of the successive constitutions of Vietnam have always stressed the history of the country and the efforts to protect it against foreign invaders.[64]

On 17 February 1979, hundreds of thousands of Chinese troops overran the northern border of Vietnam and started a bloody one-month war.[65, 66, 67] Put in the words of then Chinese Vice-Premier Deng Xiaoping, the invasion was a pre-emptive strike to discipline the "naughty kid" that was Vietnam. This border war was but one in many military conflicts between Vietnam and China throughout the two countries' thousands of years of history. From ancient times until the most recent episode, the Johnson South Reef Skirmish in 1988, armed conflicts with China have always comprised the focal points in Vietnam's history. China's role as the bad guys in Vietnam's history was replaced in the twentieth century by France and the United States during the First and Second Indochina Wars, respectively. During this period, China was portrayed by North Vietnam's propaganda as both an elder brother and a comrade. However, China has again been described as the eternal nemesis of Vietnam during the Third Indochina War and the subsequent skirmishes. More than a half of the content of history textbooks issued by the Ministry of Education and Training of Vietnam, which are used universally in all primary and secondary educational establishments within the country, is dedicated to discussing those conflicts. The identity of Vietnam as a nation and the mindset of the Vietnamese people is shaped under the conditions that they have lived under a constant state of warfare against foreign forces.

The constitutions of Vietnam have dedicated a great deal in their content to stressing the injustice caused by the French, the Americans and the Chinese, while emphasizing the heroic struggle of Vietnamese people under the guidance of the CPV. Many streets in Vietnam were named after national heroes who are known for their struggle against foreign invaders. In 2013, the Vietnamese government officially recognized fourteen historical individuals as the national heroes of Vietnam. Of those fourteen national heroes, eleven were involved in armed struggle against foreign invaders.[68]

The importance of nationalism as an aspect of legitimacy was recognized not only by the CPV, but also by their political opponents. South Vietnam's banknotes, for example, featured Tran Hung Dao and Nguyen Hue, two of the most prominent national heroes that fought against Chinese invaders as illustrated in Figure 2.1.

Bui Kien Thanh, a political advisor to President of the Republic of Vietnam Ngo Dinh Diem, said that Diem openly opposed the idea of the United States' direct military involvement in Vietnam:

Figure 2.1
South Vietnam Banknotes Featuring Tran Hung Dao and Nguyen Hue

Source: Banknotes.com, "Vietnam Banknotes", https://www.banknotes.com/vietnam/
(accessed 17 July 2024).

When the Americans wanted to send troops to Vietnam in 1962, Mr. Diem told them "You should remember that over the four thousand years of history of Vietnam, there has been no regime that invited a foreign army onto our soil and was supported by the people. Therefore, the day the United States Army sets foot on this nation is the day we stop being just, and when we are unjust then you cannot win, and we will also lose. As such, the day you set foot on this land is the day our Vietnamese justice is lost, we cannot accept that.[69]

Diem, however, was assassinated in November 1963 and was not able to prevent the direct involvement of the United States in the Vietnam War.

Some scholars argue that the anti-foreign mentality held by many Vietnamese in combination with the lack of a just cause to directly interfere in Vietnam resulted in an unwinnable situation for the United States from the very beginning and that the United Stated failed to establish a regime in South Vietnam that was considered legitimate by the people.[70] Boylan argues that the Diem administration was corrupt, dictatorial and was not able to provide a reason for the people to fight, while the communists based their legitimacy on anti-foreign nationalist sentiment that pit the Vietnamese people against "American imperialists" and were thus able to persuade millions of people to fight for them.[71]

Nationalism, as a vital element of the CPV's legitimacy, could be best described through the words of Daniel Ellsberg, a former United States military analyst who sparked a national political controversy in 1971 when he released the Pentagon Papers, a top-secret Pentagon study of US government decision-making about the Vietnam War, to the media:

> It's no surprise that in a very poor country you can find people who will wear foreign uniforms. What has always surprised us, what we've never been willing to predict or understand, is that the Vietnamese communist leadership can find enough people to live in the tunnels, fight for nothing wearing ragged shorts, year after year under the American bombs. A war in which one side is entirely financed and equipped and supported by foreigners is not a civil war. The only foreigners in that country were the foreigners we financed in the first part of the war and the foreigners we were in the second half of the war. Basically, we didn't want to acknowledge the scale of our involvement there. We didn't want to realize that it was our war, because that would have been to say that every casualty on both sides was a casualty caused by our policy. The question used to be "Might it be possible that we were on the wrong side in the Vietnamese war?" We weren't on the wrong side. We are the wrong side.[72]

Ho Chi Minh's Charismatic Leadership

Charismatic legitimacy, as the name suggests, emanates from the leader's charisma. The leadership of a regime with charismatic legitimacy is justified because people perceive the leader of that regime as worthy of being followed. Weber dedicated a significant portion of his essay to discussing the idea of charismatic legitimacy and believed that this charisma is "resting on devotion to the exceptional sanctity, heroism, or exemplary character of an individual person, and of the normative patterns or order revealed or ordained by him".[73] Riesebrodt echoed this point and further argued that Weber believed that charisma is important to, even inseparable from, a traditional authority system.[74] As charismatic legitimacy heavily relies on the persona of the leader himself, a regime that draws from this type of legitimacy usually has fragile political and administrative institutions. If the leader in question dies or falls from grace, the legitimacy of the regime will also suffer. However, if the charismatic leader has a widely acknowledged heir, this source of legitimacy may be prolonged. In certain cases, dead leaders continue to serve as the source of charismatic legitimacy for the regime they once ruled. This scenario is commonplace in post-World War II communist countries, with examples being Mao Zedong in China, Kim Il Sung in North Korea, and Vladimir Lenin and Joseph Stalin in the Soviet Union. This type of legitimacy usually manifests in the form of numinous legitimacy, such as the imperial cult in ancient Rome, the mandate of heaven in Eastern Asia or the divine rights of kings in medieval Europe. In such cases, the monarch is the focal point of the government's legitimacy. Numinous legitimacy shares similarities with traditional legitimacy in the sense that this source of legitimacy can be passed down from generation to generation.

In the case of Vietnam, charismatic legitimacy is embodied in the cult of personality that centres on the revolutionary leader Ho Chi Minh. This source is supplementary to other sources of the Party's legitimacy.

Ho Chi Minh emerged as a symbol of national liberation and independence when he read the Declaration of Independence of the Democratic Republic of Vietnam on 2 September 1945 at the Ba Dinh Square in Hanoi. Even before that milestone, Ho had been working restlessly to lay the foundation for the CPV. Ho's revolutionary career has been the main source of the legitimacy that is derived from his charismatic leadership.

The CPV's official sources, such as the Ho Chi Minh's Presidential Palace Historical Site's official website, have been consistently maintaining that Ho became a diehard socialist due to the experience he gained travelling the world while doing odd jobs.[75] He joined the Socialist Party of France in 1919 and was among the founders of the French Communist Party in December 1920.[76] Ho was invited by Dmitry Manuilsky, a prominent Bolshevik revolutionary, to work for the Comintern and rose quickly among its ranks.[77] In February 1930, Ho met with representatives from the People's Revolutionary Party of South Vietnam and Workers' Party of North Vietnam in Hong Kong and founded the CPV by merging these two organizations. Ho travelled to many countries including the Soviet Union, China, Thailand, the United States and India from 1923 until he eventually returned to Vietnam to lead the Viet Minh in 1941. Under Ho's leadership, the Viet Minh launched the August Revolution in 1945 that gave birth to the Democratic Republic of Vietnam. Although the Viet Minh under communist leadership won the National Assembly election in January 1946, Ho was forced to nominally disband the CPV when the victorious Allies entered Vietnam to disarm the Japanese army stationed there. From 1945 until his death in 1969, Ho served as the chairman of the Central Committee of the Workers' Party of Vietnam and the president of the Democratic Republic of Vietnam. During this period, the CPV fought two wars against the French colonial empire and the United States backed South Vietnam.

Although some scholars argued that Le Duan replaced Ho as the main decision-maker in Hanoi from the 1960s,[78, 79] Ho remained the figurehead of the CPV and could still maintain a certain level of influence over the decision-making process until his death. Throughout his life and even after his death, Ho has been made the symbol of Vietnamese national independence and unification by the CPV, even to the point that the Party went against his will and built a mausoleum in the centre of Hanoi to preserve and display his embalmed body.[80, 81]

The CPV has made great efforts to promote Ho's image as a benevolent grandfather figure, almost God-like, with whom all Vietnamese people, from children to the elderly, can deeply identify and the founding father of an independent Vietnamese state. In Vietnam, instead of being addressed by titles like "great leader" or "comrade", which are usually associated with communist leaders, Ho Chi Minh is both officially and unofficially addressed as *Bác* (Great Uncle). Ho Chi Minh's influence over the political environment of Vietnam is visible from the highest level. With the sole exception of the 1946 Constitution of the Democratic Republic of Vietnam, all of the constitutions of communist-controlled North Vietnam and a unified Vietnam from 1976 mention his name in their preambles.[82]

Ho's followers in the CPV have also created policies that ensure that Ho's legacy will not be forgotten. The final stage of the 1975 Spring Offensive was named the Ho Chi Minh Campaign as a tribute to him and to raise the morale of North Vietnamese troops. More than one year after the fall of the city, on 2 July 1976, the National Assembly of Vietnam passed a resolution that changed the name of the former capital city of South Vietnam from Sai Gon-Gia Dinh to Ho Chi Minh City. Ho's other names including Nguyen Ai Quoc, Nguyen Sinh Cung and Nguyen Tat Thanh, are also honoured by being used to name various streets, universities, institutions and schools across Vietnam. The youth wing of the CPV and the largest social-political organization of youth in Vietnam is officially named the Ho Chi Minh Communist Youth Union. Ho's birthday on 19th of May is a widely celebrated national holiday in Vietnam. Ho's portrait can also be found on the front of all of the banknotes of North Vietnam and unified Vietnam from 1976 as illustrated in Figure 2.2.

In addition to the mausoleum that was built in Hanoi to house Ho's embalmed body, several museums across Vietnam are dedicated to display the relics related to his revolutionary life and work, most notably Ho Chi Minh Museum in Hanoi (see Figure 2.3) and its branches in Ho Chi Minh City, Da Nang and Phan Thiet. Ho's childhood house in Nghe An was also remodelled into a museum. Ho Chi Minh busts and portraits are usually displayed visibly in many public and private establishments in Vietnam, from the National Assembly Hall to small classrooms in remote elementary schools. Posters, banners and billboards praising Ho and his achievements can be seen everywhere

Figure 2.2
Banknotes Featuring Ho Chi Minh

(*Top*) The front of the 100 dong banknotes issued by the Ministry of Finance and the Central Treasury of the Democratic Republic of Vietnam after the August Revolution in 1945, as displayed in the National Museum of Vietnamese History. (*Bottom*) The front of the 500,000 dong banknotes currently in circulation in Vietnam. Both feature Ho Chi Minh.

Sources: Vietnam National Museum of History, "Giấy bạc Cụ Hồ - Đồng tiền đầu tiên của nước Việt Nam độc lập" [Uncle Ho's banknotes - the first currency of independent Vietnam], 8 September 2014, https://baotanglichsu.vn/vi/Articles/3096/16932/giay-bac-cu-ho-djong-tien-djau-tien-cua-nuoc-viet-nam-djoc-lap.html (accessed 17 July 2024); State Bank of Vietnam, "Tiền đang lưu hành" [Current circulating currency], https://www.sbv.gov.vn/webcenter/portal/vi/menu/trangchu/pht/dtvn/tdlh (accessed 17 July 2024).

in Vietnam with the most common ones repeating phrases such as "we are eternally grateful to Chairman Ho"[83] or "Uncle Ho lives forever in our revolutionary struggle".[84]

Most Vietnamese history textbooks dedicate a significant amount of content to teach Ho's revolutionary life and work. It is arguable that Ho Chi Minh is the most taught historical figure in Vietnamese schools, more than other important national heroes by a wide margin. Furthermore, Ho's poetry and essays and those by others that praise him are extensively taught in literature class from the elementary

Figure 2.3
Ho Chi Minh Museum in Hanoi

Source: Wikimedia Commons, Ho Chi Minh Museum, Hanoi, Vietnam, 2014, https://vi.wikipedia.org/wiki/B%E1%BA%A3o_t%C3%A0ng_H%E1%BB%93_Ch%C3%AD_Minh#/media/T%E1%BA%ADp_tin:Ho_Chi_Minh_Museum_-_Hanoi,_Vietnam_-_DSC03496.JPG (accessed 17 July 2024).

levels. It should be noted that when Ho is addressed using the third-person singular personal pronouns *Bác* (Uncle) or *Người* (He), the first letter is always capitalized regardless of its position in the sentence. Referring to Ho using a neutral pronoun such as *ông* (Mr) is considered to be an insult and can sometimes result in reprimand. The following passage is the first lesson from the ninth-grade literature textbook in an essay titled "Ho Chi Minh's style".

> In his eventful life, Chairman Ho Chi Minh had the opportunity to experience the cultures of many countries and regions in both the East and the West. He was fluent in several foreign languages, including French, English, Chinese, and Russian, and had many skills. Few leaders can match Chairman Ho Chi Minh's extensive knowledge of people and cultures around the world. Wherever he travelled, he made a conscious effort to study the local culture and arts at a deep level. He absorbed the best aspects of all cultures while remaining highly critical of capitalism. What was remarkable about Ho Chi Minh was his ability to blend all foreign influences into his Vietnamese cultural heritage, making him both very Vietnamese, stoic, and Oriental, yet also very modern.[85]

The government-sponsored cult of personality of Ho Chi Minh includes religious elements, more so than just being a revolutionary and communist leader. Vietnamese tradition involves venerating the dead, where respect is paid to deceased family members. However, many Vietnamese believe that the dead continue to exist as supernatural beings who can positively or negatively influence the lives of the living. The government of Vietnam has essentially canonized Ho Chi Minh to maintain his role as the focal point of the regime's charismatic authority. He is revered as a supernatural deity that watches over the country, and his altars can be found in many government offices and buildings. Even in Vietnamese embassies overseas, Ho's altars are often located at the centre, with diplomats and visitors frequently paying homage to him. Using its massive propaganda and censorship machinery, the CPV has established Ho Chi Minh's cult of personality and elevated his status to that of an immortal saint. Some people worship Ho as a divine being, and his portraits and altars can be found above the ancestral altar of many households, especially in rural and remote areas. Figure 2.4 shows a portrait of Ho Chi Minh

Figure 2.4
Ho Chi Minh's Portrait in a Ha Giang Province's Classroom

Source: Voice of Vietnam, "Classroom in a Remote Area", 2017, https://photo-cms-vovworld.zadn.vn// uploaded/vovworld/jaigtn/2017_11_20/media/lophocvungcao-11_ofsd.jpg (accessed 17 July 2024).

hanging in a classroom in the mountainous Ha Giang Province, one of the poorest provinces in Vietnam. To the left of the blackboard, a panel displaying "Five Things Taught by Uncle Ho" can be seen.[86]

People who openly express disrespect or deliberately insult him would usually become victims of harassment, detainment and even persecution by the public and the law enforcement apparatus even though there is no law in Vietnam that explicitly prohibits such actions.[87] Publications and statements with negative elements about Ho Chi Minh, especially about his romantic relationships and marriages, are strictly banned in Vietnam to maintain his image as a puritanical founding father whose entire life was devoted to the people of Vietnam.[88] The authors of such publications could face monetary fines, detainment or even arrest for "opposing the people's revolution". One of the most prominent cases of such "reactionary behaviours" was that of Vu Kim Hanh, the former editor-in-chief of *Tuoi Tre*, a major daily newspaper in Vietnam. She was sacked for allowing an article acknowledging Ho Chi Minh's early marriage to a Chinese woman, Zeng Xueming, to be published.[89] The government of Vietnam requested William Duiker to remove a significant portion written about Ho and his personal relationships in his book *Ho Chi Minh: A Life* for the book to be allowed to be translated to Vietnamese and published in Vietnam. Upon Duiker's refusal, the Vietnamese government prohibited the publication of the book inside the country altogether.

Ho's popularity in Vietnam during the First Indochina War helped immensely in establishing a support base among the common people of Vietnam. His image of a humble, benevolent, intimate and patriotic grandfather stands in quite stark contrast with his political opponents. For example, Bao Dai, despite being the rightful emperor of the Nguyen dynasty and, as such, a prominent inheritor of traditional legitimacy, was dwarfed by Ho in terms of popularity. The emperor, being born into royalty and spending too much time as a companion of the French colonizers, appeared to be a distant figure to many Vietnamese at that time. His questionable political attitude would damage the loyalty that Vietnamese had towards his dynasty and later his position as the Chief of State of Vietnam. Then–President of the United States Eisenhower admitted that:

> I have never talked or corresponded with a person knowledgeable in Indochinese affairs who did not agree that had elections been held as of the time of the fighting, possibly eighty per cent of the population would have voted for the communist Ho Chi Minh as their leader rather than Chief of State Bao Dai.[90]

Another of Ho's major political contenders was Ngo Dinh Diem. While widely known for his nationalistic tendency, Diem was deemed unfamiliar to the common Vietnamese, as he was an "alien ruler on [sic] his new country, a wealthy, Catholic, urban, mandarin from New Jersey", while during that time, most Vietnamese were "poor, Buddhist, rural peasants".[91] Diem was adamantly against a national election to unify Vietnam as mandated by the Geneva Accords because he could foresee that he could not beat Ho Chi Minh in a popular vote. Diem declared that South Vietnam was not bound by the Geneva Accords and, with the support from the United States, refused to let the elections be held.[92]

Even though communism was a distant and unfamiliar concept to the average Vietnamese during the 1940s and 1950s, it was Ho's close-to-your-heart image and personal charisma that made this alien ideology become accepted by the common Vietnamese. Ho would explain communism very simply to the Vietnamese farmers as something that would make their lives better and avoided using the entirely complicated concept that a philosophical approach of Marxism would entail. In Duiker's description, Ho, despite being the founder of the Indochina Communist Party and a high-ranking member of the Soviet Comintern, was

> ... not as dominant a personality as many other modern revolutionary leaders, such as Lenin, Stalin, or Mao Zedong; he appeared to lead by persuasion and consensus rather than by imposing his will through force of personality. Nor did he write frequently about his ideas or inner motivations. In contrast to other prominent revolution figures, Ho Chi Minh expressed little interest in ideology or intellectual debate and focused his thoughts and activities on the practical issue of freeing his country and other colonial societies from western imperialism.[93]

To many Vietnamese, the image of Ho reading the Declaration of Independence had become the symbol of Vietnamese independence. It was written by the contemporary newspapers *Cuu Quoc* (published 5 September 1945) and *Trung Bac Tan Van* (published 9 September 1945) that during the day of the reading, huge crowds gathered in both Hanoi and Saigon. Some said that they walked dozens of kilometres merely to look at Ho. Upon seeing Ho for the first time in flesh and blood, many broke into tears.[94, 95] More than twenty years later, defying the terrible transportation conditions that resulted from constant bombing and poor infrastructure, hundreds of thousands of people would again march many kilometres to Hanoi to attend Ho Chi Minh's funeral. Footage shows masses of people crying while marching along Ho's hearse.[96] Even in death, Ho Chi Minh would have lasting influence on Vietnam's politics as Ellsberg admitted, "Ho Chi Minh, dead, could beat any candidate we (the United States) have ever put up in Vietnam."[97]

The task of evaluating Ho Chi Minh's legacy after 1975 is a great obstacle for two reasons. First, since virtually all political opposition to Ho and the CPV within Vietnam has been eliminated, there is no longer any valid entity with which to compare Ho's popularity. Ho was officially made the single focal point of charismatic legitimacy of the CPV and, as such, has remained unchallenged until this day in terms of charismatic legitimacy. Secondly, the government presents Ho's image as an immortal saint who is universally loved by Vietnamese and thus studies about people's perception of him are considered taboo, except for biased research conducted for propagandistic purposes. As mentioned earlier, negative comments, publications and statements about Ho's life and works in government-controlled media outlets are usually suppressed. Criticism of Ho, however, can be found on channels that the Vietnamese government cannot control entirely, such as on the internet, often voiced anonymously or by overseas Vietnamese. A divisive figure, Ho Chi Minh has been linked to both the CPV's achievements and its failures as illustrated in Figure 2.5.

Perception of Ho Chi Minh also varies from north to south. The further north, the more people seem to be enamoured with him. In

Figure 2.5
Achievements and Failures of the CPV and Ho Chi Minh

Clockwise from top left: (1) A trial of a landlord during the land reform in North Vietnam. Ho's portrait can be seen at the top left. (2) Ho apologizing for the damage caused by CPV cadres during the land reform. (3) A Hanoi's street few days before the 2016 National Assembly Election. (4) A victory parade after the fall of Saigon in 1975.

Sources: hinnhanhlichsu.org, "Cải cách ruộng đất tại miền Bắc Việt Nam" [Land reform in Northern Vietnam], *Hình Ảnh Lịch Sử*, August 2019, https://www.hinhanhlichsu.org/2019/08/cai-cach-ruong-dat-tai-mien-bac-viet-nam.html (accessed 25 December 2024); Phan Thanh Hau, "Tư tưởng Hồ Chí Minh: Đã nhận biết sai lầm phải ra sức sửa chữa" [Ho Chi Minh Thought: once we have admitted our mistakes, we must try our best to correct them], Ho Chi Minh Mausoleum Official Website, 16 June 2017, https://www.bqllang.gov.vn/chu-tich-ho-chi-minh/nghien-cuu-hoc-tap-tu-tuong-ho-chi-minh/6282-tu-tuong-ho-chi-minh-da-nhan-biet-sai-lam-phai-ra-suc-sua-chua.html (accessed 17 July 2024); Tien Phong, "Đường phố Hà Nội rực rỡ trước ngày bầu cử" [Hanoi streets brightly decorated before election day], 16 May 2021, https://tienphong.vn/duong-pho-ha-noi-ruc-ro-truoc-ngay-bau-cu-post1337026.tpo (accessed 17 July 2024); National Defence Journal, "Cần vạch mặt những kẻ thù địch xuyên tạc bản chất và ý nghĩa của Chiến thắng 30-4-1975" [We need to denounce the enemies who have distorted the nature and the meaning of the 30-4-1975 victory], 16 April 2015, http://tapchiqptd.vn/vi/binh-luan-phe-phan/can-vach-mat-nhung-ke-thu-dich-xuyen-tac-ban-chat-va-y-nghia-cua-chien-thang-3041975/7284.html (accessed 17 July 2024).

the south, while there is a sustainable proportion of the populace that hold positive attitudes towards him, people who worked for the South Vietnam government or people who were victims of communist repression tend to be hostile towards communism and to an extent, to Ho Chi Minh himself. Younger generations are more indifferent about this topic. Most passively accept the teachings and propaganda of the government as facts and hold a positive attitude towards Ho, especially people from Ho's hometown, Nghe An, and nearby provinces. Most people would refrain from speaking ill of Ho openly, partly out of fear of being judged by their peers and partly because of their respect for Ho. Many overseas Vietnamese, in particular boat people that managed to escape Vietnam after the Vietnam War and their descendants, seem to hold negative views towards Ho.

It should be noted that the cult of personality of Ho Chi Minh is not without its ebb and flow. Marxism, the school of thought that the Vietnamese version of communist ideology is based upon, is anti-personalist in nature as Karl Marx had expressed his attitude against the cult of personality on many occasions.[98] The cadres of the CPV, as faithful followers of Marxism, are not exceptions to this tendency. This sentiment was especially emphasized in Vietnam during the late 1950s and early 1960s after Nikita Khrushchev delivered his famous speech "On the Cult of Personality and Its Consequences" to denounce Joseph Stalin. Ho Chi Minh himself was quoted loudly speaking against cults of personality: "From the central to the local level, (everybody) must strictly follow the collective leadership, individual responsibility principle and must do their utmost to fight against the cult of personality and the bureaucratic mentality."[99] In Article 38 of the 1980 Constitution of the Socialist Republic of Vietnam, only Marxism–Leninism is recognized as the "political ideology that should guide the development of Vietnamese society".

The introduction of Ho Chi Minh Thought as the official political ideology of the CPV more than a decade after his death perhaps can be explained through the CPV's need for a renewal of socialism as a state building ideology. The fall of communism in Eastern Europe is recognized by the CPV and domestic scholars as a "huge loss"[100] and that "The citadel of socialism has fallen. The great support for international communist and workers' movements is no more. The remaining socialist countries had to face the brutal consequences left by the collapse (of communism in Eastern Europe)."[101]

While the initiation of *Doi Moi* could revive the economy of Vietnam and strengthen the CPV's legitimacy in the short term, in the long term, the CPV has been struggling to justify the pursuit of communism. One of the strategies employed by the CPV's leadership to explain the fall of communism in Eastern Europe has been to call it a temporary backtrack and a failure of a single faulty model of communism. Nong Duc Manh[102] claimed in one of his speeches in 2007 that:

> Like other revolutions, the road ahead of our socialist revolution is not an easy one but is a road with many obstacles and sometimes we have to retrace our historical course. There are temporary backtracks but ultimately humankind will reach socialism for that is the law of evolution of history. The failure of socialism in the Soviet Union and Eastern Europe is only the failure of a particular model of realist socialism and is not the failure of socialism as a more advanced step to capitalism in the progress of history.[103]

Nevertheless, without distinguishing Vietnam's model of communism and the so-called Eastern European faulty model, the pursuit of communism in Vietnam was facing objections even from within the CPV.[104, 105] To maintain the validity of communism in Vietnam, the CPV created Ho Chi Minh Thought based on Ho's works. Ho Chi Minh Thought is usually used as a theoretical framework for the Party's application of Marxist-Leninist policies in the context of Vietnam. Although the Party has been actively using Ho Chi Minh's guidance to justify its general political direction, Ho Chi Minh Thought was only discussed as an official ideology of the CPV from its Seventh National Congress in June 1991.[106] The Ninth and Eleventh National Congress continued to define and develop this concept.[107]

Ho Chi Minh Thought is explained by the CPV as a version of Marxism that is applicable only in the context of the Vietnamese revolution. As the cult of personality of Ho Chi Minh has been a persistent characteristic of Vietnamese politics, the creation and adoption of this ideology as the official ideology of the CPV more than one decade after Ho's death does not necessarily point to a rise of this cult. Rather, it was one of the CPV's attempts to theoretically justify the pursuit of communism while distancing itself from failed communist regimes.

Socialism as a State-Building Ideology and Performance Legitimacy

Performance legitimacy can be linked to the concept of rational-legal legitimacy proposed by Weber. Rational-legal legitimacy is delivered from the legal system and institutions by the ruling regime to serve the public. While Weber did not emphasize economic aspects, he did indicate that this type of legitimacy revolves around the benefits to the regime's subjects. Weber paid more attention to the legal aspect of legitimacy and stressed that if the legal establishment and enforcement is considered to be beneficial to the people then the rule of the regime would also be deemed justifiable. The source of rational-legal legitimacy does not come from tradition or the charisma of any particular leader, but rather is empowered by public consent regarding the ruling regime's legality and rationality. This form of authority could be frequently found in the modern state and its establishments and institutions, such as city governments, private and public corporations, and various voluntary associations.[108] As Weber put it, "development of the modern state is identical indeed with that of modern officialdom and bureaucratic organizations just as the development of modern capitalism is identical with the increasing bureaucratization of economic enterprise". In other words, rational-legal legitimacy and bureaucracy often go hand in hand. However, organizations with rotating office holders, such as "parliamentary and committee administration and all sorts of collegiate and administrative bodies" could have non-bureaucratic legal authority.

On its own, performance legitimacy is originally suggested by Easton to be the only source of outcome-based legitimation strategies employed by states. Easton considers performance as an outcome source of legitimacy because it is based on the outcomes of the regime's policies to fulfil its citizens' basic needs.[109, 110] While economic development is the backbone of performance legitimacy, there is more to it. Certain criteria of performance legitimacy can be statistically evaluated through indices such as GDP per capita, annual economic growth, inflation and the unemployment rate.[111]

Other criteria are harder to estimate in numbers, for example income gaps and social inequality. Using propaganda to broadcast economic development to make citizens feel that they are enjoying gradually better living standards and social equality has been a legitimation strategy employed widely by political regimes. Regimes that lack noteworthy economic improvements would use false claims to compensate.[112] This is especially true in post-Cold War socialist regimes like Vietnam where social equality, which is based on economic equality, is one of the most important factors to the regime's legitimacy.

The CPV has consistently claimed legitimacy based on the argument that it is a party that represents workers and farmers, who made up around 90 per cent of Vietnam's population at the time of its establishment. This claim has been reiterated in all of the Party's political charters, from its founding to the present day. In the view of Ho Chi Minh and his colleagues, in the first half of the twentieth century, Vietnam was a half-feudalist colonial country where most people were living in poverty as the result of French domination and the Nguyen dynasty's exploitation. The CPV's leadership has clearly indicated on many occasions that, in addition to national independence, their priority was to ensure social equality and eliminate the federalists and the bourgeoisie by imposing socialist socioeconomic policies wherever and whenever possible.[113]

However, socialism, as a state-building ideology, failed to enhance the CPV's legitimacy due to socialist economic policies that led to a crumbling economy on the brink of collapse. The shift to a market model saved Vietnam's economy, yet the CPV continues to justify its pursuit of socialism by linking social and economic betterment to socialist policies and making promises about a utopian socialist future.

The Political Report presented at the Ninth National Congress in 2001 summarized three major accomplishments of the CPV throughout its seventy-one-year history: the August Revolution in 1945, which led to the establishment of the Democratic Republic of Vietnam and the dismantling of the feudal colonial system, ushering in an era of national independence and socialism; victorious resistance efforts to liberate the people and defend the Fatherland; and advancements during the transition period towards socialism.[114]

The first achievement highlights the CPV's success in overthrowing an oppressive regime and establishing a functional political system, thereby reinforcing its rational-legal authority. The second accomplishment—the victories in the First and Second Indochina Wars—is often associated with a strong sense of nationalism. The third achievement reflects the effectiveness of the market-oriented reforms implemented during the *Doi Moi* policy. The achievements that stemmed from the regime's socioeconomic policies can be linked to socialism as those achievements do not encompass only economic development, but also include any social equality that socialism entails. The Party has been very consistent in attributing its achievements to both human efforts and its socialist ideology, while failures have been blamed on human mistakes only.

Criticism of socialism as a failed economic model is often forbidden even within the inner circle of the Politburo. Take the land reform in North Vietnam between 1953 and 1956 as an example. Ho Chi Minh blamed the humanitarian crisis caused by the extrajudicial actions of communist cadres on their lack of education and the failure to clearly tell the differences between friends and foes. Likewise, party leader Le Duan admitted that the failure of pre-*Doi Moi*'s economic policies was due to mistakes made by the Party leadership, himself included, and not because communism was a flawed theory.[115]

The narrative that attributes achievements to the superiority of socialism and failures to human errors has persisted until recent years. According to the Resolution of the Thirteenth National Congress of the CPV in 2021, the COVID-19 pandemic was progressively mitigated and overcome through strong national solidarity, the advantages of socialism and the vigorous participation of the entire political system under the insightful leadership of the Party, supported by the populace. However, the same document attributes shortcomings and failures to the occasional underutilization of the full potential of national unity and socialism.

In this book, land reform in North Vietnam and during *Doi Moi* are discussed at length due to their importance as case studies about the conflict between theory and implementation of socialist policies. The CPV's attempts to justify their failure (in the case of land reform) and success (in the case of *Doi Moi*) to make them more compatible with their socialist ideology are also worth mentioning.

Only three years after the adoption of the Guideline of the Vietnam Workers' Party in 1951, land reform was carried out in North Vietnam. Land reform and the redistribution of land promised by the CPV were very attractive to common Vietnamese rural dwellers who had lived under French colonial rule. Although land reform in North Vietnam in the 1950s ultimately turned out to be a disaster and a heavy blow to the legitimacy of the CPV, at the beginning, the promise of giving more social rights and land to the peasants, who then constituted more than 80 per cent of the population, was well received. The Party considered the friction between the landowners and landless peasants as one of the most deep-rooted problems in Vietnam that needed urgent correction.

It is generally agreed among Vietnamese scholars that in feudal Vietnam, the State, with the emperor at its head, was the ultimate owner of all the land in the country. As such, individuals were not allowed to own land. However, the fact that private transactions were recorded in the Complete Annals of Dai Viet suggests that common people in Vietnam at that time were able to cultivate and sell land, and the right to own and sell equitable interests in the land was protected by law. In feudal Vietnam, commune ownership and private ownership of land were also allowed, which created friction between the landowner class and the landless peasant class.[116]

Marxist adherents, in principle, consider private land ownership to be "evil". Discussing private land ownership, Marx writes, "one of the specific evils of small-scale agriculture, where it is combined with free land ownership, arises from the cultivator's investing capital in the purchase of land".[117]

Following Marx's teachings and China's example, the Viet Minh launched a series of land reforms in North Vietnam, lasting three years from 1953 to 1956. Prior to 1953, there were already several attempts at land reform in communist-controlled territories in North Vietnam. However, during this time, the CPV's aim was to unite all the social classes of Vietnam against the French under the banner of national independence and salvation, and as such it was very lenient towards landlords.[118] As the war against the French was prioritized over class struggle, the CPV implemented land policies which were basically negotiations to lower land rent between landlords and farmers. However, from 1953, the Party was more radical in carrying out its land reforms for several reasons. First, the pre-1953 half-hearted land reform did not provide the peasants with a significantly better standing position in the society and failed to serve their interests. Landlords were allowed to become party members and in certain committees had become the dominant political force.[119] Secondly, the Chinese communists had become powerful after the Chinese Civil War and started to support the Vietnamese communists' struggle against the French while interfering with the CPV's domestic policies, in particular land reform policies, by training Vietnamese cadres and sending over Chinese political advisors.[120] The Chinese communists initiated their own land reform in the winter of 1950–51 and believed that their model should be copied by other communist regimes, including Vietnam. Thirdly, with the defeat of the French in May 1954, the Viet Minh gained control of North Vietnam and could focus on their class struggle mission.

Land reform was carried out in two main campaigns. The first campaign aimed to coerce landlords into reducing land rent. In accordance with decree 150/SL issued by the president of the Democratic Republic of Vietnam in April 1955, provisional people's tribunal courts, which consisted mostly of illiterate farmers who knew nothing about legal procedures, were established to persecute people who protested this policy. Many people were forced to denounce their family members to appear loyal to the Party. The second campaign was carried out even more violently, with as many as five times the number of victims in comparison to the first campaign.[121] Coercive expropriation was commonplace during this second phase of the land reform.[122] The land reform resulted in the persecution, exile and deaths of tens of thousands, leaving profound effects on Vietnamese society.

The CPV hastily carried out land reform in the areas it controlled while allocated the rest of its resources to the war effort against the French to strengthen the Party's legitimacy in the eyes of the poor peasants. In the CPV's own narrative, despite its shortcomings, the land reform was successful with "334,100 hectares of agricultural lands distributed among farmers, complete elimination of the landlord class and the remnant of feudalism in the North, empowerment of the farmers in rural areas", and the mistakes of the land reform were quickly corrected.[123]

In 2014, for the first time, an exhibition about the land reform was held within the borders of Vietnam.[124] Rather than focusing on the consequences, this exhibition emphasized the class struggle between the peasants and the landlords with the attempt to justify the implementation of the land reform as one of the most important socialist policies carried out by the CPV. Figure 2.6 shows an article from an old newspaper displayed at the exhibition titled "The Party Has Saved My Life".

Figure 2.6
The Party Has Saved My Life

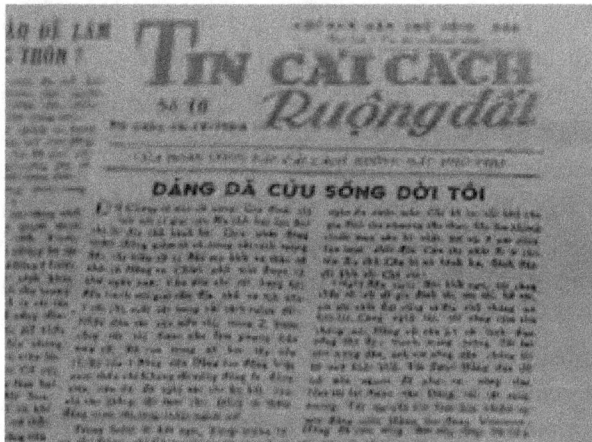

Title of an article in Land Reform News, no. 16. This article was displayed in the exhibition.

Source: Ngo Vuong Anh, "Trưng bày chuyên đề 'Cải cách ruộng đất 1946–1957'" ["Land reform 1946–1957" exhibition], *Nhandan*, 9 September 2014, https://nhandan.vn/trung-bay-chuyen-de-cai-cach-ruong-dat-1946-1957-post212689.html (accessed 17 July 2024).

Following the disastrous land reform, the CPV attempted to push towards socialism by carrying out a series of economic initiatives known as the three-year and five-year plans.[125] The CPV, determined to make a successful transition to socialism while skipping capitalism, implemented a centralized planned economy in North Vietnam from 1958 until 1965 in two separate initiatives. The first initiative lasted three years, from 1958 until 1960, and as such was named the Three-Year Plan. The second initiative followed the first one and lasted five years, from 1961 until 1965, and thus was named the First Five-Year Plan. Due to the escalation of the Second Indochina War, the Second Five-Year Plan was postponed until 1976. In 1976, after the unification of Vietnam, the National Congress of the CPV convened and decided to continue the five-year plans with the aim of standardizing the economic systems in both North and South Vietnam with an eye towards socialism.

Efforts to organize farmers into collective farming units between the 1960s and the 1980s were largely unsuccessful. The CPV forcefully relocated farmers to these collectives, disregarding the inherent contradiction between socialist policies and the traditional mindset of Vietnamese peasants. While farmers displayed little resistance, they failed to conform to the authorities' expectations. When assigned to collective work, farmers would comply but perform tasks hastily and inefficiently, as compensation remained the same regardless of their effort.[126] In contrast, farmers exhibited a markedly greater diligence when allocated individual plots of land. Additionally, farming communes in Vietnam often operated in isolation, adhering to their own rules, which frequently superseded those imposed by the central government. This phenomenon is encapsulated in the Vietnamese proverb "the law of the king must yield to the customs of the village".[127] Such divergent practices have presented formidable obstacles to the CPV's efforts to enforce uniform socialist policies across all villages.

From 1976 to 1978, Vietnam's industry saw some development, but from 1979 to 1989, industrial production experienced stagnation. The Second Five-Year Plan only saw Vietnam's industry grow by 0.1

per cent.[128] From 1975 to 1985, the consumer price index in Vietnam increased almost 40 times, peaking in 1982 and 1985, when prices doubled. Between 1986 and 1988, the inflation rate was 401.1 per cent.[129] As early as 1979, only four years after the end of the Vietnam War, Le Duan, the de facto leader of Vietnam at that time, publicly recognized the economic hardship resulting from the poor policies of the leadership.[130] Later, in 1982, he further admitted in his report that the Second Five-Year Plan had been a failure, and he endorsed reform.[131] Duan also pushed to strengthen both the centrally planned and local economies.[132]

However, prior to 1986, these changes had little effect, if any at all. After the death of Le Duan and the change of leadership in 1986, along with taking responsibility for the perilous situation that the country was in at that time, Hanoi would issue several economic measures: Decree 217 HDBT in 1987, which granted state-owned companies more autonomy and responsibilities; the 1988 Land Law, which recognized land right ownership; and the 1990 Law of Private Enterprises, which legalized private joint-stock companies and limited liability companies. These policies would soon transform the country and bring about positive results.

During the late 1980s and early 1990s, the decline and consequently the collapse of the Soviet Union and the Eastern Bloc posed a serious economic threat to Vietnam. China and the Soviet Union had been the two largest economic and military aid providers to Vietnam during the Vietnamese War. However, with the Sino-Soviet split in the 1960s and Vietnam's Soviet-leaning attitude, Chinese aid to Vietnam started to drop. Until the mid-1980s, the Soviets continued to provide Vietnam with US$1 billion annually. With that reconstruction aid gone from the mid-1980s, Vietnam struggled to recover. Furthermore, the invasion and occupation of Cambodia was a diplomatic disaster as Vietnam was denounced and isolated by the international community. China was the most responsive country towards Vietnam's invasion of Cambodia as the Khmer Rouge was a close Chinese ally. China ceased diplomatic relations and shut off aid to Vietnam in retaliation and went as far as to launch a full invasion against Vietnam in 1979.

This war did not only further devastate the already ruined economy of Vietnam but also completely severed Vietnam's ties with China and consequently left no chance for economic cooperation and aid. Furthermore, the normalization of diplomatic relations with the United States was stalled and the United States continued to enforce its trade embargo on Vietnam. Vietnam was also denied entrance to important international financial organizations and thus was unable to access funds much needed for reconstruction.

The fall of communism in Eastern Europe posed a serious legitimacy challenge to the CPV. For many years, the Soviet Union had been the model of socialism that Hanoi had strived to follow. Vietnam's communist leadership went as far as to mention the Soviet Union as a role model and trusted partner in its 1959 and 1980 constitutions.[133]

Prior to the collapse of the Soviet Union, phrases like "capitalism is dying" were frequently repeated in communist propaganda to persuade people that the Soviet Union's political and economic model would prevail. Despite the evident failures of socialist economic policies, the determination to progress directly to socialism without the transition through capitalism was reaffirmed while the market economy, individual ownership of property and capitalism were demonized and explicitly forbidden by the CPV.[134]

This view started to change during the late 1980s, however. The Guideline on Nation Building in the Transition Period to Socialism, which was approved by the CPV in 1991, suggests that the CPV had long been fully aware of both the failure of the socialist economic model in Vietnam and the success of the newly introduced market economy. Nguyen Phu Trong attributed this change in the CPV leadership's attitude to the domestic and international political climate at that time, in particular the decline and collapse of the Socialist model in the Soviet Union and many Eastern European countries, economic crisis Vietnam was experiencing and the disillusion of a proportion of cadres and party members.[135, 136]

Nevertheless, the leadership of the Party, while admitting the systematic collapse of the Eastern Bloc, refused to acknowledge the failure of communism as a state ideology. Socialism remained the focal point of this guideline. While pointing out the difficulties the CPV had to face, the guideline reaffirmed that the Party would not give up on its goal to achieve socialism. Trong claims that while "the world's history is taking some steps back, but humankind will ultimately reach socialism as it is the law of nature".[137]

In addition to the usual emphasis on the need to maintain socialism as Vietnam's state building ideology and future goal, the importance of concurrent economic development was clearly indicated in the 1991 Guideline. Economic crises due to disastrous socialist policies, which was noticed by the leadership of the CPV from as early as the late 1970s, were mentioned in the guideline and economic development was recognized as a means to reach true socialism and to maintain national independence.

It was not until the Ninth National Congress of the CPV in 2001 that the CPV started to use the term "socialist-oriented market economy"[138] to explain the adoption of the market economy model under the socialist ideology. The Resolution of the Ninth National Congress claims that the introduction of socialist-oriented market economy should reflect the perception of the Party on the relationship between production and productive forces; the Party also dictated that the newly introduced socialist-oriented market economy should be the "overall economic model of Vietnam in the transition period to socialism".[139] The CPV put further emphasis on justifying the socialist-oriented market economy in the 2008 Resolution on the Continuation of the Completion of Socialist-Oriented Market Economy. It could be observed that although the CPV launched *Doi Moi* in 1986, the need to clarify the contradiction between the socialist political system and the then newly established market economy came much later and has been undergoing a gradual theoretical evolution.

The Sixth National Congress of the CPV in 1986 acknowledged significant challenges in Vietnam's economy, noting sluggish production growth, low investment and manufacturing effectiveness, unequal goods distribution, widening economic gaps and prevalent issues of bad governance and corruption, sometimes to an extreme extent.[140] Nevertheless, the market economy model was not mentioned in the

Resolution of the Sixth National Congress. Rather than comprehensively reforming the economy, the CPV put more emphasis on the need to strengthen the production of three groups of products: food, consumer goods and goods for export. The economy would then be restructured to optimize the production of those goods.[141] The congress maintained that socialist economy must be strengthened and, while it admitted that the petite bourgeoisie class and small business in certain areas is acceptable, private commercial capitalism must be eliminated.

Looking back at the theoretical evolution regarding the market economy of the CPV, the deputy editor-in-chief of the *Communist Review Journal*[142] noted that while during the first stage of *Doi Moi*, the Party only mentioned the development of the planned multi-sector commodity economy towards socialism and did not mention the market mechanism and the development of the market economy, this was an important landmark in the theoretical renovation of the Party about the road to socialism.[143]

In 1991, the Seventh National Congress reflected on the economic progress made in the three years following the Sixth National Congress, acknowledging the establishment of a foundation for a multi-sector commodity economy. It noted significant production improvements, marking the initial stage of a market mechanism-driven economy under state management. The Congress also recognized the economy's ability to mobilize productive resources internally while reducing inflation and enhancing the living standards for a portion of the population.[144]

The Seventh National Congress further set the direction towards socialism and urged for the development of productive forces "in accordance with the socialist relations of production from low to high level along with a variety of ownership" and the advancement of the multi-sector commodity economy which followed market mechanisms under the management of the State.

This direction was maintained during the Eighth National Congress of the CPV in 1996 as no further elaboration was put into defining the economic model. The target was set by the Eighth National Congress to gradually establish the socialist-oriented market mechanism under the control of the State. However, this National Congress acknowledged individual capitalism as a legitimate economic sector along with state economy, collective economy, state capitalism, individual economy and small business owners.[145] During this stage, the CPV did not use the term market economy to directly describe Vietnam's economy. The Eighth National Congress of the CPV is noteworthy because the Party reinterpreted the relationships between commodity production and socialism.

> Commodity production is not the opposite of socialism. Commodity production is an achievement of human civilization and has been existing objectively and is necessary for the construction of socialism and (will still exist) when socialism will be firmly established.[146]

During the Ninth National Congress of the CPV in 2001, the concept of a socialist-oriented market economy was officially recognized. The Document of the Ninth National Congress devoted an entire section to discussing the concept of a socialist-oriented market economy, mentioning it eleven times. The CPV defined the socialist-oriented market economy as "a multi-sector commodity economy operating based on market mechanisms under the socialist-oriented management of the State" and advocated for its sustained and consistent development. The Ninth Congress recognized private ownership and private economic sectors while asserting the state economy as the leading force. It emphasized that the entire economy must be managed by the State to leverage the advantages and mitigate the disadvantages of the market mechanism, thereby safeguarding the interests of the working population and the Vietnamese populace. The Ninth Congress also recognized that these changes reflect a shift in the Party's understanding of the compatibility between the relations of production and the nature and level of the productive forces.[147]

After the Ninth National Congress, the CPV put considerable efforts into theoretically justifying the existence of the market economy in Vietnam both to its cadres and to the public. The adoption of the market economy within the framework of socialism in Vietnam is reinterpreted as follows:

> Classical Marxism and Leninism scholars reject the notion of the market economy within socialism; however, we acknowledged that market economies

can exist within socialism. The reason is that there was a change in our perception about socialism. The change in our perception about socialism came from the change in our perception about social equality. Before Doi Moi, we maintained that a market economy cannot exist in parallel with common ownership; without common ownership, there won't be equality; without equality there won't be socialism; as such socialism also cannot exist in parallel with a market economy. After Doi Moi, we acknowledged that even without common ownership there can be social equality and, as such, socialism can be reached.[148]

The Tenth National Congress of the CPV in 2006 was even more liberal in its conceptualization of the market economy and assured that "the right to the ownership of property and the freedom to engage in business dealings of every citizen are guaranteed by the law".[149] This is the first time that an official document issued by the CPV recognized the vital importance of the private economic sector as one of the driving forces of the economy.[150] The Tenth National Congress requested that clear distinctions be made between the public administration function of the State and the economic management function of the firms, and between the bureaucratic bodies and the state-owned businesses.[151]

The Eleventh National Congress of the CPV prioritized the development of the socialist-oriented market economy as one of the three strategic breakthroughs of national development along with human resource development and infrastructure development. The Eleventh National Congress defined socialist-oriented market economy as "a variant of market economy that follows the principles of market economy while operating based on the basic principles and the nature of socialism".[152] The Eleventh National Congress was laxer towards the private sector of the economy as it encouraged the formation of several private economic groups and allowed private individuals or enterprises to invest in state-owned companies and groups.[153]

Resolution TW5, adopted by the Twelfth National Congress of the CPV in 2016, further refined the concept of a socialist-oriented market economy as a fully functional economic model operating according to free market principles while ensuring a socialist orientation. The economy must be managed by a law-governed socialist state led by the CPV, with the ultimate goals of achieving "wealthy people, a strong country, and a democratic, equal, and civilized society".

The Resolution of the Thirteenth National Congress of the CPV in February 2021, while not introducing new concepts, reaffirmed the CPV's commitment to pursuing socialism alongside maintaining a market economy. It set targets for socioeconomic development by 2023, emphasizing the need to continue to maintain balance among various factors. These include stability, innovation and development; economic and political innovation; adherence to market rules while progressing towards socialism; and the development of productive forces alongside the gradual completion of production relations.

The brief overview above about the directions laid by the National Congresses of the CPV between 1986 and 2021 indicates that the CPV has become increasingly liberal in their policies towards the market economy. This attitude sharply contradicts the official view of the CPV before 1986.

To conclude, before the start of *Doi Moi*, the CPV based their performance legitimacy on social changes such as the removal of the feudal landowners and the bourgeoisie and the empowerment of the peasantry and working class. They also based their performance legitimacy on the promise of revolutionary advancement to socialism. After the beginning of *Doi Moi*, however, the CPV changed their tone and attempted to rely on economic development and the betterment of the people's living standard to buttress their obedient worthiness. The Party also recognized the market economy as an important transition period between the current economy of Vietnam and true socialism in contrast with the anti-capitalism attitude that was emphasized before *Doi Moi*. The perception of the CPV's leadership about the role of the market economy had also become more liberal over time. During the first half of the 1980s, the Party outrightly rejected the market economy as an inseparable element of capitalism. During the late 1980s, the Party started to accept small business owners as a legitimate sector of the economy. From the early 1990s, the Party has considered Vietnam's economy to be the first step towards a full-fledged socialist-oriented multi-sector commodity economy. This commodity economy would fully mature into a market economy and then advance towards a socialist economy. The concept of a socialist-oriented market economy was officially adopted by the CPV in the early 2000s.

Thanks to the initiation of *Doi Moi*, Vietnam had enjoyed three decades of quick economic development and political stability. The government's policies to promote free market with financial incentives and to encourage the establishment of private businesses and attract foreign investment had led to major improvement in the private sectors. By the late 1990s, with the success of the reform in the business and agricultural sectors, more than 30,000 private businesses were created, Vietnam's GDP increased at an annual rate of more than 7 per cent, and poverty being nearly halved by the early 2000s.[154] Vietnam signed several bilateral and multilateral trade agreements with its business partners and in 2007, the country became an official member of the World Trade Organization, which allowed it to further strengthen its trade ties with other countries. As a result, Vietnam's exports grew by as much as 20 to 30 per cent per year throughout the 1990s and, at the beginning of the twenty-first century, exports accounted for 40 per cent of the country's GDP while other Asian countries were still struggling to recover from the 1997 Asian financial crisis.

In 2011, the CPV updated the 1991 Guideline on Nation Building in the Transition Period to Socialism, which emphasizes its traditionally based achievements, Ho Chi Minh's charismatic leadership, economic achievements and the determination to proceed towards socialism. The timely introduction of *Doi Moi* provided the CPV with a new and much needed source of legitimacy that was actively utilized to buttress its deteriorating legitimacy, which is acknowledged by the Twelfth National Congress of the CPV.[155] Nguyen Phu Trong claimed that the adoption of a socialist-oriented market economy has not only improved the economy, but also led to the resolution of many social issues and consolidation of the people's trust in the leadership of the CPV.[156]

More than thirty years after the collapse of the Eastern Bloc and the start of *Doi Moi*, socialism as a state-building ideology remains closely linked to social and economic development in the legitimization strategies of the CPV. The CPV has consistently promoted socialism as its official state-building ideology since its establishment in 1930. The only exception to this was the period between 1945 and 1946 when the Party sought popular support for its efforts to fight against the return of the French colonial empire. Before *Doi Moi*, the Party tried to address the lack of significant economic development by implementing land reform and other social changes to reduce social inequality between rich landlords and poor peasants. While the land reforms successfully redistributed land among farmers, they also had long-lasting negative effects on Vietnamese society. The Party also implemented the Three-Year Plan from 1958 to 1960 and the first five-year plan from 1961 to 1965, but most of the resources produced by the economy of North Vietnam were directed towards the war efforts in the South until 1975, and as a result, there were no significant improvements in people's living standards.

The recently discovered diaries of North Vietnamese soldiers who died in the line of duty during the Vietnam War indicated that most of them believed that socialism would be realized in North Vietnam.[157] However, as wars ended, socialism as a state-building ideology became less attractive since the lack of economic development could no longer be attributed to the mobilization of society's resources for the war effort. Many who survived the war felt disillusioned and betrayed by the Party's policies and questioned the continuation of socialism. This included prominent military officers, writers, journalists, lawyers and politicians.

The CPV leadership is well aware of the strife from within. Resolution No. 04-NQ/TW of the Twelfth Central Committee of the CPV in 2016, approved by General Secretary Nguyen Phu Trong, identified the following internal threats within the Party: fading revolutionary ideals, wavering belief in the goals of national independence and socialism, and a lack of trust in Marxism-Leninism and Ho Chi Minh Thought; a departure from the Party's principles and objectives, failure to firmly adhere to the path towards socialism and being misled by distorted perceptions and incorrect viewpoints; a distorted understanding of the importance of political theory and a reluctance to study Marxism-Leninism and Ho Chi Minh Thought; rejection of

Marxism-Leninism and Ho Chi Minh Thought, and the Party's principle of democratic centralism, coupled with demands for the implementation of a multiple-party system; refutation of socialist democracy and the rule of law, calls for the implementation of separation of powers and the development of civil societies, and denial of the market-oriented socialist economy and the people's collective ownership of land.

While the CPV steadfastly asserts that economic development and progress towards socialism are complementary, serving to justify its governance, this narrative finds limited acceptance among the populace. This is particularly true when party leadership, self-identified as communists, disproportionately benefit from economic growth resulting from market-oriented policies, often through bribery and embezzlement, while workers and farmers are marginalized and impoverished. This reality is reflected in the rising number of worker protests demanding liveable wages and improved working conditions since the mid-1990s, coinciding with the tangible effects of *Doi Moi*.[158]

The younger generation in Vietnam has been growing increasingly indifferent to socialist ideology despite grassroots-level indoctrination. Children aged between nine and fifteen years old are almost uniformly required to join the Ho Chi Minh Young Pioneer Organization, a subordinate organization of the CPV, which is tasked with educating young children with the State's ideology of Marxism-Leninism and Ho Chi Minh Thought. Most teenagers from the age of fifteen are required to join the Ho Chi Minh Communist Youth Union, the young wing of the CPV. Communist ideology is also instilled in children and young people through mandatory subjects at all education levels. Nevertheless, state-controlled media admitted that young people are distancing themselves to the socialist ideology and have become more materialistic.[159] The Party, however, continues to reaffirm that Karl Marx's theory was not faulty and that it will not give up socialism.[160, 161]

Conclusion

The CPV has meticulously constructed its legitimacy through a combination of tradition-based achievements and values, Ho Chi

Minh's charismatic leadership and performance legitimacy supported by socialism as a state-building ideology. However, these sources of legitimacy often conflict with each other and within themselves, necessitating significant efforts to justify their coexistence.

Throughout the First and Second Indochina Wars, the CPV relied on nationalism and socialism as the pillars of its propaganda strategy, despite their conflicting nature. Following the August Revolution in 1945, the Party temporarily deviated from socialist principles to garner support from nationalist factions, only to later implement land reforms to solidify support from the peasantry.

The CPV portrays itself as the defender of Vietnam's sovereignty against foreign invaders such as the French and the Americans and as steadfast followers of authentic socialism during conflicts with former allies like the Khmer Rouge. The Sino-Vietnamese War was used to emphasize the CPV's struggle against both foreign invaders and traitors of the socialist ideal. China is also depicted as the stock antagonist in most Vietnamese textbooks, and the thousands of years of conflict with China have shaped a significant part of the Vietnamese identity.

Constant warfare and disastrous socialist policies pushed Vietnam to the brink of collapse. Only the timely introduction of *Doi Moi* saved the country's economy. Initially overlooked, the imperative to reconcile market economic policies with socialist ideology became increasingly urgent for the CPV. Despite significant propaganda efforts, this task proved daunting. Nevertheless, the Party remained steadfast in defending its ideology.

To bolster its authority, the CPV built a cult of personality around revolutionary leader Ho Chi Minh despite cults of personality being antithetical to socialism. While many northern Vietnamese, especially those from Ho's hometown and nearby provinces, revered Ho, this sentiment was not shared among some southerners. Balancing cults of personality with socialism, the Party also needed to ensure that new leadership was not overshadowed by Ho while still portraying them as loyal to his ideals.

It can be argued that, following *Doi Moi*, the most vital source of legitimacy for the CPV is performance legitimacy. As long as the regime can placate its subjects with material benefits and distractions, they will remain tolerant of its rule. However, nationalism as a pillar of the CPV's legitimacy should be overlooked, as the Vietnamese identity is built upon a history of struggle against foreign invaders. While socialism and Ho Chi Minh's leadership remain somewhat relevant, they are less influential, particularly among the younger generation of Vietnamese. In recent years, as a supplement to Ho Chi Minh's charismatic leadership, the veneration of other prominent communist figures such as Vo Nguyen Giap and Nguyen Phu Trong have also been promoted by the CPV.

The evolving global landscape and internal sociopolitical dynamics have posed significant threats to the CPV's legitimacy, emanating from both external pressures and internal dissent. As explored in the subsequent chapter, these changes compel the CPV to intensify its propaganda efforts to safeguard its legitimacy amid mounting challenges.

Notes

1. Ho Chi Minh, *Hồ Chí Minh Toàn Tập* [Ho Chi Minh's complete works], vol. 5 (Hanoi: National Political Publishing House, 2000), p. 232.
2. Wolfgang Mommsen, *The Political and Social Theory of Max Weber* (Oxford: Blackwell, 1989), p. 20.
3. Max Weber, *The Theory of Social and Economic Organization*, edited by Talcott Parsons (New York: The Free Press, 1964), p. 382.
4. Max Weber, "The Three Types of Legitimate Rule", translated by Hans Gerth, in *Berkeley Publications Society and Institutions* 4 (1958): 1–11.
5. Arthur Ripstein, "Authority and Coercion", *Philosophy and Public Affairs* 32, no. 1 (2004): 2–35.
6. John Rawls, *Political Liberalism* (New York: Columbia University Press, 1993), p. 34.
7. Ibid.
8. Schmidt (2003) maintained that any political regime, from absolute monarchy to liberal democracy, must ensure that it is considered legitimate by its subjects to remain in power over the long term. In the words of Easton (1965) and Brady (2009), if a ruling regime is perceived as worthy of obedience, its actions and policies will be less costly. This is because they are less likely to be resisted by the population and violent repression involving the military or law enforcement in most cases will thus not be needed. Less costly and more widely accepted policies would translate

into more easily sustainable governance and, consequently, more durability. Burnell (2006) brought up the case of the Roman Empire, where even the emperor needed the loyalty of the praetorian guard as a bare minimum to maintain his power. In more democratic and liberal societies, this bare minimum is broadened. For example, in the case of the United States, a presidential candidate first needs to be nominated by his or her own party to run with their endorsement in presidential elections, and then would need to win a majority of votes from the Electoral College, representing the entire population, to be elected. In the case of Japan, although the de facto leader of the country, the prime minister, does not have to be elected in a universal election, he must secure the support of the dominant party or the dominant coalition to be designated as leader by the National Diet of Japan.

Gilley (2009) argued that almost every sovereign state in the modern world claims that its legitimacy stems from the right and just political and social order created under its rule. However, in this study, legitimacy is understood to be "the capacity of a political system to engender and maintain the belief that existing political institutions are the most appropriate or proper ones for the society" (Lipset 1959). Grauvogel and von Soest (2014) argued that there are three ways through which those claims to legitimacy can have actual impact on the social and political structure of a country, namely elite cohesion, opposition movements and regime popularity.

Firstly, Barker (2001) and LeBas (2013) pointed out that strong claims to legitimacy could potentially improve elite cohesion. Cohesion is generated through a collective identification of the ruling elite as a group that shares several similarities. This collective identification is created through emphasis on the process of legitimation. The more effort put into legitimation, the more reliable and more powerful this collective identification is. Alagappa (1995) added that relationships among the ruling elite can be further enhanced by using tactics of legitimacy improvement, such as the imposition of socioeconomic performance goals. Secondly, by employing certain legitimation strategies, the ruling regime can control the opposition's criticism by determining who may criticize the government and via which channels. If effectively used, legitimation strategies could marginalize dissidents and actors deemed undesirable by the ruling regime, restrict their access to the public and distort their portrayal in the mass media in a way that favours the regime. Case (1995) added that skilfully presented claims to legitimacy can help the ruling regime steer perception of the masses in a desirable direction. As a result, even during periods of upheaval, such as economic decline or political crisis, widely accepted claims to legitimacy could be crucial to the survival of a ruling regime. This perception, subsequently, would define the political vessel through which the regime could practise its rule. Thirdly, according to Burnell (2006), legitimacy also determines how vulnerable a regime is to internal crises and external pressures. As a result, in addition to organizational power, legitimacy is another crucial factor that defines the internal resilience of a political regime.

Nevertheless, Alagappa (1995) and Burnell (2006) pointed out that while elections masquerading as democracy have been held frequently in many post-Cold War Eurasian countries as one of their most important legitimation strategies, these by no means could be their sole sources of legitimacy because these elections fail to meet Western democratic standards. In fact, the CPV has frequently employed all three of the aforementioned strategies to buttress its legitimacy while sidelining and demonizing its political opposition.

See Vivien Schmidt, "The European Union: Democratic Legitimacy in a Regional State?", *IHS Political Science Series* 91 (2003); David Easton, *A Framework for Political Analysis* (Englewood Cliffs, NJ: Prentice-Hall, 1965); Anne-Marie Brady, "Mass Persuasion as a Means of Legitimation and China's Popular Authoritarianism", *American Behavioural Scientist* 53 (2009): 434–57; Peter Burnell, "Autocratic Opening to Democracy: Why Legitimacy Matters", *Third World Quarterly* 27 (2006): 545–62; Bruce Gilley, *The Right to Rule: How States Win and Lose Legitimacy* (Columbia: Columbia University Press, 2009); Seymour Martin Lipset, "Some Social Requisites of Democracy: Economic Development and Political Legitimacy", *American Political Science Review* 53, no. 1 (March 1959); Julia Grauvogel and Christian von Soest, "Claims to Legitimacy Count: Why Sanctions Fail to Instigate Democratization in Authoritarian Regimes", *European Journal of Political Research* 53 (2014): 635–53; Rodney Barker, *Legitimating Identities: The Self-Presentations of Rulers and Subjects* (Cambridge: Cambridge University Press, 2001); Adrienne LeBas, *From Protest to Parties: Party-Building and Democratization in Africa* (Oxford: Oxford University Press, 2013); Muthiah Alagappa, *Political Legitimacy in Southeast Asia: The Quest for Moral Authority* (Stanford, CA: Stanford University Press, 1995); William Case, "Malaysia: Aspects and Audiences of Legitimacy", in *Political Legitimacy in Southeast Asia*, edited by Muthiah Alagappa (Stanford, CA: Stanford University Press, 1995).

9. Schmidt, "The European Union: Democratic Legitimacy in a Regional State?", p. 10.
10. Lipset, "Some Social Requisites of Democracy: Economic Development and Political Legitimacy", p. 86.
11. Brady, "Mass Persuasion as a Means of Legitimation and China's Popular Authoritarianism", pp. 434–57.
12. Burnell, "Autocratic Opening to Democracy: Why Legitimacy Matters", pp. 545–62.
13. Grauvogel and von Soest, "Claims to Legitimacy Count: Why Sanctions Fail to Instigate Democratization in Authoritarian Regimes", pp. 635–53.
14. Barker, *Legitimating Identities: The Self-Presentations of Rulers and Subjects*.
15. LeBas, *From Protest to Parties: Party-Building and Democratization in Africa*.
16. Alagappa, *Political Legitimacy in Southeast Asia: The Quest for Moral Authority*.
17. Ibid., p. 4.
18. Case, "Malaysia: Aspects and Audiences of Legitimacy", p. 104.
19. Burnell, "Autocratic Opening to Democracy: Why Legitimacy Matters", p. 545.

20. Alagappa, *Political Legitimacy in Southeast Asia: The Quest for Moral Authority*, pp. 31–35.
21. Johannes Gerschewski, "The Three Pillars of Stability: Legitimation, Repression, and Co-optation in Autocratic Regimes", *Democratization* 20 (2013): 13–38.
22. Easton, *A Framework for Political Analysis*.
23. Lipset, "Some Social Requisites of Democracy: Economic Development and Political Legitimacy".
24. Timur Kuran, "Chameleon Voters and Public Choice", *Public Choice* 53 (1987): 53–78, https://doi.org/10.1007/BF00115654.
25. In Kuran's works, preference falsification is described as a phenomenon whereby individuals have the tendency to alter their preferences to be more acceptable to society, even if that means hiding their true preferences. The resulting misinterpretation is termed "preference falsification". For example, a person born to a family of communists would have the tendency to support communism. See Timur Kuran, *Private Truths, Public Lies: The Social Consequences of Preference Falsification* (Cambridge, MA: Harvard University Press, 1995).
26. Gilley, *The Right to Rule: How States Win and Lose Legitimacy*, p. 12.
27. Grauvogel and von Soest, "Claims to Legitimacy Count: Why Sanctions Fail to Instigate Democratization in Authoritarian Regimes", pp. 635–53.
28. Michael Wahman, Jan Teorell, and Axel Hadenius, "Authoritarian Regime Types Revisited: Updated Data in Comparative Perspective", *Contemporary Politics* 19 (2013): 19–34, https://doi.org/10.1080/13569775.2013.773200.
29. Easton, *A Framework for Political Analysis*.
30. Burnell, "Autocratic Opening to Democracy: Why Legitimacy Matters".
31. Fritz W. Scharpf, *Governing in Europe: Effective and Democratic?* (Oxford: Oxford University Press, 1999).
32. Edward Schatz, "Access by Accident: Legitimacy Claims and Democracy Promotion in Authoritarian Central Asia", *International Political Science Review* 27, no. 3 (2006): 263–84.
33. Julia Grauvogel and Christian von Soest, "How Do Non-democratic Regimes Claim Legitimacy? Comparative Insights from Post-Soviet Countries", GIGA Working Papers 277 (2015).
34. Le Hong Hiep, "Performance-Based Legitimacy: The Case of the Communist Party of Vietnam and *Doi Moi*", *Contemporary Southeast Asia* 34, no. 2 (2012): 145–72.
35. Nguyen Khac Vien, "Confucianism and Marxism in Vietnam", in *Tradition and Revolution in Vietnam* (Berkeley, CA: Indochina Resource Center, 1975), pp. 15–52.
36. William Duiker, *The Rise of Nationalism in Vietnam, 1900–1941* (Ithaca, NY: Cornell University Press, 1976), p. 127.
37. John T. McAlister and Paul Mus, *The Vietnamese and Their Revolution* (New York: Harper & Row, 1970).

38. Stephen B. Young, "Unpopular Socialism in United Vietnam", *Orbis – A Journal of World Affairs* 21 (1977): 227–39.

39. Thaveeporn Vasavakul, "The Changing Models of Legitimation", in *Political Legitimacy in Southeast Asia: The Quest for Moral Authority*, edited by Muthiah Alagappa (Stanford, CA: Stanford University Press, 1995), pp. 257–89.

40. Sungmoon Kim, *Public Reason Confucianism: Democratic Perfectionism and Constitutionalism in East Asia* (Cambridge: Cambridge University Press, 2016), p. 233.

41. The three principles (*tam cương*) are the bonds between father and son (*cha-con*), ruler and subject (*vua-tôi*) and husband and wife (*chồng-vợ*). The five virtues (*ngũ thường*) are benevolence (*nhân*), righteousness (*nghĩa*), propriety (*lễ*), wisdom (*trí*) and trustworthiness (*tín*).

42. Mary T. Kelleher, "San-ts'ung ssu-te", in *The Illustrated Encyclopedia of Confucianism: N-Z*, vol. 2, edited by Rodney L. Taylor and Howard Y.F. Choy (New York: The Rosen Publishing Group, 2005), p. 496.

43. Craig Calhoun, James Gerteis, Joe Moody, Steven Pfaff, and Indermohan Virk, eds., *Classical Sociological Theory* (Chichester, UK: John Wiley & Sons, 2012), p. 23.

44. Patricia Springborg, "Karl Marx on Democracy, Participation, Voting, and Equality", *Political Theory* 12 (1984): 537–56.

45. It should be noted that while this concept is quite similar to the concept of divine right of kings in the West, there is no all-powerful god in Chinese traditional belief unlike in Christianity and thus this mandate is not granted to an emperor by a single omnipotent deity, but rather by a supernatural council of godheads representing the laws of nature.

46. *Thắng làm vua, thua làm giặc* [in Vietnamese].

47. Karl Marx, "Critique of the Gotha Programme", in *Karl Marx, Frederick Engels: Collected Works*, vol. 24 (1989): 75–99.

48. Ho Chi Minh, *Hồ Chí Minh Toàn Tập* [Ho Chi Minh's complete works], vol. 5, p. 304.

49. Ibid., pp. 570–71.

50. Vietnam Defense, "Cuộc kháng chiến chống Mỹ, cứu nước (1954–1975)" [National salvation and resistance war against America (1954–1975)], 14 September 2009, http://vietnamdefence.com/Homc/quansuvietnam/khoinghiachientranh/Cuoc-khang-chien-chong-My-cuu-nuoc-19541975/20099/48704.vnd (accessed 10 July 2024).

51. Ho Chi Minh, *Hồ Chí Minh Toàn Tập* [Ho Chi Minh's complete works], vol. 2, p. 511.

52. Ibid., pp. 291–92.

53. D. C. Lau, trans., *The Analects* (Harmondsworth, Middlesex, England: Penguin Books, 1979), p. 102.

54. There have been heated discussions among Vietnamese scholars on whether the army should be loyal to the nation or the Party. Certain sources claim that Ho Chi Minh explicitly stated that the army must remain loyal to the Party while others claim that he only mentioned the nation.

55. *Quân Đội Nhân Dân Online*, "Mười Lời thề danh dự của quân nhân" [Ten oaths of enlistment for military service], 6 April 2014, https://www.qdnd.vn/van-hoa-giao-duc/doi-song-van-hoa/muoi-loi-the-danh-du-cua-quan-nhan-412982 (accessed 10 July 2024).

56. Decree 09/2008/QĐ-BCAX11.

57. Kai Nielsen, "Liberal Nationalism, Liberal Democracies and Secession", *University of Toronto Law Journal* 48 (1998): 253–95, https://doi.org/10.2307/825982.

58. The first aspect requires a more thorough explanation about the concept of nationhood and national identity. In other words, when should a political entity be considered a nation? Furthermore, should membership in a nation be considered involuntary or voluntary? When the identity of one's nation comes into conflict with one's religion or loyalty, which should take precedence? For more discussion on this topic, see Isaiah Berlin, "Nationalism: Past Neglect and Present Power", *Partisan Review* 46, no. 3 (1979): 337–58; Anthony D. Smith, *Ethno-symbolism and Nationalism: A Cultural Approach* (Abingdon: Routledge, 2009); and Chaim Gans, *The Limits of Nationalism* (Cambridge: Cambridge University Press, 2003).

    The second aspect is concerned with the definition of sovereignty and to what extent the sovereignty of a state should be considered complete. See Hudson Meadwell, "Nationalism chez Gellner", *Nations and Nationalism* 18 (2012): 563–82; and David Miller, *Citizenship and National Identity* (Cambridge: Polity Press, 2000).

59. Reuters, "Soccer: Wild Celebrations in Hanoi as Vietnam Wins the Regional Title", 16 December 2018, https://www.reuters.com/article/soccer-asean-idINKBN1OF027 (accessed 10 July 2024).

60. Hans Kohn, "Nationalism as Group Consciousness", in *The Dynamics of Nationalism*, edited by Louis L. Snyder (Princeton, New Jersey: D. Van Nostrand Company, 1964).

61. William Ball, "Nationalism and Communism in Vietnam", *Far Eastern Survey* 21 (1952): 21–27, https://doi.org/10.2307/3024534.

62. Paul Giran, *Psychologie du peuple annamite: Le caractère national. L'évolution historique, intellectuelle, sociale et politique* (1904).

63. Stephen B. Young, "Who Were the Real Nationalists in Vietnam?", *New York Times*, 9 March 2018, https://www.nytimes.com/2018/03/09/opinion/who-were-the-real-nationalists-in-vietnam.html (accessed 10 July 2024).

64. For more information, see the 1959 Constitution of the Democratic Republic of Vietnam, the 1980 Constitution of Socialist Republic of Vietnam, the 1992 Constitution of Socialist Republic of Vietnam and the 2013 Constitution of Socialist Republic of Vietnam. The first words of the preamble of the constitutions have always been more

or less as follows: "Over their thousands of years of history, the Vietnamese people have always been working diligently and creatively, fighting bravely to build and to protect the Vietnamese nation and civilization."

65. Xiaoming Zhang, "China's 1979 War with Vietnam: A Reassessment", *The China Quarterly* 184 (2005): 851–74.

66. Chinese sources claim at least 200,000 (Zhang 2005), while Vietnamese sources claim 600,000 (Phuong 2017).

67. Hoang Phuong, "Remembering Vietnam's Bloody Border War with China", *VnExpress*, 16 February 2017. https://e.VnExpress.net/news/news/remembering-vietnam-s-bloody-border-war-with-china-3542147.html (accessed 10 July 2024).

68. In 2013, the Ministry of Culture, Sports and Tourism issued Decree 2296/BVHTTDL-MTNATL, which names fourteen individuals who were officially recognized by the Vietnamese government as the heroes of the people. Of those fourteen people, only three were not directly involved in wars against foreign forces, namely Hung Kings (the founding fathers of the country of Vietnam), Dinh Bo Linh (the warlord who unified Vietnam in the tenth century) and Ly Cong Uan (the founder of the later Ly Dynasty). The rest of the national heroes were military leaders who directly engaged in wars against foreign invaders. Those wartime heroes were the Trung sisters who rebelled against the Han Dynasty; Ly Nam De, a warlord who fought against the Chinese Liang Dynasty; Ngo Quyen, who reclaimed Vietnam's independence from the Southern Han Dynasty; Le Hoan, who warded off invaders from the Song Dynasty; Ly Thuong Kiet, who drove back the armies of the Song Dynasty almost 100 years after Le Hoan; Tran Nhan Tong, the emperor of the Tran Dynasty; Tran Hung Dao, the commander-in-chief of the army during the second and third Mongolian invasions of Vietnam; Le Loi, the leader of the victorious Lam Son rebellion against the Ming Dynasty; Nguyen Trai, the strategist of the same rebellion; Nguyen Hue, who defeated the Siamese navy and later the massive army sent by the Qianlong Emperor of the Qing Dynasty; and Ho Chi Minh, the founder of the CPV.

69. Mac Lam, "Tại sao phải giết Tổng thống Ngô Đình Diệm?" [Why must President Ngô Đình Diệm be eliminated?], Radio Free Asia, 29 October 2015, https://www.rfa.org/vietnamese/in_depth/why-president-ngo-dinh-diem-should-be-killed-ml-10292015135932.html (accessed 10 July 2024).

70. Robert Freeman, "Why the US Lost the Vietnam War", Common Dreams, 9 October 2017, https://www.commondreams.org/views/2017/10/09/why-us-lost-vietnam-war (accessed 10 July 2024).

71. Kevin Boylan, "Why Vietnam Was Unwinnable", *New York Times*, 22 August 2017, https://www.nytimes.com/2017/08/22/opinion/vietnam-was-unwinnable.html (accessed 10 July 2024).

72. Peter Davis, "Hearts and Minds", 1974, video, 27:13–27:20, https://vimeo.com/126567345 (accessed 10 July 2024), 1:14:13–1:15:15.

73. Max Weber, "Politics as a Vocation", in *From Max Weber: Essays in Sociology*, edited by Hans Gerth and Charles Wright Mills (London: Routledge, 1991), p. 215.

74. Martin Riesebrodt, "Charisma in Max Weber's Sociology of Religion", *Religion* 29, no. 1 (1999): 1–14.

75. Ho Chi Minh's Presidential Palace Historical Site, "Cuộc đời và sự nghiệp Chủ tịch Hồ Chí Minh" [The life and career of Chairman Ho Chi Minh], 2015, https://ditichhochiminhphuchutich.gov.vn/cuoc-doi-va-su-nghiep-692 (accessed 24 November 2024).

76. William J. Duiker, *Communist Road to Power in Vietnam* (London: Westview Press, 1981), p. 16.

77. Ton That Thien, "Ho Chi Minh and the Comintern: Was Ho Chi Minh a Nationalist?" (1990), http://www.tonthatthien.com/wp-content/uploads/2015/07/1990-Was-Ho-Chi-Minh-A-Nationalist.pdf (accessed 24 November 2024).

78. Cheng Guan Ang, *The Vietnam War from the Other Side: The Vietnamese Communists' Perspective* (Abingdon: Routledge, 2013), p. 21.

79. Lien Hang Nguyen, "Who Called the Shots in Hanoi?" *New York Times*, 14 February 2017, https://www.nytimes.com/2017/02/14/opinion/who-called-the-shots-in-hanoi.html (accessed 25 November 2024).

80. In his will, Ho Chi Minh explicitly stated that his body should be cremated with the remains being divided into three boxes, each buried at a hill in Northern, Central and Southern Vietnam. See the transcripts of Ho Chi Minh's original will (2017). His will and the date of his death had been kept hidden by the inner circle of the CPV for twenty years.

81. Ho Chi Minh, "Nguyên văn các bản di chúc của Chủ tịch Hồ Chí Minh" [President Ho Chi Minh's original wills], 2017, http://dangcongsan.vn/tu-lieu-van-kien/ho-so-su-kien/books-191820152384256/index-0918201523332569.html (accessed 10 July 2024).

82. For example, in the preamble of the 1959 Constitution of the Democratic Republic of Vietnam, Ho's name was mentioned two times, both with the title of president. The 1959 Constitution claims that under Ho's clear-sighted leadership, the Vietnamese people will "surely win glorious success in the building of socialism in North Vietnam and the struggle for national reunification".

    In the preamble of the 1980 Constitution of the Socialist Republic of Vietnam, Ho's name was mentioned four times as the founder of the ruling CPV. Furthermore, Ho Chi Minh Thought was also mentioned twice in the body of the 1992 Constitution as the official ideology of Vietnam. In the 2013 Constitution of Vietnam, Ho was mentioned in the preamble as the founding father of Vietnam and Ho Chi Minh Though is again recognized as the state ideology.

83. *Đời đời nhớ ơn ơn chủ tịch Hồ Chí Minh* [in Vietnamese].

84. *Bác Hồ sống mãi trong sự nghiệp cách mạng của chúng ta* [in Vietnamese].

85. Le Anh Tra, "Phong cách Hồ Chí Minh" [Ho Chi Minh's style], in *Hồ Chí Minh và văn hóa Việt Nam* [Ho Chi Minh and the Vietnamese culture] (Hanoi: Vietnam National Institute of Culture and Arts Studies, 1990).

86. The five things taught by Uncle Ho to Vietnamese youth are as follows:

    Love the fatherland, love fellow countrymen.

    Study hard, work hard.

    Maintain solidarity and discipline well.

    Maintain hygiene well.

    Be humble, honest, and courageous.

87. VOA Tiếng Việt, "Trần Hoàng Phúc 'không xúc phạm ông Hồ Chí Minh'" [Trần Hoàng Phúc 'did not insult Hồ Chí Minh'], 5 July 2017, https://www.voatiengviet. com/a/tran-hoang-phuc-bi-bat-vi-xuc-pham-ong-ho-chi-minh/3929217.html (accessed 10 July 2024).

88. Hoang Thuy, "Vì sao 20 năm mới công bố ngày mất Chủ tịch Hồ Chí Minh?" [Why was President Ho Chi Minh's date of death only disclosed after 20 years?], *VnExpress*, 30 August 2014, https://VnExpress.net/tin-tuc/thoi-su/vi-sao-20-nam-moi-cong-bo-ngay-mat-chu-tich-ho-chi-minh-3037443.html (accessed 10 July 2024).

89. Robert Banks, "Việt Nam News luôn đến từ hôm qua?" [Vietnamese news always comes from yesterday?], BBC, 2014, https://www.bbc.com/ vietnamese/forum/2014/09/140908_state_media_vietnam_news.shtml (accessed 10 July 2024).

90. Dwight D. Eisenhower, *Mandate for Change, 1953–1956*, vol. 1 (New York: Doubleday, 1963), p. 372.

91. Freeman, "Why the US Lost the Vietnam War".

92. Alan Watt, "The Geneva Agreements 1954 in Relation to Vietnam", *The Australian Quarterly* 39 (1967): 7–23, https://doi.org/10.2307/20634125.

93. William Duiker, *Ho Chi Minh: A Life* (New York: Hachette Books, 2012), p. 13.

94. Le Ai, "Báo Cứu Quốc và bản Tuyên ngôn Độc lập" [Cuu Quoc newspaper and the Declaration of Independence], *Dai Doan Ket*, 2 September 2019, https://daidoanket. vn/bao-cuu-quoc-va-ban-tuyen-ngon-doc-lap-10230750.html (accessed 10 July 2024).

95. It should be noted that both sources potentially possess bias as the *Cuu Quoc* was founded by the Viet Minh, while the *Trung Bac Tan Van* was left leaning.

96. *VietNamNet*, "Nhìn lại Quốc tang Chủ tịch Hồ Chí Minh hơn 40 năm trước" [Looking back at President Hồ Chí Minh's state funeral more than forty years ago], 16 October 2013, http://vietnamnet.vn/vn/doi-song/nhin-lai-quoc-tang-chu-tich-ho-chi-minh-hon-40-nam-truoc-144900.html (accessed 10 July 2024).

97. Davis, "Hearts and Minds".

98. Hewlett Johnson, *Marxism and the Individual* (London: Lawrence & Wishart, 1943).

99. Ho Chi Minh, *Hồ Chí Minh Toàn Tập* [Ho Chi Minh's complete works], vol. 5, p. 50.

100. Tran Nguyen Viet, "Quan điểm và cách nhìn nhận của học giả Việt Nam về sự sụp đổ của Liên Xô và tiền đồ chủ nghĩa xã hội" [The views of Vietnamese scholars on the collapse of the Soviet Union and the prospect of socialism], *Chung Ta*, 30 July 2010, https://www.chungta.com/nd/tu-lieu-tra-cuu/hoc_gia_viet_nam_sup_do_lien_xo_tien_do_chu_nghia_xa_hoi-2.html (accessed 10 July 2024).

101. Nguyen Van Bao, "Bài học từ sự sụp đổ của chủ nghĩa xã hội ở Liên Xô và Đông Âu" [Lessons from the failure of socialism in the Soviet Union and Eastern Europe], *Nhân Dân*, 7 November 2017, https://nhandan.vn/bai-hoc-tu-su-sup-do-cua-chu-nghia-xa-hoi-o-lien-xo-va-dong-au-post308642.html (accessed 10 July 2024).

102. Nong Duc Manh was the general secretary of the CPV between 2001 and 2011.

103. Nong Duc Manh, "Tư tưởng vĩ đại của Cách mạng Tháng Mười đã chiếu sáng con đường đấu tranh giải phóng dân tộc và tiến lên chủ nghĩa xã hội của Cách mạng Việt Nam" [The glorious ideology of the October Revolution lights up the way for the struggle for national liberation and the advancement towards socialism of the Vietnamese revolution], *Nhân Dân*, 7 November 2007, https://nhandan.vn/tu-tuong-vi-dai-cua-cach-mang-thang-muoi-da-chieu-sang-con-duong-dau-tranh-giai-phong-dan-toc-va-tien-len-chu-nghia-xa-hoi-cua-cach-mang-viet-nam-post477388.html (accessed 10 July 2024).

104. Nguyen Van Dai, "Tại sao cứ tiếp tục giương cao ngọn cờ Xã hội chủ nghĩa?" [Why must the pursuit of socialism be continued?], VOA Tiếng Việt, 20 June 2019, https://www.voatiengviet.com/a/tai-sao-tiep-tuc-giuong-cao-ngon-co-xa-hoi-chu-nghia/4966754.html (accessed 10 July 2024).

105. Phuong Vinh, "Chủ nghĩa xã hội và con người xã hội chủ nghĩa" [Socialism and the human of socialism], *Tuyen Giao*, 25 May 2019, https://tuyengiao.vn/chu-nghia-xa-hoi-va-con-nguoi-xa-hoi-chu-nghia-127251 (accessed 10 July 2024).

106. Ministry of Education and Training, *Giáo Trình Tư Tưởng Hồ Chí Minh* [Ho Chi Minh Thought textbook], 10th ed. (Hanoi: National Political Publishing House, 2017), p. 5.

107. The official document of the Ninth National Congress stated that "The Party and the Vietnamese people are determined to build our socialist nation based on Marxism-Leninism and Ho Chi Minh Thought". The same document also gave a detailed definition of Ho Chi Minh Thought as follows:

> Ho Chi Minh Thought is a comprehensive and insightful system of doctrines about the most fundamental issues of the Vietnamese revolution. It is the result of the flexible application and development of Marxism-Leninism in the Vietnamese context. Ho Chi Minh Thought also inherits and develops the lofty traditional traits and values held by the Vietnamese people and incorporates the quintessence of human wisdom. Ho Chi Minh Thought is an ideology that revolves around the

liberation of nations, classes, and humanity. It is an ideology that establishes the links between national independence and socialism, the combination of the people's potential and the opportunity of an era, the power that arises from the solidarity of the Vietnamese people, democracy, and a government that genuinely belongs to the people, created by the people and works for the people. Additionally, it is about the people's national defense, the establishment and improvement of a people's armed force, economic development, cultural enrichment, improving the people's daily life, and the revolutionary virtues of hardworkingness, prudence, honesty, fairness, and incorruptibility.

See Communist Party of Vietnam, *Báo cáo chính trị của Ban Chấp hành Trung ương Đảng khoá VIII tại Đại hội đại biểu toàn quốc lần thứ IX của Đảng* [Political report of the Eighth Central Committee of the Communist Party of Vietnam at the Ninth National Congress of the Communist Party of Vietnam] (2001), https://tulieuvankien.dangcongsan.vn/ban-chap-hanh-trung-uong-dang/dai-hoi-dang/lan-thu-ix (accessed 25 November 2024).

108. Weber, "The Three Types of Legitimate Rule".
109. Easton, *A Framework for Political Analysis*.
110. David Easton, "A Re-assessment of the Concept of Political Support", *British Journal of Political Science* 5 (1975): 435–57.
111. Grauvogel and von Soest, "Claims to Legitimacy Count: Why Sanctions Fail to Instigate Democratization in Authoritarian Regimes".
112. Martin K. Dimitrov, "Popular Autocrats", *Journal of Democracy* 20 (2009): 78–81.
113. Those priorities were stressed in the first political guidelines of the Indochinese Communist Party in 1930. The second guideline, composed by Tran Phu and approved by the Central Committee of the CPV, states:

The most important missions of the democratic capitalist revolution in our country are to overthrow French imperialism and (Vietnamese) feudalism, to establish a workers-peasants' government, to confiscate lands from the hands of foreign and domestic landowners and the Catholic Church and to distribute them among farmers, to ensure that land ownership belong to the workers-peasants' government, to seize all major properties that belong to foreign capitalists, to eliminate current taxes, to establish a progressive tax system, to ensure an eight-hour work day, to improve living conditions for workers and laborers, to ensure a completely independent Indochina, to acknowledge national rights to self-determination, to promote gender equality, to support the Soviet Union, and to cooperate with global working class and colonial revolution and semi-colonial revolution movements.

See Communist Party of Vietnam, *Các Cương Lĩnh Cách Mạng của Đảng Cộng Sản Việt Nam* [The revolutionary guidelines of the Communist Party of Vietnam] (Hanoi: National Political Publishing House, 1991), p. 33.

The Second Political Guideline of the Indochinese Communist Party in October 1930 reaffirmed two priorities: to gain national independence for Vietnam; and to lay the foundation for a socialist economy and to improve the living standards of the proletariats. The Party had consistently pursued these goals into the First Indochina War.

The Guideline of the Vietnam Workers' Party, formulated by Ho Chi Minh and Truong Chinh and ratified by the Second National Congress of the CPV in February 1951 (third guideline), outlines the following key objectives for the Vietnamese revolution: overthrowing imperialism, reclaiming independence, eradicating feudal remnants, ensuring land distribution to farmers, promoting democracy, and laying the groundwork for socialism, with workers, farmers and intellectuals leading the charge, emphasizing a transition from a new democratic capitalist revolution to socialism without civil war (Guideline of the Vietnam Workers' Party).

It should be noted that this guideline was more inclusive than the previous guidelines perhaps because it was drafted during the First Indochina War when the Viet Minh needed the support of every class in the society. As a result, in contrast to the first two guidelines that only emphasize the revolutionary role of farmers and workers, the new guideline of the Vietnam Workers' Party included petit bourgeoisie, nationalist bourgeoisie, and patriotic and progressive intellectuals in the revolutionary ranks. The determination to pursue national independence and socialism is again affirmed in this guideline. The CPV would follow this guideline over the next forty years before adopting the Guideline on Nation Building in the Transitional Period to Socialism at the Seventh National Congress of the CPV in June 1991.

114. Communist Party of Vietnam, Official Documents of the Ninth National Congress of the Communist Party of Vietnam (Hanoi: National Political Publishing House, 2001).

115. Ronald Bruce St. John, Revolution, Reform and Regionalism in Southeast Asia: Cambodia, Laos and Vietnam (London: Routledge, 2006), p. 45.

116. Nguyen Van Thao and Nguyen Huu Dat, Một số vấn đề về sở hữu ở nước ta hiện nay [A number of issues on possession in current Vietnam] (Hanoi: National Political Publishing House, 2004), p. 75.

117. Karl Marx, Capital: A Critique of Political Economy, vol. 1, translated by Ben Fowkes, contributed by Ernest Mandel (New York: Penguin Publishing Group, 1976), p. 342.

118. Nguyen Ngoc-Luu, Peasants, Party and Revolution: The Politics of Agrarian Transformation in Northern Vietnam 1930–1975 (Amsterdam: Universiteit van Amsterdam), pp. 258–59.

119. Ibid.

120. Qiang Zhai, China and the Vietnam Wars, 1950–1975 (Chapel Hill: University of North Carolina Press, 2000), pp. 39–41.

121. Hoang Van Chi, *From Colonialism to Communism: A Case History of North Vietnam* (London: Pall Mall, 1964), p. 164.

122. Ibid., pp. 195–97.

123. Government Portal, "Hoàn thành cải cách ruộng đất và khôi phục kinh tế quốc dân (1955–1957)" [The completion of land reform and restoration of the national economy (1955–1957)], n.d., https://chinhphu.vn/giai-doan-1955-1975-xay-dung-cnxh-va-dau-tranh-thong-nhat-dat-nuoc/1-hoan-thanh-cai-cach-ruong-dat-va-khoi-phuc-kinh-te-quoc-dan-1955-1957-10001592 (accessed 10 July 2024).

124. Thanh Tu, "Lần đầu tiên công bố hình ảnh cải cách ruộng đất" [First exhibition of images and items of land reform], *VnExpress*, 9 September 2014, https://VnExpress.net/thoi-su/lan-dau-tien-cong-bo-hinh-anh-cai-cach-ruong-dat-3076449.html (accessed 10 July 2024).

125. In other communist regimes, such as the Soviet Union and China, similar five-year plans were also carried out. In this chapter, unless otherwise indicated, the term "five-year plan" refers to the five-year plans of Vietnam.

126. Benedict J. Tria Kerkvliet, "Everyday Politics in Peasant Societies (and Ours)", *The Journal of Peasant Studies* 36 (2009): 227–43, https://doi.org/10.1080/03066150902820487.

127. *Phép vua thua lệ làng* [in Vietnamese].

128. David G. Marr, *Postwar Vietnam: Dilemmas in Socialist Development*, vol. 3 (Ithaca, NY: SEAP Publications, 1988), pp. 81–87.

129. Ngoc Duong, "Lạm phát do đâu?" [What are the reasons for inflation?], *VnEconomy*, 12 September 2011, http://vneconomy.vn/thoi-su/lam-phat-do-dau-20110912100018354.htm (accessed 10 July 2024).

130. St. John, *Revolution, Reform and Regionalism in Southeast Asia: Cambodia, Laos and Vietnam*, p. 45.

131. Vo Nhan Tri, *Vietnam's Economic Policy Since 1975* (Singapore: Institute of Southeast Asian Studies, 1990), p. 107.

132. St. John, *Revolution, Reform and Regionalism in Southeast Asia: Cambodia, Laos and Vietnam*, p. 48.

133. For example, it is stated in the 1959 Constitution of Vietnam that "our people are resolved to strengthen further solidarity and unity of mind with the brother countries in the socialist camp headed by the great Soviet Union and to strengthen solidarity with the peoples of Asia and Africa and peace-loving people all over the world."

134. Article 15 of the 1980 Constitution mandates that Vietnam's economy comprises primarily two elements: the state-owned economic sector and the cooperative economic sector, with the former being the dominant element and receiving prioritization and the latter being collectively owned by the working class (Article 18). The State holds a monopoly on foreign trade with other countries (Article 21).

The government promotes and facilitates the integration of individual farmers, handicraftsmen and labourers into cooperatives and unions. Additionally, it guides small business owners towards transitioning into manufacturing or other more suitable occupations (Article 24). Moreover, within the borders of the Socialist Republic of Vietnam, economic establishments owned by feudal landowners and comprador capitalists are subject to confiscation without compensation (Article 25). The State also undertakes the re-education of capitalist individuals in both urban and rural settings employing appropriate methods (Article 26).

135. Nguyen Phu Trong, "Cương lĩnh xây dựng đất nước trong thời kỳ quá độ lên chủ nghĩa xã hội (bổ sung, phát triển năm 2011)" [Guideline on building the country during the transitional period towards socialism (revised and improved on 2011)], *Communist Review*, 2011, http://www.tapchicongsan.org.vn/Home/Quan-triet-thuc-hien-nghi-quyet-dai-hoi-dang-XI/Noi-dung-co-ban-van-kien/2011/1689/Cuong-linh-xay-dung-dat-nuoc-trong-thoi-ky-qua-do-len.aspx (accessed 10 July 2024).

136. In particular, Trong wrote as follows:

The (1991) Guideline was written amidst the decline and collapse of the Socialist model in the Soviet Union and many Eastern European countries, many communist parties lost their direction or faced insurmountable obstacles while the hostile forces were fiercely on their offense. Domestically, the socialist economy was in deep crisis and a proportion of the cadres and party members were disillusioned (about socialism).

137. Ibid.

138. *Kinh tế thị trường định hướng xã hội chủ nghĩa* [in Vietnamese].

139. Communist Party of Vietnam, "Báo cáo chính trị của Ban Chấp hành Trung ương Đảng khoá VIII tại Đại hội đại biểu toàn quốc lần thứ IX của Đảng" [Political report of the Eighth Central Committee of the Communist Party of Vietnam at the Ninth National Congress of the Communist Party of Vietnam], 2001, http://chinhphu.vn/portal/page/portal/chinhphu/NuocCHXHCNVietNam/ThongTinTongHop/noidungvankiendaihoidang?categoryId=10000714&articleId=10038377 (accessed 10 July 2024).

140. Communist Party of Vietnam, "Văn Kiện Đại Hội Đảng Thời Kỳ Đổi Mới (Đại Hội VI, VII, VIII, IX)" [Official documents of the National Congress of the CPV in the transition period (Sixth, Seventh, Eighth, Ninth National Congress)] (Hanoi: National Political Publishing House, 2005), p. 43.

141. Ibid., p. 57.

142. This journal is the organ of political theory of the Vietnam Communist Party's Central Committee.

143. Ha Van Vinh, "Phát triển nền kinh tế thị trường định hướng XHCN: Sự sáng tạo của Đảng Cộng sản Việt Nam" [The development of a socialist-oriented market economy: the creativeness of the CPV], *Tai Chinh Online*, 4 March 2019, http://

tapchitaichinh.vn/nghien-cuu-trao-doi/phat-trien-nen-kinh-te-thi-truong-dinh-huong-xhcn-su-sang-tao-cua-dang-cong-san-viet-nam-303661.html (accessed 10 July 2024).

144. Communist Party of Vietnam, *Văn Kiện Đại Hội Đảng Thời Kỳ Đổi Mới (Đại Hội VI, VII, VIII, IX)*, p. 274.

145. Ibid., p. 178.

146. Ibid., p. 180.

147. Ibid., p. 637.

148. Nguyen Ngoc Ha, "Kinh tế thị trường với chủ nghĩa xã hội" [Market economy and socialism], *Triet hoc* [Philosophy] 8 (2005): 19–25.

149. Communist Party of Vietnam, "Văn Kiện Đại Hội Đảng X" [Official documents of the Tenth National Congress of the CPV] (Hanoi: National Political Publishing House, 2008), p. 86.

150. Ibid., p. 83.

151. Ibid., p. 79.

152. Communist Party of Vietnam, *Văn Kiện Đại Hội Đảng XI* [Official documents of the Eleventh National Congress of the CPV] (Hanoi: National Political Publishing House, 2011), p. 205.

153. Ibid., p. 209.

154. Arsenio Balisacan, Ernesto Pernia, and Gemma Estrada, *Economic Growth and Poverty Reduction in Viet Nam* (Manila: Asian Development Bank, 2003).

155. Voice of Vietnam, "Đại hội Đảng toàn quốc lần thứ XII: Những ấn tượng lịch sử" [Twelfth National Congress of the Communist Party of Vietnam: historical impressions], 2016, https://vov.vn/chinh-tri/dang/dai-hoi-dang-toan-quoc-lan-thu-xii-nhung-an-tuong-lich-su-473945.vov (accessed 10 July 2024).

156. Nguyen Phu Trong, "Một số vấn đề lý luận và thực tiễn về chủ nghĩa xã hội và con đường đi lên chủ nghĩa xã hội ở Việt Nam" [Some theoretical and practical issues about socialism and the path to socialism in Vietnam], *Communist Review*, 16 May 2021, https://www.tapchicongsan.org.vn/media-story/-/asset_publisher/V8hhp4dK31Gf/content/mot-so-van-de-ly-luan-va-thuc-tien-ve-chu-nghia-xa-hoi-va-con-duong-di-len-chu-nghia-xa-hoi-o-viet-nam (accessed 10 July 2024).

157. The prospect of a prosperous socialist North Vietnam was repeated many times, which indicates that the writers, who were young people when they perished in the war, truly believed in the better future that socialism promised to deliver. See Dang Vuong Hung, *Tuyển tập những lá thư thời chiến Việt Nam* [A collection of wartime letters in Vietnam] (Hanoi: National Political Publishing House, 2023).

158. Benedict J. Kerkvliet, "Workers' Protests in Contemporary Vietnam (with Some Comparisons to Those in the Pre-1975 South)", *Journal of Vietnamese Studies* 5 (2010): 162–204. Republished with some revisions as "Workers' Protests in Contemporary Vietnam", in *Labour in Vietnam*, edited by Anita Chan (Singapore: Institute of Southeast Asian Studies, 2011), pp. 160–210.

159. *Quân Đội Nhân Dân*, "Không để một bộ phận giới trẻ lún sâu vào những suy nghĩ, hành vi lệch lạc" [(We must) not allowing a portion of young people to sink deeply into deviant thoughts and behaviours], 7 December 2017.

160. Vo Oanh, "Vì con người xã hội chủ nghĩa!" [For the people of socialism], *Communist Review*, 2013, http://www.tapchicongsan.org.vn/Home/Tri-thuc-viet-nam/Tri-thuc/2013/20369/Vi-con-nguoi-xa-hoi-chu-nghia.aspx (accessed 10 July 2024).

161. Ha Dang, "Từ bỏ chủ nghĩa xã hội là một sai lầm lớn" [To give up on socialism would be a great mistake], *Quân Đội Nhân Dân*, 7 November 2017, http://www.qdnd.vn/chong-dien-bien-hoa-binh/tu-bo-chu-nghia-xa-hoi-la-mot-sai-lam-lon-522845.

3

Factors Contributing to the Cpv's Need to Improve Its Legitimacy

Although it is difficult, we must do it, because it is closely tied to the very existence of the Party and the survivability of the regime.

Nguyen Phu Trong,
General Secretary of the Communist Party of Vietnam,
on strengthening and reforming the Party[1]

After more than three decades of economic reform and integration into the international community, the standard of living in Vietnam has experienced significant improvements. However, as Vietnam diversified its economic and diplomatic relationships, it became increasingly susceptible to Western influence, while other sources of its legitimacy began to show signs of deterioration. Decades after the last war on

Vietnamese soil, military victories gradually lost their impact on people's perception of the ruling party. Additionally, the collapse of the Soviet Union and the Eastern Bloc, coupled with the success of the Vietnamese market economy, severely damaged socialism's reputation as a state-building ideology.

The CPV quickly became aware of these emerging challenges that threatened its authority. Six years after the initiation of *Doi Moi*, during its Seventh National Congress in December 1994, the CPV identified four major threats to its survival: falling further behind economically, misdirection towards socialism, corruption and bureaucratic misconduct, and the risk of "Peaceful Evolution".

Thayer posits that the foundation of the regime's legitimacy is challenged on four fronts: ideology, economic performance, rational-legal and nationalism by southern war veterans, communist intellectuals, non-party elites, peasants, retired high-ranking military officials and pro-democracy advocates, with a specific emphasis on the era following the disintegration of socialism in Eastern Europe and the Soviet Union during 1989–91.[2] During the 2000s, Thayer raised three challenges to the legitimacy of the CPV: opposition to bauxite mining in the Central Highlands, which tested the State's performance legitimacy; widespread demonstrations by the Catholic Church regarding land ownership disputes, which questioned the State's legitimacy grounded in rational-legal principles; and resurging political opposition led by pro-democracy activists and bloggers, which calls for democracy and raised environmental concerns, as well as issues regarding relations with China, posed a challenge to the State's legitimacy founded on nationalism.[3] He also argues that despite the regime's inclination towards repression as its default stance, it has also demonstrated a capacity for accommodation and adaptation in addressing criticisms originating from grassroots movements.[4] The Party leadership also engages in ongoing negotiations concerning the extent and pace of political transformations.[5]

According to Kerkvliet, starting from the mid-1990s the phenomenon of public criticism directed towards the government in Vietnam gained momentum, eventually becoming a significant aspect of the country's political landscape. While some critics believe that the CPV leadership should spearhead the transition to a more democratic political system, others opt to establish organizations aimed at openly and directly challenging the regime. Alternatively, some advocate for reforming the current system by actively engaging with it, while others prioritize the expansion of civil society to democratize the nation.[6]

This chapter examines the factors that compelled the CPV to adopt a new propaganda paradigm emphasizing its legitimacy through institutionalized and procedural means. These factors include increasing linkages and leverage from the West, corruption and poor governance, the CPV's handling of the territorial dispute in the South China Sea with China and the proliferation of the internet, which amplifies the effects of the other factors.

Linkage and Leverage for Democratization

In the wake of the demise of the Soviet Union, military and economic aid to both Soviet and United States-backed authoritarian regimes plummeted. The rising military and economic power of the West in combination with the post-Cold War realignment of governments towards political alternatives to the collapsing communist regimes led to the unprecedented level of adoption of Western-style institutions by leaders in the developing world.[7] Seizing this opportunity created by the power vacuum left by the dissolution of the Soviet Union, the West increased diplomatic and military pressure to promote democracy. Assistance and loans were provided to struggling regimes by both government agencies and international organizations on the conditions that they respect human rights, hold free and fair elections and allow civil societies to thrive.[8] The West also imposed strict conditions to ensure the permanent establishment of a framework for democracy, for instance the onerous conditionality of the European Union's membership or the collective sanction mechanisms of the Organization of American States.[9]

Since the end of the Cold War, a great number of organizations and networks have been established to contribute to the proliferation of human rights and democracy. Those organizations usually form networks for human right monitoring and encourage Western governments to interfere should violations be found.[10] Levitsky and Way (2006), however, argue that outside of the European Union, the role of external pressure for democratization should not be overestimated. Evidently, according to the Economist's Democracy Index, in 2017, almost three decades after the collapse of the Soviet Union, many regimes have remained non-democratic.[11] Although the lack of internal incentive for democratization was the major factor, Levitsky and Way also attribute the failure of democratization to the inconsistency in democracy promotion outside of Europe and the overemphasis on the holding of elections while overlooking other aspects of democracy, such as human rights and civil liberties. They conclude that even though external pressure has been one of the prominent factors in undermining non-democratic regimes, its role in promoting democracy has not been as effective.[12]

Western leverage is defined as a non-democratic regime's leadership's vulnerability to pressure to democratize from the West.[13] There are several ways through which such pressure may be applied, including democratic conditionality, economic sanctions, diplomatic engagements and military threats. The main factors that decide the level of success of Western leverage are the differences in economic, military and diplomatic power between the actors. A powerful country with a strong military and a substantial economy, such as China or Russia, would be more resilient to Western pressure than countries in sub-Saharan Africa or Latin America. Western leverage makes the maintenance of authoritarian regimes costlier. After the collapse of the Eastern Bloc, countries that are deprived of economic assistance and are strategically unimportant often find themselves the victims of pro-democracy pressure from the West. Refusal to comply may result in punishment, which could prove critical to their regimes.[14]

Levitsky and Way argue that there are two main factors that could negatively affect Western leverage.[15] First, economic, military and diplomatic assistance provided by a regional power could mitigate the effectiveness of Western pressure. Such anti-democratic support is termed black knights' support.[16] This kind of support does not exclusively come from non-democratic regimes like China or Russia. The United States, for example, has been notorious for funding dictatorships across the world to serve its national interests. The second factor is the contradicting interests of external forces. Pressure on authoritarian regimes in countries where different western powers are competing to protect their national interests can be nullified if these Western powers are pitted against one another. By casting itself as the only political force that can maintain and balance these interests, the authoritarian regime could prevent the West from collectively carrying out economic sanctions or military threats.[17] Due to these inherent shortcomings, the actual effectiveness of Western cooperation in promoting democracy has been largely compromised. Often, authoritarian regimes can escape punitive actions from the West unscathed. In many regimes, nominal reforms or rigged elections have been held without any substantial changes in the political system. Crawford studied twenty non-democratic regimes in the 1990s and found that Western leverage only contributed significantly to the democratization of two, and this even took into account regions where authoritarian regimes are most vulnerable to Western pressure, such as those in sub-Saharan Africa.[18]

In Levitsky and Way's words, linkage is "the density of ties and cross-border-flows between a particular country and the United States, the European Union, and Western-dominated multilateral institutions".[19] Levitsky and Way divide linkage into five categories: economic linkage, geopolitical linkage, social linkage, communication linkage and transitional civil society linkage, of which geographic proximity is the most important factor. Being in close geographic proximity to the United States and the European Union allows countries to have robust economic, social and communication ties. Other factors also contributed to the intensity of linkage include military occupation, geopolitical alliances and colonial heritage. Similarities in culture, religion and ethnicity may strengthen linkage, while socioeconomic development would naturally lead to cross-border flows that would result in the same outcome.

Linkage to the West can put pressure on non-democratic governments in several ways. First, in the modern era, extensive communication, the flow of people and far-reaching media coverage make it more likely than ever that unjust acts committed by a regime would be exposed to the global community.[20] As a result, a given government's abuses, considering the deep penetration of media and the amplification of transnational advocacy networks, have the potential to incite uproar overseas. Second, a stronger linkage means it is more probable that Western countries will interfere if abuses are exposed due to public opinion roused by media coverage, lobbying carried out by pro-democracy organizations or the appeals of exiles and their supporters. Third, as economic ties develop, there are more incentives for a country to remain on good terms with the West. Firms and organizations usually benefit greatly from a good relationship with the Western community. Sanctions may be deadly for companies and investors, so business leaders would try their best to maintain a positive relationship with the West by urging the regime to follow democratic norms, a condition favourable to democratization.[21] Furthermore, through cross-border flows, the number of Western-educated elites also increases. As those technocratic elites often maintain their ties with their Western alma maters, international isolation would prove unbeneficial for them personally, and they would attempt to pressure their governments to adhere to widely accepted democratic norms. Finally, linkage to the West could possibly upset the balance of power within a non-democratic regime in several ways.[22] (1) International media coverage and the interference of nongovernmental organizations often serve as deterrence that protects political minorities from government oppression and abuse. (2) Non-governmental and governmental ties to the West could be translated into political, financial and organizational support for opposition. (3) Having strong linkages to the West could improve the domestic reputation and political standing of pro-democracy opposition groups. (4) Even within the ruling regime, linkage encourages pro-democratic and reformist movements.[23]

Linkage and leverage can be understood as external "hardware" and "software", respectively, as they work in tandem to increase the costs of maintaining an authoritarian regime. While leverage is more visible and some of its features, such as differences in the sizes of economies or military forces, can be statistically estimated, linkage is a subtler dimension akin to the concept of "soft power" that contributes to the proliferation of democracy by "shaping preference".[24]

Contemporary Vietnam can be considered a case of moderate linkage and low leverage. During the late 1970s and early 1980s, Vietnam was isolated due to several disastrous mistakes in terms of foreign relations. According to Tran Quang Co, former first vice-minister of foreign affairs of Vietnam,[25] those mistakes were

(1) Vietnam was unable to strike a balance between China and the Soviet Union, resulting in a devastating border war with the former.

(2) Vietnam missed the chance to normalize relations with the United States in 1977, when the Carter administration offered unconditional normalization.

(3) Vietnam failed to join ASEAN in 1976, despite the interest of all six members, who were motivated by their own national interests, to include Vietnam.

(4) Vietnam became excessively involved in the Cambodian conflict for too long a time.

The implementation of *Doi Moi* in 1986 represented a turning point in the country's relationships, not just with the Soviet Union, the United States and China, but also with many new actors. *Doi Moi* ushered in a shift towards a more market-oriented economy and greater openness to the world, including increased engagement with the United States and other Western nations. The collapse of the Soviet Union in 1991 and the rise of a more pragmatic and economically driven China greatly impacted Vietnam's standing in the region and its connections with major global and regional powers. Despite these changes, the Cold War mentality continues to have a lingering impact on Vietnam's post-*Doi Moi* diplomatic policies.

With the collapse of the Soviet Union and Eastern Bloc, Vietnam lost its major sources of aid and became isolated from the international community. Despite the introduction of the *Doi Moi* policy and subsequent efforts to reintegrate with the world, the damage from the fall of the Eastern Bloc and the failure of socialism as a state-building ideology was only partially mitigated. Vietnam became more vulnerable to pressure to democratize from the West.[26] The CPV is fully aware of this external pressure and has given it the name *Peaceful Evolution*,[27] which is defined by the Vietnam Academy of Social Sciences as

> ... a scheme employed by imperialism and international reactionary forces which is being carried out under new disguises and methods to undermine, sabotage, and destroy socialism. The targets of Peaceful Evolution are the countries with non-capitalist tendencies. The nature of Peaceful Evolution is anti-socialist and anti-national independence. The main target of Peaceful Evolution is to destroy socialist countries' politics, ideologies, economies, cultures, and societies. The main method is to promote internal reactionary and counter-revolutionary elements to push the socialist countries into crisis. From then, they would step-by-step change the political system to a capitalist one or use brute force to overthrow the government.[28]

Before *Doi Moi*, Vietnam's main trading partners were Eastern Bloc countries. Following the introduction of *Doi Moi*, trade and the flow of people between Vietnam and the West surged. On 13 July 2000, the first bilateral trade agreement between Vietnam and the United States was signed. In the same year, the total bilateral trade volume between Vietnam and the United States amounted to a modest US$1.18 billion.[29] As of 2020, the bilateral trade volume between the two countries totalled US$92.2 billion,[30] an increase of more than seventy-eight times over a short twenty years. In 2020 Vietnam was the United States' twenty-eighth largest export market for goods and the United States' sixth largest supplier of goods. In 2017, total investment stock purchased by European investors reached US$21.86 billion, making the European Union home to one of the largest groups of investors to Vietnam. Vietnam is also the second largest trading partner of the European Union in ASEAN, after Singapore.[31] As of 2020, top ODA providers to Vietnam include Japan, the World Bank, Asian Development Bank, the European Union, the United States and South Korea. Top investors in Vietnam are Singapore, South Korea, Japan and China.[32] As shown in Figure 3.1, the trading volume between Vietnam and Russia in 2020 was completely dwarfed by that with

Figure 3.1
vietnam's Imports and Exports with Major Trading partners in 2020

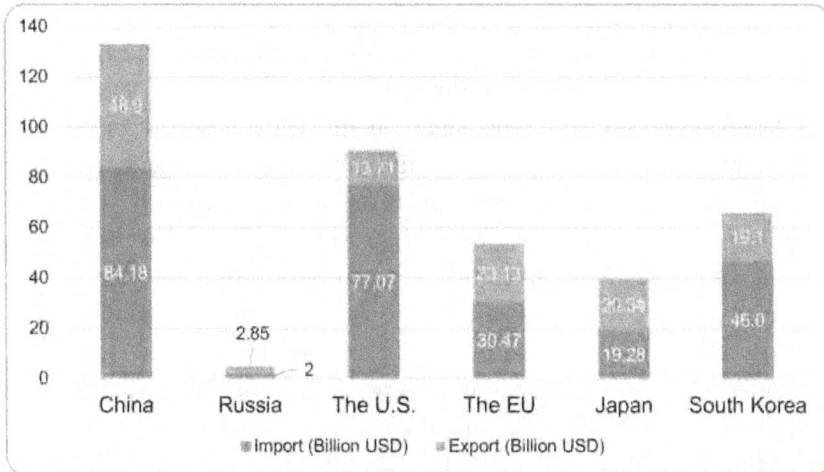

Source: General Statistics Office of Vietnam, "Số liệu xuất nhập khẩu các tháng năm 2020" [Import-export data by month for 2020], 29 January 2021, https://www.gso.gov.vn/du-lieu-va-so-lieu-thong-ke/2020/10/tri-gia-xuat-nhap-khau-phan-theo-nuoc-va-vung-lanh-tho-chu-yeu-so-bo-cac-thang-nam-2020-2/ (accessed 17 July 2024).

other major trading partners such as the United States, South Korea and Japan.

Not only has the flow of money changed drastically, but also the flow of people. Eastern Bloc countries used to be the most popular destinations for cross-border migration from Vietnam from labour export to elite education. Most post-war party leaders who were trained overseas received their education in the Soviet Union. This includes many current and recent top leaders such as president and general secretary of the CPV, Nguyen Phu Trong, who graduated from the Russian Academy of Sciences. However, since the implementation of the *Doi Moi* policy, the pattern of migration has substantially shifted.

According to data from the International Cooperation Department of the Ministry of Education and Training, in 2019, around 190,000 Vietnamese students were studying abroad. Of these, 40,000 were in Europe, with the majority in the United Kingdom (12,000), followed by Germany (7,500), France (6,500), Russia (6,000) and Finland (2,500). In North America, there were approximately 50,000 Vietnamese students, with 29,000 in the United States and 21,000 in Canada.[33] In Asia, by 2021 there were 70,000 Vietnamese students, 49,000 of these students were in Japan alone.[34]

Vietnamese students who study in the United States, the United Kingdom or Australia generally fall into one of three categories: academically gifted students or researchers who have received scholarships from the host country; researchers and teachers from Vietnamese educational institutions or government officials who receive funding from the Vietnamese government; and students from families that can afford the cost of studying in a Western country. As a result, a significant proportion of Vietnamese students in Western countries belong to the social or academic elite. An increasing number of young Vietnamese technocrats are taking advantage of Western education, which could potentially strengthen Vietnam's connections with the West in the future.

Using its leverage, the West has been putting pressure on Vietnam on several issues, most notably human rights violations, lack of freedom of speech and assembly, the country's one-party political system, and the government's handling of religious and ethnic minority groups and land disputes.

Several Western countries, most notably the United States have expressed disapproval of Vietnam's poor human rights record and its suppression of political and religious freedoms. Between 2004 and 2006, Vietnam was on the list of "countries of particular concern" of the United States for its perceived arbitrary arrests, torture and other forms of mistreatment of political activists, as well as growing restrictions on freedom of speech, assembly and religion.[35] As of 2024, the United States Commission on International Religious Freedom still has Vietnam on its recommendation list of countries of particular concern.[36]

The 2022 Department of State report on Vietnam highlighted numerous human rights violations. These included reports of unlawful killings, torture and inhumane treatment by government agents, arbitrary arrests and detention. It also noted issues with judicial independence, privacy infringements, severe limits on expression and media, including the arrest of critics and censorship. Additionally, the report mentioned substantial restrictions on internet access, assembly, association and political participation. Other concerns raised were corruption, trafficking, restrictions on workers' rights and the use of compulsory child labour.

In January 2019, the European parliament passed a resolution condemning the Vietnamese government for its human rights record, particularly in relation to the cases of journalists Pham Chi Dung, Nguyen Tuong Thuy and Le Huu Minh Tuan, who were arrested and given prison sentences on charges of spreading propaganda against the State.

In Vietnam, expressing explicit opinions against the CPV, the government or the State can lead to harassment and prosecution. The internet is one of the few channels through which dissidents can express their viewpoints, but it is also monitored by the CPV's security apparatus, notably the Ministry of Public Security's Department of Cyber Security and the Ministry of Information and Communications. The domestic flow of information is also under the strict scrutiny of the Central Propaganda Department of the CPV. Dissidents can face warnings or prosecution depending on the severity of their actions, and prominent dissidents are often put under surveillance by the Ministry of Public Security, with their rights and access to public services being restricted.

Chapter 8 of the 2015 Penal Code of Vietnam is devoted to discussing offenses against national security, among which Article 117 is frequently used to prosecute dissidents. This article prohibits the creation, storage and distribution of information and materials that contain distorted information about the people's government, which can cause dismay among the public or amount to psychological warfare. The punishment for this offense can be up to twenty years of imprisonment. Additionally, preparing to commit this offense can result in a penalty of up to five years of imprisonment.[37]

To make matters worse, dissidents are sometimes put under a long period of detention for investigation under bogus claims. According to Article 173 of the 2015 Criminal Procedure Code of Vietnam, the maximum temporary detention period for suspects under investigation varies based on the severity of the crime: two months for less serious crimes, three months for serious crimes and four months for very serious and especially serious crimes.

Furthermore, this detention period could be extended twice, each time up to four months for extremely serious crimes. Article 9 of the 2015 Penal Code of Vietnam defines extremely serious crimes as crimes with a maximum sentence from over fifteen years to twenty years' imprisonment, life imprisonment or death.

As the upper punishment for extremely serious cases of spreading propaganda against the State is twenty years of imprisonment, the detention period of extremely serious crimes and its extended period could be applied to cases that fall under Article 117 of the Penal Code. As such, a suspect charged with violation of Article 117 could be theoretically put under detention for one year just for investigation.

Even nonviolent dissent in Vietnam could lead to job loss, intimidation, social isolation and even imprisonment.[38] However, repression is not uniform; some critics face no detention despite years of criticism, while others are imprisoned but not rearrested upon resuming dissent. Analysis offers no clear explanation for varying repression levels, but factors like advanced age and prior government service may reduce arrest likelihood. Examining the case of Le Cong Dinh, a prominent pro-democracy lawyer sentenced to five years imprisonment for activities aimed at overthrowing the People's Government, Thayer suggests that if the State's treatment of dissidents is perceived as unjust, its legitimacy faces pressure from multiple fronts—rational-legal, performance and nationalism.[39]

Dissidents and political civil society actors within Vietnam sometimes receive moral and financial support from overseas state and non-state entities opposing the CPV. Thayer cites the case of Viet Tan, arguing that this group has renounced violence and is currently backing pro-democracy movements in Vietnam through non-violent means. He posits that the collaboration between domestic groups like Bloc 8406 and external support will elevate the role of civil society in Vietnam.[40] However, the extent to which these efforts remain peaceful is subject to debate, given Viet Tan's history of violence and recent events like the Dak Lak Attack or the Dong Tam Land Dispute, demonstrating that external support can escalate situations into deadly conflicts with the state apparatus.

In certain cases, some compromise could be reached between Vietnam and the West, particularly the United States, in disputed areas such as the treatment of dissidents in the form of under-the-table agreements. According to Human Rights Watch, as of 2022, the Vietnamese government has detained at least 145 individuals who have exercised their fundamental rights without resorting to violence. Some prominent dissidents who were arrested for serious charges such as conducting propaganda against the State, abusing the rights to freedom and democracy to infringe upon the interests of the State, or carrying out activities to overthrow the People's Government have been released to the United States. One of the most well-known cases is Cu Huy Ha Vu. Vu is one of the most outspoken critics of the Vietnamese government's human rights record and land policies and was sentenced to seven years in prison on charges of spreading anti-government propaganda. However, in 2014, Vu was released to the United States before the end of his sentence.[41] While Vu's arrest and trial was widely reported by domestic news agencies, his release to the United States was not covered inside Vietnam. Another case was Nguyen Ngoc Nhu Quynh, better known by her moniker Mother Mushroom, who was a high-profile dissident and anti-government blogger. In 2017, Quynh was sentenced to ten years in prison for spreading propaganda against the State. However, in October 2018, Quynh was quietly released from prison and sent to the United States.[42] In May 2022, Ho Duc Hoa and Tran Thi Thuy, two dissidents who were sentenced to prison terms on carrying out activities to overthrow the People's Government, were prematurely released before Prime Minister Pham Minh Chinh's visit to the United States.[43] As with Vu's case, the other dissidents' premature release was not reported by domestic news outlets despite their arrest and trial was widely covered.

Another aspect that Vietnam has been moving closer to the West is regard to its relations with Russia. On the surface, the bilateral relation between Vietnam and Russia is still as strong as ever. During his visit to Russia in July 2022, Nguyen Phu Trong, the then-general secretary of the CPV, stated that he considers the relations with Russia as the extension of the relations with the Soviet Union. This comment was well received by Russia's Foreign Minister Sergey Lavrov.[44] Official media outlets such as the website of the Embassy of the Socialist Republic of Vietnam in Russia also echoes this sentiment.[45] After his re-election as president of the Russian Federation in 2024, Vladimir Putin chose Vietnam as the destination for one of his first state visits, following visits to China, Belarus, Uzbekistan and North Korea.

While mutual trade between Vietnam and Russia has been falling consistently since the 1990s, military cooperation between the two countries has remained strong as between 1995 and 2001 roughly 80 per cent of Vietnam's imported arms is from Russia, according to data from the Stockholm International Peace Research Institute.[46] While Vietnam has been making progress in diversifying its arms import, Russian remains an important trading partner of Vietnam in national defence.[47]

The CPV has consistently maintained its stance of non-interference in other countries' internal affairs as an excuse to avoid friction with Russia. Vietnam was among the five countries that voted against the suspension of Russia from the United Nations' Human Rights Council in April 2022 following the Russian invasion of Ukraine and abstained when the UN General Assembly voted to pass a resolution to condemn the invasion in October 2022. In February 2023, again, Vietnam was among the thirty-two countries abstained on a UN resolution that called for Russian's immediate and unconditional withdrawal from Ukraine. This non-interference stance has been invoked in similar situations in the past. For instance, in July 2008, Vietnam was among the members of the United Nations Security Council that voted against sanctions against Zimbabwean President Robert Mugabe for the regime's human rights violation and crimes against humanity. Defending its negative vote, the Ministry of Foreign Affairs of Vietnam said that "Vietnam does not support the interference of the UN into the internal affairs of sovereign nations."[48] The Twelfth Congress of the CPV in 2016 maintained that Vietnam would maintain its foreign policies.

In contrast to Vietnam's close relationship to Russia, domestic media outlets are allowed to show support for Ukraine. For example, during the onset of the 2022 Russian invasion of Ukraine, the *Communist Party of Vietnam Online Newspaper* published an article on the looming humanitarian crisis that would likely follow the invasion.[49] In December 2022, the official mouthpiece of the Vietnamese Youth Federation published an article estimating that Russia's material losses from the invasion are three times higher than Ukraine's. Comments that support the independence and integrity of Ukraine on domestic news outlets are not completely censored.[50] In comparison, most Vietnamese news outlets report very little about subjects such as the Tiananmen Square protests or the Xinjiang concentration camps if anything at all. As all domestic news agencies must be scrutinized by the Central Propaganda Department of the CPV, perhaps the liberty that the Vietnamese press is enjoying in covering the Russian invasion of Ukraine somehow reflects a change in the CPV's attitude towards Russia. In May 2022, during a meeting between Vietnamese Prime Minister Pham Minh Chinh and his Japanese counterpart Kishida Fumio, Vietnam pledged to provide Ukraine with $500,000 in humanitarian aid.[51]

Despite warmer relations between Vietnam and the West, the CPV remains distrustful of Western interference and motivations. Colonel General Nguyen Tri Vinh, a member of the CPV Central Committee and deputy minister of defence, argues that Vietnam must resolutely combat efforts to undermine the CPV's authority arguing that hostile forces are leveraging globalization and international integration to subvert the Vietnamese revolution through peaceful evolution, ultimately aiming to destabilize and overthrow the Party.[52]

Nhan Dan, the official mouthpiece of the CPV has blamed the West for interfering in Vietnam's domestic affairs under the guise of human rights and democracy.[53] Overall, while Vietnam has been trying to stay in line with the Western rule-based order for its economic and security benefits, at times Vietnam has shown significant defiance to the

West when it comes to regime security. One of the most surprising, if not perplexing, instances was the abduction of Trinh Xuan Thanh on German soil. Thanh, a former Vietnamese government official, made headlines in 2017 when he was kidnapped from Germany and brought back to Vietnam to stand trial for corruption charges. Thanh had served as the chairman of a state-run construction company in Vietnam but fled to Germany in 2016 amid allegations of financial mismanagement. In July of that year, he was allegedly abducted in Berlin by Vietnamese intelligence agents and taken back to Vietnam, where he was eventually sentenced to life in prison for corruption. The Vietnam government claimed that Thanh turned himself in and refused to release him.[54] While perhaps Thanh's abduction was meant to send a message to corrupt officials that they cannot escape justice, it backfired terribly as the incident caused a diplomatic crisis between Germany and Vietnam, with Germany's prosecutors calling the abduction a state-organized kidnapping.

Factors contributing to Vietnam's resilience to Western linkage and leverage include its economy's size, politico-geography and the contradicting national interests of foreign actors. According to the World Bank, as of 2020, Vietnam is the thirty-fifth largest economy in the world by nominal GDP and has been enjoying an annual growth of more than 6 per cent prior to being hit by the COVID-19 pandemic.[55] Vietnam is also projected to be one of the top twenty economies in the world by 2050.[56] Although GDP per capita remains low, the sheer size of an economy with a population of almost one hundred million people could afford Vietnam some independence from foreign aid. The vast geographic distance between Vietnam and the United States and the European Union is another factor that limits Western influence. The proximity, similar culture and political system to China has often made observers consider Vietnam to be under China's sphere of influence. The CPV has also been following the survival strategy laid by its predecessors, which centred on Vietnam's diplomatic submission and vassalage to China. Throughout Vietnam's history, despite its military struggle against its northern nemesis, Vietnam's successive dynasties would immediately seek diplomatic reconciliation after a war by formally accepting Chinese nominal rule. The modern version of this story, however, is quite different, as the appearance of other regional and global powers has upset the power balance between Vietnam and China. Some scholars consider maintaining a balance between China and the United States to be one of the most important diplomatic dilemmas facing the CPV.[57] As Beech puts it, "if geography is destiny, then the fate of Vietnam is to be an expert in bargaining with Beijing and balancing between superpowers".[58] The CPV, however, has been quite successful in mitigating pressure from the outside by pitting regional and global powers against each other, thus reducing the risk of regime change.

Corruption and Bad Governance

Corruption remains a persistent challenge in Vietnam and has a significant impact on the country's economic development and overall well-being of its citizens. Despite efforts by the government to address the issue, corruption continues to permeate many aspects of society, including the public sector, business and everyday life.

Corruption has been a prevalent characteristic in both Vietnam's business and political environment even long before the start of *Doi Moi*. In 1945, when asked by To Huu[59] whether the Chinese or the French were a greater threat, Ho Chi Minh was famously quoted as saying "The biggest threat is you, the cadres",[60, 61] implying that the greatest threat was from within the machinery of the CPV. During wartime, stories told in letters and diaries of fallen soldiers mentioned excessive bureaucracy, corruption and infighting among the ranks of North Vietnamese officials. For example, in Dang Thuy Tram's diary,[62, 63] she expresses rage because

> Injustice still exists in our society and (cases of injustice) are still occurring on a daily basis. There are still pests that are damaging the reputation of the Party. If they are not exterminated, those pests would cause significant damage to the Party's credibility (p. 24) ...
>
> ... no matter how honest you are, you will painfully realize that there are people who are willing to use scams and schemes to rob you of your

reputation, and your rights, although those can be as little as a meal or a simple object (p. 26).

Nevertheless, during wartime, corruption and bad governance tended to be overlooked as the CPV had to concentrate their resources and efforts aimed at winning the war. During the period before the start of *Doi Moi*, which is known in Vietnam as the Subsidy Period, corruption and bad governance were so rampant and prevalent that they were known to and frequently mentioned by the documents penned by the leadership of the CPV.[64]

Looking back at the Subsidy Period, some considered the period between 1975 and 1985 to be one of the darkest periods in Vietnam's history.[65] Nevertheless, before *Doi Moi*, Vietnamese considered bad governance and excessive bureaucracy inherent features of the centralized economic model of Vietnam and were quite tolerant of them. In the book "Subsidy Period's Stories", the authors recounted their experience during this period and most of them considered corruption and bad governance to be inevitable results of the centralized socialist economy and nothing extraordinary. For example, one story went:

> The salary of a shopkeeper in the 1980s was around a few dozen Dong, and the salary of a shop manager is only a few Dong higher. However, they enjoyed so much power. Ms. Bui Thi Nguyet, a former shopkeeper at a food store during the Subsidy Period recounted her story: "The salary was not high but during that period, shopkeepers were respected. Perhaps it was only during that period that shopkeepers could receive gifts and commissions. Family members (of a shopkeeper) always received the freshest food and high-quality goods."[66]

Although this kind of petty corruption was rampant in Vietnam before *Doi Moi*, the impact of corruption and bad governance on the legitimacy of the CPV has become more visible recently; there are three reasons for this. The first reason is the mindset of the people that link corruption and bad governance to the socialist centrally planned economy. After the abolishment of the centrally planned economy, this kind of mindset has been slowly disappearing. In the market economy, people tend to emphasize the harmful effects of corruption and bad governance on economic development, an important source of the legitimacy of the Party. Secondly, the proliferation of the internet has made information about prosecuted, suspicious and perceived corruption cases more accessible to the public, further negatively affecting the credibility of the CPV. Thirdly, the state-owned media are allowed to make more critical reports regarding corruption and bad governance in Vietnam as of recent.

Corruption in the form of facilitation payments, extortion, abuse of office, attempted corruption, fraud, money laundering, and active and passive bribery is a crime according to both the Vietnamese Penal Code and the Anti-Corruption Law. Depending on the severity of the corruption case, if found guilty, the defendant may face punitive measures ranging from monetary fines to capital punishment. However, companies in all economic sectors are prone to be involved in bribery, political interference and facilitation payments. Corruption is most likely to occur in land administration, the construction sector and public administration.[67]

During its history, the CPV has consistently recognized that corruption is one of the major threats to its legitimacy and survival and has passed several resolutions and laws as well as started many anti-corruption campaigns.[68] The 2011 Political Guideline of the CPV mentioned corruption several times while stressing the grave danger it posed to the regime, stating "Red tape, corruption, and departing from the people would lead to unimaginable damage to the fate of the country, the socialist regime and the Party." The guideline suggested that the government must "establish mechanisms and measures to control, prevent, and punish bureaucracy and corruption". Furthermore, party members themselves must "frequently criticize and self-criticize to guard against individualism, opportunism, bureaucracy, corruption, wastefulness, and acts of division and factionalism".[69]

The Resolution of the Thirteenth National Congress of the CPV in 2021 considered corruption and bad governance to be gravely detrimental to the CPV and mentioned that one of the most important tasks facing the CPV is to combat against "bureaucracy, corruption, wastefulness, bad governance, and interest groups". On 20 November 2018, the National Assembly passed the 2018 Anti-corruption Law, which prohibits violations such as embezzlement of assets, accepting bribes, abuse of power and authority to misappropriate assets, and abusing power while on duties for personal gain.

Nevertheless, despite open acknowledgement of rampant corruption, the enforcement of anti-corruption frameworks has been deemed lacking. *Tuoi Tre*, the official mouthpiece of the Ho Chi Minh Communist Youth Union, compared the Anti-corruption Law with a toothless tiger due to the lack of better regulations on transparency and an effective mechanism to monitor government officials' property.[70] Vietnam has been consistently considered to be one of the more corrupt countries in the world by Transparency International.

From the early 2000s, several massive corruption scandals involving government officials have come to light, seriously damaging the image of the CPV. One of the earliest and most prominent cases was the Project Management Unit 18[71] corruption scandal. In early January 2006, just three months before the Tenth National Congress of the CPV, the executive director of Project Management Unit 18 was detained on charges of embezzlement and gambling. He was reportedly accused of spending as much as US$1.8 million to gamble on football matches. Following a series of other accusations, including bribery and abuse of office, Deputy Minister of Transport Nguyen Viet Tien was also arrested, and his home searched. In April 2006, after several attempts at rejecting his responsibilities, under political pressure from the Party, Transport Minister Dao Dinh Binh resigned.[72] Official news outlets estimated the total damage caused in this case was at least US$1.6 million,[73] although the real number could be much higher. Project Management Unit 18 was detrimental to the legitimacy of the CPV, not only because it involved the resignation of a minister, a rare occurrence in Vietnam, and that a massive amount of taxpayers' money was embezzled, but also because of the inconsistent reactions from the leadership of the CPV.

Prior to this scandal, corruption involving high ranking officials in Vietnam had been rarely prosecuted, let alone extensively covered by state-controlled media. Initially the press was allowed, even encouraged, to report extensively about the Project Management Unit 18 case.

The author still remembers vividly the massive news coverage of the case by government-run news outlets during the first quarter of 2006. VTV, the national television broadcaster, carried several reports on the case and major newspapers openly criticized the officials involved and called for their resignations and prosecution. The reporters who discovered the case were hailed as heroes for their investigation.

However, in mid-2007, the situation was turned upside down. Police started to track down and interrogate journalists who reported on the case about their sources. Among the reporters, two were arrested and tried for "abuse of power for personal gain" and seven others were stripped of their press credentials.[74] The arrests sparked a confrontation between the media and the government as media outlets unleashed a torrent of protests. However, the protests proved to be short-lived as the government quickly reasserted its control over the press. Furthermore, there was upheaval within the police force as several senior police officers involved in the investigation of the case, including one major general, were detained for "leaking confidential information to the press".[75] Deputy Minister Nguyen Viet Tien was cleared of all charges and released in April 2008 and his party membership was restored later in May.[76] However, in August of the same year, the Party Central Committee disciplined and removed Tien from all of his positions and requested the prime minister to dismiss him from his role as the deputy minister of transport. Later, in September 2009, Pham Tien Dung, an important official involved in the case who was arrested earlier on corruption and abuse of office charges, unexpectedly died while in detention. Media coverage of his death was kept to a minimum and no formal investigation was carried out. His death was ruled an asthma attack.[77] The timing of the investigation, combined with the suspicious turn of events and the CPV's bewildering reactions, led some observers to believe that this was just a masquerade for factional infighting within the CPV, which further weakened the legitimacy of the CPV's efforts in fighting corruption.

Another notorious scandal is the Pacific Consultants International bribery scandal. In August 2008, Japanese authorities arrested four officials working for Pacific Consultants International, a Japanese consultant company, on charges of paying bribes to Vietnamese government officials. Vietnamese authorities remained silent about the issue for several months after the arrests of the Japanese officials, and Huynh Ngoc Si, the chief recipient of the bribes, managed to keep his position. The Vietnamese government only started to investigate the case after the Japanese government announced that it would suspend official development aid to Vietnam. Despite attempts by the Vietnamese authorities to remedy the delay in dealing with the issue through the hasty detainment of Huynh Ngoc Si, the scandal severely damaged the image of the communist regime in the eyes of both ODA donors and the Vietnamese public.[78]

In 2010, the Vinashin scandal, the largest corruption scandal to date, was uncovered, which not only deeply shook the public's trust in the CPV's transparency and credibility, but also revealed inner conflicts among the top-ranking members of the Politburo. Vinashin was the largest state-owned shipbuilding holding group in Vietnam. Prior to 2010, the group had suffered several consecutive years of financial loss. In July 2010, the Government Inspectorate investigated the financial situation of the group and found that, as of December 2009, Vinashin was roughly US$4 billion in debt. Several senior officials of the debt-laden group and its subordinate companies were arrested. In 2017, Tran Van Lien, Vinashin's former head, and Giang Kim Dat, an official of one of its subsidiaries, were given the death penalty due to corruption and abuse of office charges.[79]

Then Chairman of the National Assembly of Vietnam Nguyen Van An reportedly commented on the scandal, placing the blame on socialism:

> (The Vinashin case) was a consequence of the global financial crisis, however, (the cause of this incident) was due to the systematic errors deep-rooted in the instruction and direction of the Central Committee and the Politburo which is founded on the belief that a socialist society must be built upon public ownership of the means of production. This model itself took root from a radical theory that asserts that private ownership of the means of production is the seed of all exploitation. It is a radical and unmotivated economic theory that has been rejected by reality. The government was the

one who carried out the Party's direction. Is any responsibility attached to the authority and power wielded by the Central Committee (of the CPV) and the Politburo? With the current political regime, both success and failure can be traced back to the CPV.[80]

After being re-elected as the general secretary of the CPV at its Twelfth National Congress in 2016, in order to regain public trust in the CPV's governance, Nguyen Phu Trong started a campaign against corruption, which resulted in many high-ranking officials being arrested and prosecuted, most notably Transport Minister Dinh La Thang, Police General Phan Van Vinh, Chairman of the People's Council of Hanoi Nguyen Duc Chung, Information and Communications Minister Nguyen Bac Son, Science and Technology Minister Chu Ngoc Anh and the ambassador of Vietnam to Japan Vu Hong Nam. Trong's campaign was compared to a blazing furnace. State-controlled news agencies are also allowed to cover those scandals.[81]

Nguyen Phu Trong's "blazing furnace" anti-corruption campaign appeared to reach its peak in 2023 when State President Nguyen Xuan Phuc resigned and two deputy prime ministers, Pham Binh Minh and Vu Duc Dam, were dismissed.[82] Prior to Dam's dismissal, one of his advisors was arrested on corruption charges. The resignation of a state president and dismissal of two deputy prime ministers, which was widely covered by state-controlled media, is unprecedented in the history of the CPV. Phuc, Minh and Dam were held accountable for major corruption scandals that happened under their management during the COVID-19 pandemic with Phuc admitting that he must take political responsibility as the head of the State.[83] While the official reason was "due to personal issues", the unusual manner in which the dismissals have been carried out prompted suspicion that those high-ranking officials were dismissed due to their incompetence or even direct involvement in the aforementioned corruption cases.[84]

The anti-corruption campaign extended into 2024, resulting in the discipline, dismissal and prosecution of even more top leaders. In May 2024, former Chief of the Government Office Mai Tien Dung was arrested and charged with bribery. Dung's party membership was also revoked.[85] Between March and April 2024, following the arrest of several of their subordinates in a corruption scandal, Chairman of the National Assembly of Vietnam Vuong Dinh Hue and State President Vo Van Thuong were dismissed.[86, 87] They were reprimanded by the Party for violating regulations that outline prohibited actions for party members, particularly members of the Politburo, the Party Central Committee and heads of organizations who are held accountable for their subordinates' action under party regulations and state laws.

In Vietnamese politics, the term "four pillars"[88] refers to the positions of general secretary of the Communist Party, president, prime minister and chairman of the National Assembly. Collectively, they are officially known as the "Key Leaders of the Party and the State"[89, 90] and represent the highest echelon in Vietnam's political hierarchy, historically considered untouchable. The consecutive dismissals of two such officials have shocked the public. However, possibly due to the perceived "too big to fail" nature of their positions, they were allowed to resign and avoided prosecution.[91]

Trong's anti-corruption campaign has received positive recognition, not only from state-controlled media outlets, but also from some foreign commentators.[92, 93, 94] The campaign has shown that even Politburo members are not exempt from being held accountable. However, the widespread and persistent nature of corruption in Vietnam has caused the anti-corruption drive to disrupt the functioning of the government, particularly in sectors where many officials have been prosecuted, such as medical equipment procurement, visa examination, vehicle inspection and urban planning. Many officials are avoiding decision-making to avoid responsibility, leading to shortages of medicine and medical equipment and delays in critical infrastructure projects.[95] The author experienced this first hand upon returning to Vietnam in September 2022, when a friend from the upper-middle class complained about his inability to purchase a decent apartment despite his high salary. Despite the high demand for apartments in Hanoi, no new apartment buildings have been constructed in the last three to four years. This friend pointed to the many unfinished high-rise buildings in the outskirts of Hanoi and explained that the officials responsible for urban planning in Hanoi have not approved any major residential building projects since the start of the blazing furnace campaign. Construction projects, ranging from small shops to massive skyscrapers, are often approved only when substantial bribes are provided, and many are plagued by safety and planning violations. Fearing prosecution for approving such projects, most officials have adopted a self-preservation mindset, hoping for a "safe landing".[96]

Another example of the negative impact of the campaign can be seen in the car registration issue. In January 2023, Tran Ky Hinh, former director of the Vietnam Register, was arrested on bribery charges. Investigations have determined that from 2014 to August 2021, Hinh, as the head of the Vietnam Register, accepted bribes from several directors of inspection centres in exchange for granting them registration codes and certificates, even though the centres did not meet the required standards. Additionally, during his tenure as the head of the Vietnam Register, Hinh relaxed management practices, neglected to enforce proper supervision and ignored violations in the granting of registration certificates to vehicles that did not meet technical safety and environmental protection standards, in exchange for bribes from vehicle owners and brokers. The Ho Chi Minh City police have arrested and detained eighty-nine individuals, including directors, deputy directors, employees of inspection centres and intermediaries, on charges of bribery, intermediary bribery and fraud.[97] One of the arrested directors has been discovered to be unable to even read or write Vietnamese.[98] This large-scale prosecution of officials has resulted in a significant backlog in car registration in major cities, as many inspection centres have been shut down and the remaining centres are struggling to keep up with the increased demand, sometimes ten-fold their capability. This has had a serious impact on the livelihood of many drivers and their families.[99]

Tatarski points out that while the crackdown is useful in improving the system to some extent, it has generated fear and unease among both the public and private sectors.[100] Recently, there has been a significant crackdown on fraudulent business practices by prominent private property developers, causing concerns that the real estate industry could crumble. Guarascio argues that combating corruption is typically regarded as a positive development in the long run, but it can cause short-term disruptions in business operations, particularly if the implementation of anti-bribery measures is perceived as unclear and influenced by political factors.[101]

Nguyen Phu Trong himself maintained that the campaign is not politically driven and that he "does not enjoy disciplining and prosecuting his own comrades and brothers-in-arms, it even hurts, but it must be done". Regarding the lack of officials after the purge, Trong said that there are always good candidates and that it is better to take time to choose a capable and incorruptible official rather than hastily find a replacement for the vacant positions.[102]

Trong's tenure had received positive evaluations from state media,[103] the general populace in Vietnam and scholars alike.[104] Following his death in July 2024, Trong is perhaps the most mourned leader since Ho Chi Minh and Vo Nguyen Giap. However, Western sources, while recognizing Trong's economic and diplomatic achievements, have criticized him for his harsh treatment of dissidents and his departure from a collective leadership towards a more autocratic rule.[105, 106]

Endemic corruption in Vietnam is in many ways detrimental to the legitimacy of the communists, who have been trying to portray themselves as the transparent and responsible representatives of the interests of the people, especially the working class. For a developing country with low GDP per capita like Vietnam, the enormous economic damage caused by a single corruption case is hard to defend. The Vinashin case's loss reported by state-controlled media alone accounted for almost 4 per cent of the total GDP of Vietnam in 2009. Corruption cases involving foreign investors and donors were particularly harmful to the image of Vietnam worldwide and this could discourage future investment and financial support from the international community. As such, those cases not only directly damaged the economy of Vietnam, but also left long-lasting negative effects. Furthermore, the delayed, conflicting and inconsistent reactions of the CPV and the Politburo in dealing with certain cases hinted at efforts to cover up the scandals and even infighting between factions within the Party itself.[107]

Petty and medium-scale corruption is even more prevalent and widespread within the society than large-scale corruption. Petty and medium-scale corruption range from police officers asking for bribes, abuse of office for monetary gain, to nepotism. The author, for example, on a few occasions was stopped by the police due to bogus traffic infractions but was let go after paying them some money "to buy a drink". On another occasion, the author had to give the official at the municipal office one million VND (US$40) as "lucky money" when he applied for a copy of his No Record of Marriage Certificate. Since this kind of corruption could be encountered by anybody and visibly influences their livelihood, it could be argued that they are as harmful as large-scale corruption to the image of the CPV, if not more.

As paradoxical as it may sound, petty and medium-scale corruption is often considered tolerable and even acceptable by officials and ordinary citizens. In Vietnam, greasing palms is seen by many small businesses as a cost of doing business.[108] If stopped for a traffic infraction, most people would likely be advised by police officers to offer a bribe and would likely comply with that suggestion.

Vietnamese people are willing to bribe officials to achieve their goals or to use essential services. The common reasons cited for this compromise are to avoid "cumbersome procedures", to "not be bothered", or to "conduct business smoothly". As shown in Figure 3.2, most Vietnamese believe that they must bribe to gain access to public services from using medical services to acquire permission.[109]

The 2018 PAPI Report highlights that the level of tolerance for corruption dramatically increased from 2011 to 2017. In 2011, the average threshold for reporting bribery was around VND 5 million (US$210), meaning that if the bribery amount exceeded this, the victim was likely to report it to the police. By 2017, this figure had increased fivefold to VND 27.5 million (US$1,200). From 2017 to 2021, this amount remained stable at around VND 27 million. Considering the low average income in Vietnam, this indicates that people are willing to spend up to half a year's income to bribe officials.[110]

Figure 3.2
perception on Corruption in public Sector, 2011–21

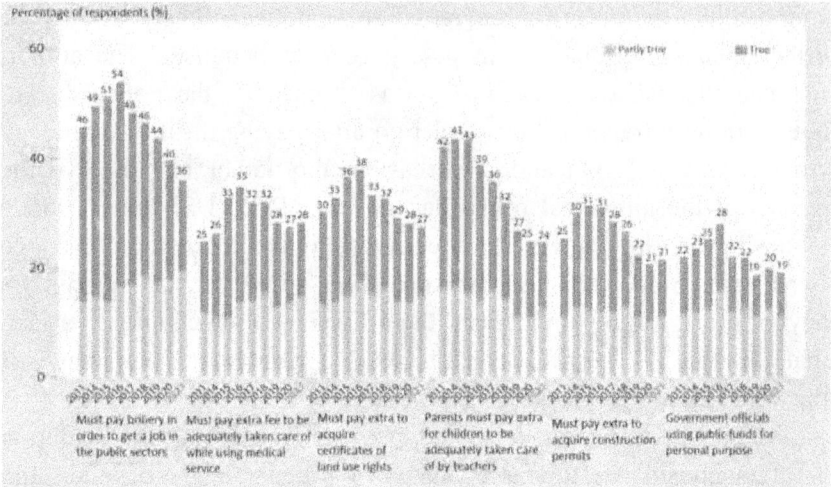

Source: Viet Nam Provincial Governance and Public Administration Performance Index (PAPI), "2021 Annual Report", 2022, https://papi.org.vn/eng/bao-cao/?year-report=2021 (accessed 17 July 2024).

From the perspective of the bribe taker, this figure also far exceeds the prosecutable threshold for the crime of bribery (VND 2 million or US$86).[111] High inflation is the main reason cited to justify this tolerance, meaning that when prices rise sharply, people tend to accept paying more when being extorted by officials. This reflects a prevalent mindset among Vietnamese that bribing officials is as normal as paying a service fee. According to the PAPI 2017 report, the percentage of people who report witnessing corrupt behaviour is also very low, decreasing from 9 per cent in 2011 to only about 3 per cent in 2017. Those who do not report say they do not know how to report (14 per cent), fear retaliation or revenge (11 per cent) or believe that reporting will not bring any benefit (53 per cent). In 2020 and 2021, the percentage of people who would report corrupt behaviour are 3.65 per cent and 5.03 per cent, respectively.

The Global Corruption Barometer carried out by Transparency International, which studied Vietnamese perceptions and experiences regarding corruption gave the country a Corruption Perception score of 42/100 in 2022 and suggested that

- 64 per cent of people think government corruption is a big problem;
- 15 per cent of public service users paid a bribe in the previous twelve months.

Although the score has been significantly improving in the past decade,[112] corruption on all levels has remained a deep-rooted issue within Vietnamese society. Enforcement of the anti-corruption legal framework is lacking. Facilitation payments and private gifts over US$25 to government officials are criminalized by law but common in practice.

Land Disputes

Land conflict has been a prominent issue in Vietnam since the early 1990s. Perhaps nothing undermines the legitimacy of the CPV more than instances of bad governance and corruption revealed through deadly confrontations between authorities and local peasants during land confiscations.

Private landownership is not legally recognized in Vietnam. Land is regarded as a public asset; thus, only land use rights can be granted. The State reserves the right to acquire land for national defence, security or socioeconomic development purposes. In such cases, land user is entitled to compensation by the government.

Land confiscation is a significant source of grievance, particularly in contexts marked by corruption and inept management, as evident in Vietnam.[113, 114] Since the start of *Doi Moi*, most complaints lodged with authorities are land-related, consistently exceeding 65 per cent, and reaching as high as 98 per cent in 2019, according to a report from the CPV's official mouthpiece.[115] Protests related to land conflicts are a frequent sight in certain areas of Hanoi where government headquarters are situated.

Kerkvliet observed the land confiscation for the construction of a high-tech industrial zone in District Nine, Ho Chi Minh City and concludes that the residents based their protests on four claims. The first is the illegality of the confiscations. Local authorities seized land without adhering to required procedures, applied an outdated land law, neglected to consult residents, intimidated those who resisted, disrupted demonstrations and violated democratic procedures in various ways. Many residents attributed these shortcomings to corruption, the second reason for their protests. Suspicions arose that local authorities hurried to confiscate land, intending to sell it later at inflated prices for personal gain. Additionally, protesters claimed that the compensation payments for their land were unjustly low, constituting a form of land theft by the government. Lastly, forcibly taking land against people's will was deemed unfair, particularly when the victims and their families are people who had made great sacrifices for the nation during the First, Second and Third Indochina Wars.[116]

Most of land-related protests share those same grievances. However, they can become significantly more complex and potentially severe when intertwined with religious and ethnic issues, as seen in conflicts such as the land dispute in Thai Ha, Hanoi[117] and the land disputes in Central Highland Vietnam.[118] Kerkvliet argues that while many protests were peaceful and aligned with the rightful resistance theory,[119, 120] exceptions exist.

One such example that has led to deadly consequences is the Dong Tam Commune Land Dispute. On 14 September 2020, the Hanoi High People's Court issued two death sentences, one life imprisonment and three prison terms to six Dong Tam commune villagers in Hanoi on charges of murder. Another twenty-three defendants received sentences of up to six months in prison for resisting law enforcement officers on duty.[121] These charges stem from a land dispute in the Dong Tam commune, initiated when villagers claimed that the local government had unlawfully allocated their agricultural land.[122] During clashes with police in April 2017, thirty officers were taken hostage. They were released a few days later after the villagers received concessions from then Hanoi mayor Nguyen Duc Chung.[123] Additionally, fourteen government officials were prosecuted for unlawfully issuing land use certificates to the villagers.[124]

Three years later, on 9 January 2020, police conducted a raid in Dong Tam commune, resulting in the death of the protest leader, an eighty-four-year-old CPV member, and three police officers. Chief of the Government Office Mai Tien Dung later acknowledged that the dispute stemmed from faults of the Hanoi government.[125] The hostage crisis, raid and subsequent trials faced scrutiny and criticism from both overseas and domestic Vietnamese observers, significantly undermining the authority of the CPV.

Thayer argues that land-related disputes is the most serious challenge to the rule of the CPV.[126] Despite the substantial financial losses to taxpayers resulting from massive corruption cases detailed earlier in this chapter, there were minimal demonstrations initiated in response, let alone violent clashes with state law enforcement. However, land-related disputes, if poorly managed by local governments, can escalate into deadly confrontations between local people and the state police. This is because people are tolerant to corruption, whether petty or large-scale, due to the perceived high costs associated with openly challenging governmental authority. Land confiscation, on the other hand, threatens the people's livelihoods, prompting extreme responses. Two Vietnamese proverbs perfectly describe this situation "a worm that is trampled on will wriggle"[127] and "a cornered dog will fight back fiercely".[128] This tendency is exacerbated when religious and ethnic factors come into play. Moreover, protestors may receive backing and guidance from overseas opposition to the CPV, further complicating the situation and intensifying their resistance.

Nepotism

Nepotism, which is the practice of favouring family connections over merit or qualifications, is a pervasive issue in Vietnam. Nepotism and corruption are two sides of the same coin, as up-and-coming officials often require powerful backers and must pay a large sum of money to secure their positions. In turn, these officials then tend to favour their own relatives and accept bribes in order to maximize the benefits of their positions, which were obtained through costly and questionable means.

According to PAPI (2022), most Vietnamese believe that personal relationships are either important or very important when looking for jobs in the public sector, as illustrated in Figure 3.3. The same report indicates that roughly half of Vietnamese respondents surveyed in 2020 and 2021 reported that they would have to resort to bribery to secure their position in the government. On a scale of one to five, with one being utmost important and five being unimportant, having a powerful backer is given the score of 1.59 in 2020 and 1.61 in 2021 by respondents, meaning Vietnamese think that having strong personal relationship to government officials is very important to be recruited as a civil servant.

Figure 3.3
personal Ties in State Sector Job Applications, 2011–21

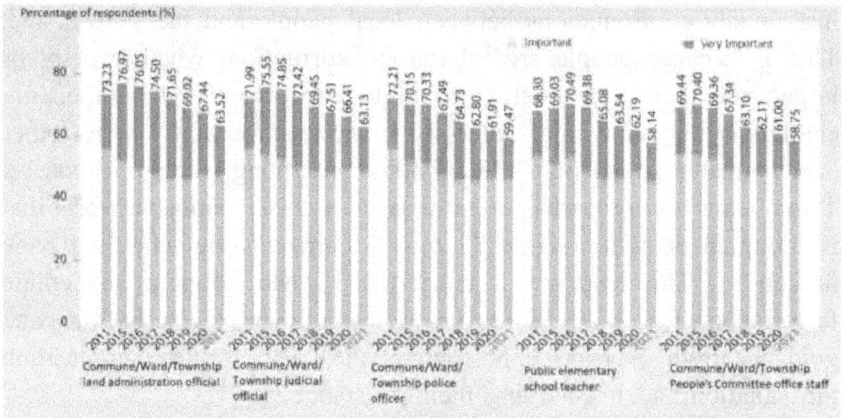

Source: Viet Nam Provincial Governance and Public Administration Performance Index (PAPI), "2021 Annual Report", 2022, https://papi.org.vn/eng/bao-cao/?year-report=2021 (accessed 17 July 2024).

Two factors contribute to the widespread nepotism, which has been particularly problematic in the public sector, are the tolerant mindset of both ordinary people and government officials and the lack of an effective legal mechanism to deter and punish nepotism.

Along with the Chinese theory of statecraft and imperial examination system, the mindset "when one member becomes an official, the whole clan benefits"[129] was also introduced into Vietnam centuries ago. In feudal Vietnam, a male student must spend years, even decades of rigorous studying to have a chance at passing the imperial examination to be employed as mandarins. As such, they would have had to sacrifice their time working the fields and would have needed the support from their whole family. As a result, the whole family expects that they would benefit in case one of their members passes the imperial examination and becomes an official. This mindset survived into the Subsidy Period, when government clerks had privileges, such as giving good quality food to their family members with impunity.

As this mindset became entrenched in modern Vietnam, many officials now assume as standard practice that their relatives will receive preferential treatment when applying for government positions influenced by them. While positions themselves are not hereditary, this unwritten norm is widely accepted among government officials due to its personal benefits for themselves and their families. Ordinary citizens, whose children face limited opportunities for advancement as civil servants, also exhibit considerable tolerance towards this unwritten practice. The public's indifference to overt nepotism can be attributed to the belief that if one person in the family is fortunate enough to secure public sector employment, the entire family stands to benefit from this practice.

To secure a government position, candidates typically need personal connections with a patron and are often required to pay a fee ranging from tens of millions to multiple billions of VND, depending on the perks associated with the position. This practice extends to career advancement as well. It should be noted that even individuals with a powerful patron and the financial means to pay a substantial fee must still meet certain requirements before applying for specific positions. For example, usually only deputy ministers and equivalents can apply for a vacant minister position. Although there are few candidates, the competition is often very intense due to the lucrative nature of such positions. Officials appointed through nepotism and bribery view the money spent to acquire their position as an investment and will often abuse their position to get back the invested money. They would also try to consolidate power and strengthen their hold on the position.

The most obvious method to make money from one's position while strengthening it is to appoint loyal subordinates from among their relatives and acquaintances.[130]

Relatives of officials also enjoy certain privileges such as their applications are usually processed much more quickly when they have to do administrative formalities. The amount of bribery also depends on the relationship between the official in charge and the backer. For example, if the applicant is an immediate family member of a direct supervisor of the official in charge, usually they would not have to pay bribery at all. Relatives of police officers are usually let off without a ticket for traffic infractions. It is not uncommon for a Vietnamese to walk into a government office and declare to the clerk that they are a relative to such and such high-ranking officials before submitting their documents.

The persistent existence of nepotism in Vietnam is widely acknowledged and was even debated in the National Assembly many times.[131] Nevertheless, nepotism is so widespread in the Vietnamese public sector that it is hard to find a government employee without a personal link to a higher-ranking official. While there have been cases of nepotism exposed by the state-controlled media,[132] most people who are recruited based on their personal relationship rather than merits remain firmly seated on their position. For example, Nguyen Thanh Nghi, the firstborn son of former Prime Minister Nguyen Tan Dung, became the youngest deputy minister in Vietnam's history when he was appointed in 2011 at the age of only thirty-five.[133] Furthermore, usually the beneficiaries of nepotism cases are only exposed after their patrons fall out of favour. As such, the exposed cases of nepotism are often considered to be a byproduct of factional infighting rather than real efforts in combating corruption.

In addition to the Vietnamese people's deep-rooted tolerance of nepotism, the lack of an effective mechanism to punish it only worsens the situation. The 2018 Anti-Corruption Law, the 2018 Officials and Civil Servants Law[134] and the 2015 Penal Code of Vietnam make no mention of nepotism or cronyism and their punishments. Decision 205-QĐ/TW on Preventing Abuse of Power and Authority while on Duty and Controlling Nepotism and Cronyism is one of the few documents that explicitly mentions nepotism and cronyism. This decision prohibits the abuse of relationships, money and other unjust leverage to gain a position or benefits. It also prohibits enabling, aiding and abetting in bribery for position or power. Nevertheless, the punishments for such actions are rather lacking, with the most severe punishment being expulsion from the CPV and dismissal from one's position. As such, even in cases of exposed nepotism, the perpetrators are usually named and shamed or faced internal discipline rather than being prosecuted as criminals.

Another reason that explains the tolerance towards corruption and nepotism is the abysmal salary of civil servants in Vietnam. The highest-paid officials receive a monthly salary of VND 14,400,000 (US$610) following a nation-wide raise from July 2023. At the opposite end of the spectrum, a newly recruited government janitor or driver's salary would be VND 3,690,000 (US$157).[135] In comparison, the average monthly salary of an employee of the top ten banks in Vietnam varies from VND 27,000,000 (US$1,150) to VND 48,000,000 (US$2,045).[136]

While in addition to the monthly salary and yearly bonus, government officials also enjoyed other benefits, such as insurance and housing benefits, even state-controlled media admitted that government officials would struggle to make ends meet as the mouthpiece of the National Assembly alleged that the salary of newly recruited government officials is lower than that of factory workers.[137] To make up for the low salary, government officials would have to abuse their position for monetary gains. In the aforementioned corruption scandals, an official may pocket sums that are thousands of times his annual legal salary through bribery and embezzlement. Petty corruption, which is widely tolerated as it is not as massive, remains significant. In 2018, an interviewed police officer reported that around 50 to 70 per cent of his income comes from stopping traffic infractions.

Newly recruited government officials may be asked by their supervisor to carry out small favours, such as overlooking minor infractions or reissuing a document within a short time frame for their relatives. The recruit might find it difficult to refuse such requests out of fear of upsetting their boss. In some cases, the request may be accompanied by a gesture of gratitude, such as an envelope of "lucky money". Over time, the frequency and seriousness of such requests may escalate, along with the compensation offered. This could lead to officials making similar requests for themselves or their family members to other colleagues in return. Refusing to comply with such requests may result in the official being ostracized and subjected to bullying and significantly harm their chances of advancing in their career.

In combination with the compromising mindset and government official's low salary, this practice has resulted in the fact that virtually all government officials have abused their positions either for monetary gains or to improve their relationship with their colleagues. Although such actions often go unpunished, officials may occasionally be held responsible for their abuse of power. For instance, although most police officers accept bribes to overlook traffic infractions with impunity, there have been rare cases where officers have been prosecuted for doing so.[138] Another example was that after the arrest of the former director of Vietnam Register, many inspectors refused to go to work in fear that they would be arrested by the police for their previous violations.[139] The arrest of the former ambassador of Vietnam in Japan on corruption charges also sent shockwaves among employees of the Ministry of Foreign Affairs, many of whom bribed for a tenure in a Western country hoping to recoup their "investment" through consulate work.

Nguyen Phu Trong's "blazing furnace" campaign has significantly changed government officials' perception of what is considered tolerable. Violations that would previously have been overlooked or dealt with leniently are now being prosecuted, and offenders may face life sentences or even the death penalty. Although the campaign has increased transparency within the government, it is likely to cause discord and friction within the CPV and the government, potentially eroding partisan loyalty. Low salaries, combined with the loss of informal benefits, have led to an exodus of workers from the public sector to the private sector in recent years. According to a report from

Vietnam's Ministry of Home Affairs, more than 40,000 government workers have resigned to take up jobs in the private sector from 2020 to June 2022.[140]

Some Vietnamese express their suspicions that Nguyen Phu Trong's campaign is merely another internal purge and will have no lasting impact on the corruption situation and the improvement of governance in Vietnam. Although Trong's leadership has enhanced the legitimacy of the CPV, the initial absence of notable successors after the tumultuous final years of his tenure has left his supporters concerned that his anti-corruption campaign may not continue. Nevertheless, In December 2024, under the leadership of General Secretary To Lam, the Politburo disciplined former Prime Minister Nguyen Xuan Phuc and former Standing Deputy Prime Minister Truong Hoa Binh with warnings, and issued a reprimand to Truong Thi Mai, former Head of the Central Commission for Mass Mobilization, for violations and shortcomings that had caused "serious consequences, negative public opinion, and affected the reputation of the Party and State".[141] This development may indicate that the anti-corruption campaign will continue under To Lam's tenure.

The Territorial Disputes in the South China Sea

Throughout the course of its history, overall, Vietnam was under Chinese domination for more than one thousand years. Even when not occupied as a province of China, Vietnam was put under significant Chinese influence due to proximity. This has left a long-lasting effect on the country's culture, from statecraft theory to local rituals. While nominally submitting to the Chinese emperors as a vassal, the succeeding Vietnamese dynasties fought constantly both militarily and diplomatically against China to maintain the country's independence. This complex relationship continued under the rule of the CPV. The Chinese Communist Party provided the Viet Minh with much needed military aid during the early 1950s when even the Soviet Union showed no interest in getting involved in the war in Indochina. China also sent advisors to instruct the CPV to carry out land reforms following the Chinese model. Chinese aid to North Vietnam continued until the relations between the two countries fell apart during the Vietnam War. Even when their survival depended on Chinese aid, the CPV fought to maintain their self-determination in decision making.

Founder of the CPV, Ho Chi Minh, was educated by his father, a mandarin, spent many years living in China, and was an accomplished writer of Chinese poems. However, on many occasions, he showed his disdain towards China. According to Karnow,[142] during a meeting with his government in 1946, explaining his decision to let the French return, Ho allegedly said that

> You fools! Don't you realize what it means if the Chinese remain? Don't you remember your history? The last time the Chinese came, they stayed a thousand years. The French are foreigners. They are weak. Colonialism is dying. The white man is finished in Asia. But if the Chinese stay now, they will never go. As for me, I prefer to sniff French shit for five years than eat Chinese shit for the rest of my life.

When interviewed by the French Broadcasting and Television Office in June 1967 and asked about the possibility of an isolated North Vietnam becoming a satellite state to China, Ho responded in French *"Jamais"* (never).[143]

After the 1979 Sino-Vietnamese War, the CPV considered the Chinese Communist Party their greatest enemy. The pro-Chinese faction led by Politburo member and then Vice Chairman of the National Assembly of Vietnam Hoang Van Hoan was purged. In his speech during the first session of the Seventh National Assembly of Vietnam on 25 June 1981, Le Duan, then general secretary of the Central Committee of the CPV, chastised China for supporting the Khmer Rouge and invading Vietnam. Duan accused China of committing two wars of aggression against Vietnam, one from the north by themselves and one from the south through the Pol Pot regime. Duan claimed that China had long nurtured the ambition to annex Vietnam and the Indochinese Peninsula to pave the way for realizing their dream of expansion and becoming the hegemonic power in Southeast Asia. Even worse, Duan claimed that China had colluded with the United States to destroy Vietnam and called China "a direct and dangerous enemy of our people". He condemned China's actions, stating that they exposed to the world the "extremely brutal and cunning nature of the expansionist and hegemonic ideology and the largest international reactionary force that threatens the independence, peace, and stability in Indochina and Southeast Asia".[144]

Despite the official normalization of relations in 1991 and stronger economic ties, the Vietnamese leadership remains distrustful of China. The distrust towards China is not only harboured by elite politicians but also by common people in Vietnam. According to a survey conducted by the Pew Research Centre in 2017, 64 per cent of Vietnamese respondents considered China's economic growth a bad thing for Vietnam, while 90 per cent considered China's growing military a threat to Vietnam. Furthermore, 80 per cent of the surveyed Vietnamese viewed China's rising power and influence as a major threat to Vietnam.[145]

The South China Sea dispute, which has a long history dating back to the French colonial period, resurfaced and became one of the most discussed issues in Vietnam in 2005. To most Vietnamese, this is just another chapter in the thousands of years of conflict between them and their northern nemesis.

The South China Sea dispute started to emerge in the wake of the Second World War, during the formation of many nation states in East and Southeast Asia, with Vietnam being one of those. The significantly important geographic location and the rich fishery of the South China Sea were the origin reason for the dispute. Later, the discovery of massive amounts of crude oil and natural gas ripe for exploitation in the seabed further intensified the conflict. Parts of the sea are claimed by China, Vietnam, Taiwan, the Philippines, Malaysia, Indonesia and Brunei; with Vietnam, China, Taiwan and the Philippines being the most active parties. Since the mid-2000s, several noteworthy incidents have occurred in the disputed waters between Vietnam and China, resulting in both anti-China and anti-government protests in major cities in Vietnam. Initially, the Vietnamese government allowed limited press reports on those incidents while attempting to curb the protests.

One of the earliest incidents that ignited widespread anti-Chinese sentiment in Vietnam was the killing of Vietnamese sailors on 8 January 2005. Armed Chinese ships attacked two Vietnamese fishing boats in the Gulf of Tonkin in the northern part of the South China Sea, killing nine people and injuring seven others. Chinese ships also detained a ship with eight Vietnamese onboard. Five days later, on January 14, the Vietnamese government issued an official statement through its Ministry of Foreign Affairs spokesperson, condemning the shooting and requesting that China investigate and punish the perpetrators.[146] According to Chinese foreign ministry spokesman Kong Quan, several Chinese fishing boats were operating on the Chinese side of the Beibu Gulf when three unidentified armed vessels attempted to rob and fire at them.[147] Kong maintained that "the Chinese maritime police were forced to take necessary actions. They shot dead several armed robbers, seized one of the armed vessels and eight robbers along with their weapons and ammunition and tools", and called it a "serious armed robbery case at sea". The Chinese government did not provide any further information on the case and no investigation was carried out. This incident sparked anti-China protests first among overseas Vietnamese and then domestically. The Vietnamese government responded to those protests by enacting the 38/2005/ND-CP Decree which carried out several measures to ensure public order in March 2005.[148]

In November 2007, the plan to establish a city-level administrative unit under the name Sansha, which incorporates South China Sea islands, including most of the disputed islands, was approved by the People's Republic of China's State Council. In response to this, the Ministry of Foreign Affairs of Vietnam issued a statement during a press conference on December 3 to assert Vietnam's authority over the disputed islands and reject China's claims.[149]

Domestic media coverage of the incident was allowed by the government to a broad degree. Upon hearing the news, on December 9, hundreds of people, mostly students, gathered in front of the Embassy and Consulate of the People's Republic of China in Hanoi and Ho Chi Minh City, respectively, to protest China's decision.

Protesters communicated with one another via social media. The protests in Hanoi and Ho Chi Minh City were peaceful in general with people waving Vietnamese flags and singing the Vietnamese national anthem. However, police quickly dispersed the protesters in both cities.[150] The conflicting reactions of the government sparked dissatisfaction among protestors.

On 26 May 2011, a Vietnamese oil and gas survey ship named Binh Minh 02 belonging to the Vietnam National Oil and Gas Group clashed with three Chinese maritime patrol vessels in the water some 120 km off the south-central coast of Vietnam and roughly 600 km south of Hainan Island. The clash resulted in the destruction of the survey ship's cable. The deputy director of Vietnam Oil and Gas Group maintained that the Vietnamese survey ship had attempted to communicate with the three invading Chinese ships before the incident but received no response and that the former's cables were deliberately cut by the latter. He also added that the incident occurred inside Vietnam's non-disputed exclusive economic zone. The next day an official from the Ministry of Foreign Affairs of Vietnam met with a diplomat from the Embassy of the People's Republic of China to deliver a diplomatic note requesting China to refrain from violating the sovereignty of Vietnam and demanding compensation for the damage caused to the Vietnamese survey ship by Chinese ships.[151]

Chinese authorities, however, claimed that Vietnam had violated Chinese sovereignty. In response to Vietnam's condemnation, the spokeswoman of the Ministry of Foreign Affairs of the People's Republic of China maintained that "China's position on the South China Sea is clear and consistent. We strongly object to Vietnam's exploitation of oil and natural gas as it is against the interests and sovereignty of China in the South China Sea as well as violating the consensus agreed upon by both sides on this issue." She further added that "the actions carried out under Chinese authority were legal law-enforcing activities within Chinese waters".[152]

The Vietnamese public reacted fiercely. In the span of more than ten weeks, from early June until late August, many waves of protest were organized in Hanoi and Ho Chi Minh City.[153] The scale and duration of those protests were unprecedented. Campaigns that advocated a boycott of Chinese-made products were started and some Vietnamese tourism companies reportedly refused service to Chinese tourists.[154, 155] The Vietnamese government, on the other hand, reacted cautiously by trying to curb the hostility of the public towards China. Police were deployed to control the protest by quietly dispersing the protesters. In the weeks following the incident, as the protests occurred more frequently and with more participants, several protesters and journalists who were working for foreign media companies, such as Asahi Shimbun, Japan Broadcasting Corporation and Associated Press, were arrested.[156] Video clips taken by protesters showed dozens of people detained by what appeared to be police officers in plain clothes.[157] After ten weeks of continuous protests, the People's Committee of Hanoi officially demanded its citizens to "completely refrain from spontaneous demonstrations, protests, rallies, and gatherings within the boundaries of the city". Committee officials called the protests the result of "domestic and foreign reactionary forces' manipulation, provocation, and organization to disturb public safety of Hanoi"[158] and that "the spontaneous protests, demonstrations, and rallies had badly damaged social safety and the image of Hanoi, a city under the name The City for Peace. The unrest could also potentially lead to political tension, and is harmful to Vietnam's foreign relations."[159] The Vietnamese government's attempts to control and minimize the impact of the protests inevitably led to anti-Chinese protesters' loss of confidence. On 24 July 2011, protesters gathered in front of the headquarters of *Hanoi Moi* newspaper to express dissatisfaction about an article praising General Xu Shiyou, the commander in chief of the People's Liberation Army of China during the 1979 Sino-Vietnamese War. The protestors also showed their support for the *Dai Doan Ket* newspaper, the only paper in Vietnam at that point to suggest that the Republic of Vietnam's soldiers and sailors who died during the Battle of the Paracel Islands in 1974 should be recognized as martyr war soldiers.[160]

On 2 May 2014, China National Offshore Oil Corporation relocated its Hai Yang Shi You 981 oil rig, worth over US$1 billion, to a new drilling location seventeen nautical miles from the southwestern-most island of the Paracel Islands.[161] Vietnamese sources claimed that China had been moving the oil rig to several locations from that point and the rig was accompanied by a fleet of six warships. The initial location of the oil rig was on the Vietnamese continental shelf, which was claimed by Vietnam.

Vietnam responded by sending a fleet of ships to monitor the situation. The Vietnamese fleet and the fleet protecting the rig consequently clashed. Video clips released by the Vietnamese government show Chinese ships ramming into and firing water cannons at the Vietnamese vessels. Vietnamese officials reported that at least six Vietnamese sailors onboard had been injured during those standoffs. Chinese officials admitted to the use of water cannons against Vietnamese ships, but they maintained that the Vietnamese side attacked first, and they were forced to respond accordingly. Yi Xian Liang, deputy director general of the foreign ministry's Department of Boundary and Ocean Affairs, said in a press briefing that China is "deeply surprised and shocked" by Vietnam's actions and "from May 3 to May 7, in a short period of five days, Vietnam has dispatched thirty-five vessels of various kinds which rammed into Chinese ships as many as 171 times". Yi also added that China's operation of the oil rig was "legitimate, justified, and lawful" and such actions had been going on for a decade. He consequently said that the Chinese government would continue such operations.[162] On May 26, a Vietnamese fishing boat was sunk in the waters near the oil rig after colliding with a Chinese vessel. Xinhua News Agency reported that the Vietnamese fishing boat was sunk because it provoked Chinese coast guard ships, and the Ministry of Foreign Affairs of the People's Republic of China had officially sent a diplomatic note to protest to the Vietnamese.[163]

The incident was quickly made known to the Vietnamese public and it was followed by unprecedented protests in twenty-two major cities and towns throughout Vietnam, continuing from May to June of 2014. The demonstrations attracted thousands of participants.[164] In an unusual move, the CPV turned a blind eye to the protests, an act that could be understood by the protesters as a sign of approval. While in the major cities the protests were more or less non-violent, in the industrial parks in Binh Duong and Dong Nai, what started as peaceful demonstrations quickly escalated into violent riots that resulted in the deaths of five people.[165] The rioters then turned to foreign-owned factories, regardless of whether they were Chinese-owned or not. Hundreds of factories were vandalized, burned, destroyed and looted as the rioters proved to be uncontrollable. Overseas Vietnamese communities also organized large scale anti-Chinese demonstrations. In Binh Duong, the province most heavily damaged by the riots, only fourteen of the 351 factories affected were owned by Chinese corporations.[166] More than one thousand people were arrested following this calamity.[167] This turn of events forced the Vietnamese government to adopt stricter measures against the protests. On May 15, Prime Minister Nguyen Tan Dung issued Official Order No. 697/CĐ-TTg regarding the restoration of public order and safety, urging local authorities to urgently implement measures to maintain order and strictly deal with rioters and provocateurs. The order prioritizes the protection of enterprises, especially foreign enterprises, ensuring that their properties are safe, and their production remains undisrupted.

The Vietnamese government became more and more cautious as the demonstrations in the big cities were progressing and becoming increasingly radical. On May 23, a Vietnamese woman died after immolating herself near the Independence Palace in Ho Chi Minh City to protest against China.[168] Escalation in the aggressiveness of the protests-turned-riots prompted the Chinese government to evacuate citizens from Vietnam and put strong diplomatic pressure on the Vietnamese government. From the middle of May, law enforcement agencies started to crack down on anti-China protests and arrested several protesters.[169] The response of the Vietnamese government inevitably led to disapproval from anti-Chinese protesters and deepened the CPV's legitimacy crisis.[170]

To many Vietnamese, the identity of Vietnamese nationhood is based on the fight to maintain independence against foreign invaders, particularly the struggle against China. As such, the escalating tension in the South China Sea was an important reality check regarding the legitimacy of the CPV, which often claims to be the defender of Vietnamese national independence. While the Party's handling of the crisis was deemed inadequate by a proportion of the population, a notion that was amplified by both domestic and overseas opposition, some scholars suggest that the CPV may use this opportunity to boost its legitimacy or even distract the public from other issues.[171]

The proliferation of the Internet

The internet has been significantly influencing the relationships between governments and their citizens, and Vietnam is no exception. The dissemination of information through a network of vibrant communication channels has long been one of the most crucial requirements for democracies to be functional.[172] The introduction of the internet allows information to flow freely, which benefits businesses and enables a more efficient passage of political discussions among citizens. The internet provides citizens a channel to keep check on their government's transparency and governance, and allows them to voice their own opinions, which, in large numbers, could influence the outcomes of elections in democracies. As such, in countries with freer and broader access to information, citizens tend to be more active in carrying out their political rights and duties by participating in elections and petitions to influence the decision-making mechanism of the government. An ideal network of information would theoretically allow all involved parties to be heard equally and indiscriminately.[173]

In non-democratic regimes where the flow of information is often controlled, censored and distorted by the government, the internet is even more important as a channel of information exchange. In contrast with conventional domestic media, which is usually monopolized by the government, the internet reduces blockages from gatekeepers and facilitates citizen journalism, which otherwise could be expensive.[174] The proliferation of the internet allows information to be posted and accessed by virtually any person who has access to a computer and an internet connection. This thus provides alternative sources of information, weakening the monopoly of information often enjoyed by authoritarian regimes.

Thanks to the internet, even under the strict surveillance of the government, citizens gain the potential to freely expose and discuss a ruling party's bad governance, misuse of power, corruption and violation of human rights, which have a negative effect on the regime's reputation.[175] The internet as a channel of communication is so powerful that in many cases a regime has to invest a great deal of effort in attempts to control it. One of the most noteworthy examples is the combination of legislative actions and technologies, known as the Great Firewall of China, employed by the Chinese Communist Party to censor the internet within its borders.

The internet was first introduced in Vietnam in November 1997.[176] After just more than twenty years, more than two out of every three Vietnamese have access to the internet. This massive number of internet users serves as fertile soil for perhaps hundreds of thousands of websites to sprout up.

Kerkvliet contends that since 1990, public political criticism which centred around four groups of critics: factory workers advocating for improved wages and living conditions; rural residents protesting against corruption and land seizures; individuals voicing opposition to China's territorial encroachments and criticizing Sino-Vietnamese relations; and dissidents challenging the Party-State regime and advocating for democratization, have emerged as a significant aspect of Vietnam's political landscape, noting a transformation from discreet conversations within families to widespread utilization of electronic media platforms.[177]

Despite the efforts of the Central Propaganda Department to regulate the internet, a significant number of websites share views that contradict those of the CPV. Dissidents establish websites and utilize social media networks, most notably Facebook, to voice dissatisfaction with the Party's governance and to disclose scandals involving top communist leaders. Internet sites that criticize the actions and leadership of the CPV can be roughly divided into four types:

Vietnamese versions of foreign news agencies such as VOA, BBC and Radio Free Asia; websites of overseas Vietnamese political parties and groups, such as Viet Tan, the People's Action Party of Vietnam and the Vietnamese National Party; websites and blogs started and maintained by Vietnamese individuals and groups, such as Me Nam, Co Gai Do Long and Dieu Cay; and anonymous blogs and websites that discuss Vietnamese politics, such as Chan Dung Quyen Luc, Dan Lam Bao and Nguyentandung.org. Some of these websites are quite popular and are among the most accessed websites by Vietnamese.[178]

As the creation of those websites often involves people who are antagonistic, disillusioned and unsatisfied, their biases are not without question. Furthermore, due to difficulty in fact-checking, the truthfulness of a significant proportion of the information provided by those sources cannot be confirmed. Some commentators suspect that many such websites are started by communist leaders themselves as weapons to be used in factional infighting.[179]

As the most frequently discussed topics on such sites are the Party's bad governance, corruption, violation of human rights, handling of territorial disputes with China and environment issues, the internet is significant in the sense that it acts as an amplifier of other issues that force the CPV to review its paradigm of political legitimacy. Although in many cases the sources of the news can be difficult to verify, this kind of information could incite robust discussions and negatively affect the legitimacy of the Party. Websites, blogs and social networks also act as tools to gather dissidents for meetings and demonstrations. Most of the major demonstrations in Vietnam in the last decade were arranged in this way. These include the 2014 Vietnam anti-China protests and 2016 anti-Formosa Ha Tinh protests.

The CPV has recognized the risks posed to its rule by the introduction of the internet. While Kerkvliet points out that while Vietnamese authorities are quite tolerant and responsive to public criticisms, the CPV is not unlike other party-state regimes in the methods they use to repress potential threats.[180] Although the CPV has been consistently claiming that there has been no censorship or state-sanctioned oppression on the internet,[181] it has been using a combination of legal, technical and even extra-legal methods to scrutinize and control actions deemed harmful to the regime.

Several government bodies are assigned to this mission. The Ministry of Information and Communications is tasked with monitoring domestic information flow under the supervision of the Central Propaganda Department of the CPV while the Ministry of Public Security is tasked with carrying out law enforcement against dissidents who are charged with violating the legal framework imposed by the government. In August 2014, the Ministry of Public Security established the Cyber Security Department, which is responsible for maintaining order online.[182] The Department of Domestic Security, Ministry of Public Security also engages in activities to control people who are deemed by the government as overseas and domestic counter-revolutionary individuals, many of whom have been actively using the internet as a channel to voice their opinions.

As early as March 1997, even before the internet was officially introduced to Vietnam, the government issued Decree 21-CP Provisional Rules on the Establishment, Management, and Usage of the Internet in Vietnam. Article 1 of this decree states that the government manages and controls the internet and its services in Vietnam, oversees gateways to the international internet and regulates the content of information transmitted on the network.

According to this decree, information on the internet must not distort, slander, deny the people's government; fabricate, cause panic among the people; disseminate information that divides between social classes, between the people and the people's government, with the people's armed forces, with political organizations, sociopolitical organizations or distort history; deny revolutionary achievements; or offend ethnic groups and national heroes.

Article 3 of Decree 21-CP prohibits actions against the Socialist Republic of Vietnam and that internet providers must have effective measures to prevent the spreading of such information and that if such information is found, it must be reported to the authority as soon as possible.

More recently legal documents, such as Decree 72/2013/NĐ-CP on the Management, Provision, and Use of the Internet and Information on the Internet in 2013 and Document 09/2014/BTTTT on Detailed Regulations on the Management, Provision, and Use of Websites and Social Networks in 2014 prohibit roughly the same transgressions but in more details.

Article 4 of the 2018 Law on Cybersecurity states that cybersecurity must be put under the leadership of the CPV and prohibits actions such as mobilizing and training people to act against the government; rejecting revolutionary accomplishments and disrupting national unity; spreading misinformation and causing chaos among citizens; disrupting socioeconomic activities; and obstructing the operations of government agencies.

Spreading information harmful against the State or the government is also criminalized in Article 88 of the 1999 Penal Code of Vietnam and Article 117 of the 2015 Penal Code of Vietnam. As such, law enforcement would be backed by a strong legal basis in dealing with dissidents online. Many dissidents who voiced their dissatisfaction with the CPV online were arrested and prosecuted using this article. Vietnam was called the enemy of the internet by Reporters Without Borders,[183] who accused the regime of taking a stricter stance towards its critics, which was accompanied by a severe wave of repression targeting those who express their opinions freely and putting immense pressure on dissidents.

The Vietnamese government also asked internet providers to impose a technical blockage against sites deemed hostile. Wilkey suggests that Vietnam had its own version of China's "Great Firewall", which is called "Bamboo Firewall".[184] The Vietnamese government has been actively blocking sites with contradictory political views to its own. Facebook was blocked for a time in the past but could be accessed from inside Vietnam from the 2010s; however, content in Vietnamese is still under the surveillance of the government. While the technical blockage imposed by government sanctioned internet providers could be overcome using simple tools, the use of those tools is also prohibited.[185]

In addition to legal and technical mechanisms, the government is not above using extra-legal methods to deter dissidents. Reporters Without Borders and Human Rights Watch report that dissidents were routinely harassed and threatened by the police. Furthermore, the government was condemned for mounting cyberattacks against "counter-revolutionary websites" as Lt. Gen. Vu Hai Trieu of the public security ministry announced that they (the police) have "destroyed 300 web pages and blogs with bad content" using this method.[186]

The Vietnamese government also employs internet propagandists to promote a pro-communist narrative and counter criticism against the CPV. This tactic is not new, as the Chinese and Russian governments is also known for using fake social media accounts to manipulate information online.[187, 188] In December 2012, Ho Quang Loi, the head of the Propaganda Committee of the Hanoi Municipal Party Committee, proudly shared his experience of creating a propaganda writer group to "combat distorted information from hostile forces".[189 190] While there are many Facebook pages that criticize the CPV, there are also many pages with pro-CPV leanings. Both groups constantly engage in online debates while referring to each other using derogatory terms. For instance, anti-CPV netizens are often called "reactionary", "traitor", "loser" or "three-stripes" referring to the three red stripes on South Vietnam's flag, while pro-CPV netizens are referred to as "red cows" or "propagandists".[191] Although some of these pro-CPV netizens are unofficially supported by CPV officials, it is unclear whether they are on the government payroll. Moreover, it seems that many netizens support the CPV because of their personal connections to the Party. For example, their grandparents fought for North Vietnam, their parents or they themselves work for the government, or they simply find anti-CPV netizens to be intolerable.

Conclusion

In this chapter, the major threats to the legitimacy of the CPV are identified as pressure for democratization from the West, corruption and bad governance, the CPV's perceived mishandling of the territorial disputes in South China Sea and the amplifying effect of the internet on these issues. Recognizing the mounting challenges posed by both domestic and global shifts, the CPV has adopted a multifaceted approach to address these threats.

The Party has demonstrated a willingness to engage in compromise with certain Western countries with enough economic and diplomatic ties to Vietnam while simultaneously seeking to mitigate external pressures. Initiatives such as anti-corruption campaigns, spearheaded by CPV leadership, have shown that the CPV can respond positively to feedback from its subjects and garnered favourable reception among many Vietnamese, although some perceive them as glorified factional infighting. Nevertheless, the CPV is not above resorting to both legal and extra-legal methods through its law enforcement apparatus to suppress dissent and deploying propagandists to counter criticism.

However, despite wielding a range of tools—from "hard" to "soft"—the CPV continues to grapple with maintaining its legitimacy, particularly due to its perceived lack of mass mandate. In response, the CPV has increasingly emphasized its democratic credentials, particularly through electoral processes and the functioning of the National Assembly. It is worth noting that the CPV's claim to democratic legitimacy is contentious, as its interpretation of democracy diverges significantly from Western norms.

The forthcoming chapter will delve into the CPV's assertion of democratic legitimacy, exploring the nuances and contradictions inherent in its claims.

Notes

1. Nguyen Phu Trong, "Toàn văn phát biểu của Tổng Bí thư Nguyễn Phú Trọng tại Hội nghị về công tác xây dựng, chỉnh đốn Đảng" [Full text of General Secretary Nguyen Phu Trong's speech at the Conference on Strengthening and Reforming the Party], *Socialist Republic of Vietnam Government News*, 9 December 2021, https://baochinhphu.vn/toan-van-phat-bieu-cua-tong-bi-thu-nguyen-phu-trong-tai-hoi-nghi-ve-cong-tac-xay-dung-chinh-don-dang-102305259.htm (accessed 10 July 2024).

2. Carlyle A. Thayer, "Political Legitimacy in Vietnam Under Challenge", in *Political Legitimacy in Asia: New Leadership Challenges*, edited by John Kane, Hui Chieh Loy, and Haig Patapan (New York: Palgrave Macmillan, 2011), pp. 39–59.

3. Carlyle A. Thayer, "Political Legitimacy of Vietnam's One Party-State: Challenges and Responses", *Journal of Current Southeast Asian Affairs* 28 (2010): 47–70.

4. Ibid.

5. Carlyle A. Thayer, "Political Legitimacy in Vietnam: Challenge and Response", *Politics & Policy* 38 (2010): 423–44.

6. Benedict J. Kerkvliet, "Regime Critics: Democratization Advocates in Vietnam, 1990s–2014", *Critical Asian Studies* 47 (2015): 359–87.

7. Richard Joseph, "The Reconfiguration of Power in Late Twentieth-Century Africa", in *State, Conflict, and Democracy in Africa*, edited by Richard Joseph (Boulder, CO: Lynne Rienner Publishers, 1999), pp. 61–78.

8. Joan M. Nelson, "Promoting Policy Reforms: The Twilight of Conditionality?", *World Development* 24 (1996): 1551–59.

9. Frank Schimmelfennig and Ulrich Sedelmeier, eds., *The Europeanization of Central and Eastern Europe* (Ithaca, NY: Cornell University Press, 2005).

10. Margaret E. Keck and Kathryn Sikkink, *Activists beyond Borders: Advocacy Networks in International Politics* (Ithaca, NY: Cornell University Press, 2014).

11. According to The Economist Democracy Index, in 2017, only 11.4 per cent of the countries in the world could be classified as full democracies, 34.1 per cent as flawed democracies, 23.4 per cent as hybrid regimes and 31.1 per cent as authoritarian regimes.

12. Steven Levitsky and Lucan A. Way, "Linkage versus Leverage: Rethinking the International Dimension of Regime Change", *Comparative Politics* 38 (2006): 379–400.

13. Ibid.

14. Gordon Crawford, *Foreign Aid and Political Reform: A Comparative Analysis of Democracy Assistance and Political Conditionality* (London: Springer, 2000), p. 2.

15. Levitsky and Way, "Linkage versus Leverage: Rethinking the International Dimension of Regime Change".

16. Jakob Tolstrup, "Black Knights and Elections in Authoritarian Regimes: Why and How Russia Supports Authoritarian Incumbents in Post-Soviet States", *European Journal of Political Research* 54 (2015): 673–90.

17. Joan M. Nelson and Stephanie J. Eglinton, *Encouraging Democracy: What Role for Conditioned Aid?* (Berkeley, CA: University of California Libraries, 1992).

18. Gordon Crawford, "Foreign Aid and Political Conditionality: Issues of Effectiveness and Consistency", *Democratization* 4 (1997): 69–108.

19. Levitsky and Way, "Linkage versus Leverage: Rethinking the International Dimension of Regime Change".

20. Ibid.

21. Ibid.
22. Ibid.
23. Ibid.
24. Joseph S. Nye, "Soft Power", *Foreign Policy* 80 (1990): 153–71, https://doi.org/10.2307/1148580.
25. Trần Quang Cơ served in the Ministry of Foreign Affairs (MOFA) of Vietnam for forty-four years, from 1954 to 1997. In 1966, he was a member of the delegation of the Socialist Republic of Vietnam at the Paris Peace Conference. He was responsible for negotiating US-Vietnamese relations from 1976 and served as the ambassador to Thailand from 1982 to 1986. During the twelve years from 1979, Cơ participated in negotiations to resolve the conflict in Cambodia. After the Vietnam War, he was involved in negotiations to normalize relations with the United States, Laos and China. In 2001, Cơ wrote the memoir "Memories and Thoughts", which chronicled his experiences in post-war foreign affairs. He submitted the memoir to the MOFA leadership as "internal reference materials", but due to his critical view of the CPV's handling of foreign affairs in the 1970s, the book was not published. The author was given a copy of the memoir by a senior MOFA official with the note, "Every Vietnamese diplomat must read this."
26. In the case of Vietnam, the West is defined as the United States, European Union, and, to some extent, Australia. Japan and South Korea have consistently been Vietnam's two largest investors and trading partners. However, despite their alliance with the United States and their democratic political systems, aid from Japan and South Korea does not often come with pro-democratic conditions.
27. *Diễn biến hòa bình* [in Vietnamese].
28. Vietnam Academy of Social Sciences, "Diễn biến hòa bình" [Peaceful Evolution], n.d., http://bachkhoatoanthu.vass.gov.vn/noidung/tudien/Lists/GiaiNghia/View_Detail.aspx (accessed 10 July 2024).
29. United States Census Bureau, "Trade in Goods with Vietnam", 2018, https://www.census.gov/foreign-trade/balance/c5520.html (accessed 10 July 2024).
30. Office of the United States Trade Representative, "Vietnam", 2022, https://ustr.gov/countries-regions/southeast-asia-pacific/vietnam (accessed 10 July 2024).
31. European Commission, "EU Trade Relations with Vietnam", n.d., https://policy.trade.ec.europa.eu/eu-trade-relationships-country-and-region/countries-and-regions/vietnam_en (accessed 10 July 2024).
32. Angelo Alpuerto, "Vietnam FDI in 2022: Biggest Investors and Top Recipients", *Vietcetera*, 6 January 2022, https://vietcetera.com/en/vietnam-fdi-in-2022-biggest-investors-and-top-recipients (accessed 10 July 2024).
33. *Tiền Phong Online*, "190.000 lưu học sinh Việt Nam đang ở nước ngoài: Bộ GD&ĐT khuyến cáo khẩn" [190,000 Vietnamese students abroad and Ministry of Education's urgent warning], 20 March 2020, https://tienphong.vn/190000-luu-

hoc-sinh-viet-nam-dang-o-nuoc-ngoai-bo-gddt-khuyen-cao-khan-post1223601.tpo (accessed 10 July 2024).

34. Ministry of Education, Culture, Sports, Science and Technology (MEXT), "外国人留学生在籍状況調査」及び「日本人の海外留学者数」等について" [Survey of enrolment status of foreign students and number of Japanese students studying abroad] (in Japanese), 30 March 2021, https://www.mext.go.jp/a_menu/koutou/ryugaku/1412692_00003.htm (accessed 10 July 2024).

35. Reuters, "Vietnam FDI in 2022: Biggest Investors and Top Recipients", 12 April 2010, https://www.reuters.com/article/idINIndia-47625020100412 (accessed 10 July 2024).

36. United States Commission on International Religious Freedom, *2024 Annual Report*, 2024, https://www.uscirf.gov/sites/default/files/2024-05/2024%20Annual%20Report.pdf (accessed 29 November 2024).

37. Sometimes Article 116, entitled "Sabotaging the Implementation of Solidarity Policies", is used in cases that are related to minor ethnic groups, and Article 118, entitled "Disruption of Security", is used in cases where demonstrations are held.

38. Benedict J. Kerkvliet, "Government Repression and Toleration of Dissidents in Contemporary Vietnam", in *Politics in Contemporary Vietnam*, edited by Jonathan London (Houndmills, Basingstoke: Palgrave Macmillan, 2014), pp. 100–134.

39. Carlyle A. Thayer, "The Trial of Le Cong Dinh: New Challenges to the Legitimacy of Vietnam's Party-State", *Journal of Vietnamese Studies* 5 (2010): 196–207.

40. Carlyle A. Thayer, "Vietnam and the Challenge of Political Civil Society", *Contemporary Southeast Asia* 31 (2009): 1–27.

41. Matthew Brown, "Vietnamese Dissident Arrives in US after Early Release from Prison", VoA, 6 May 2014, https://www.voanews.com/a/vietnamese-dissident-arrives-in-us-after-early-release-from-prison/1888486.html (accessed 10 July 2024).

42. BBC, "Mother Mushroom: Vietnam Releases Well-Known Dissident into US Exile", 18 October 2018, https://www.bbc.com/news/world-asia-45898203 (accessed 10 July 2024).

43. Radio Free Asia, "Vietnamese Dissident Arrives in US after Early Release from Prison", 12 May 2022, https://www.rfa.org/english/news/vietnam/usa-dissident-05122022164959.html (accessed 10 July 2024).

44. *Nhân Dân*, "Việt Nam coi trọng quan hệ đối tác chiến lược toàn diện với Liên bang Nga" [Vietnam values the comprehensive strategic partnership with the Russian Federation], 6 July 2022, https://nhandan.vn/viet-nam-coi-trong-quan-he-doi-tac-chien-luoc-toan-dien-voi-lien-bang-nga-post704174.html (accessed 10 July 2024).

45. The Embassy of the Socialist Republic of Vietnam in the Russian Federation, "Quan hệ Đối tác chiến lược toàn diện Việt Nam-Nga với những điểm nhấn" [Vietnam-Russia Comprehensive Strategic Partnership with highlights], n.d., https://vnembassy-moscow.mofa.gov.vn/vi-vn/News/EmbassyNews/Trang/Quan-hệ-Đối-

tác-chiến-lược-toàn-diện-Việt-Nam-Nga-với-những-điểm-nhấn.aspx (accessed 10 July 2024).

46. Stockholm International Peace Research Institute (SIPRI), SIPRI Arms Transfers Database, n.d., https://www.sipri.org/databases/armstransfers (accessed 10 July 2024).

47. Francesco Guarascio and Khanh Vu, "Vietnam Shifts Gears on Arms Trade as It Loosens Ties with Russia", *Japan Times*, 9 December 2022, https://www.japantimes. co.jp/news/2022/12/09/asia-pacific/vietnam-arms-russia-trade/ (accessed 10 July 2024).

48. *Socialist Republic of Vietnam Government News*, "Việt Nam không ủng hộ việc HĐBA can thiệp vào công việc nội bộ của các quốc gia có chủ quyền" [Vietnam does not support the Security Council to interfere into the domestic affairs of sovereign states], 12 July 2008, https://baochinhphu.vn/viet-nam-khong-ung-ho-viec-hdba-can-thiep-vao-cong-viec-noi-bo-cua-cac-quoc-gia-co-chu-quyen-10214331.htm (accessed 10 July 2024).

49. Khanh Linh, "Nguy cơ khủng hoảng nhân đạo nghiêm trọng tại Ukraine" [The risk of terrible humanitarian crisis in Ukraine], *Communist Party of Vietnam Online Newspaper*, 28 February 2022, https://dangcongsan.vn/the-gioi/nhung-van-de-toan-cau/nguy-co-khung-hoang-nhan-dao-nghiem-trong-tai-ukraine-604853.html (accessed 10 July 2024).

50. *Thanh Niên*, "Nga tổn thất thiết bị quân sự gấp 3 lần Ukraine?" [The military equipment loss of Russia is triple that of Ukraine], 31 December 2022, https://thanhnien.vn/nga-ton-that-thiet-bi-quan-su-gap-3-lan-ukraine-1851537598.htm (accessed 10 July 2024).

51. Voice of Vietnam, "Việt Nam hỗ trợ nhân đạo 500.000 USD cho Ukraine" [Vietnam to provide Ukraine with US$500,000 in humanitarian aid], 1 May 2022, https://vov. vn/chinh-tri/viet-nam-ho-tro-nhan-dao-500000-usd-cho-ukraine-post940992.vov (accessed 10 July 2024).

52. Nguyen Vinh, "Quán triệt nguyên tắc 'Bảo đảm lợi ích tối cao của quốc gia - dân tộc, trên cơ sở các nguyên tắc cơ bản của luật pháp quốc tế, bình đẳng, cùng có lợi' trong quan hệ đối ngoại thời kỳ hội nhập quốc tế" [Fully implement the principle of 'ensuring the highest interests of the nation and the people, based on the fundamental principles of international law, equality, and mutual benefit' in foreign relations during the period of international integration], *National Defense Journal*, 6 September 2020, http://tapchiqptd.vn/vi/quan-triet-thuc-hien-nghi-quyet/quan-triet-nguyen-tac-bao-dam-loi-ich-toi-cao-cua-quoc-gia-dan-toc-tren-co-so-cac-nguyen-t/15960.html (accessed 10 July 2024).

53. *Nhân Dân*, "Thúc đẩy nhân quyền hay can thiệp vào công việc nội bộ?" [Promotion of human rights or interference?], 18 August 2014, https://nhandan.vn/thuc-day-nhan-quyen-hay-can-thiep-vao-cong-viec-noi-bo-post211110.html (accessed 10 July 2024).

54. Vu Anh, "Vietnam Denies Returning Jailed Oil Executive to Germany", *VnExpress*, 8 November 2018, https://e.VnExpress.net/news/news/vietnam-denies-returning-jailed-oil-executive-to-germany-3836453.html (accessed 10 July 2024).

55. World Bank, "Vietnam Gross Domestic Production", 2018, https://data.worldbank. org/indicator/NY.GDP.MKTP.CD?locations=VN (accessed 10 July 2024).

56. PricewaterhouseCoopers (PwC), "The Long View: How Will the Global Economic Order Change by 2050?", February 2017, https://www.pwc.com/gx/en/world-2050/assets/pwc-world-in-2050-summary-report-feb-2017.pdf (accessed 10 July 2024).

57. Ngo Di Lan, "Vietnam between China and the United States: The Next Balancing Test Beckons", *The Diplomat*, 16 October 2015, https://thediplomat.com/2015/10/vietnam-between-china-and-the-united-states-the-next-balancing-test-beckons/ (accessed 10 July 2024).

58. Hannah Beech, "Vietnam, in a Bind, Tries to Chart a Path between U.S. and China", *New York Times*, 11 November 2017, https://www.nytimes.com/2017/11/11/world/asia/vietnam-china-us.html (accessed 10 July 2024).

59. One of Vietnam's most famous revolutionary poets and a member of the Politburo from 1976–1986.

60. Nguyen Dang Manh, *Hoi Ky Nguyen Dang Manh* [Nguyen Dang Manh's memoirs], n.d., http://www.geocities.ws/xoathantuong/ndm_vehcm.htm (accessed 10 July 2024).

61. This anecdote was recorded by Nguyen Dang Manh, a Vietnamese scholar and author, in his memoirs. It was not mentioned in the volumes of *Ho Chi Minh's Complete Works*, which was published by the Vietnamese government.

62. Dang Thuy Tram, *Nhật Ký Đặng Thùy Trâm* [The diary of Dang Thuy Tram] (Hanoi: Nha Nam, 2005).

63. Dang Thuy Tram was a medic who fought and died for North Vietnam during the Vietnam War. Her diary was posthumously published and has drawn international attention.

64. For example, Resolution 25-NQ/TW on price, salary and money that was approved by the Fifth Central Committee of the CPV in June 1985, stated: "Due to our closed-mindedness and excessive bureaucracy, faulty leadership and management, over-reliance on international aid, we have been slow to improve the economic policies and managerial mechanism."

Resolution 10-NQ/HNTW on the Direction of the Planning of the Socio-economic Development in 1991, which was approved by the Sixth Central Committee of the CPV in November 1991, stated:

Subjectively speaking, due to poor leadership, especially from the macro-level, we have not been able to catch up with the demands of the new managerial mechanism and have failed to carry out policies in a timely manner that ensure the implementation of effective and efficient production and business management. We have also been slow to correct our mistakes and fill the gaps in certain policies, irresponsive to cases of discipline violation and neglected our duty to uphold the discipline. Our organization is cumbersome and ineffective.

65. Tran Van Tho, "Việt Nam 40 năm qua và những năm tới: Cần một nền kinh tế thị trường định hướng phát triển" [Vietnam over the last 40 years and the coming years: a direction for the development of the market economy is needed], *Thoi Dai*, July 2015, www.tapchithoidai.org/ThoiDai33/201533_TranVanTho.pdf (accessed 10 July 2024).

66. Vietnam News Agency Publishing House, *Những câu chuyện thời bao cấp* [Stories of the Subsidy's period] (Hanoi: Vietnam News Agency Publishing House, 2014), p. 64.

67. Business Anti-Corruption Portal, "Vietnam Corruption Report", 2017, http://www.business-anti-corruption.com/country-profiles/vietnam (accessed 10 July 2024).

68. On 23 November 1945, President Ho Chi Minh signed Order No. 64-SL to establish a Special Inspection Committee to supervise all government officials and employees. This was the first legal document aimed at preventing and combating corruption in Vietnam. A special court was to be established in Hanoi to prosecute corrupt government officials, who could be sentenced to death.

In 1963, the Central Committee of the CPV launched the "Three Builds, Three Preventions" campaign, which aimed to fight against corruption, wastefulness and red tape bureaucracy to ensure that all resources were channelled to the war in South Vietnam and the economic reconstruction in North Vietnam. Several legal documents for preventing and combating corruption were issued, such as Resolution No. 207/CP dated 6 December 1962 of the Council of Ministers on the establishment of the Central Steering Committee for the campaign "Enhancing responsibility awareness, strengthening economic and financial management, fighting against corruption, waste, and bureaucracy"; Directive No. 84-TTg/3X dated 9 September 1964, which summarized the situation of corruption, waste and bureaucracy in North Vietnam; Ordinance No. 149-LCT dated 21 October 1970 of the Standing Committee of the National Assembly on punishing offenses against socialist property.

On 20 May 1981, the National Assembly Standing Committee passed the Ordinance on Bribery Penalties. This ordinance consists of thirteen articles, which define corruption as receiving bribes, giving bribes and acting as a bribe mediator, with a relatively high penalty of imprisonment. In addition, a number of anti-corruption decisions and directives were passed, including Decision No. 240/HĐBT dated 26 June 1990 on the fight against corruption; Directive No. 416/CT dated 3 December 1990 on strengthening inspection and handling of corruption and smuggling; Official Document No. 08/CT-TATC dated 6 December 1990 on the handling of some crimes caused by civil servants; Decision No. 114/TTg dated 21 November 1992 on urgent measures to prevent corruption and smuggling; Directive No. 171/TTg dated 16 December 1992 on combating corruption, waste and loss in construction. The

1986 Criminal Law also criminalized embezzlement, giving and accepting bribery, and abuse of power for personal gain.

On 26 February 1998, the Ordinance on Anti-Corruption was issued. This ordinance defines the act of corruption as well as its punishment. Furthermore, on 21 December 1999, the National Assembly passed the Criminal Law of 1999, which stipulated seven corruption-related offences.

On 29 November 2005, the National Assembly passed the 2005 Anti-Corruption Law, which was intended to fix the shortcomings and inadequacies of the 1998 Ordinance on Anti-Corruption.

On 30 June 2009, the president signed Decision No. 950/2009/QD-CTN "On the approval of the United Nations Convention against Corruption". Accordingly, Vietnam officially became a member of the Convention from 19 August 2009.

In 2013, the Eleventh Party Congress established the Central Steering Committee on Anti-Corruption led by the general secretary with the goal of "preventing and pushing back corruption".

On 20 November 2018, the National Assembly passed the 2018 Anti-Corruption Law. The law consists of ten chapters and ninety-six articles, replacing the 2005 Anti-Corruption Law.

69. *Xây Dựng Đảng*, "Cương Lĩnh Xây Dựng Đất Nước Trong Thời Kỳ Quá Độ Lên Chủ Nghĩa Xã Hội (Bổ Sung, Phát Triển năm 2011)" [Political direction for national construction towards socialism (enhanced and improved in 2011)], 2011, http://www.xaydungdang.org.vn/Home/vankientulieu/Van-kien-Dang-Nha-nuoc/2011/3525/CUONG-LINH-XAY-DUNG-DAT-NUOC-TRONG-THOI-KY-QUA-DO-LEN.aspx (accessed 10 July 2024).

70. Le Kien, "Luật phòng chống tham nhũng vẫn là 'cọp không răng' nếu..." [Anti-corruption law will still be just a toothless tiger if...]", *Tuoi Tre*, 21 November 2017, https://tuoitre.vn/luat-phong-chong-tham-nhung-van-la-cop-khong-rang-neu-20171121090222508.htm (accessed 10 July 2024).

71. This scandal is referred to using its abbreviation PMU 18 by both state-controlled and private media in Vietnam. Project Management Unit 18 (PMU 18) is a department under the direct management of the Ministry of Transportation that is entrusted with a budget of US$2 billion for its multiple infrastructure projects. In addition to this state-provided budget, PMU 18 also received money from overseas donors, including from Australia, Japan and the World Bank (Harkey 2006).

Clare Harkey, "Crisis Dogs Vietnam Congress", *BBC News*, 2006, http://news.bbc.co.uk/2/hi/asia-pacific/4917466.stm (accessed 29 November 2024).

72. Pham Hieu and Anh Thu, "Bộ trưởng Đào Đình Bình từ chức" [Transport Minister Dao Dinh Binh resigned], *VnExpress*, 4 March 2006, https://VnExpress.net/tin-tuc/thoi-su/bo-truong-dao-dinh-binh-tu-chuc-2067716.html (accessed 10 July 2024).

73. *Tuoi Tre*, "Vụ PMU18 gây thiệt hại ít nhất 37 tỉ đồng" [Damage caused by the PMU 18 case is estimated to be at least 37 billion VND], 8 May 2006, https://tuoitre.vn/vu-pmu18-gay-thiet-hai-it-nhat-37-ti-dong-99985.htm (accessed 10 July 2024).

74. *Thanh Niên*, "2 nhà báo Thanh Niên và Tuổi Trẻ bị bắt vì đưa tin vụ PMU 18" [Two journalists from *Thanh Niên* and *Tuoi Tre* arrested for investigating the PMU 18 case], 13 May 2008, https://thanhnien.vn/thoi-su/2-nha-bao-thanh-nien-va-tuoi-tre-bi-bat-vi-dua-tin-vu-pmu-18-209439.html (accessed 10 July 2024).

75. *VnExpress*, "Tướng Phạm Xuân Quắc bị khởi tố" [General Pham Xuan Quac prosecuted], 13 May 2008, https://VnExpress.net/phap-luat/tuong-pham-xuan-quac-bi-khoi-to-2104292.html (accessed 10 July 2024).

76. *VnExpress*, "Ông Nguyễn Việt Tiến được khôi phục Đảng" [Mr Nguyen Viet Tien's party membership restored], 9 May 2008, https://VnExpress.net/phap-luat/ong-nguyen-viet-tien-duoc-khoi-phuc-dang-2104000.html (accessed 10 July 2024).

77. *VnExpress*, "Pham Tien Dung, a Suspect in the PMU 18 Case, Suddenly Died", 14 July 2009, https://VnExpress.net/phap-luat/pham-tien-dung-bi-can-vu-pmu-18-dot-tu-2129929.html (accessed 10 July 2024).

78. Xuan Linh, "Nhật tạm dừng một phần ODA cho Việt Nam" [Japan partially stops providing ODA to Vietnam], *VietNamNet*, 2008, http://vietnamnet.vn/chinhtri/2008/12/816866/ (accessed 10 July 2024).

79. Ha An and Minh Chien, "Vụ án tham ô ở Vinashinlines: Tuyên án tử hình Giang Kim Đạt và Trần Văn Liêm" [Vinashinlines embezzlement case: Giang Kim Dat and Tran Van Liem sentenced to death], *Thanh Niên*, 22 February 2017, https://thanhnien.vn/thoi-su/vu-an-tham-o-o-vinashinlines-tuyen-an-tu-hinh-giang-kim-dat-va-tran-van-liem-793999.html (accessed 10 July 2024).

80. Nguyen Nam, "Vinashin: Vỡ nợ hay phá sản về chiến lược?" [Vinashin: default or bankrupt due to strategic mistakes?], Radio Free Asia, 23 December 2011, http://www.rfa.org/vietnamese/in_depth/vinashin-bankrupt-or-strategic-failure-12232011102754.html (accessed 10 July 2024).

81. Most prominent among those are the following corrupt scandals:

1. In January 2018, former Minister of Transport Dinh La Thang and twenty-one others were prosecuted for deliberately violating the state rules on economic management resulting in serious consequences and embezzlement charges. According to the indictment, as chairman of the board of directors of the state-owned Vietnam National Oil and Gas Group, Thang illegally granted the bid of the EPC project, a part of the Thai Binh 2 coal-fired power project to PetroVietnam Construction Joint Stock Corporation (PETROCONs), a member of the Vietnam National Oil and Gas Group. Thang also directed his subordinates to approve the illegal distribution of funds to PETROCONs, which had resulted in the maldistribution of more than VND 1,312 billion (US$51,8 million) and US$6.6 million. Upon receiving the funds provided by Thang, Trinh Xuan Thanh, former chairman of the board

of directors and CEO of PETROCONs had used those funds for activities other than the original purpose and was wanted for deliberately violating the state rules on economic management resulting in serious consequences and embezzlement charges. Thanh escaped to Germany but was later held under custody of Vietnamese authorities (*Tuoi Tre* 2021).

2. In a highly publicized online gambling case in Vietnam, two high-ranking police officers were arrested in April 2018 on multiple charges, including abuse of the internet to appropriate property, operating a gambling business, gambling, making unlawful purchases of receipts, money laundering, bribery and fraud by abuse of position. According to the indictment, Lieutenant General Phan Van Vinh took bribes and ordered Major General Nguyen Thanh Hoa to establish a front company with the guise of criminal investigation. However, the company was used to run an online gambling operation. The two officers allegedly actively suppressed into their gambling activities and have personally benefitted VND 4,700 billion (equivalent to US$20 million) (*VietNamNet* 2021).

3. In mid-2019, Nhat Cuong Mobile, one of the leading consumer electronics retailers in Vietnam was investigated for smuggling and tax evasion. In August 2020, Nguyen Duc Chung, the then Chairman of the People's Council of Hanoi and a major general of the Vietnam People's Public Security was arrested for unlawful possession of the state's confidential documents in relation to the Nhat Cuong Mobile case. He was found guilty of unlawful possession of the state's confidential documents, and two counts of abusing positions and/or powers while performing official duties and was sentenced to a total of sixteen years in prison (Hung 2020).

4. In April 2020, Nguyen Bac Son, former Minister of Information and Communications, pledged guilty to and received life sentence for mismanagement of investment causing serious consequences and receiving bribes. Son had allegedly received US$3 million in bribes to help MobiFone, a major Vietnamese mobile network operator, to unlawfully acquire 95 per cent of the share of AVG, a television service provider. The transaction was estimated to cause a loss of VND 7,000 billion (US$350 million) to the State (Phi 2018).

5. In December 2021, two directors general of the Ministry of Health of Vietnam were prosecuted for abusing positions and/or powers while performing official duties. The two directors general were accused of taking bribes from Viet A, a pharmaceutical company specialized in making COVID-19 testing kits. The company was under investigation for importing COVID-19 testing kits and selling them at exorbitant prices. In relation to this scandal, two high-ranking officials from the Centers for Disease Control and Prevention in Vietnam were arrested under the suspicion of violating law on bidding causing serious consequences (Du 2021). As investigation progressed, more and more high-ranking officials were found involved with the scandal. On 6 July 2022, Nguyen Thanh Long, then Minister of Health, was charged

with "abusing position and power while performing official duties" for his gross violation while issuing registration numbers for circulation, pricing and conducting price inspection of those COVID-19 test kits. On the same day, Chu Ngoc Anh, former Minister of Science and Technology, then incumbent chairman of Hanoi People's Committee was arrested on "violating regulations on management and use of state assets causing losses and waste" (Phung 2022).

6. In January 2022, the head of the Consular Department of the Ministry of Foreign Affairs, her deputy, and her chief of staff were arrested for taking bribes from travelling agencies. The arrested officials would then allow those agencies to sell "rescue flights" tickets to Vietnamese citizens overseas at exorbitant prices. In April 2022, a deputy minister of the Ministry of Foreign Affairs was also arrested in relation to this case. In December 2022, Vu Hong Nam, former ambassador of Vietnam to Japan was suddenly arrested on bribery charges (Onishi 2022). This case was noteworthy because although the financial damage was not as devastating as other cases mentioned earlier, the Ministry of Foreign Affairs was considered to be untouchable.

Tuoi Tre, "Ông Đinh La Thăng lãnh 11 năm tù, Trịnh Xuân Thanh 18 năm tù" [Former minister Dinh La Thang sentenced to 11 Years, former executive Trinh Xuan Thanh sentenced to 18 Years], 15 March 2021, https://tuoitre.vn/ong-dinh-la-thang-lanh-11-nam-tu-trinh-xuan-thanh-18-nam-tu-20210315145118336.htm (accessed 10 July 2024).

VietNamNet, "Lời khai chi tiết tấn công cho Ông Phan Văn Vinh, Nguyễn Thanh Hóa" [Statement of details attacking Mr Phan Van Vinh, Nguyen Thanh Hoa], 15 March 2021, https://vietnamnet.vn/loi-khai-chi-tien-tan-cho-ong-phan-van-vinh-nguyen-thanh-hoa-464099.html (accessed 10 July 2024).

Nguyen Hung, "Những vụ án tham nhũng nghiêm trọng đã xét xử năm 2020" [Prominent corrupt scandals prosecuted in 2020], *Công an Nhân dân*, 30 December 2020, https://cand.com.vn/Phap-luat/Nhung-vu-an-tham-nhung-nghiem-trong-da-xet-xu-nam-2020-i593028/ (accessed 10 July 2024).

Hoai Phi, "Mobifone mua AVG làm thất thoát 7.006 tỉ như thế nào?" [How Mobifone buying AVG caused a 7,006 billion loss], *Tuoi Tre*, 15 March 2018, https://tuoitre.vn/mobifone-mua-avg-lam-that-thoat-7-006-ti-nhu-the-nao-20180315163551347.htm (accessed 10 July 2024).

Pham Du, "Hai vụ trưởng Bộ Y tế bị khởi tố do liên quan vụ Việt Á" [Two directors general of the Ministry of Health of Vietnam were prosecuted in relation to Viet − a criminal case], *VnExpress*, 31 December 2021, https://VnExpress.net/giam-doc-cdc-nghe-an-binh-duong-bi-khoi-to-4409142.html (accessed 10 July 2024).

Tuan Phung, "Ông Chu Ngọc Anh và ông Nguyễn Thanh Long bị bắt" [Chu Ngoc Anh and Nguyen Thanh Long arrested], *Dan Tri*, 7 June 2022, https://

tuoitre.vn/cuc-dang-kiem-noi-gi-vu-giam-doc-trung-tam-dang-kiem-khong-biet-chu-20230104155949498.htm (accessed 10 July 2024).

Tomoya Onishi, "Vietnam Arrests Former Ambassador to Japan on Bribery Charges", *Nikkei Asia*, 23 December 2022, https://asia.nikkei.com/Politics/Vietnam-arrests-former-ambassador-to-Japan-on-bribery-charges (accessed 10 July 2024).

82. Thanh Chung, "Lý do miễn nhiệm Phó Thủ tướng Phạm Bình Minh, Vũ Đức Đam" [Reason for dismissing Deputy Prime Ministers Pham Binh Minh and Vu Duc Dam], *Tuoi Tre Online*, 9 January 2023, https://tuoitre.vn/ly-do-mien-nhiem-pho-thu-tuong-pham-binh-minh-vu-duc-dam-2023010916265009.htm (accessed 10 July 2024).

83. Luan Dung, "Nguyên Chủ tịch nước Nguyễn Xuân Phúc: 'Tôi chịu trách nhiệm chính trị của người đứng đầu'" [President Nguyen Xuan Phuc: 'I take political responsibility as the leader'], *Tiền Phong Online*, 12 April 2022, https://tienphong.vn/nguyen-chu-tich-nuoc-nguyen-xuan-phuc-toi-chiu-trach-nhiem-chinh-tri-cua-nguoi-dung-dau-post1507424.tpo (accessed 10 July 2024).

84. Le Hong Hiep, "What Recent Changes at the Top Mean for Vietnam", *The Interpreter*, 27 February 2023, https://www.lowyinstitute.org/the-interpreter/what-recent-changes-top-mean-vietnam?fbclid=IwAR3YeWNcQIIOhIM3of3hoF Ef9_gKeUkrcB6isJRX5SAFNJG-yCwY2uDSCS8 (accessed 10 July 2024).

85. Than Hoang, "Khởi tố ông Mai Tiến Dũng, cựu Bộ trưởng, Chủ nhiệm Văn phòng Chính phủ" [Prosecution of Mai Tien Dung, former minister and head of the government office], 27 March 2024, https://tuoitre.vn/khoi-to-ong-mai-tien-dung-cuu-bo-truong-chu-nhiem-van-phong-chinh-phu-20240327140908199.htm (accessed 10 July 2024).

86. Son Ha, "Trung ương đồng ý ông Vương Đình Huệ thôi chức Chủ tịch Quốc hội" [Central Committee agrees for Vuong Dinh Hue to resign as chairman of the National Assembly], *VnExpress*, 26 April 2024, https://VnExpress.net/trung-uong-dong-y-ong-vuong-dinh-hue-thoi-chuc-chu-tich-quoc-hoi-4735654.html (accessed 10 July 2024).

87. Hoai Thu, "Trung ương đồng ý cho ông Võ Văn Thưởng thôi chức Chủ tịch nước" [Central Committee agrees for Vo Van Thuong to resign as president], *Dan Tri*, 20 March 2024, https://dantri.com.vn/xa-hoi/trung-uong-dong-y-cho-ong-vo-van-thuong-thoi-chuc-chu-tich-nuoc-20240316162235699.htm (accessed 10 July 2024).

88. *Tứ trụ* [in Vietnamese].

89. *Cán bộ chủ chốt của Đảng và Nhà nước* [in Vietnamese].

90. Conclusion 35-KL/TW.

91. Some commentators believe that Hue and Thuong were granted *hạ cánh an toàn* (safe landing), a Vietnamese slang that means an uneventful retirement; however, officials who are officially dismissed for their violations are usually not considered to have landed safely. Nevertheless, it is true that Hue and Thuong avoided criminal prosecution despite their alleged involvement in corruption.

92. Thuy Thi Lan, "Vietnam and the Fight Against Corruption", *Nikkei Asia*, 4 March 2019, https://asia.nikkei.com/Opinion/Vietnam-and-the-fight-against-corruption (accessed 10 July 2024).

93. Bruno Pedroletti, "In Vietnam, the Anti-Corruption Fight Is in Full Swing", *Le Monde*, 28 June 2022, https://www.lemonde.fr/en/economy/article/2022/06/28/in-vietnam-the-anti-corruption-fight-is-in-full-swing_5988162_19.html (accessed 10 July 2024).

94. Philip J. Heijmans, "How Vietnam's Anti-corruption Fight Keeps Expanding", *Washington Post*, 10 January 2023, https://www.washingtonpost.com/business/how-vietnams-anti-corruption-fight-keeps-expanding/2023/01/10/1606e0c6-90df-11ed-90f8-53661ac5d9b9_story.html (accessed 10 July 2024).

95. Michael Tatarski, "Unintended Consequences of Vietnam's Anti-corruption Drive", *Asia Society*, 17 November 2022, https://asiasociety.org/magazine/article/unintended-consequence-vietnams-anti-corruption-drive (accessed 10 July 2024).

96. *Hạ cánh anh toàn* [In Vietnamese]

97. Quoc Thang, "Nguyên cục trưởng Đăng kiểm Việt Nam và nhiều người bị bắt" [The director of Vietnam Register and many others were arrested], *VnExpress*, 17 January 2023, https://VnExpress.net/nguyen-cuc-truong-dang-kiem-viet-nam-va-nhieu-nguoi-bi-bat-4558989.html (accessed 10 July 2024).

98. Tuan Phung, "Cục Đăng kiểm nói gì vụ giám đốc trung tâm đăng kiểm không biết chữ?" [What did Vietnam Register comment about the illiterate director of the inspection center?], *Tuoi Tre*, 1 April 2023, https://tuoitre.vn/cuc-dang-kiem-noi-gi-vu-giam-doc-trung-tam-dang-kiem-khong-biet-chu-20230104155949498.htm (accessed 10 July 2024).

99. Luu Duyen, "Tái diễn cảnh tài xế ăn ngủ trên xe để chờ đăng kiểm" [Drivers sleeping in car waiting for inspection], *Tuoi Tre Online*, 7 March 2023, https://tuoitre.vn/tai-dien-canh-tai-xe-an-ngu-tren-xe-de-cho-dang-kiem-20230307084002022.htm (accessed 10 July 2024).

100. Tatarski, "Unintended Consequences of Vietnam's Anti-corruption Drive".

101. Francesco Guarascio, "Analysis: Vietnam's Anti-graft Crackdown Chills Supply Chains, Investment", Reuters Japan, 28 November 2022, https://jp.reuters.com/article/vietnam-economy-corruption-analysis-idAFKBN2SI0F5 (accessed 10 July 2024).

102. *An ninh Thủ đô*, "Tổng Bí thư Nguyễn Phú Trọng trả lời băn khoăn 'kỷ luật nhiều cán bộ như vậy thì lấy ai làm việc?'" [General Secretary Nguyen Phu Trong answered the question 'if we discipline many officials, then who will do the work?'], 23 June 2022, https://www.aninhthudo.vn/tong-bi-thu-nguyen-phu-trong-tra-loi-ban-khoan-ky-luat-nhieu-can-bo-nhu-vay-thi-lay-ai-lam-viec-post508542.antd (accessed 10 July 2024).

103. Vietnam News Agency, "Dấu ấn sâu sắc của Tổng Bí thư Nguyễn Phú Trọng trong lòng người dân" [The deep impression of General Secretary Nguyen Phu Trong in the hearts of the people], 20 July 2024, https://baotintuc.vn/thoi-su/dau-an-sau-sac-

cua-tong-bi-thu-nguyen-phu-trong-trong-long-nguoi-dan-20240720164134501.htm (accessed 17 July 2024).

104. Le Hong Hiep and Nguyen Khac Giang, "Nguyen Phu Trong's Incomplete Legacy in Vietnam", *Fulcrum*, 27 September 2023, https://fulcrum.sg/nguyen-phu-trongs-incomplete-legacy-in-vietnam/ (accessed 17 July 2024).

105. BBC Vietnamese, "Tổng Bí thư Nguyễn Phú Trọng qua đời ở tuổi 79" [General Secretary Nguyen Phu Trong dies at age 79], 5 July 2023, https://www.bbc.com/vietnamese/articles/c903v280jyno (accessed 17 July 2024).

106. Joshua Kurlantzick, "What Nguyen Phu Trong's Death Means for Vietnam", Council on Foreign Relations, 14 May 2023, https://www.cfr.org/blog/what-nguyen-phu-trongs-death-means-vietnam (accessed 17 July 2024).

107. For obvious reasons, factional infighting has never been recognized by official media outlets controlled by the CPV. Hung (2017) argues that there have always been conflicts between the progressive faction and the conservative faction within the CPV and claims that the campaign against "revisionism" launched by the conservative Le Duan in 1967 was the climax of such infighting. Grossheim (2006) argues that the purge was necessary for Duan's faction to consolidate their power so that they could step-up their military struggle in South Vietnam. Likewise, political commentators have been sceptical about the nature of investigation and prosecution process of the PMU 18 scandal and many considered it to be the result of infighting rather than impartial law enforcement (AsiaSentinel 2008). Interviews with party members reveal that most of them believe that factional infighting exists within the CPV and had experienced this themselves. However, the perceived scope varies from person to person. Interviewees agree that the survivability and safety of the CPV as a whole have always been prioritized over uncertain progress. This may explain the domination of the conservative faction. State controlled media acknowledges that rumours about infighting do exist but deny the existence of such infighting.

Le Anh Hung, "Phe cấp tiến từng trỗi dậy ngoạn mục ra sao?" [The rise of the progressive faction], *Voice of America*, 13 January 2017, https://www.voatiengviet.com/a/phe-cap-tien-trong-dang-csvn-tung-troi-day-ngoan-muc-nhu-the-nao/3721008.html (accessed 29 November 2024).

Martin Grossheim, "Revisionism in the Democratic Republic of Vietnam: New Evidence from the East German Archives", *Cold War History* 5, no. 4 (2005): 451–77.

Asia Sentinel, "Vietnam: Behind the Journalists' Jailings", 25 October 2008, https://www.asiasentinel.com/politics/vietnam-behind-the-journalists-jailings/ (accessed 29 November 2024).

108. *Al Jazeera*, "In Vietnam, Feeding the Police Is Just a Cost of Doing Business", 23 December 2021, https://www.aljazeera.com/economy/2021/12/23/in-vietnam-feeding-the-police-just-a-cost-of-doing-business (accessed 10 July 2024).

109. PAPI, *2021 Annual Report*, 2022, https://papi.org.vn/eng/bao-cao/?year-report=2021 (accessed 10 July 2024).

110. PAPI, *2017 Annual Report*, 2018, https://papi.org.vn/eng/bao-cao/?year-report=2017 (accessed 10 July 2024).

111. Under Article 354 of the 2015 Penal Code, anyone who accepts bribes from VND 2 million to below VND 100 million shall be sentenced to imprisonment from two to seven years.

112. Transparency International gives Vietnam the following score: 31 in 2012; 31 in 2013; 31 in 2014; 31 in 2015; 33 in 2016; 35 in 2017; 33 in 2018; 37 in 2019; 36 in 2020; 39 in 2021; 42 in 2022.

113. Benedict J. Tria Kerkvliet, "Protests over Land in Vietnam", *Journal of Vietnamese Studies* 9, no. 3 (Summer 2014): 19–54, https://doi.org/10.1525/vs.2014.9.3.19.

114. Huong Giang, "Khiếu nại, tố cáo liên quan đến đất đai dự báo sẽ tiếp tục là điểm nóng" [Land-related complaints and accusations expected to continue being a hot spot], n.d., https://thanhtra.com.vn/khieu-nai-to-cao/khieu-nai-to-cao-lien-quan-den-dat-dai-du-bao-se-tiep-tuc-la-diem-nong-201766.html (accessed 10 July 2024).

115. Khanh Thi, "Khiếu nại trong lĩnh vực đất đai chiếm 98%" [Land-related complaints account for 98%], *Communist Party of Vietnam Online Newspaper*, 26 July 2019, https://dangcongsan.vn/y-te/khieu-nai-trong-linh-vuc-dat-dai-chiem-98---529832.html (accessed 10 July 2024).

116. Kerkvliet, "Protests over Land in Vietnam".

117. Parishioners in Thai Ha, Hanoi, filed complaints to reclaim church land acquired by the communist government in 1961. When the complaints were dismissed, parishioners broke into the land and began placing their worship objects there. Police were dispatched to handle the protestors, leading to a scuffle. Opinions polarized, with state-owned media branding the protestors as lawless, while religious groups accused the government of heavy-handed oppression during the protest. *Nhân Dân*, "Cần chấm dứt những hành vi vi phạm pháp luật ở giáo xứ Thái Hà" [Illegal activities at Thai Ha Parish must stop], 19 August 2008, https://nhandan.vn/can-cham-dut-nhung-hanh-vi-vi-pham-phap-luat-o-giaoxu-thai-ha-post587426.html (accessed 10 July 2024).

118. On 11 June 2023, a group armed with guns, knives, Molotov cocktails and grenades attacked a People's Committee headquarters in Dak Lak province, Central Highlands, Vietnam. The perpetrators killed nine people, injured two and took three hostages. Two hostages were later rescued, while one escaped independently. Authorities arrested 100 people in connection with the attack, and in January 2024, ten of them received life imprisonment and the remaining defendants received varying prison sentences. Although anti-government protests are not uncommon in the Central Highlands of Vietnam, the severity of this attack shocked the public. While domestic

media outlets describe the attack as an attempt to overthrow the government and establish a separatist Montagnard state, allegedly incited and financially supported by terrorists living in the United States, land disputes were among the direct reasons that led to the attack. *Socialist Republic of Vietnam Government News*, "Xét xử vụ khủng bố tại Đắk Lắk: Tòa tuyên phạt 10 án chung thân" [Trial for the terrorist incident in Đắk Lắk: court sentences 10 to life imprisonment], 20 January 2024, https://baochinhphu.vn/xet-xu-vu-khung-bo-tai-dak-lak-toa-tuyen-phat-10-an-chung-than-102240120195613365.htm (accessed 10 July 2024).

119. The term "rightful resistance" generally refers to the justified or legitimate opposition or defiance against perceived injustice, oppression or unlawful actions by authorities or entities in power.

120. Kerkvliet, "Protests over Land in Vietnam".

121. *Socialist Republic of Vietnam Government News*, "Y án sơ thẩm với 6 bị cáo vụ án tại Đồng Tâm, Hà Nội" [First instance sentences upheld for 6 defendants in the Dong Tam case, Hanoi], n.d., https://baochinhphu.vn/y-an-so-tham-voi-6-bi-cao-vu-an-tai-dong-tam-ha-noi-102288829.htm (accessed 10 July 2024).

122. Government of the Socialist Republic of Vietnam, "Nội dung họp báo Chính phủ thường kỳ tháng 4/2017" [Contents of the government's regular press conference in April 2017], 4 May 2017, https://vpcp.chinhphu.vn/noi-dung-hop-bao-chinh-phu-thuong-ky-thang-4-2017-11517857.htm (accessed 10 July 2024).

123. *VietNamNet*, "Người dân Đồng Tâm trao trả hết 19 cán bộ, chiến sỹ" [Dong Tam residents release all 19 officers], n.d., https://vietnamnet.vn/nguoi-dan-dong-tam-trao-tha-het-19-can-bo-chien-sy-368112.html (accessed 10 July 2024).

124. *Tuoi Tre*, "Sai phạm liên quan vụ đất Đồng Tâm: Hà Nội gần 30 cán bộ bị xử lý" [Violations related to Dong Tam land case: nearly 30 officials in Hanoi disciplined], 25 November 2019, https://tuoitre.vn/sai-pham-lien-quan-vu-dat-dong-tam-ha-noi-gan-30-can-bo-bi-xu-ly-20191125195718643.htm (accessed 10 July 2024).

125. *VnExpress*, "Ông Mai Tiến Dũng: Vụ Đồng Tâm bên nào sai thì phải chịu trách nhiệm" [Mai Tien Dung: in the Dong Tam case, whoever is wrong must be held accountable], 4 May 2017, https://vnexpress.net/ong-mai-tien-dung-vu-dong-tam-ben-nao-sai-thi-phai-chiu-trach-nhiem-3579826.html (accessed 10 July 2024).

126. Carlyle A. Thayer, "Weak States and Strong Societies in Southeast Asia", in *Weak States, Strong Societies: Power and Authority in the New World Order*, edited by Amin Saikal (London and New York: I. B. Tauris & Co. Ltd., 2016), pp. 149–72.

127. *Con giun xéo lắm cũng phải quằn* [in Vietnamese].

128. *Chó cùng rứt dậu* [in Vietnamese].

129. *Một người làm quan cả họ được nhờ* [in Vietnamese].

130. Vuong Tran, "Cán bộ 'chạy chức, chạy quyền' sẽ tìm mọi cách 'tận thu, hoàn vốn' đầu vào" [Officials appointed through corruption would use every tool to get their

bribery back], *Lao Dong*, 24 August 2022, https://laodong.vn/thoi-su/can-bo-chay-chuc-chay-quyen-se-tim-moi-cach-tan-thu-hoan-von-dau-vao-1084467.ldo (accessed 10 July 2024).

131. Quoc Toan, "Bổng lộc, quyền lực khiến cán bộ tham quyền, cố vị" [Benefits and power make officials cling firmly on to power], *Giao Duc*, 21 November 2016, https://giaoduc.net.vn/bong-loc-quyen-luc-khien-can-bo-tham-quyen-co-vi-post172618.gd (accessed 10 July 2024).

132. For example, *Phap Luat*, a Vietnamese domestic newspaper, listed four cases of nepotism: (1) In early 2015, Vu Quang Hai (the son of Vu Huy Hoang, former Minister of Industry and Trade who was dismissed from his position) was appointed deputy CEO and member of the board of directors of Sabeco, a state-owned enterprise under the Ministry of Industry and Trade. Hai was only twenty-eight years old at the time of his appointment. His appointment was later investigated by the Central Inspection Commission, and in early 2017, Hai was dismissed from all his positions. (2) Pham Van Khang who is the son of Pham Van To, director of the Provincial Internal Affairs Department, was appointed as the deputy head of the same department without meeting the requirements for such a position. This incident was later investigated by the Provincial Party Committee's Inspection Commission. (3) Le Phuoc Hoai Bao, son of Le Phuoc Thanh, former secretary of the Quang Nam Provincial Party Committee, was appointed as director of the Department of Planning and Investment when he was only thirty years old. The Central Inspection Commission concluded that this appointment "did not meet the standards, conditions, and violated recruitment procedures". (4) Dinh Van Thu, former chairman of Quang Nam Provincial People's Committee, was investigated by the Central Inspection Commission for unlawfully bypassing the recruitment procedure to employ his son.

Trong Phu, "Những vụ con ông cháu cha thăng tiến thần tốc" [Cases of Nepotism Leading to Rapid Promotions], *Phap Luat Online*, https://plo.vn/nhung-vu-con-ong-chau-cha-thang-tien-than-toc-post466379.html (accessed 29 November 2024).

133. There are countless examples of people who are suspected of nepotism as they are promoted to positions far beyond their expertise. In addition to Nguyen Thanh Nghi, below are a few of the most notable cases. Nghi's brother Nguyen Minh Triet, who was born in 1988, has also enjoyed fast advancement in his political career and is currently chairman of the Central Committee of the Vietnam Students' Association. Official sources rarely mention the brothers' ties to Nguyen Tan Dung. Dung's daughter, Nguyen Thanh Phuong, was appointed the chairman of the board of directors of Viet Capital Commercial Joint Stock Bank in 2012, when she just turned thirty. To Linh Huong, the daughter of To Huy Rua, chairman of the Propaganda Department of the Communist Party of Vietnam and chairman of the Theoretical Council, was appointed the chairman and CEO of state-running real estate company

Vinaconex in 2021 when she freshly graduated from university. While these cases of nepotism are widely known and discussed by the public, they are not usually covered by state-run media outlets.

134. According to Article 38 (2018), the recruitment process of officials and civil servants must

(1) ensure publicity, transparency, objectivity and compliance with the law;
(2) ensure competitiveness;
(3) select the right person who meets the requirements of the task and position;
(4) prioritize the recruitment of talented people, those who have made contributions to the country and people of ethnic minorities.

However, violations and prohibitions during the recruitment process of officials and civil servants were not mentioned.

135. In Vietnam, the salary of a government official is calculated using the following formula:

Salary = Base salary x Multiplier

Of which, the base salary is decided by the government while the multiplier includes the official's rank and seniority.

The base salary has increased more than six times over the years from VND 290,000 (US$19, adjusted to 2004 exchange rate) in 2004 to VND 1,800,000 (US$77, adjusted to 2023 exchange rate) in 2023 (Decree 204/2004/NĐ-CP). Given that the Vietnamese government has set the target GDP per capita in 2023 to be US$4,400, Vietnam's GDP per capita would have increased almost eight times during the same period (Dong 2022).

Pham Dong, "Năm 2023, mục tiêu GDP bình quân đầu người đạt khoảng 4.400 USD" [In 2023, the target for GDP per capita is about 4,400 USD], *Lao Dong*, 19 November 2022, https://laodong.vn/thoi-su/nam-2023-muc-tieu-gdp-binh-quan-dau-nguoi-dat-khoang-4400-usd-1118194.ldo (accessed 29 November 2024).

According to Article 34 of the 2019 Law on Cadres and Civil Servants, civil servants are classified into the following corresponding ranks: Rank A, high-ranking specialist; Rank B, senior specialist; Rank C, specialist; Rank D, cadre and employee. Civil servants are paid based on their profession, specialization and expertise with Rank A being the most well-paid and Rank D being the least. Each rank is further divided into subclasses depending on their expertise. For example, Rank A is classified into Rank A1, Rank A2 and Rank A3 with Rank A3 being the most well-paid and Rank A1 being the least. Those ranks could be divided further, for example Rank A3 can be sub-rank into A3.1 and A3.2.

Each sub-rank has its own salary tier that progresses as the official becomes more senior. For example, Rank A alone has eight tiers. These salary tiers increase by one after three years of service without any reprimand. The highest paid public servants are Rank A3.2 officials. Their monthly salary from July 2023 would be

VND 14,400,000 (US$610). At the opposite end of the spectrum, a newly recruited driver's salary would be VND 3,690,000 (US$157) (Decree 204/2004/NĐ-CP). It should be noted that it is extremely demanding to become a Rank A3 official, and the majority of government officials belong to the lower ranks.

An official would need to pay social insurance for at least twenty years to be able to receive pension at the lowest rate at 45 per cent of their average monthly salary in those twenty years. An official who had paid at least thirty-five years of social insurance would receive the full pension at 75 per cent of their average monthly salary (Article 54 of the 2019 Labour Code of Vietnam and Article 56 of the Law on Social Insurance). An average official would retire with a monthly pension of about VND 7,000,000 (US$298) after at least thirty-five years of service.

Ministers and those above them have their own multiplier, which is independent of ranks and seniority. For example, the salary of the big four (general secretary of the CPV, state president, prime minister and chairman of the National Assembly) will be VND 23,400,000 (US$1,000) from July 2023. Minister equivalent's salary will be VND 17,280,000 (US$736) (Decree 730/2004/NQ-UBTVQH11). Military and police officers with the rank lieutenant general and above also have their own salary tier. Accordingly, from July 2023, the highest paid officers with the rank of full general will have a salary of VND 18,720,000 (US$798) (Circular 224/2017/TT-BQP). As an average 50 m² apartment in Hanoi would have cost VND 2,350,000,000 in 2023 (An 2023), the most high-ranking officials of Vietnam would have struggled to buy one.

Thuy An, "Căn hộ tại Hà Nội có giá bán trung bình 47 triệu đồng/m2" [The average selling price of apartments in Hanoi is VND 47 million per square meter], *VTV*, 11 January 2023, https://vtv.vn/kinh-te/can-ho-tai-ha-noi-co-gia-ban-trung-binh-47-trieu-dong-m2-20230111060212142.htm (accessed 20 November 2024).

136. VTV, "Lương và thu nhập nhân viên ngân hàng nào 'khủng' nhất?" [Which bank pays the highest income], 2 November 2022, https://vtv.vn/kinh-te/luong-va-thu-nhap-nhan-vien-ngan-hang-nao-khung-nhat-20221102091409 71.htm (accessed 10 July 2024).

137. Xuan Tung, "Công chức, viên chức không được sống được bằng lương sẽ gây nhiều hệ lụy" [There would be consequences if civil servants and public employees could not live on their salaries], *Đại Biểu Nhân Dân*, 22 October 2022, https://daibieunhandan.vn/dien-dan-quoc-hoi-va-cu-tri/cong-chuc-vien-chuc-khong-song-duoc-bang-luong-se-gay-nhieu-he-luy-i304466/ (accessed 10 July 2024).

138. VTV, "Tham ô tiền tỷ, hai cựu cảnh sát giao thông lĩnh án" [Embezzlement of billions of VND, two former traffic police officers receive sentence], 26 January 2022, https://vtv.vn/phap-luat/tham-o-tien-ty-hai-cuu-canh-sat-giao-thong-linh-an-20220126051757391.htm (accessed 8 April 2023).

139. Anh Duy, "Nhiều đang kiểm viên không dám đi làm vì sợ công an bắt" [Many registration inspectors are afraid to go to work because they fear being arrested by the police], *VnExpress*, 26 February 2023, https://VnExpress.net/nhieu-dang-kiem-vien-khong-dam-di-lam-vi-so-cong-an-bat-4575072.html (accessed 10 July 2024).

140. Vietnam News Agency, "Bộ Nội vụ giải thích nguyên nhân gần 40 nghìn công chức, viên chức thôi việc" [Ministry of Home Affairs explains why almost 40,000 civil servants have quitted their job], 1 October 2022, https://baotintuc.vn/thoi-su/bo-noi-vu-giai-thich-nguyen-nhan-gan-40-nghin-cong-chuc-vien-chuc-thoi-viec-20221001182651948.htm (accessed 10 July 2024).

141. Vuong Tran, "The Politburo Disciplines Mr. Nguyễn Xuân Phúc and Ms. Trương Thị Mai", *Lao Động*, 13 December 2024, https://news.laodong.vn/thoi-su/bo-chinh-tri-ky-luat-ong-nguyen-xuan-phuc-ba-truong-thi-mai-1434771.ldo (accessed 25 December 2024).

142. Stanley Karnow, *Vietnam: A History* (New York: Viking Press, 1983), p. 153.

143. Office de Radiodiffusion Télévision Française (ORTF), "Interview avec Ho Chi Minh", YouTube, 5 June 2019, https://www.youtube.com/watch?v=ROgYHCYU9Zk&ab_channel=2010vietnam2011 (accessed 10 July 2024).

144. The Complete Compilation of the National Assembly of the Socialist Republic of Vietnam's Document VI 1981–1983, "Document VI 1981–1983", website of the National Assembly of the Socialist Republic of Vietnam, 25 June 1981, https://quochoi.vn/tulieuquochoi/anpham/Pages/anpham.aspx?AnPhamItemID=3261 (accessed 10 July 2024).

145. *Pew Research Center*, "How People in Asia-Pacific View China," October 16, 2017, https://www.pewresearch.org/short-reads/2017/10/16/how-people-in-asia-pacific-view-china/ (accessed 29 November 2024).

146. *VnExpress*, "Tàu Trung Quốc tấn công giết hại ngư dân Việt Nam" [Chinese ships attack and murder Vietnamese fishermen], 14 January 2005, https://VnExpress.net/thoi-su/tau-trung-quoc-tan-cong-giet-hai-ngu-dan-viet-nam-2017091.html (accessed 10 July 2024).

147. *Xinhua News*, "Vietnamese Sea Bandits Shot, Captured", 15 January 2005, http://www.chinadaily.com.cn/english/doc/2005-01/15/content_409326.htm (accessed 10 July 2024).

148. The decree prohibits "abusing democratic civil liberties to carry out or manipulate, provoke, bribe, force other people to gather in order to disturb public order or to do other illegal action", and "illegal gathering on the streets, or on the pavement in front of governmental offices or near the venue of international conferences, the National Assembly Congresses, people's councils meeting and locations where political activities are being carried out by the CPV, the Vietnamese government, the Fatherland's Front and other socio-political organizations or any other public places" (Decree 8/2005/ND-CP).

149. *Ministry of Foreign Affairs (MOFA)*, "Việt Nam phản đối việc Trung Quốc thành lập thành phố hành chính Tam Sa thuộc tỉnh Hải Nam" [Vietnam objects the establishment of Sansha, a prefecture-level city of Hainan province], 2007, http://www.mofa.gov.vn/vi/tt_baochi/pbnfn/ns071204081718 (accessed 10 July 2024).

150. *BBC*, "Biểu tình phản đối Trung Quốc" [Anti-China protest], 9 December 2007, http://www.bbc.com/vietnamese/vietnam/story/2007/12/071209_china_protest.shtml (accessed 10 July 2024).

151. Nguyen Dinh, "Toàn cảnh vụ Trung Quốc xâm phạm Việt Nam" [An overview of China's violation of Vietnam's sovereignty], *VnExpress*, 1 June 2011, https://VnExpress.net/tin-tuc/the-gioi/tu-lieu/toan-canh-vu-trung-quoc-xam-pham-viet-nam-2196467.html (accessed 10 July 2024).

152. *BBC*, "Trung Quốc nói về cáo buộc của Việt Nam" [What China commented on Vietnam's accusation], 29 May 2011, http://www.bbc.com/vietnamese/vietnam/2011/05/110529_china_response_vietnam.shtml (accessed 10 July 2024).

153. *BBC*, "Dân chúng Hà Nội lại biểu tình chống Trung Quốc" [Hanoi citizens demonstrated against China again], 3 July 2011, http://www.bbc.com/vietnamese/av/2011/07/110703_fifthantichinaprotest.shtml (accessed 10 July 2024).

154. Mac Lam, "Doanh nghiệp du lịch Việt Nam tẩy chay Trung Quốc" [Vietnamese tourist companies boycott Chinese clients], *Radio Free Asia*, 2 June 2011, http://www.rfa.org/vietnamese/in_depth/boycott-china-tour-ml-06022011162537.html (accessed 10 July 2024).

155. *BBC*, "Kêu gọi chống Trung Quốc ở Việt Nam" [Calling for anti-China actions in Vietnam], 2 June 2011, http://www.bbc.com/vietnamese/vietnam/2011/06/110602_viet_antichina.shtml (accessed 10 July 2024).

156. *BBC*, "HRW chỉ trích VN bắt người biểu tình" [Human Rights Watch condemn Vietnam's arrests of protesters], 11 July 2011, http://www.bbc.com/vietnamese/vietnam/2011/07/110711_hrw_vietarrests.shtml (accessed 10 July 2024).

157. *BBC*, "Biểu tình Hà Nội 'hàng chục' người bị bắt" [Dozens of protesters in Hanoi arrested], 21 August 2011, http://www.bbc.com/vietnamese/vietnam/2011/08/110821_hanoi_protest.shtml (accessed 10 July 2024).

158. Pham Thao, "Hà Nội yêu cầu chấm dứt biểu tình, tuần hành tự phát" [Hanoi's authority demanded citizens to stop demonstrations and parades], *Dan Tri*, 18 August 2011, http://dantri.com.vn/xa-hoi/ha-noi-yeu-cau-cham-dut-bieu-tinh-tuan-hanh-tu-phat-1313973489.htm (accessed 10 July 2024).

159. Nguyen Hop, "Thông báo về công tác đảm bảo an ninh trật tự trên địa bàn thành phố Hà Nội" [Report on security and order in Hanoi], *Hanoi Portal*, 19 August 2011, http://hanoi.gov.vn/ubndthanhpho/-/hn/AlBuH0bMcRAB/2807/55743/3/thong-bao-ve-cong-tac-am-bao-an-ninh-trat-tu-tren-ia-ban-thanh-pho-ha-noi.html (accessed 10 July 2024).

160. *BBC*, "Hà Nội có biểu tình phản đối TQ lần thứ tám" [Eighth wave of anti-China in Hanoi], 24 July 2011, http://www.bbc.com/vietnamese/vietnam/2011/07/110724_hanoi_protest_24july.shtml (accessed 10 July 2024).

161. Edward Wong, "Q & A: M. Taylor Fravel on China's Dispute with Vietnam", *New York Times*, 8 May 2014, https://sinosphere.blogs.nytimes.com/2014/05/08/q-and-a-m-taylor-fravel-on-chinas-dispute-with-vietnam/ (accessed 10 July 2024).

162. Jonathan Kaiman, "China Accuses Vietnam of Ramming Its Ships in the South China Sea", *The Guardian*, 8 May 2014, https://www.theguardian.com/world/2014/may/08/china-accuses-vietnam-ships-south-china-sea-oil-rig (accessed 10 July 2024).

163. *Vietnam News Agency*, "Tàu cá Trung Quốc đâm chìm tàu cá của ngư dân Đà Nẵng" [Chinese fishing ship sunk Da Nang's fishing ship], 26 May 2014, https://www.vietnamplus.vn/tau-ca-trung-quoc-dam-chim-tau-ca-cua-ngu-dan-da-nang/261833.vnp (accessed 10 July 2024).

164. Ha Thanh, "Trung Quốc sơ tán 3.000 người khỏi Việt Nam" [China evacuated 3,000 people from Vietnam], *Radio France Internationale*, 18 May 2014, http://vi.rfi.fr/viet-nam/20140518-trung-quoc-so-tan-3000-nguoi-khoi-viet-nam (accessed 10 July 2024).

165. Paddock R. Christopher and Eva Dou, "Behind Vietnam's Anti-China Riots, a Tinderbox of Wider Grievances", *Wall Street Journal*, 17 June 2014, https://www.wsj.com/articles/behind-vietnams-anti-china-riots-a-tinderbox-of-wider-grievances-1403058492 (accessed 10 July 2024).

166. Ng Kang-chung and Phila Siu, "Just 14 Factories Targeted in Vietnam's Anti-China Protests Belonged to Mainland Chinese", *South China Morning Post*, 19 May 2014, http://www.scmp.com/news/asia/article/1515912/few-factories-hit-vietnams-anti-china-riots-were-mainland-chinese-owned (accessed 10 July 2024).

167. Nguyet Trieu, "Hơn 1.000 người bị bắt trong cuộc biểu tình quá khích" [More than 1,000 rioters arrested], *VnExpress*, 20 May 2014, https://VnExpress.net/tin-tuc/phap-luat/hon-1-000-nguoi-bi-bat-trong-cuoc-bieu-tinh-qua-khich-2992939.html (accessed 10 July 2024).

168. *The Guardian*, "Vietnamese Woman Dies in Self-Immolation Protest against China", 23 May 2014, https://www.theguardian.com/world/2014/may/23/vietnamese-woman-dies-self-immolation-protest-china (accessed 10 July 2024).

169. Matthew Brown, "Vietnam Cracks Down on Anti-China Protests", VoA, 18 May 2014, https://www.voanews.com/a/hanoi-changes-tack-over-anti-china-protests-/1916973.html (accessed 10 July 2024).

170. Christopher and Dou, "Behind Vietnam's Anti-China Riots, a Tinderbox of Wider Grievances".

171. Dien Nguyen An Luong, "How Hanoi is Leveraging Anti-China Sentiments Online", *ISEAS Perspective*, no. 2020/115, 13 October 2020, https://www.iseas.edu.sg/wp-content/uploads/2020/09/ISEAS_Perspective_2020_115.pdf (accessed 10 July 2024).

172. Ben Etling, Robert Faris, and John Palfrey, "Political Change in the Digital Age: The Fragility and Promise of Online Organizing", *SAIS Review of International Affairs* 30, no. 2 (2010): 37–49.

173. Ibid.

174. Ibid.

175. Michael L. Best and Keegan W. Wade, "The Internet and Democracy: Global Catalyst or Democratic Dud?", *Bulletin of Science, Technology & Society* 29, no. 4 (2009): 255–71.

176. Vietnam Posts and Telecommunications Group, "10 năm Internet Việt Nam: Những bước tiến dài ấn tượng" [Ten years of internet in Vietnam: impressive steps forward], 2007, http://www.vnpt.vn/News/Tin_Tuc/ViewNews/tabid/85/newsid/9220/seo/10-nam-Internet-Viet-Nam-Nhung-buoc-tien-dai-an-tuong/Default.aspx (accessed 10 July 2024).

177. Benedict J. Kerkvliet, *Speaking Out in Vietnam: Public Political Criticism in a Communist Party-Ruled Nation* (Ithaca, NY: Cornell University Press, 2019).

178. *VOA Vietnamese*, "Trang về Thủ tướng Dũng 'làm mưa làm gió' trên mạng" [Website about Prime Minister Nguyen Tan Dung has been drawing attention on the internet], 1 January 2016, https://www.voatiengviet.com/a/trang-ve-thu-tuong-dung-lam-mua-lam-gio-tren-mang/3127300.html (accessed 10 July 2024).

179. Hoang Long, "Trang 'phản động' nào đáng sợ nhất?" [What are the most dangerous 'counter-revolutionary websites'?], *BBC*, 3 February 2015, https://www.bbc.com/vietnamese/forum/2015/02/150203_dang_so_trang_mang_nao_forum (accessed 10 July 2024).

180. Kerkvliet, *Speaking Out in Vietnam: Public Political Criticism in a Communist Party-Ruled Nation.*

181. CPV, "Văn Kiện Đại Hội Đảng XIII" [Official documents of the 13th National Congress of the CPV] (Hanoi: National Political Publishing House, 2021), p. 41.

182. *An ninh Tiền tệ*, "Thành lập Cục An ninh mạng trực thuộc Bộ Công an" [The establishment of a cyber-security department under the Ministry of Public Security], 29 August 2014, http://antt.vn/thanh-lap-cuc-an-ninh-mang-truc-thuoc-bo-cong-an-2109.htm (accessed 10 July 2024).

183. *Reporters Without Borders*, "Vietnam", 17 March 2011, https://web.archive.org/web/20110317075418/http://en.rsf.org/Internet-enemie-vietnam,39763.html (accessed 10 July 2024).

184. Robert Neil Wilkey, "Vietnam's Antitrust Legislation and Subscription to E-ASEAN: An End to the Bamboo Firewall over Internet Regulation", *Journal of Computer & Information Law* 20 (2002): 631.

185. Document 02/2005/TTLT-BCVT-VHTT-CA-KHĐT.

186. Human Rights Watch, "Vietnam: Stop Cyber-Attacks against Online Critics", 26 May 2010, https://www.hrw.org/news/2010/05/26/vietnam-stop-cyber-attacks-against-online-critics (accessed 10 July 2024).

187. Henry Farrell, "The Chinese Government Fakes Nearly 450 Million Social Media Comments a Year. This Is Why", *Washington Post*, 19 May 2016, https://www.washingtonpost.com/news/monkey-cage/wp/2016/05/19/the-chinese-government-fakes-nearly-450-million-social-media-comments-a-year-this-is-why/ (accessed 10 July 2024).

188. Francis Carmichael, "How a Fake Network Pushes Pro-China Propaganda", *BBC*, 5 August 2021, https://www.bbc.com/news/world-asia-china-58062630 (accessed 10 July 2024).

189. *Lao Dong*, "Tổ chức nhóm chuyên gia bút chiến trên Internet" [Creating a propaganda writer group on the internet], 9 January 2013, https://laodong.vn/archived/to-chuc-nhom-chuyen-gia-but-chien-tren-Internet-698587.ldo (accessed 10 July 2024).

190. Propagandists are called *Chuyên gia bút chiến* [in Vietnamese] by government sources.

191. *Bò đỏ* and *dẫn luận viên* [in Vietnamese], respectively.

4

The Cpv's Claim to Democratic Legitimacy

Many forms of government have been tried, and will be tried in this world of sin and woe. No one pretends that democracy is perfect or all-wise. Indeed, it has been said that democracy is the worst form of government except for all those other forms that have been tried from time to time.

Winston Churchill[1]

Democracy in its broadest sense refers to a collective method of decision-making that involves all participants equally. The term originated in ancient Greece from as early as the fifth century BC to denote the notion of a political system that is "ruled by the common people", in contrast to the term aristocracy, which basically means "ruled by the few".[2] Although the concept of democracy has been known to political scientists for thousands of years, up until the twentieth century, virtually all regimes who branded themselves democratic failed to practise full enfranchisement. Women, minor ethnic groups and slaves were often denied the right to vote. Contemporary definitions of democracy are distinctively different in the sense that universal suffrage is considered to be a fundamental requirement. The autonomous Grand Duchy of Finland was the first modern state to grant universal suffrage to all of its citizens in 1906.[3]

In modern politics, although there has been no universal consensus on what exactly democracy entails, most political scientists use the term to denote a political system in which each citizen can practise their political power through voting. In a direct democracy, each individual represents themselves by casting their own vote directly. In a representative democracy, representatives are elected to represent an electorate. These democratically elected representatives would then convene to make a decision-making institution, such as a national assembly or a state parliament.[4] As a decision is often made depending on the majority of the votes, democracy is sometimes referred to as the "rule of the majority". Because of this "rule of majority", democracy has been criticized for its two inherent flaws: negligence of the rights of the minority and the irrationality of the decisions made through a democratic decision-making mechanism. To address the former, a constitutional democracy employs a constitutional framework to control the power of the majority and ensure the rights of the minority.[5]

According to the United Nations, universal and equal suffrage and human rights protection are the two fundamental requirements for democracy.[6] The legal basis for democracy is also protected by international law, in particular by the 1966 International Covenant on Civil and Political Rights.[7]

Diamond suggests that a democracy must fulfil four requirements: a fair and free electoral system that allows government to be democratically chosen and replaced; the active involvement of citizens in both politics and civic life; the guarantee of universal basic human rights; and a rule of law which is practised impartially towards all citizens.[8]

Many contemporary political philosophers maintain that democracy is a requirement for a regime in modern times to be considered legitimate, especially in the West. The legitimacy of a democracy is typically evaluated based on the quality of the people's consent, which can be realized in various ways.[9] One way is through electoral authorization, which encompasses factors like the inclusivity of the voting process, the fairness of political competition and the integrity of the election procedures.[10, 11] Another way is through direct citizen participation, such as through referendums, public consultations or access to elected officials.[12, 13, 14] The third approach involves informed and reasoned agreement generated through deliberation,[15] while the fourth involves substantive representation of citizens' preferences and concerns.[16, 17] The fifth approach involves consent that is limited by liberal-constitutional elements, such as checks and balances, individual rights and procedural safeguards.[18]

Even regimes that are clearly authoritarian tend to label themselves democratic by adding the words such as Democratic, Republic or the People's to the country's name. Examples being Democratic People's Republic of Korea, People's Republic of China or Lao People's Democratic Republic. Vietnam is not an exception, with North Vietnam being called the Democratic Republic of Vietnam from 1945 until 1976 and a unified Vietnam being called the Socialist Republic of Vietnam from 1976 until now.

The CPV has been consistently claiming to be democratic throughout its history, as democracy, under different wordings, has been mentioned in many important documents penned by its leadership. However, the CPV espouses centralism,[19] which is fundamentally different to the Western concept of democracy. Democratic centralism is first defined as "freedom of discussion, unity of action" in the political pamphlet "What is to be done", penned by Vladimir Lenin in 1901.[20] This concept was adopted and interpreted by Ho Chi Minh as a system of government that "belongs to the people and is under the leadership of the people", in which the people can vote for their representatives; however, the government must be under a centralized and unified leadership. Ho called this system "both democratic and centralized".[21]

The Charter of the CPV devotes an entire article to explain the core principles of democratic centralism that it adheres which entails the election of decision-makers and the rule of the majority.[22] The CPV argues that democracy is practised at all levels within its system-based elections as a means of selecting representatives; and decision-making through debating and voting. Elections are commonly cited as a method for selecting representatives, from hamlets to national levels, to appoint individuals to positions of authority. Nevertheless, these elections and voting are often more symbolic than substantive, with outcomes predetermined through internal consensus.

This Vietnamese version of democracy is introduced to children as early as middle school to shape their preferences. The 2023 ninth grade Citizenship Education Textbook defines democracy as a process through which individuals can lead and shape the collective and society by actively participating in discussions, contributing to implementation and overseeing communal and societal affairs.[23] The 2023 Citizenship Education Textbook for eleventh grade students provides a more detailed explanation of the concept of democracy imposed by the CPV, which is termed "socialist democracy". This concept of democracy is founded on five key principles: Vietnamese democracy is a working-class democracy; the economic system is based on state ownership of the means of production; the ideology underpinning Vietnamese democracy is Marxism-Leninism; socialist democracy belongs to the working people; and socialist democracy must be accompanied by the rule of law, discipline and order.[24]

Even though both conceptions are based on the principle of majority rule, there are several clear distinctions between the concept of democracy acknowledged in the West and the concept of democratic centralism adopted by the CPV. While the Western concept puts strong emphasis on individual rights, equality and the rule of law, the concept adopted by the CPV tends to emphasize the importance of a centralized system under the name of majority rule. In this system only few can actually yield power. The hierarchical organization structure of the Party ensures that every single party cell and party member ultimately answer to the National Congress and the Central Committee. It could be put simply that at both the national and party level, democratic centralism is a form of representative democracy that concentrates power in the hands of the Party's leadership and that a chain of command is always maintained.

Socialism, as a foundational state-building ideology, and the leadership of the working class are regarded as fundamental to Vietnam's concept of democracy. This perspective is somewhat ironic, given that after *Doi Moi*, the individuals comprising the leadership of the CPV can scarcely be considered working-class people. Nevertheless, the CPV continues to employ this narrative to justify its monopoly on power.

When the CPV was founded in 1930, it focused mainly on the peasant and worker classes to capitalize on the class struggle inside the semi-colonial and semi-feudal Vietnamese society. As a result, universal democracy was ignored. The 1930 Political Guideline of the Indochinese Communist Party indicates that the objective of the revolution was to set up a peasant-worker government and a peasant-worker army. In the same document, the proletariats and the peasants were mentioned as the main driving forces of the revolution. This political guideline declared that proletariats, however, must be in charge of leadership in order for the revolution to be victorious. The guideline also mentioned the possibility of neutralizing or incorporating the petit bourgeoisie into the rank of the revolution. However, it maintained a very hostile standing against the bourgeoisie class and the Vietnamese who worked for the French-colonialists.

After seizing power in 1945, the CPV attempted to include other classes in its political struggle. The Proclamation of Independence of the Democratic Republic of Vietnam started by denouncing French colonial rule and announcing the birth of the Democratic Republic of Vietnam, a state which was claimed to exist under a democratic republic government. Nationalism, however, was the centrepiece of this declaration and a socialist ideology addressing class struggle was completely left out to rally the support of the multitude of factions within Vietnamese society at that time.

In the short preamble of the 1946 Constitution of the Democratic Republic of Vietnam, which was approved by the newly elected National Assembly in the January 1946 election, the democratic claim of the regime was repeated four times while class struggle was omitted. Furthermore, the third article of the same constitution emphasized democracy as one of the most important elements of the newly elected government's claim to legitimacy. Given the political environment and the composition of the National Assembly of Vietnam in 1946, in which the Viet Minh and its allies the Democratic Party of Vietnam and the Socialist Party of Vietnam only occupied 57 per cent of the total seats, this was understandable.

Article 22 of the 1946 Constitution of the Democratic Republic of Vietnam recognized the National Assembly, which was mentioned under the name the People's Parliament, as the most powerful institution of the Democratic Republic of Vietnam. According to Article 23 of the same constitution, the National Assembly has the power to exercise constitutional and legislative powers, decide significant national affairs, make and amend laws, decide on the fundamental national financial and monetary policies and ratify international treaties signed with foreign governments. In other words, the first constitution of Vietnam not only acknowledged democracy as the core value of the Democratic Republic of Vietnam but also maintained the critical role of the National Assembly in the country's political system.

The 1951 Political Guideline of the Vietnam Workers' Party, penned by Ho Chi Minh six years after the declaration of independence and amidst the height of the First Indochina War, while mostly devoted to discussing the ongoing war against the French, also mentioned democracy as one of the core values of the government established by the Viet Minh and that the Vietnamese revolution is the conflict between "the people's democratic regime of Vietnam and the reactionary factions in order to push forward socialism". However, this people's democratic regime was not a universal regime as the guideline also branded Vietnamese feudalists, in particular "the reactionary feudalists", as the secondary enemies of the regime, with the primary enemies being the French colonial empire and the American interferers. Building a people's democratic regime is also listed as one of the main objectives of the revolution, along with driving out the colonialists, unifying the country, completely removing the remnants of feudalism and redistributing land among farmers, all of which ultimately aim to achieve socialism.

In addition to mentioning peasants and workers as the backbone of the revolution, the 1951 Political Guideline of the Vietnam Workers' Party also enlisted the support of petit bourgeois, nationalist bourgeois and progressive and patriotic landowners. However, the guideline maintained that the leadership must be firmly placed in the hands of the proletariats with the intellectuals, along with the peasants and the workers being the core of the mass. The guideline further described that the Party aimed to create a true people's democratic government belonging to the aforementioned social classes and to eradicate the imperialists and those who were branded traitors. The principle of the people's democratic government was democratic centralism, which should be practised by the local authorities, namely the people's committees and bureaucracy committees. The guideline acknowledged the National Assembly and the government as the ultimate decision-makers.

In 1959, a constitution was approved by a National Assembly consisting mostly of members of the Vietnam Workers' Party and their satellite parties. This constitution was explicitly communist in nature and differed significantly from its 1951 predecessor, which had refrained from mentioning any political party. The 1959 constitution acknowledged the leading role of the Vietnam Workers' Party, the government of the Democratic Republic of Vietnam and President Ho Chi Minh, claiming that under their clear-sighted leadership, Vietnam would ultimately become a socialist society.

Nevertheless, while recognizing the political domination of the CPV, like its predecessor, the 1959 Constitution of Vietnam did mention democracy as one of the core values of the regime, stating that the Democratic Republic of Vietnam is a people's democratic state.

Furthermore, the 1959 Constitution acknowledged the National Assembly as the "highest body of state authority" and the "only legislative authority of the Democratic Republic of Vietnam". The 1959 Constitution describes how the National Assembly was granted the power to exercise state authority to fulfil its functions, which consisted of a wide range of important tasks from enacting and amending the constitution to deciding upon national economic plans and approving the state budget.

The 1959 Constitution can be considered an effort by the CPV to combine its socialist ideology, the struggle for national independence and the task of rebuilding Vietnam. Over the next two decades the political direction of the CPV remained the same as the Party's foremost priority was to unify the country. In the draft of his will in 1965, Ho Chi Minh expressed his determination for national unification despite overwhelming losses:

> The war of resistance against America perhaps will continue for another several years. We would lose more resources and men. Nevertheless, we must uphold our determination to fight the American invaders until the final victory. We still have our country; we still have our men. After our triumph over the American invaders, we will rebuild our country ten times better than today.[25]

The CPV implemented a three-year plan from 1958 to 1960, followed by a five-year plan, both heavily geared towards socialism. Informed by the violent and unjust experiences of prior land reforms, their execution displayed greater flexibility. Particularly, the approach to forming agricultural cooperatives during the three-year plan was notably more lenient.

The Resolution of the 16th Central Committee Conference recognized that while poor and middle-class farmers generally supported the cooperatives, in principle, wealthy farmers and landowners opposed them, with many actively avoiding participation and some even sabotaging government efforts. The CPV instructed its cadres to promote the formation of farming collectives based on three principles: voluntarism, mutual benefit and democracy. Specifically, the Resolution forbade any form of coercion or command to force farmers into cooperatives, to keep them in or to bar re-entry into cooperatives.[26]

The cooperatives were categorized into low-level and high-level collectives, based on their degree of cooperation and the distribution of agricultural products. Unlike lower-level cooperatives, which might permit some private plots or individual farming activities, high-level cooperatives were characterized by extensive collectivization. Almost all land and resources were pooled and managed collectively. While the CPV was determined to gradually integrate all farmers into cooperatives, the methods employed were less coercive and more flexible than those used during land reform.

With the Second Indochina War coming to an end in April 1975, on 29 September 1975, the CPV adopted Decree No. 247-NQ/TW titled "Completion of National Unification and Our Quick, Vigorous, and Steady Development Towards Socialism". The collapse of the Republic of Vietnam and all of its parties left the CPV without any political opposition, allowing it to quickly consolidate power in South Vietnam. The other two holdover political parties in Vietnam, the Socialist Party of Vietnam and the Democratic Party of Vietnam, were only politically functional in name as they were constitutionally bound to follow the leadership of the CPV.

Decree No. 247-NQ/TW shows a strong determination to achieve socialism "under the leadership of the CPV, the dictatorship of the proletariat, the national united front, and the revolutionary government which are empowered by the unification of the workers and the peasants". The success of the August Revolution and the victory over the French and the Americans were attributed to the CPV, and, as such, the Party entrusted itself with the mission "to unify and lead the proletariat class and the Vietnamese people to build a socialist Vietnam with modern agriculture and industries, a powerful military, and progressive culture and science". According to the decree, military victories justified the dictatorship of the proletariat and the concentration of political power in the hands of the CPV; as a result, the role of the National Assembly was not mentioned.

Nevertheless, the decree claims repeatedly that the Vietnamese revolution is a people's national democratic revolution and a part of a larger global movement for national independence, democracy and progress. However, the decree also claims that the Party needed to strengthen the authority of the central communist government and that "a centralized and unified leadership must be ensured". The decree encouraged "individual responsibility" and the practice of "collective democracy". Overall, this decree cemented the dictatorial leadership of the CPV and explicitly expressed a strong communist tendency.

More than ten years after the unification of Vietnam, facing an unprecedented economic and legitimacy crisis, the CPV carried out a series of reforms known as *Doi Moi*. This change in policies was constitutionalized in the 1992 Constitution of the Social Republic of Vietnam, which was adopted two decades after its most recent predecessor. The 1992 Constitution was an effort by the Party to restore its legitimacy, which was heavily damaged by disastrous economic policies amidst the collapse of communism worldwide. The constitution focused mostly on nationalism, Ho Chi Minh's charismatic leadership and the promise of economic development and socialism as the three main pillars of the Party's legitimacy. Nevertheless, the word "democracy" was repeated six times in the 1992 Constitution.[27]

The role and functionality of the National Assembly are also defined in detail in this constitution. Article 83 recognized the National Assembly as the "highest representative body of the people, the highest state authority in the Socialist Republic of Vietnam" and the only political body vested with constitutional and legislative powers and that it can decide on key domestic and foreign policies, national socioeconomic, defence and security tasks, and the main principles of the state apparatus and social relations. The National Assembly also holds supreme supervisory authority over all state activities. The link between democracy and the National Assembly, however, was only vaguely mentioned in Article 6, where Vietnamese democracy is defined as democratic centralism.[28]

The 1992 Constitution of the Socialist Republic of Vietnam was clearly aimed at promoting the nationalistic and socialist achievements of the CPV and Ho Chi Minh's heritage while attempting to add economic development as a new dimension of the Party's legitimacy. Although democracy was mentioned, it was not the focal point of this constitution.

Several years after the initiation of *Doi Moi*, the inherent tensions between socialist policies and market-driven economic reforms began to surface. While certain segments, particularly government officials and entities with state backing, accrued substantial wealth, others were marginalized. This disparity led to widespread discontent, culminating in a series of protests, with the Thai Binh disturbances being the most notable. Local government officials in Thai Binh were implicated in fund misappropriation, bribery and inequitable land distribution, which intensified the economic struggles of farmers and eroded trust in local governance. Thousands of villagers engaged in protests, confronted police forces and called for the removal of corrupt officials. Hai examines the Thai Binh disturbances, noting that the CPV responded by promoting grassroots democracy, which ostensibly mitigated corruption and reduced inequality.[29] However, the efficacy of grassroots democracy relied heavily on local authorities, often leading to nominal rather than substantive democratic practices. Although the CPV has learned from these past experiences, it has not sufficiently addressed the underlying issues of inequality.[30] Hai argues that unless the CPV commits to genuine democratic reforms and cultivates a strong democratic ethos at the local level, the legitimacy of its one-party rule and the broader social stability may be at risk of further challenges.[31]

The 1997 disturbances were not the last confrontation between the government and the locality in Thai Binh. In 2008, another series of confrontations broke out. The 2008 disturbances, dubbed "the Jumon Army" because they coincided with the broadcast of the popular South Korean historical series of the same name in Vietnam, are best described through the firsthand account of the author's father-in-law, who is a native of Thai Binh:

> The local officials took the land that was supposed to be used to build a football field and a cultural centre for the local people. They then sold it to a gasoline company to build a gas station. The people were livid; they gathered and clashed with the police. They brought portraits of Uncle Ho and the Fatherland Flag. They used loudspeakers to play revolutionary songs day and night. I was there; a person next to me picked up a rock and smashed a police car window with it. He was arrested on the spot. The central government intervened. They arrested the leader of the demonstration group, who was a war veteran. First, they tried to bribe him by promising him a veteran's pension. When he refused, they threatened his family and

his son, who is a government official, saying that if he could not calm his father down, then both father and son would suffer. The leader was jailed for a few years. The central government also bribed his lieutenants with land and other benefits. Then they arrested the responsible chairman of the local people's committee, the land administrators, and some local police officers. The situation has improved since then; government officials are still asking for bribes to provide services without hindrance, and land disputes occasionally surface, but nothing of that scale has happened again. The people are given more rights and face less hassle when doing paperwork. There is also a sports court and a cultural centre in every commune now.

Although they are reported by foreign media outlets and studied by scholars outside of Vietnam, both the 1997 and the 2008 disturbances in Thai Binh receive little coverage from the domestic press, if any at all. The case of the disturbances in Thai Binh is a good illustration of the conflict between the local people and the corrupt local government over land use and land ownership. It required the intervention of the central government, which used a combination of strategies, from coercion to the introduction of grassroots democracy and other benefits to appeal to the local people.

Several legal changes were subsequently adopted in an attempt to introduce a framework for democratic practices. The 2013 Constitution of the Socialist Republic of Vietnam ratified twenty-six years after the initiation of *Doi Moi* put a stronger emphasis on democracy. In Article 2, the Socialist Republic of Vietnam is stated to be a socialist state "of the People, by the People and for the People", and that "The people are the masters of the Socialist Republic of Vietnam; all state powers belong to the people whose foundation is the alliance between the working class, the peasantry and the intelligentsia."[32]

Article 6 of the 2013 Constitution stipulates that "The people exercise state power under the forms of direct democracy and representative democracy through the National Assembly, the people's councils and other state agencies." Article 8 further adds that all state agencies, officials and employees must respect, serve and stay connected with the people, listen to their opinions and accept their supervision. They must also fight against corruption, wastefulness, bureaucracy, arrogance and authoritarianism.

Other articles in this constitution guarantee universal, equal, direct and secret suffrage (Article 7); human rights (Article 3 and Chapter 2); and rule of law (Article 16 and other articles). Nevertheless, the 2013 Constitution also guarantees the role of the CPV as the leading force of the State and the society in Article 4.

In addition to the 2013 Constitution, one of the most important landmarks to Vietnam's legal framework on democracy is the ratification of the Law on the Implementation of Grassroots Democracy in November 2022. This law is not the first of its kind, being preceded by the Ordinance on the Implementation of Grassroots Democracy in Communes, Wards, and Townships in 2007, and earlier by Resolution 79/2003/NĐ-CP on the Implementation of Democracy in Communes in 2003. Nonetheless, the 2022 Democracy Law provides a comprehensive legal framework on grassroots democracy. It secures human rights and the right to be informed about significant government decisions such as planning and development. Additionally, it affirms citizens' rights to reap benefits from socioeconomic reforms and growth, social security and the provision of safety and stability (Article 7). Furthermore, the 2022 Democracy Law prohibits any actions that impede citizens from exercising their democratic rights at the grassroots level, including repression or negligence in addressing petitions and complaints. It also safeguards against the disclosure of information concerning whistleblowers or informants of offenses related to the implementation of grassroots democracy (Article 9). Moreover, the law stipulates the responsibilities of local governments, which include the disclosure of information, engaging in public consultation and soliciting public comments, all under public scrutiny and supervision. State enterprises are similarly required to maintain equivalent responsibilities towards the public and their employees.

Nevertheless, the same law also prohibits the misuse of democratic rights to commit acts that infringe upon national security, public order, state interests and the legal rights of others. It further forbids exploiting grassroots democratic rights to distort facts, provoke conflicts, incite violence or engage in discrimination resulting in harm to others.

Such actions are also criminalized in Article 331 of the 2015 Penal Code, which stipulates that any individual exploiting liberal rights to undermine the State's interests or the lawful interests of others will face sanctions ranging from a warning and re-education without detention up to seven years of imprisonment in severe cases.

Article 331 of the Penal Code can be used as a means to penalize dissidents and whistleblowers who express opposition to the State, the ruling party and its leadership, and it has indeed been used to prosecute many such individuals. For instance, one defendant was sentenced to six months of imprisonment for displaying the flag of South Vietnam and disseminating anti-government content on his Facebook account.[33]

While the CPV has endeavoured to enhance its rational-legal authority through improvements to the legal framework concerning citizens' democratic rights, the implementation of this framework can be impeded by existing laws and, more critically, by their interpretation. Consequently, the effectiveness of these frameworks in safeguarding citizens' democratic rights and facilitating legal political opposition to the ruling party remains a subject of debate. Against the backdrop of the fervent anti-corruption campaign, while the 2022 Democracy Law can be utilized at the grassroots level to combat corruption and poor governance in certain cases, it would be unrealistic to expect that it grants Vietnamese citizens the same level of political and freedom rights as those in Western democracies.

The CPV maintains that the Vietnamese-styled democracy is superior to Western democracy and that one-party political system does not necessarily mean the country is non-democratic. The official mouthpiece of the Armed Forces of Vietnam claims that there are many one-party states where people live happily while in many countries with a multiparty political system, the people lack fundamental democratic rights and argues that the current political system is the most suitable to the situation of Vietnam.[34] According to the CPV Online Newspaper, the people are the masters and leaders in all aspects of social life, guided by the principles of the CPV. The people can exercise self-determination through direct and indirect means within the political system, centred on a socialist rule of law and a state of the people, by the people and for the people, with the state sector playing a leading role.[35]

Nguyen Phu Trong, the previous paramount leader of Vietnam, in his lengthy essay "Some Theoretical and Practical Issues Regarding Socialism and the Path Towards Socialism in Vietnam", claimed that "in contrast to Western democracy, Vietnam is building a society in which development truly serves humanity, rather than prioritizing profits that exploit and undermine human dignity".[36]

The CPV also offers criticism of Western democracy, in particular American democracy. *Nhan Dan*, the official newspaper of the CPV, published a series of articles claiming that Western democracy is facing a crisis of faith. The series criticizes the Western democratic system for perpetuating and protecting the interests of the wealthy at the expense of the less privileged.[37] According to *Nhan Dan*, in the West, the bourgeoisie can influence politics using their massive wealth and as such enjoy a disproportionate amount of power while individuals from marginalized communities, such as low-income individuals or racial and ethnic minorities, often face barriers to political participation. Nguyen Phu Trong also claimed that in the West only one per cent of the whole population control more than three-fourths of the resources and media and as such control the whole society.[38] The official mouthpiece of the Ministry of Public Security of Vietnam claims that American politics is dominated by big companies for their own interests through lobbying.[39]

The National Defence Journal, the official newspaper of the Ministry of National Defence of Vietnam, criticizes the West for attempting to "export" democracy through a series of colour revolutions. According to the journal, the goal of the West, especially the United States, is to destabilize other countries in order to exploit their resources. As a result, the West's influence has led to significant consequences, including political instability and humanitarian crises. The journal claims that the West has blatantly interfered in domestic affairs and undermined democracy in countries across the world when the results of elections did not turn out the way they wanted.[40]

The CPV Online Newspaper maintains that the West still wants to overthrow the CPV under the guise of spreading democracy and freedom through fundings terrorists and criminals to undermine Vietnam's political stability and that the CPV must remain vigilant against peaceful evolution. Human Rights Watch, Freedom House and Amnesty International are among the organizations named and shamed for allegedly distorting information and defaming the CPV.[41]

Conclusion

As the mandate of the masses plays a pivotal role in modern political legitimacy, most dictatorial regimes claim to be democratic and the CPV is not an exception. Documents produced by the Party's leadership or under their auspices consistently assert the CPV's role as the rightful representative of the Vietnamese people's authority.

Democracy has always been a component in the claim to legitimacy of the CPV; however, before the 2010s, it was rarely seen as a focal point of the regime's propaganda paradigm other than during the short period just after the August Revolution when democracy was, in fact, alongside nationalism, the centrepiece of the Declaration of Independence and the 1951 Constitution of the Democratic Republic of Vietnam. The rationale behind this was that the CPV needed to share power with several other political parties and was trying to mobilize their support for the coming tumultuous period that would inevitably come after the end of the Second World War.

Pressure to democratize from the West, economic slowdown as the result of global economic crises combined with domestic corruption and bad governance, the South China Sea disputes and the proliferation of the internet have all contributed to the increasing need for the CPV to improve its rule and adopt a more responsive approach to the population's grievances. The CPV has also been putting significant efforts into incorporating democracy into its propaganda to enhance the legitimacy of its rule. This improvement in policy was signalled by the 2011 addition to the 1991 Guideline on National Building in the Transition Period to Socialism.[42]

The concept of democracy advocated by the CPV is fundamentally different from the definition espoused by the West. The CPV advocates for a form of democratic centralism that primarily serves to centralize power in the hands of the Party elite rather than empowering the masses. In line with the CPV's socialist ideology, the working class is often emphasized as the leading force in the society while the role of other classes is marginalized. However, it is rather ironic that less than one per cent of the most recent three National Assembly members list their occupations as farmers or factory workers, highlighting a disparity between theory and reality. Furthermore, the Party also resorts to repression against individuals and groups perceived as posing threats to its political hegemony or national stability.

Nevertheless, Vietnam's CPV-led government exhibits a degree of responsiveness to various pressures and grievances emanating from both organized and unorganized sectors of society. Furthermore, the CPV's central leadership has also shown willingness to allow local governments some leeway to carry out experiments to improve grassroots democracy.[43, 44, 45] As such, while some dissidents have been advocating for direct confrontation with the CPV and replace it with a more democratic government, some views the State's responsiveness as a potential avenue for incremental democratic reforms through constructive engagement.[46] The legislative elections in Vietnam represent one of the most, if not the most, important channels for such engagement. In the next chapter, we will explore how the exercise of democratic rights of the ordinary people is permitted—or restricted—in practice through the quinquennial elections of the National Assembly.

Notes

1. Richard Langworth, ed., *Churchill by Himself: The Definitive Collection of Quotations* (New York: Public Affairs, 2011), p. 574.
2. Nigel Wilson, *Encyclopedia of Ancient Greece* (New York: Routledge, 2013), p. 511.
3. Irene Sulkunen, "The General Strike and Women's Suffrage", n.d. http://www.aanioikeus.fi/en/articles/strike.htm (accessed 10 July 2024).
4. The Stanford Encyclopaedia of Philosophy (2017) offers a philosophical definition of democracy that includes the following four dimensions: democracy is a collective

decision-making process that means that all members of the group must be involved; the scope of democracy varies from families to corporations, to states, and to international organizations; the definition of democracy itself does not include any normative element, that is, it is not related to any evaluating or descriptive standards; and the level of political equality required by the definition of democracy varies. To some, a one-person one-vote decision-making mechanism is sufficient, while others may require deliberation, discussion and coalition building to be involved. Any political activity from the grassroot level of representative election to the direct involvement in law making can be considered to be democracy.

5. W. Frederick, *Encyclopaedia Britannica* (1970), pp. 215–23.

6. According to Article 21 of the Universal Declaration of Human Rights,

     The will of the people shall be the basis of the authority of government; this shall be expressed in periodic and genuine elections which shall be by universal and equal suffrage and shall be held by secret vote or by equivalent free voting procedures.

7. According to the International Covenant on Civil and Political Rights, citizens enjoy the following inseparable rights: "the right to freedom of expression" (Article 19); the right to "peaceful assembly" and "association with others" (Article 21 and Article 22, respectively); the right to direct participation in the implementation of public affairs, or indirectly through democratically elected representatives; and the right to "vote and to be elected at genuine periodic elections which shall be by universal and equal suffrage and shall be held by secret ballot, guaranteeing the free expression of the will of the electors" (Article 25) (OHCHR 1976). The United Nations also emphasizes the importance of the civil society in democracy and encourages inclusive and active participation in political activities (United Nations 2017).

     United Nations Human Rights Office of the High Commissioner (OHCHR), *International Covenant on Civil and Political Rights* (1976), https://www.ohchr.org/en/professionalinterest/pages/ccpr.aspx (accessed 30 November 2024).

     United Nations, *Democracy* (2017), http://www.un.org/en/sections/issues-depth/democracy/index.html (accessed 30 November 2024).

8. Larry Diamond, "What Is Democracy?", Hilla University for Humanistic Studies, 21 January 2004, https://diamond-democracy.stanford.edu/events/lecture/what-democracy (accessed 10 July 2024).

9. John Dunn, ed., *Democracy: The Unfinished Journey, 508 BC to AD 1993* (Oxford, England: Oxford University Press, 1992).

10. Adam Przeworski, "Constraints and Choices: Electoral Participation in Historical Perspective", *Comparative Political Studies* 42, no. 1 (2009): 4–30, https://doi.org/10.1177/0010414008324991.

11. Pippa Norris, *Why Electoral Integrity Matters* (Cambridge, England: Cambridge University Press, 2014).

12. Jan W. van Deth, "What Is Political Participation?", Oxford Research Encyclopedia of Politics, 2016, https://doi.org/10.1093/acrefore/9780190228637.013.68.
13. Paul Lucardie, *Democratic Extremism in Theory and Practice: All Power to the People* (Abingdon, England: Routledge, 2014).
14. Hannah Arendt, *On Revolution* (London: Faber and Faber, 1963).
15. Antonio Floridia, *From Participation to Deliberation: A Critical Genealogy of Deliberative Democracy* (Colchester, England: ECPR Press, 2017).
16. Bernard Manin, *The Principles of Representative Government* (Cambridge, England: Cambridge University Press, 1997).
17. Hanna Fenichel Pitkin, *The Concept of Representation* (Berkeley, CA: University of California Press, 1967).
18. William H. Riker, *Liberalism Against Populism* (San Francisco, CA: W.H. Freeman, 1982).
19. *Dân chủ tập trung* [in Vietnamese].
20. Vladimir I. Lenin, *Report on the Unity Congress of the R.S.D.L.P.*, 1906.
21. Ho Chi Minh, *Hồ Chí Minh Toàn Tập* [Ho Chi Minh's complete works], vol. 3 (Hanoi: National Political Publishing House, 2000), p. 553.
22. The 2001 Charter of the CPV listed the core principles of democratic centralism as follows:

    1. The decision-making bodies at all levels of the Party are elected.
    2. The highest authority within the CPV is the National Congress. Between the two congresses, the highest authority of the CPV is the Central Committee. At lower levels, there are also Party congresses and executive committees corresponding to the National Congress and the Central Committee.
    3. The executive committees must report their activities to same-level congresses and to the higher and lower-level committees. The committees must also periodically report their activities to related party organizations and duly carry out criticism and self-criticism.
    4. Organizations under the leadership of the CPV and its members must follow the Party's resolutions. The minority must follow the decisions of the majority, subordinates must submit to their supervisors, individuals must follow the decisions of the group, and organizations belonging to the Party must follow the leadership of the National Congress and the Central Committee.
    5. Resolutions by decision-making organizations need more than half of the vote by all the members of such organizations to be approved. Before voting, each member is entitled to express their own opinion. Party members whose opinions are in the minority can keep their opinions and report them to higher-level executive committees, including the National Congress. However, such members must duly accept the resolution and must not spread sentiments that go against the Party's

resolution. Executive committees must carefully consider every opinion, regardless of whether that opinion belongs to the majority or the minority.

6. Party organizations can work within their own authority; however, their decisions must not go against the principles, directions and policies of the Party, the rule of law of the government and the resolutions of the higher-level committees.

23. Ministry of Education and Training of Vietnam, *Sách Giáo Khoa Giáo Dục Công Dân Lớp 9* [Ninth Grade Citizenship Education Textbook] (Hanoi: Viet Nam Education Publishing House, 2023), p. 10.

24. Ministry of Education and Training of Vietnam, *Sách Giáo Khoa Giáo Dục Công Dân Lớp 11* [Eleventh Grade Citizenship Education Textbook] (Hanoi: Viet Nam Education Publishing House, 2023), p. 81.

25. Ho Chi Minh, "Confidential: Ho Chi Minh's 1965 Written Will", 1965, http://hochiminh.vn/news/pages/news.aspx (accessed 10 July 2024).

26. Communist Party of Vietnam, "Nghị quyết của Hội nghị Trung ương lần thứ 16 (mở rộng), tháng 4 năm 1959 về vấn đề hợp tác hóa nông nghiệp" [Resolution of the 16th Central Committee Conference (expanded), April 1959 on the issue of agricultural cooperation], https://tulieuvankien.dangcongsan.vn/van-kien-tu-lieu-ve-dang/hoi-nghi-bch-trung-uong/khoa-ii/nghi-quyet-cua-hoi-nghi-trung-uong-lan-thu-16-mo-rong-thang-4-nam-1959-ve-van-de-hop-tac-hoa-nong-nghiep-804 (accessed 10 July 2024).

27. In the preamble of the 1992 Constitution, similar to the 1959 Constitution, the CPV claimed that the Vietnamese revolution should be a people's national democratic revolution. In Article 14, the constitution claimed that Vietnam had pursued a line of policies that "actively supports and contributes to the common struggle of the peoples of the world for peace, national independence, democracy and social progress". Article 20 infused the concept of economic collectivism and democracy as follows: "economic collectives set up through the contribution of funds and manpower by citizens for cooperation in production and business will be organized under different forms on the basis of voluntariness, democracy and mutual benefit". Article 47 maintained that one of the main purposes of the government was to "ensure political stability and citizen's rights to freedom and democracy". Article 82 guaranteed the right of asylum for any individuals who "are persecuted for taking part in the struggle for freedom and national independence, for socialism, democracy and peace".

28. Article 6 of the 1992 Constitution:

> The people exercise state power through the National Assembly and the people's councils, bodies representing the will and aspirations of the people and which are elected by and accountable to the people. The National Assembly, the people's councils and other state bodies are organized and function according to the principle of democratic centralism.

29. Nguyen Hong Hai, "Grassroots Democracy and Inequality Reduction in Rural Vietnam: The Case of Thái Bình in 1997 and Now", *Asian Journal of Political Science* 22, no. 3 (2014): 221–39, https://doi.org/10.1080/02185377.2013.879067.

30. Ibid.

31. Ibid.

32. Translation taken from ConstitutionNet: https://constitutionnet.org/sites/default/files/tranlation_of_vietnams_new_constitution_enuk_2.pdf.

33. Supreme People's Court of the Socialist Republic of Vietnam, "Bản án số: 94/2019/HS-PT" [Case No. 94/2019/HS-PT], 28 August 2019, https://congbobanan.toaan.gov.vn/2ta342180t1cvn/chi-tiet-ban-an (accessed 10 July 2024).

34. *Quân Đội Nhân Dân*, "Ngăn chặn và đẩy lùi biểu hiện 'đòi thực hiện đa nguyên, đa đảng" [Prevent and push back the manifestations of "demanding pluralism and multi-party system"], 2017, https://www.qdnd.vn/phong-chong-tu-dien-bien-tu-chuyen-hoa/ngan-chan-va-day-lui-bieu-hien-doi-thuc-hien-da-nguyen-da-dang-512223 (accessed 10 July 2024).

35. Nguyen Nham, "Không có chuyện Việt Nam 'đàn áp mạng xã hội'" [Vietnam does not oppress social networks], *Communist Party of Vietnam Online Newspaper*, 2 April 2021, https://dangcongsan.vn/bao-ve-nen-tang-tu-tuong-cua-dang/khong-co-chuyen-viet-nam-dan-ap-mang-xa-hoi-576601.html.

36. Nguyen Phu Trong, "Một số vấn đề lý luận và thực tiễn về chủ nghĩa xã hội và con đường đi lên chủ nghĩa xã hội ở Việt Nam" [Some theoretical and practical issues regarding socialism and the path towards socialism in Vietnam], *Communist Review*, 16 May 2021, https://www.tapchicongsan.org.vn/media-story/-/asset_publisher/V8hhp4dK31Gf/content/mot-so-van-de-ly-luan-va-thuc-tien-ve-chu-nghia-xa-ha-con-duong-di-len-chu-nghia-xa-hoi-o-viet-nam (accessed 10 July 2024).

37. Ho Ngoc Thang, "Nền dân chủ phương Tây và sự khủng hoảng niềm tin" [Western democracy and the crisis of faith], *Nhân Dân*, 7 December 2015, https://nhandan.vn/nen-dan-chu-phuong-tay-va-su-khung-hoang-niem-tin-ky-1-post242022.html (accessed 10 July 2024).

38. Nguyen Phu Trong, "Thành tựu phát triển nền kinh tế thị trường định hướng xã hội chủ nghĩa ở Việt Nam qua hơn 35 năm đổi mới" [Achievements of the socialist-oriented market economy development in Vietnam over more than 35 years of *Doi Moi*], *Communist Review*, 2 March 2023, https://www.tapchicongsan.org.vn/media-story/-/asset_publisher/V8hhp4dK31Gf/content/thanh-tuu-phat-trien-nen-kinh-te-thi-truong-dinh-huong-xa-hoi-chu-nghia-o-viet-nam-qua-hon-35-nam-doi-moi (accessed 10 July 2024).

39. Nguyen Bao Duong, "Phê phán quan điểm cho rằng: 'Việt Nam kiên định con đường đi lên chủ nghĩa xã hội là sai lầm, đi theo vết xe đổ của Liên Xô'" [Critique of the opinion that "the determination to head toward socialism is a

mistake and would only copy the Soviet Union's failure"], *Public Security News*, 2018, http://hvctcand.edu.vn/phe-phan-quan-diem-cho-rang-%E2%80%9Cviet-nam-kien-dinh-con-duong-di-len-chu-nghia-xa-hoi-la-sai-lam-di-theo (accessed 10 July 2024).

40. Nguyen Trung, "'Cách mạng sắc màu' – một biện pháp chiến lược phi dân chủ, ngược dòng thời đại" ["The color revolution" – an anti-democratic, out-of-date strategic measure], *National Defence Journal*, 16 September 2011, http://tapchiqptd.vn/vi/an-pham-tap-chi-in/cach-mang-sac-mau-%E2%80%93-mot-bien-phap-chien-luoc-phi-dan-chu-nguoc-dong-thoi-dai/2210.html (accessed 10 July 2024).

41. Nguyen Thi Minh Hue and Le Trung Kien, "Lợi dụng dân chủ, nhân quyền, thủ đoạn nguy hiểm của thế lực thù địch" [Exploiting democracy, human rights: dangerous tactics of hostile forces], *Communist Party of Vietnam Online Newspaper*, 17 March 2022, https://dangcongsan.vn/bao-ve-nen-tang-tu-tuong-cua-dang/loi-dung-dan-chu-nhan-quyen-thu-doan-nguy-hiem-cua-the-luc-thu-dich-606069.html (accessed 10 July 2024).

42. The second lesson listed by the Party in the 1991 Guideline on National Building in the Transition Period to Socialism states:

    Our revolution is devoted to the people, by the people, and for the people. The Vietnamese people are the ones who created our victorious history. The entire activity of the Party must be based on the rightful interests and wishes of the people. The power of the Party lies in its close ties to the people. Bureaucracy, corruption, and departure from the people will result in unimaginable damage to the fate of our country, our socialist system, and our party (2011 addition to the 1991 Guideline on National Building in the Transition Period to Socialism).

43. Nguyen Hong Hai, *Political Dynamics of Grassroots Democracy in Vietnam* (Houndmills, Basingstoke, Hampshire; New York, NY: Palgrave Macmillan, 2016).

44. Hai is particularly impressed by Nguyen Ba Thanh, the Party secretary and president of the people's council of Da Nang city, for his reforms and his willingness to challenge party-imposed rules. However, Thanh garnered many rivals within the CPV due to his actions. Following Thanh's death in 2015 after seeking cancer treatment in the United States and Singapore, rumours circulated on the internet alleging that he was poisoned. Subsequently, many of his former subordinates were arrested on corruption charges, revealing that Thanh was the mastermind behind one of the most damaging land-related corruption cases in Da Nang during his tenure. The case of Nguyen Ba Thanh serves as an example of the complexity of inner-party politics.

45. Nguyen Hung, "Nguyên Bí thư Nguyễn Bá Thanh có ý kiến cho Vũ 'nhôm' mua đất công giá rẻ" [Former Secretary Nguyen Ba Thanh allowed Vu 'Nhom' to buy public land at a low price], *Công An Nhân Dân*, 2023, https://cand.com.vn/Phap-luat/Nguyen-Bi-thu-Nguyen-Ba-Thanh-co-y-kien-cho-Vu-nhom-mua-dat-cong-gia-re-i549536/ (accessed 10 July 2024).

46. Benedict J. Kerkvliet, "Governance, Development, and the Responsive-Repressive State in Vietnam", *Forum for Development Studies* 37 (March 2010): 33–60.

5

Elections and Improvements in the Functionality of the National Assembly

The National Assembly is the highest representative body of the People and the highest body of State power of the Socialist Republic of Vietnam.

Article 69 of the 2013 Constitution of the Socialist Republic of Vietnam

As discussed in the previous chapter, democracy has always been one of the elements of the CPV's claims to legitimacy. Democratic centralism is embedded at all levels of the party's structure, from the Politburo to the people's councils in small hamlets. Significant attention has been devoted to highlighting the National Assembly's significance as a symbol of democracy from the early 1990s. This chapter explores the National Assembly election process and recent endeavours to bolster its credibility through improvements in specific areas of its functioning.

Why Do Most Authoritarian Regimes Hold Elections?

One might argue that during wartime, military victories take precedence over elections and other democratic activities, as was the case in the United Kingdom during the Second World War when the 1940 General Election was cancelled. Nevertheless, despite the extreme conditions of constant warfare that Vietnam faced, efforts were made to ensure that elections were held in the North from 1960 until 1975, and from 1976 in a newly unified Vietnam.

In peacetime, while democratic legitimacy takes more priority, holding elections is not a trivial expense. In Vietnam, the entire electoral process is financed through the state budget, which has become increasingly expensive. Election expenses increased by 50 per cent from 2007 to 2011 and almost doubled from 2011 to 2016.[1] The cost of the 2021 Election was roughly $59 million, 20 per cent higher than that of the 2016 Election,[2] despite previous forecasts of 2.6 times increase in expenses. Put in perspective, the 2021 election expenses were comparable to the budgets assigned to the Ministry of Home Affairs ($49 million), the Ministry of Construction ($67 million) and the Ministry of Information and Communications ($58 million).[3] Holding an election is one thing; maintaining the National Assembly and its representatives is another matter entirely. In 2021, the Standing Committee of the National Assembly allocated a total of $7.78 million to the National Assembly delegations of approximately 500 delegates, equating to about $15,500 per delegate per year.[4] This amount is almost five times the GDP per capita of Vietnam in the same year.[5]

Since the CPV has consistently claimed democratic legitimacy, it is only logical that it endeavours to hold elections even under extreme conditions and at significant expense, which could have been allocated elsewhere. In practical terms, however, what does the regime expect to gain in return from holding elections?

Gandhi and Przeworski note that elections, as an indicator of democracy, can be an important factor contributing to the resilience of authoritarian regimes.[6] Although the fairness of elections in non-democratic regimes is often doubted and the elections themselves are usually considered to be mere masquerades of democracy, they are still held to maintain connections between the ruling class and the masses. Levitsky and Way point out that in most competitive authoritarian regimes, elections are held frequently by leaders to consolidate and enhance their power.[7] Diamond[8] and Schedler[9] maintain that legislative and executive elections held in dictatorial regimes do not represent democracy; however, in the long term, those elections could be used for democratization purposes.

Several authors further add that authoritarian regimes could effectively abuse elections to improve their political legitimacy,[10] divide and weaken their political opposition,[11] create an environment for compromise with potential contenders,[12, 13] fight corruption and malfeasance,[14] improve government responsiveness and credibility,[15] and allow leaders to exit from power or make peaceful transitions of power.[16] Empirical evidence provided by Gandhi and Przeworski shows that non-democratic regimes that hold nominally democratic elections tend to endure longer than those that do not.[17] In Vietnam, legislative elections are held periodically. While the democratic values of those elections are questionable at best, they play an important role in buttressing the legitimacy of the CPV.

The election and operation of the National Assembly of Vietnam after *Doi Moi* have been extensively studied by scholars. One of the most comprehensive works on the National Assembly of Vietnam is the four-volume book series, *The History of the National Assembly of Vietnam*, edited by Han and published by the National Political Publishing House.[18] The books, which were written at the request of, and monitored by, the Office of the National Assembly, provide the most detailed and comprehensive account of the National Assembly's history from its establishment in 1946 until 2011. Goto discussed the changes that took place in the National Assembly and the people's councils during the initiation of *Doi Moi*. He concluded that even though sustainable changes were made in both the National Assembly and the local people's councils, at the central level, those changes did not weaken the CPV's ability to maintain a monopoly on political power.[19] However, he argues that at the local level, these changes might undermine the single-party political system.[20]

According to Malesky and Schuler[21, 22, 23] and Malesky, Schuler and Anh,[24, 25] the following theories can be applied to elections under communist rule, in particular the case of Vietnam: co-optation theory suggests that the presence of democratic institutions will help reduce resistance and the cost of the actions of the regime; accountability theory explains that the ruling regime could pinpoint and remove incompetent officials through the election and operation of the National Assembly and people's councils; signalling theory argues that the ruling regime could use their overwhelming victories in elections to buttress their legitimacy; and rent-distribution theory proposes that National Assembly elections provide a mechanism through which representatives from every social group can be gathered to distribute state resources to their corresponding groups, which in turn strengthen grassroot level support. The findings suggest that the CPV holds elections not to monitor local officials or to select local leaders suitable for power-sharing arrangements, but rather to maintain its supermajority in the National Assembly.[26] Elections also serve as a mechanism of bargaining between ruling elites.

Ishizuka suggests that the role of the National Assembly has remained unchanged since the start of *Doi Moi*, which is to buttress the legitimacy of the CPV of Vietnam and to maintain political stability at the highest level.[27] Nevertheless, she argues that the National Assembly has been more active in using its power and could contribute to future political changes in Vietnam. She suggests that the CPV has been actively removing undesirable candidates even before elections and, as such, does not have to resort to electoral fraud to obtain a favourable result. Malesky argues that the vote of confidence, which was introduced in 2013, serves as a method of information gathering and signalling.[28] Through the vote of confidence, the CPV can gather valuable information on the needs of citizens while warning officials with incompetent performance. He also estimated that only 30 per cent of the members of the National Assembly actively participated in a no-confidence vote, which means the rest 70 per cent only cast a very confidence or confidence vote most of the time. This inactivity can be considered a safety net to prevent the removal of top officials through this mechanism.[29] As such, the vote of confidence is not a transformative mechanism and does not significantly threaten the dominance of the CPV in the National Assembly.

In general, the role of the National Assembly in the democratization of Vietnam is not highly regarded. Nakano argues that the CPV has been paying attention only to economic development since *Doi Moi* and that democratization has been ignored for the most part.[30] Nevertheless, she maintains that it is not international pressure but domestic actors, including high-ranking officials within the CPV, Vietnamese intellectuals, religious leaders, rural residents and overseas Vietnamese, that have been motivating the CPV to embrace more democratic changes.

Kerkvliet describes the gap between theory and practice of procedural legitimacy in Vietnam and forecasts that democratization is unlikely in the foreseeable future. However, he also argues that democracy as a concept, aspiration and form of government have played a significant role in the country's political evolution, from its struggles against French colonial rule in the first half of the twentieth century to ongoing debates about its future today.[31]

Abuza focuses on democratization from inside the CPV instead of external pressure for democratization from overseas or domestic dissident groups. He claims that any hope for regime change will have to be initiated from within the Party and illustrates this point by citing the political reform efforts of several dissidents within the ranks of the Party from the 1950s until the late 1990s.[32] Efforts to democratize post-colonial Vietnam in the late 1940s and early 1950s and social and economic reforms urged by former members of the

National Liberation Front in South Vietnam after unification in 1975 were denied and repressed by the leadership of the CPV, fearing that instability and loss of power would follow.[33]

The Legal Framework for National Assembly Elections in Vietnam

While in general scholars studying Vietnamese politics agree that despite political stagnation, the CPV's leadership is still determined to reject any fundamental changes to the political system, there is evidence showing that the CPV has been making efforts to improve its rational-legal authority, with democratic legitimacy being one of the cornerstones. Between 1958 and 2015, five election laws were enacted in North Vietnam and later, in communist-controlled unified Vietnam, corresponding to the elections of 1960, 1981, 1992, 1997 and 2016. New election laws are usually enacted when the CPV leadership perceives that they need to buttress their legitimacy.

The inaugural Election Law of 1958, though basic, laid the groundwork for the first post-First Indochina War legislative elections, with the main purpose of legitimizing CPV rule in North Vietnam. Although no new election laws were introduced between 1958 and 1980, elections continued to be conducted.

The 1992 Election Law emerged during a critical period when Vietnam faced a dire situation. Despite the country's unification almost two decades earlier, forcibly implemented socialist economic policies had not achieved significant progress. Additionally, Vietnam was reeling from destructive wars with Cambodia and China, its former ideological allies. With the cessation of aid from China and reduced support from Eastern Bloc countries, which were grappling with their own economic challenges, Vietnam found itself isolated. The occupation of Cambodia also hindered Vietnam from receiving support from friendly Western countries like Japan and Sweden. Against this backdrop, bolstering the the rational-legal authority of the CPV became crucial.

The 1992 Election Law was passed almost six years after the initiation of *Doi Moi*, when the superiority of market economic policies over socialist policies within the context of Vietnam was clearly evident. The final collapse of the Soviet Union in December 1991 dealt a devastating blow to the credibility of socialism as a state-building ideology. Consequently, the CPV made every effort to justify the continuation of its communist rule. These efforts were manifested in the 1992 Constitution, which signals the resurrection of Ho Chi Minh's charismatic leadership, recognizes a multi-sector commodity economy that follows market mechanisms under state management and reaffirms the determination to adhere to socialist ideology. The 1992 Election Law is but one manifestation of these efforts.

The 1992 Election Law expanded upon the framework established by its 1958 predecessor, introducing major changes that enhanced legislative elections. Before the 1992 legislative elections, sometimes the number of candidates equalled or even fell below the number of elected representatives, rendering the elections meaningless, Article 31 of the 1992 Election Law stipulates that the number of candidates must exceed the number of elected representatives. Furthermore, the 1992 Election Law allows self-nomination, whereas the 1980 Election law required candidates to be nominated by their state-approved organizations. However, the 1992 Election Law also strengthened the scrutiny role of the CPV-dominated Fatherland Front and removed any mention of "political parties" in the plural, implicitly establishing the CPV as the only legal political party within Vietnam, whereas the 1980 Election Law allowed the participation of other political parties in the election process. This change followed the dissolution of all political parties in South Vietnam after 1975 and the disbandment of the Democratic Party of Vietnam and the Socialist Party of Vietnam, two satellite parties of the CPV, in 1988. Furthermore, while the 1992 Election Law allowed for the direct dismissal of elected representatives who lost the trust of voters; the 1992 Election Law no longer permits this practice.

Other notable additions include provisions outlined in Chapter 8, which specify the process for electing additional National Assembly members to fill vacant seats, and Chapter 9, which stipulates procedures for the dismissal of National Assembly members. The 1992 Election

Law also assigned the Fatherland Front significant responsibilities in organizing legislative elections, most notably the authority to screen candidates. Additionally, actions against the election process were classified as criminal offenses under the 1992 Election Law. Overall, the law's enactment reflects the CPV's effort to tighten its control over the National Assembly while reinforcing its central role in Vietnam's political system. The changes in the 1992 Election Law made elections more meaningful as independent candidates technically had a chance to win while party-backed candidates could lose.[34] It is possible that the CPV itself did not fully anticipate the results these changes could bring and was, therefore, not adequately prepared for the 1992 legislative elections.

In some districts where not enough candidates were nominated, election councils scrambled to find candidates to meet the quota. As a result, while not officially recognized, some candidates are understood by both electoral officials and voters as token candidates, nominated merely to fulfil legal requirements. Thus, the concept of *quân xanh, quân đỏ* (lit. blue pawn, red pawn) emerged. Blue pawns are perceived to be mere placeholders, while red pawns are more or less guaranteed election. While these terms are usually used to discuss elections, they are also applied in scenarios where the selection process may be rigged, such as bidding for a contract or taking entrance exam to a university.

Centrally nominated candidates are usually perceived as red pawns because they are expected to hold leadership positions. Malesky and Schuler note that these candidates never run against each other and usually compete against weaker, locally nominated opponents. Furthermore, centrally nominated candidates are more likely to be assigned to voting district with a 5/3 candidate-to-seat ration, which would have higher chance of victory (60 per cent of winning election) than those who are assigned to 4/2 and 6/3 districts (50 per cent).[35]

Recalling elections in the 2000s, one senior CPV member remarked: "Just by looking at the list of candidates, you immediately knew who you should vote for. It was like a professional athlete competing against a child. There was no question about who would win. Nowadays, it is not that simple. Every candidate is qualified. It is hard to tell who is red and who is blue anymore."

Koh observed voting at a polling station during the 2002 National Assembly Election and found no evidence of direct interference with the voting results.[36] This rules out completely staged elections, which combined with the changes in the 1992 Election Law, have produced some surprises. Despite overwhelming support, sometimes candidates favoured by the CPV failed to secure their seats. For example, Thayer notes that in Ho Chi Minh City three incumbents and four out of six party-endorsed candidates, including Ngo Thanh Ba, a prominent lawyer, were defeated during the 1992 Election.[37] Similarly, Malesky and Schuler analysed the 2007 legislative elections and highlight that twelve centrally nominated candidates were not elected.[38]

The 1997 and 2015 Election Laws, issued almost twenty years apart, failed to introduce any radical changes like those seen in the 1992 Election Law. The 1997 Election Law primarily improved upon its predecessors in terms of the election process, addressing complaints and reports concerning candidates, and election results, as well as activities perceived as fraudulent and illegal during the elections. Whereas the 1992 Election Law simply stated that "Everyone has the right to report illegal activities during the election of National Assembly deputies" (Article 68), the 1997 Election Law entrusted the responsibility of receiving and investigating such reports and complaints to the election councils. It also set deadlines of ten days for lodging complaints and thirty days for addressing them regarding the outcomes of the elections. The election councils have the ultimate authority in matters concerning complaints (Article 35). Consultative conference is specified to have three rounds, all of which are to be administered and conducted by the Fatherland Front (Articles 30, 37 and 40). Overall, the 1997 Election Law strengthened the CPV's control over legislative elections through a multi-layered mechanism involving the Fatherland Front, the National Election Council, the local election councils and the local people's committees.

The 2015 Election Law focuses on the promotion of equality by establishing a quota that requires 30 per cent of all candidates to be female and 18 per cent to come from ethnic minority backgrounds. Additionally, voting rights are expanded to individuals in pre-trial detention, undergoing compulsory education or in mandatory rehabilitation centres, who are permitted to register as voters and vote at their respective facilities, as opposed to previous election laws.

While the constitutions acknowledge the National Assembly as the supreme representative body of the Vietnamese populace and grants it the authority to wield the utmost state power, its power and functionality is compromised by the fact that the CPV has been able to monopolize the selection and nomination of candidates and the organization of the National Assembly elections, including vote counting and press coverage. Since the first National Assembly election after the unification of Vietnam, more than 90 per cent of the membership of the National Assembly has consistently been held by CPV members. The political domination of the CPV in the National Assembly has been so well known that many Vietnamese refer to the National Assembly as an organization "nominated by the Party, voted for by the people".[39, 40] This is especially true before the introduction of the 1992 Constitution and Election Law, when legislative elections were a blatant façade.

Following the implementation of *Doi Moi*, the CPV has undertaken notable improvements to the legislative electoral process and has endeavoured to enhance the operational effectiveness of the National Assembly. Although the improvements through subsequent election laws may make legislative elections in Vietnam appear less nominal and more genuine, the extent to which these alterations and advancements are driven by genuine efforts to enhance governance or merely serve as superficial measures to project a more democratic image remains a subject of debate.

National Assembly Elections in Vietnam

The term "Election of Deputies to the National Assembly and Deputies to People's Councils" is used officially to refer to the quinquennial legislative elections in Vietnam,[41, 42] which, as the name suggests, elect not only the National Assembly, the most powerful legislative body within the borders of Vietnam,[43] but also the local people's councils.

The term of office of members of the National Assembly is five years. However, upon consideration of the recommendations of the National Assembly's Standing Committee, the National Assembly can extend or shorten its tenure by one year. Sixty days before the duration expires, a new National Assembly must be established through an election (2013 Constitution of Vietnam, Article 71).[44]

According to the Law on Election of Deputies to the National Assembly and Deputies to People's Councils of 2015,[45] the election of representatives to the National Assembly must follow the principles of universal suffrage, equality, directness and employ a secret ballot system. Any Vietnamese citizens eighteen years of age or older, except for those who are serving prison terms, under detainment or stripped of their capacities as citizens, are permitted to vote. Likewise, any Vietnamese citizen who fulfils certain conditions regulated by the Law on the Organization of the National Assembly is entitled to be nominated as candidate for the National Assembly.[46]

The overall process of legislative elections is supervised by the National Assembly's Standing Committee. This committee is responsible for mobilizing the people's committees at all levels to organize and maintain security during the elections. Additionally, the National Assembly establishes a National Election Council to directly oversee and manage the elections. The National Election Council usually consists of fifteen to twenty-one members who are appointed by the National Assembly based on the recommendation of the National Assembly's Standing Committee (2015 Election Law, Article 12). Operating on a majority rule principle, the National Election Council is tasked with establishing election committees at the local level, organizing the National Assembly election, managing propaganda and mass mobilization, ensuring security throughout the election process and upholding election laws.

One of the key organizations involved in the National Assembly election process is the Fatherland Front of Vietnam, essentially a grassroots extension of the CPV. The Fatherland Front Central Committee is responsible for directing its local committees to conduct meetings and consultations to select and nominate candidates for legislative elections and overseeing the election process, including the counting of votes (2015 Election Law, Article 3).

The date for the National Assembly election is determined and announced by the Standing Committee of the National Assembly. The election must be held on a Sunday, and the specific date must be publicized at least 115 days prior to the election (2015 Election Law, Article 5). As shown in Table 5.1, the National Congress of the CPV typically convenes between one year and a few months before each National Assembly election to set the strategic direction for the nation for the upcoming years, which is then subsequently ratified by the incoming National Assembly.

Table 5.1
National Congresses of the CPV and Elections Date, 1986–2021

National Congress of the CPV	1986/12 (VI)	1991/6 (VII)	1996/7 (VIII)	2001/4 (IX)	2006/4 (X)	2011/1 (XI)	2016/1 (XII)	2021/2 (XII)
Legislative Elections	1987/4 (VIII)	1992/7 (IX)	1997/7 (X)	2002/5 (XI)	2007/5 (XII)	2011/5 (XIII)	2016/5 (XIV)	2021/5 (XV)
Time in between (in months)	5	13	12	13	13	4	4	3

Source: Communist Party of Vietnam, "Đảng Cộng sản Việt Nam qua các kỳ đại hội" [The Communist Party of Vietnam through the congresses], 2016, https://daihoi13.dangcongsan.vn/cac-ky-dai-hoi/tu-lieu-van-kien/dang-cong-san-viet-nam-qua-cac-ky-dai-hoi-3926 (accessed 17 July 2024); National Assembly of Vietnam, "Các kỳ quốc hội trong lịch sử" [The national assemblies in history], 2021, https://quochoi.vn/pages/tim-kiem.aspx?ItemID=50998 (accessed 17 July 2024).

The National Assembly Standing Committee will allocate the number of elected representatives to each first-tier administrative unit[47] based on two conditions: each first-tier administrative unit must have least three residing representatives, and the total number of representatives elected must be calculated based on the population and the special characteristics of each unit (2015 Election Law, Article 7).[48] Each first-tier administrative unit equals one election unit for the National Assembly election. Those election units would be further divided into smaller voting districts based on their populations.

The final composition of candidates will be decided by the Standing Committee of the National Assembly and the Standing Committee of the Central Committee of the Fatherland Front at the latest 105 days before the day of election (2015 Election Law, Article 9).

The National Assembly Election Process

Consultation[49] is a process unique perhaps to Vietnamese legislative elections. This process is organized by the Fatherland Front and its central and local committees. Essentially, the purpose of consultation is to remove undesirable and unqualified candidates from nomination. The consultation process is divided into several rounds, which are carried out at both national and local levels. Figure 5.1 shows the candidate selection process for the National Assembly elections.

Figure 5.1
Candidate Selection Process

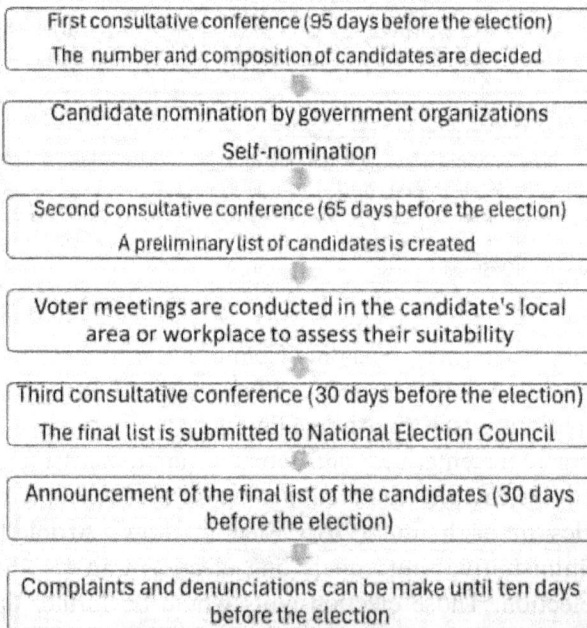

First consultative conference (95 days before the election)
The number and composition of candidates are decided

Candidate nomination by government organizations
Self-nomination

Second consultative conference (65 days before the election)
A preliminary list of candidates is created

Voter meetings are conducted in the candidate's local area or workplace to assess their suitability

Third consultative conference (30 days before the election)
The final list is submitted to National Election Council

Announcement of the final list of the candidates (30 days before the election)

Complaints and denunciations can be make until ten days before the election

The first consultative conference at the national level is regulated by law to be held by the presidium of the Fatherland Front Central Committee ninety-five days before the election day at the latest. Participants in the first consultative conference include the presidium of the Fatherland Front Central Committee, representatives from its member organizations, representatives from the National Election Council and representatives from the Standing Committee of the National Assembly. The purpose of the first consultative conference is to discuss the composition and the number of representatives from central governmental organizations to be nominated. Likewise, the first consultative conferences at the municipality and provincial levels are regulated by law to be held by the standing board of the provincial Fatherland Front Central Committee ninety-five days before the election day at the latest to discuss the composition and number of the candidate to be nominated by provincial organizations.

Depending on the outcomes of the initial consultative conferences, the Standing Committee of the National Assembly would adjust the composition, proportion and number of candidates to be nominated by central and local organizations. These adjustments must be made at least ninety days before the election day. Based on these adjustments, organizations and agencies will select and nominate individuals for the National Assembly elections.

The second consultative conferences at both central and local levels are held by the presidium of the Fatherland Front Central Committee at least sixty-five days before the election day. The participants in this consultative conference are the same as in the first consultative conference (2015 Election Law, Article 43). The purpose of this round of consultative conferences is to compose a list of prospective candidates, both nominated and independent. Opinions and comments on the candidates and nominees on this list will be gathered from voters in the candidate's residency and workplace.

The responsibility of organizing and presiding over the voters' confidence conferences in the locality where the nominee or self-nominated candidate resides is entrusted to the local standing boards of Vietnam Fatherland Front committees and the standing boards of the people's committees at the same levels. The head of the agency and the trade union executive boards of the same level convene and chair the voters' confidence conferences in designated organizations. The only exception to this rule is the voters' confidence conference in the armed forces, which is chaired by the unit's commander. The nominees or independent candidates, as well as representatives from the organizations or localities they currently reside in or work for, are invited to these conferences. Participants must be legal voters who personally know the nominees or candidates.

During the conference, the participants can either approve or disapprove of the candidates based on a list of criteria that a National Assembly member should fulfil. They can share their opinions via methods determined by the organizers such as raising their hands or casting secret ballots. The minutes of the conferences, which include information such as the number and composition of participants and detailed results, are then submitted to the corresponding standing board of the Vietnam Fatherland Front Committee. Based on these conference minutes, the Vietnam Fatherland Front Committee proceeds to prepare for the third consultative conference (2015 Election Law, Article 45).

The Election Law also regulates that should there be unresolved issues or questions related to the candidate, voters might inquire during the third consultative conference.[50] All matters pertaining to the nominee or candidate must be verified at least forty days before the election day.[51]

Thirty days before the election day at the latest, the standing boards of the Vietnam Fatherland Front Central Committee and the provincial Vietnam Fatherland Front committees must submit the minutes of the third consultative conference and the complete lists of qualified candidates nominated by the presidium of the Fatherland Front Central Committee and the provincial Fatherland Front committees, respectively, to the National Election Council. Thus concludes the consultative conferences (2015 Election Law, Article 57). Based on these lists, the National Election Council will assign candidates to suitable first-tier administrative units, typically their place of birth or their long-time place of residence. However, in cases where there are too many qualified candidates sharing the same locality, exceptions may be made. The National Election Council then sends the final lists and profiles of candidates assigned to each locality to correspondent election committees. The National Election Council must also publicize the complete list of candidates in each voting district, at the latest, twenty-five days before the election day.[52]

As late as ten days before the election date, complaints and denunciations may be made against candidates and the process of nomination (2015 Election Law, Article 61).[53] Such complaints must be submitted to the election committees or the National Election Council.[54]

The Election Law also regulates election propagation and campaigns. The National Election Council and its subordinate election committees are to be in charge of disseminating election information and propagation at their respective levels. News agencies must provide voters with coverage about meetings between candidates and voters and candidate interviews. The Provincial Fatherland Front Committee is responsible for arranging meetings between candidates and voters. The designated organizations that the candidates belong to must also, within their power, facilitate meetings and contact between candidates and voters. Campaigning activities can be carried out from the time the final lists of the candidates are published by the National Election Council, which means twenty-five days before the election day at the latest, until up to twenty-four hours before the election day. The Election Law explicitly limits campaigning activities to meetings with voters and campaigning through mass media (Article 65). Both forms of campaigning are strictly regulated by law. For example, rallies and meetings with voters must be held in cooperation with the standing board of the Fatherland Front provincial committee and the voting district's people's committee (Article 66). All of the candidates of a voting district, representatives from "certain organizations, agencies, and units" and voters are to be invited to participate in the meetings.[55] At the meetings, under the chairmanship of representatives of the Fatherland Front and the people's council, each candidate is to take turns presenting their future plans as a member of the National Assembly. Voters are then allowed to ask questions and exchange opinions with their prospective representatives. The standing board of the Fatherland Front provincial committee is responsible for writing meeting minutes and sending them to the National Election Council and the Standing Board of the Vietnam Fatherland Front Central Committee.

The candidates have limited opportunities to campaign through mass media. They are permitted to discuss their plans and be interviewed by local media and reporters working for the official website of the National Election Council. However, all mass media content regarding the candidates and the election must be approved by the National Election Council. The responsibility for local media coverage lies with the provincial people's committees (Article 67, 2015 Election Law). Nevertheless, Article 68 of the same law prohibits candidates from using their privileges and positions to gain access to mass media during their campaign. It is also forbidden for them to disseminate illegal propaganda which criticizes or insults organizations and individuals in the form of election campaigning. Since the campaign period only lasts for twenty-five days and all campaign activities must be directed and observed by the National Election Council, candidates are not expected to form a campaign staff or engage in fundraising. As specified in Article 62 of the 2015 Election Law, the expenses related to campaign propaganda are covered by the state budget.

From the enactment of the 1992 Election Law, any Vietnamese citizen twenty-one years of age or older, with a few exceptions regulated by the law, can stand for election. Candidates can be either nominated by their organizations at the central or local level,[56] or self-nominate. The right to self-nominate was allowed in the 1946 North Vietnamese National Assembly Election. Before the 1946 Election, Ho Chi Minh said about self-nomination:

> The election is an opportunity for the Vietnamese people as a whole to elect competent and virtuous representatives to carry the State's burdens. In this election, everyone who wants to participate in the State's affairs can stand for election, every citizen can vote …[57]

Article 18 of the 1946 Constitution of the Democratic Republic of Vietnam only mentions three conditions for self-nomination: must be over twenty-one years of age at the time of election; must not be suffering from mental disorders or had lost civil rights; and must also be capable of writing and reading *Quốc Ngữ*.[58]

Article 24 of the 1959 Law on Election of Deputies to the National Assembly of the Democratic Republic of Vietnam also reaffirmed that "an individual can also self-nominate for election". Nevertheless, even for self-nominated candidates, the recommendation of a state-approved organization is required (Article 33). As such, candidates without CPV backing stand no chance of being selected for election.

According to Article 22 of the 2014 Law on the Organization of the National Assembly, candidates must meet several requirements beyond the basic age qualification.[59] The candidates must submit their resumes to the electoral committee of the corresponding level. In other words, candidates nominated by national-level organizations submit their resumes directly to the National Election Council, while candidates nominated by local organizations submit theirs to the corresponding election committees. All resumes are then sent to the National Election Council for scrutiny. Qualified resumes are then sent to the Standing Board of Vietnam Fatherland Front Central Committee and to provincial standing committees of the Fatherland Front for consultation (2015 Election Law, Articles 36 and 37).

The Election Law provides only a vague definition of the types of organizations permitted to nominate candidates. In practice, non-governmental and non-partisan organizations are not given the privilege of nominating their members. The list of organizations authorized to nominate their members for the 2016 National Assembly of Vietnam was made public through Decision 1140/2016/UBTVQH. Out of the 500 members of the Fourteenth National Assembly, 198 were required to be nominated by central level organizations. The specific proportion and composition of those candidates are detailed in Table 5.2.

The remaining candidates are selected by corresponding organizations at the provincial level. Both at the central and provincial levels, the leadership of the designated organizations would hold consultative conferences to gather opinions and choose one or more of their members for nomination.

Most of these nominating organizations are directly or indirectly under the control of the CPV, with leadership positions exclusively

Table 5.2
Fourteenth National Assembly's Candidate Central Nomination

	Organization	Number of Candidates
1	Organizations under the CPV	11
2	Organizations under National Assembly	114
3	Organizations under the State President	3
4	Central government	18
5	Ministry of National Defense	15
6	Ministry of Public Security	3
7	Supreme People's Court	1
8	Supreme People's Procuracy	1
9	State Audit Office	1
10	Fatherland Front and its member organizations	31
	Total	198

Source: *VnExpress*, "Dự kiến gần 200 đại biểu Quốc hội ở Trung ương" [Nearly 200 national assembly deputies expected from the central government], 2 February 2016, https://vnexpress.net/du-kien-gan-200-dai-bieu-quoc-hoi-o-trung-uong-3351823.html (accessed 17 July 2024).

held by senior party members. As it is common for organizations to nominate their leaders as candidates, most, if not all, nominees end up being senior party members.

The practice of promoting party members to managerial positions is an unwritten law based on Article 4 of the 2013 Constitution of Vietnam. Article 4 of the Constitution of Vietnam has been interpreted that CPV members must always hold managerial positions in the organizations that have been loosely and collectively defined as being under the direct control of the government or as government-related.[60] Although the Law on Cadres and Civil Servants does not explicitly state that to hold managerial positions one must possess CPV membership, it does confirm the importance of such membership several times. For example, Article 5 clearly states that the principles of cadres and civil servant management must "ensure the leadership of the CPV and the management of the government" and that civil servants and cadres must "remain loyal to the CPV and the Socialist Republic of Vietnam" as well as "strictly observe the Party's directions and policies and the State's laws" (Law on Cadres and Civil Servants, Article 8). Likewise, Article 1 of the 2008 revision of Law on Military Officers of the PAV, while not explicitly stating that military officers must join the ranks of the CPV, repeatedly stresses that "military officers of the PAV are cadres of the CPV and the Socialist Republic of Vietnam" and that military officers must be "absolutely loyal to Fatherland and the people, the CPV, and the Socialist Republic of Vietnam" (Article 8). In Article 3 of the same law, military officers are put under the "absolute and direct command of the CPV", tasked with the duty to be "always ready to fight and to sacrifice to protect the independence, sovereignty, territorial integrity of the Fatherland, and to protect the CPV and the Socialist Republic of Vietnam".

Likewise, Article 5 of the Law on Vietnam People's Public Security Forces explicitly states that the police apparatus is "placed under the direct and comprehensive leadership of the CPV";[61] however, police officers are not explicitly required to be Party members. The author of this book has interviewed three military and police officers about this practice and all three confirmed that membership of the CPV is indeed necessary to become a full-fledged military or police officer. The two junior military officers said that they obtained Party membership prior to graduating from the Military Technical Academy and further added that it is one of the requirements for graduation. The senior police officer, who held the rank of major general prior to his retirement, became a member of the CPV during the Vietnam War while he was fighting as a guerrilla. He said that during war time, Party membership and military ranks were not always linked. However, he confirmed that in the current Vietnam People's Public Security Forces, obtaining CPV membership is an absolute necessity for one to become a police officer. According to Decree No. 73/2009/ND-CP on Commune Police, the requirements to become a commune-level police officer are relaxed, as Party membership is not required, and in certain cases, only a primary education degree is necessary. However, Party membership is mandatory to serve as the Commune Police Chief.

Junior civil servants are not absolutely required to obtain Party membership. However, as they gain seniority, they are encouraged to take a political training class and to become a Party member. At a certain point, promotion is virtually impossible without Party membership. To be promoted to even a deputy head of department position in any government agency, the cadre would need to attend advanced politics courses. Interviews with senior civil servants who are working for or previously worked for the government also confirmed this narrative. Civil servants who were interviewed confirmed that, although there have been a few exceptions, promising young civil servants are usually given the chance to take politics classes and join the CPV before being promoted. Their promotion is likely to be postponed or even called off should they refuse to do so. One of the respondents raised the example of Professor Nguyen Lan Hieu, who, despite not being a member of the CPV, rose to the position of vice-director of Hanoi Medical University Hospital, one of the most prestigious state hospitals in Vietnam, and was elected to the National Assembly in the 2016 election. However, she further commented that without obtaining party membership, Professor Hieu is extremely unlikely to progress any further in the political system of the country. Hieu himself confirms that becoming a member of the Party is the only way for him to break through in his political career and that "people who have a stable job only enrol in politics courses for promotion".[62]

The fact that only party members can rise to the highest ranks of organizations capable of fielding candidates and the universal practice of only nominating the heads of these organizations results in a reality where virtually all candidates nominated by designated organizations are party members. Figure 5.2 illustrates the complete dominance of the CPV in the membership of the National Assembly of Vietnam. Interestingly, the two National Assemblies with the highest non-CPV membership are the Sixth National Assembly (1976–81) and the Tenth National Assembly (1997–2002). Afterward, the percentage of non-CPV members in the National Assembly gradually decreased. This can be explained by the fact that the Sixth National Assembly was elected

Figure 5.2
National Assembly Membership, 1976–2026

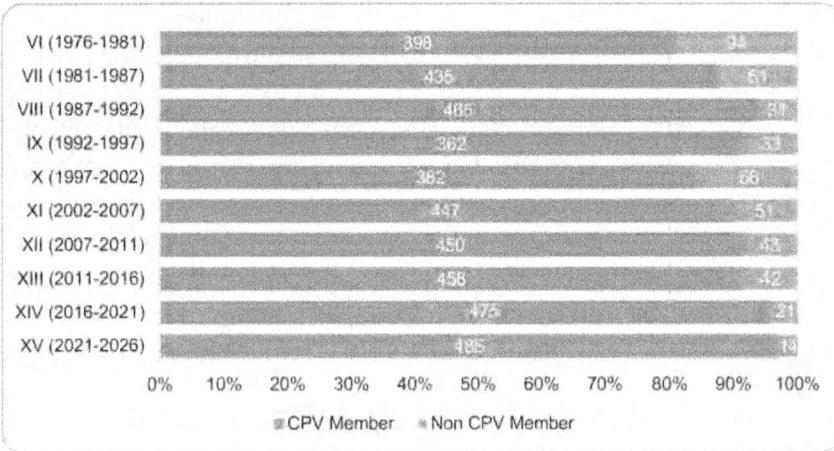

Assembly	CPV Member	Non CPV Member
VI (1976-1981)	398	94
VII (1981-1987)	435	61
VIII (1987-1992)	465	31
IX (1992-1997)	362	33
X (1997-2002)	382	66
XI (2002-2007)	447	51
XII (2007-2011)	450	43
XIII (2011-2016)	458	42
XIV (2016-2021)	475	21
XV (2021-2026)	485	14

Source: National Assembly of Vietnam, "Tư liệu bầu cử Đại biểu Quốc hội các khóa" [Election materials for national assembly deputies], 2022, https://quochoi.vn/tulieuquochoi/tulieu/baucuquochoi/Pages/bau-cu-quoc-hoi.aspx?ItemID=23986 (accessed 17 July 2024).

one year after the unification of the country, including individuals who fought for the National Liberation Front (Viet Cong) but did not hold official CPV membership. At that time, the CPV was not the only legal political party, and seats in the National Assembly were also shared by its satellite parties. The Tenth National Assembly was elected five years after the introduction of the 1992 Election Law, which brought about several more liberal changes. While those changes were not effectively utilized immediately after their introduction in the 1992 National Assembly Election, they were more successfully used by non-CPV candidates during the 1997 National Assembly Election. Perhaps this is one of the reasons that led to stricter scrutiny of candidates and the subsequent improved roles of the Fatherland Front during legislative elections.

The only viable way for non-party members to stand for election is through self-nomination. The multilevel consultative conferences are usually criticized for only serving as a tool for the CPV to remove undesirable candidates from the election process.[63] State-controlled media reported that in the 2016 National Assembly Election, there were 162 self-nominated candidates who sent applications to the National Election Council and local election committees; 154 of these were valid.[64] However, after the third consultative conference, only eleven were shortlisted to officially stand for election. In Hanoi, where almost a third of the self-nominated individuals came from, 95 per cent were disqualified.[65] Disqualified candidates report that they were put under unfair conditions and were disqualified for allegedly being politically or morally questionable. Sometimes, their supporters were barred from entering the venue of the consultative conference while the candidates were put under heavy criticism from strangers and were not allowed to defend themselves.[66] Of the eleven independent candidates who passed the third consultative conference, six were not members of the CPV. However, only two independent candidates were successfully elected to the National Assembly, and both were members of the CPV according to Decree No. 270/NQ-HĐBCQG.

The nomination, consultation and propaganda processes leading up to the election solidify the political monopoly of the CPV during legislative elections, allowing them to exert significant influence over the outcomes without resorting to vote rigging. While the National Assembly theoretically maintains independence from direct external political interference, in practice, its membership has consistently been dominated by the CPV. The only legal avenue to challenge the CPV's dominance is through constitutional and election-related law revisions, a task that falls primarily on the National Assembly. Consequently, any significant constitutional or legal changes that could undermine the CPV's political dominance are highly unlikely. This cycle ensures the CPV's unchallenged monopoly of power.

Nevertheless, there have been notable inconsistencies between official government reports and observable reality. One such discrepancy is the consistent extremely high voter turnout. Since the first election after reunification in 1976, voter turnout has consistently exceeded 98 per cent, as illustrated in Figure 5.3. Such a voter turnout is simply implausible even without taking into consideration the transportation and socio-political conditions in Vietnam following the war. Even

Figure 5.3
National Assembly Elections' Voter Turnouts, 1972–2021

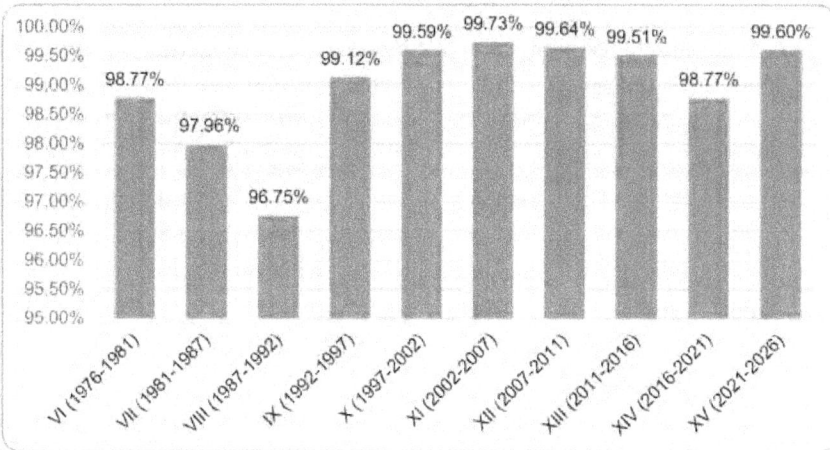

Source: National Assembly of Vietnam, "Các kỳ quốc hội trong lịch sử" [The national assemblies in history], 2021, https://quochoi.vn/pages/tim-kiem.aspx?ItemID=50998 (accessed 17 July 2024).

today, accessing certain remote areas can be extremely difficult, particularly under specific conditions—such as reaching isolated villages in Vietnam's Central Highlands during the rainy season—making the organization of elections in these regions even more challenging.

Furthermore, voters who resided outside of Vietnam are not accounted for. Vietnamese citizens living overseas are not included in the list of people who are not able to vote according to the 2015 Election Law and as such they should be eligible to vote. However, the author of this book had directly contacted the Embassy of the Socialist Republic of Vietnam in Tokyo to inquire about voting and was told that voting was not possible in Tokyo. Official sources confirmed that Vietnamese citizens residing overseas must return to Vietnam to vote.[67] No official source has confirmed or denied whether Vietnamese expatriates are included in the officially reported voter turnout. However, if we consider the eligible voters living overseas who are unable to vote, the extremely high voter turnout reported by the authorities becomes highly questionable, if not outright impossible.

Observation and Press Coverage of the National Assembly Elections

As a Vietnamese citizen, the author of this book was eligible to participate in legislative elections as a voter on four occasions: the 2007, 2011, 2016 and 2021 elections. In the 2007 election, the author voted in person after reaching the age of eighteen that same year. However, in the 2011 election, the author did not personally participate or go to the polling location. Instead, a family member cast the author's vote on his behalf, which was registered as a legal vote. Similarly, in the 2016 election the author was unable to vote in person. Again, a family member cast the author's vote for an unknown candidate, and it was registered as a legal vote.

To observe the voting process, including the atmosphere, security measures, voters and ballots, among other details, the author sent a collaborator with a camera to record the proceedings. However, recording the election was explicitly prohibited, even from a distance. After a few minutes of recording, the assistant was approached by security officials who asked them to delete the footage. The plainclothes security guards explained that video recording within the polling location premises goes against the principles established to prevent interference from reactionary individuals. It should be noted that the 2015 Election Law does not explicitly forbid taking pictures or recording videos at the polling location. State-owned media outlets have widely used pictures of Politburo members, the elderly and individuals from ethnic minorities casting their votes for propaganda purposes.

During the 2021 legislative elections, again, the author's vote was cast by a family member and registered as legal. Attempts to take pictures of the voting process, however, were allowed perhaps because the collaborator this time is one of the organizers of the election. Pamphlets, unused votes and candidate lists were also collected and are used to illustrate the voting procedure. Figure 5.4 shows a voter voting during the 2021 legislative elections.

In Vietnam, taking pictures and recording videos in public places is a grey zone. The only legal document that regulates the locations where people can take pictures, record videos and create paintings is

Figure 5.4
A Voter Voting in the 2021 Legislative Election

The three voting boxes are for the National Assembly, Hanoi's People's Council and Cau Giay District's People's Council. Ho Chi Minh's bust can be seen in the background.

Source: the author.

Circular No. 552/CA-VH 1964 issued jointly by the Ministry of Public Security and the then Ministry of Culture of Vietnam. In principle, both Vietnamese citizens and foreigners are generally permitted to photograph, film and sketch landscapes across the country. However, permission from the head of the establishment or the responsible person must be obtained before engaging in these activities within private or state-owned premises. It is strictly prohibited to take pictures, record videos or create paintings within or of military installations, national defence-related buildings and major transportation hubs like train stations, airports and seaports, as well as science and technology facilities and power plants.

Although both Circular No. 552/CA-VH 1964 and the 2015 Election Law do not explicitly forbid taking photos at polling places, Circular No. 552/CA-VH 1964 stipulates that permission is needed to take photos or record videos within the vicinity of state-owned establishments. Attempts to capture images of the elections with digital handheld devices such as cameras or smartphones may meet with hostility from the security apparatus. Furthermore, although attempts to take photos of police officers controlling demonstrations are not explicitly prohibited by law; such actions sometimes meet with hostility from the police. Elections and demonstrations are considered sensitive events in Vietnam and making graphic records are rarely approved by the authorities.

Official media outlets consistently report that the elections are completely legitimate and that no electoral fraud takes place.[68, 69] There have been no reports of illegal votes, even though the number of voters is estimated by these sources to be more than sixty-nine million. By law, voters must cast votes themselves (2015 Election Law, Article 69) and must not disclose the content of their votes to others, including family members or members of the election committee. However, it is a common practice in Vietnam for a representative to vote for the entire family and most of the time these votes are registered as legal by the election committee. Furthermore, blank votes, donkey votes and protest votes are common due to voter apathy and dissatisfaction. However, this phenomenon went completely unreported by domestic media outlets.

The author conducted interviews with two journalists employed by domestic news agencies, and both confirmed that news coverage of elections is tightly controlled by the Central Propaganda Department of the CPV. For events considered crucial for the CPV's legitimacy, such as National Assembly elections, the Central Propaganda Department goes beyond censorship and even dictates the content that journalists should write. According to the journalists, their supervisors at the news agencies hold weekly meetings to relay instructions that purportedly come from the Central Propaganda Department.

When asked about the possibility of election fraud in National Assembly elections, the responses varied. Except for a senior police officer who had previously been responsible for maintaining order and security at polling places, and one journalist who was directed to a specific polling place to gather data, and a retired governmental official who helped with organizing the 2016 and 2021 elections, most interviewees had limited experience with organizing legislative elections. Most interviewees admitted that it was challenging to draw a clear conclusion about possible fraudulent practices during beyond what was previously presented. However, they acknowledged that direct election rigging might be a last resort to ensure the successful election of individuals holding important positions, such as members of the Politburo. Many voters reported being advised by organizers to vote for specific candidates prior to the election, perhaps to ensure such measures are not resorted to. Figure 5.5 shows a valid election ballot of the 2021 National Assembly Election.

Figure 5.5
An Election Ballot of the 2021 National Assembly Election

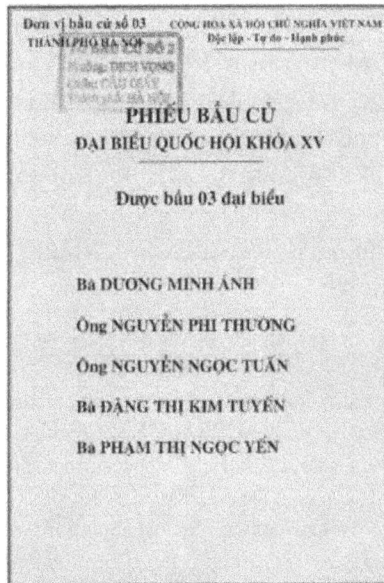

Voters were expected to select three candidates at the maximum. The names of the candidates are sorted by alphabetical order. Voters are allowed to choose three representatives at the maximum among five candidates. Candidates are listed by the alphabetical order of their given name. Vietnamese almost never refer to each other using surnames, no matter how formal the situation is.

Source: the author.

Vote counting during elections is managed by election organizing groups. These groups are established according to Article 25 of the 2015 Law on Elections. It stipulates that no later than fifty days before the election, the local people's council, with approval from the standing committee of the local government and the standing committee of the corresponding level of the Fatherland Front's committee, must set up an election organizing group for each voting district. These groups are responsible for overseeing the National Assembly elections and the election of the people's council at that level. Each election organizing group comprises eleven to twenty-one members, including a leader, a secretary and other members. These members must represent government organizations, sociopolitical organizations, social organizations and local voter representatives.

Other than that, Vietnam's Law on Elections does not go deeper into detail of the member selection process for election organizing groups. Most of the members of the election organizing group that oversaw the author's voting district in the 2016 and the 2021 elections were CPV members. As people's councils, standing committees of local governments and local committees of the Fatherland Front are all dominated by CPV members, it is logical to guess that most, if not all the election organizing groups are also dominated by CPV members. Vote counting is regulated by Article 73 of the 2015 Law on Elections as follows:

> Vote counting must be carried out at the voting location immediately after voting is over.
> Before opening the ballot box, the election organizing group must count and create documents to confirm the number of unused votes. They must also invite two voters who are not candidates to observe the vote counting process.
> Candidates, representatives of the organizations who nominated the candidates or their agents can observe the vote counting process and make claims if needed. News reporters are also permitted to observe the vote counting process.

Domestic news agencies reported that there were no frauds and claims of fraudulent practices during the 2016 and 2021 National Assembly elections. Nevertheless, most people who can observe the vote counting process are predetermined by the CPV-dominated local people's committees and Fatherland Front. Furthermore, although it is unclear if foreign reporters are permitted to observe the voting counting process or not, reporters present at the author's local polling place were from state-controlled news. Due to the restriction to the observers of the vote counting process, there has been rarely concrete proof of frauds that leaked outside.

Result of the 2016 and 2021 National Assembly Elections of Vietnam

Table 5.3 provides a side-by-side comparison of the 2016 and 2021 elections. The 2016 legislative elections of Vietnam were held on Sunday, 22 May 2016. According to official statistics, of the 67,485,482 legal voters nationwide, 67,049,091 participated in the election[70] to choose at maximum 500 congresspersons from 870 candidates approved by the Fatherland Front after three consultative conferences.[71, 72] Of the 870 candidates, 197 were registered by the central government, 673 were registered by local governments, among those only 11 were self-nominated.[73] It should be noted that after the second consultative conference, of the remaining 1,146 candidates, as many as 154 were self-nominated and 97 candidates were not members of the CPV. This means only seven per cent of the self-nominated candidates passed the third consultative conference. Counting the 66,284,625 valid votes, 496 representatives were finally elected. The election saw a significant change in the membership of the National Assembly, as 317 of the 496 seats were won by first-time assembly members. Of the successful candidates, 71 were under 40 years of age, 133 were women and 86 were ethnic minorities. Among these newly elected congresspersons, only 21 were non-communists. Only two self-nominated candidates were elected, and both were members of the CPV.[74] Explaining the gap in the numbers of independents passing the second and third consultative conferences, Chief of Office of the National Electoral Committee Nguyen Hanh Phuc commented that it was a "normal thing" as "finalists must meet certain criteria".[75] Overall, despite a new wave of representatives being voted in, the result of the election was expected as every single seat in the National Assembly was won

Table 5.3
Result of the 2016 and 2021 National Assembly Elections of Vietnam

	2016	2021	Notes
Total Legal Voters	67,485,482	69,523,133	Overseas Vietnamese voters are accounted for.
Voters Participated in the election (Voter turnout)	67,049,091 (99.35%)	69,243,604 (99.60%)	Numbers reported by official sources differ slightly.*
Total Final Candidates (Candidates for each seat)	870 (1.75)	866 (1.74)	
Candidates (Central Government)	197	203	Includes both nominated and self-nominated candidates
Candidates (Local Governments)	673	663	
Candidates after Second Consultative Conference	1,146	1,161	Most self-nominated candidates were disqualified after the Third Consultative Conference
Self-nominated Candidates after Second Consultative Conference	154	77	
Final Self-nominated Candidates	11	9	
Valid Votes (Percentage of Total Votes)	66,284,625 (98.85%)	68,650,890 (99.14%)	
Representatives Elected	496	499	
First-time Assembly Members	317	296	
Successful Candidates under 40	71	47	
Successful Female Candidates (Percentage of Elected Candidates)	133 (26.8%)	151 (31%)	In principle, at least 30 per cent of the nominated candidates must be female, and at least 18 per cent must be from ethnic minorities
Successful Ethnic Minority Candidates (Percentage of Elected Candidates)	86 (17.33%)	89 (17.83%)	
Non-CPV Elected	21	14	No self-nominated
Self-nominated Elected	2	4	All Members of CPV

* For example, although both pages belong to the official National Assembly's website, this page https://quochoi.vn/pages/tim-kiem.aspx?ItemID=50998 reports a 98.77 per cent voter turnout for the 2016 National Assembly Election, while this page https://quochoi.vn/tintuc/pages/tin-hoat-dong-cua-quoc-hoi.aspx?ItemID=31471 reports a 99.35 per cent voter turnout for the same election.

Source: See in-text description.

either by a CPV member or by an individual nominated by the pro-communist Fatherland Front.

The 2021 legislative election of Vietnam was held on Sunday, 23 May 2021. According to official statistics, of the 69,523,133 legal voters, 69,243,604 participated in the election to choose at maximum 500 congresspersons from 870 candidates approved by the Fatherland Front after three consultative conferences. Of the 866 candidates, 203 were registered by the central government, 663 were registered by local governments and only nine were self-nominated.[76] 68,650,890 votes were registered as valid.[77] A total of 499 representatives were elected. Of the successful candidates, 47 were under 40 years of age, 151 were women and 89 were ethnic minorities. Furthermore, 296 were elected for the first time. Only one did not have a college degree. Among these newly elected congresspersons, only 14 were non-communists.[78] Only four self-nominated candidates were elected, and all were members of the CPV.[79] Same with the 2021 National Assembly Election, the result of the election was expected as every single seat in the National Assembly was won either by a CPV member or by an individual nominated by the Fatherland Front.[80] Figure 5.6 shows voters lining up waiting to vote and Figure 5.7 shows a polling place in Hanoi during the 2021 National Assembly Election.

Figure 5.6
Voters at the 2021 Legislative Election Venue

Source: the author.

Figure 5.7
A Polling Place in Hanoi

Source: the author.

Recent Changes in the Elections and the Functionality of the National Assembly of Vietnam

Criticism of the National Assembly often focuses on the fact that the domination of the CPV would mean that the assembly would be more representative of the interests of the CPV rather than the interests of the Vietnamese people.[81]

The National Assembly members were criticized by Radio Free Asia for being heavily influenced by the CPV and failing to represent the voters' will or protect the nation's interests. Instead, they primarily serve to legitimize the CPV's policies, often voting in line with the party's directives rather than expressing their own views.[82] The BBC supports this view citing an independent candidate who was disqualified from the election:

> It seems that the policies are not decided based on the will of the people and the National Assembly as a whole. Rather, the decrees and directions of the CPV are the most important factor. Discussions (about law making) are just internal debates within the Party.[83]

Domestic media under the control of the CPV offers more moderate criticisms that mostly focus on the National Assembly's ineffective control and monitoring functions over other state organizations. The official mouthpiece of the PAV also acknowledges that there has been widespread criticism of the National Assembly's incompetence. Allegations include claims that, according to unwritten customs, CPV representatives provide instructions to elected delegates before National Assembly meetings. Additionaly, while only three or four per cent of the Vietnamese population are CPV members, they account for over 90 per cent of the National Assembly's membership. However, they dismiss these criticisms as "groundless accusations" and maintain that:

> The mechanism of "the Party leads, the government controls, and the people are the true owners (of the nation)" is distorted and misinterpreted into some kind of tasteless political satire: "the Party points the way, the National Assembly members raise their hands in support, the people have no choice but to...clap their hands".[84]

Nevertheless, they acknowledges that if left unattended, these criticisms could undermine the democratic legitimacy of the regime that the National Assembly represents. The CPV has been putting significant efforts into promoting the role of the National Assembly in Vietnam's politics and using its propaganda to reflect these efforts. Changes have been seen in four areas of the National Assembly's functionality, namely the vote of confidence for top leaders, law-making functionality, debate sessions, and communications between the National Assembly and the media.

Vote of Confidence

The vote of confidence is a relatively new practice in the National Assembly. It was first implemented during the fifth session of the Thirteenth National Assembly of Vietnam on 20 May 2013, when forty-nine top leaders from the government, the National Assembly, and the CPV were evaluated. According to Decree 35/2012/QH13, which the National Assembly adopted on 21 November 2012, the vote of confidence is the vote to:

> Survey the confidence towards people who are elected or appointed by the National Assembly or the people's committees. The results of the vote

of confidence can be used as the basis for the evaluation, promotion, and assignment of officials within a regulatory agency.

The second vote of confidence took place on 15 November 2014, in accordance with Decree 35/2012/QH13, which mandates an annual vote of confidence. However, no vote of confidence was conducted between 2015 and 2017. The third vote of confidence occurred in October 2018, followed by the fourth in October 2023, five years later. Although no official explanation was provided for the gap between votes of confidence, Decree 96-QĐ/TW issued by the Politburo in February 2023 changed the frequency of votes of confidence from annual to quinquennial, and that votes of confidence are to be conducted during the third year of the National Assembly's tenure.

According to Article 1 of Decree 35/2012/QH13, the vote of confidence is held to evaluate the top leadership of the State, the National Assembly, the Government, the Courts and the State Audit Office, which are categorized into four blocs. Except for the Presidency Bloc, these represent the legislative, executive and judicial branches of the State's powers, respectively. Votes of confidence employ a secret ballot with three response options: high confidence, confidence and low confidence. The results of the 2013, 2014, 2018 and 2023 votes of confidence are presented in Figures 5.8–5.11. Typically, the media employ a descriptive approach to reporting the votes; for example, a minister received 100 high confidence votes, 200 confidence votes and 30 low confidence votes. However, in this book, a different system of evaluating scores is used: a high confidence vote is counted as two points, a confidence vote as one point and a low confidence vote yields zero points. The total points are then divided by the total number of voters, with two being the highest possible confidence score and zero the lowest. With this scoring system, officials' performance can be directly compared.

Table 5.4 compares the scores from the four votes of confidence. There has been a progressive increase in average confidence scores over time. In 2013, the mean score was recorded at 1.33, ascending to 1.64 by 2023. Among the four assessed blocs, the Presidency Bloc has consistently received the highest evaluations, with the National Assembly Bloc following. In contrast, the Government Bloc has consistently garnered the lowest scores.

Figure 5.8
Results of the 2013 Vote of Confidence

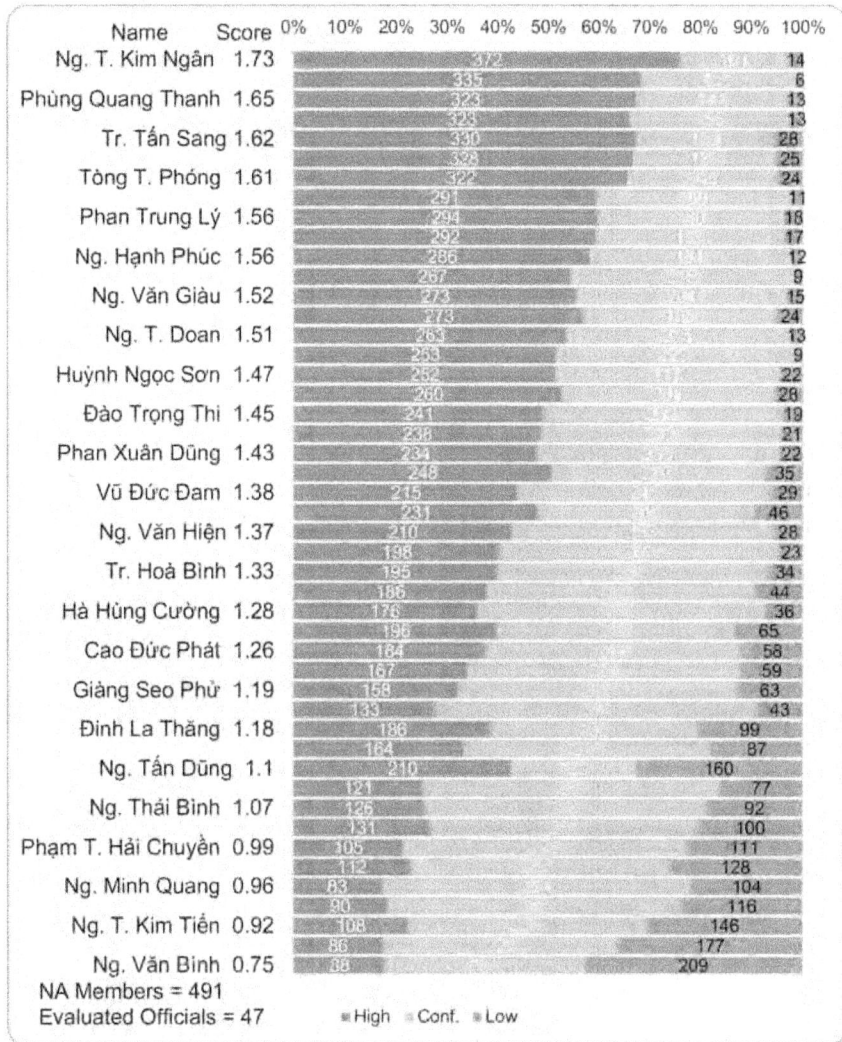

Name	Score
Ng. T. Kim Ngân	1.73
Phùng Quang Thanh	1.65
Tr. Tấn Sang	1.62
Tòng T. Phóng	1.61
Phan Trung Lý	1.56
Ng. Hạnh Phúc	1.56
Ng. Văn Giàu	1.52
Ng. T. Doan	1.51
Huỳnh Ngọc Sơn	1.47
Đào Trọng Thi	1.45
Phan Xuân Dũng	1.43
Vũ Đức Đam	1.38
Ng. Văn Hiện	1.37
Tr. Hoà Bình	1.33
Hà Hùng Cường	1.28
Cao Đức Phát	1.26
Giàng Seo Phử	1.19
Đinh La Thăng	1.18
Ng. Tấn Dũng	1.1
Ng. Thái Bình	1.07
Phạm T. Hải Chuyền	0.99
Ng. Minh Quang	0.96
Ng. T. Kim Tiến	0.92
Ng. Văn Bình	0.75

NA Members = 491
Evaluated Officials = 47

■ High   Conf.   ■ Low

Source: Thirteenth National Assembly of Vietnam, "Nghị quyết 44/2013/QH13 về kết quả lấy phiếu tín nhiệm đối với người giữ chức vụ" [Resolution 44/2013/QH13 on the results of confidence votes for office holders], 11 June 2013, https://thuvienphapluat.vn/van-ban/Bo-may-hanh-chinh/Nghi-quyet-44-2013-QH13-ket-qua-lay-phieu-tin-nhiem-doi-voi-nguoi-giu-chuc-vu-197573.aspx (accessed 17 July 2024).

Figure 5.9
Result of the 2014 Vote of Confidence

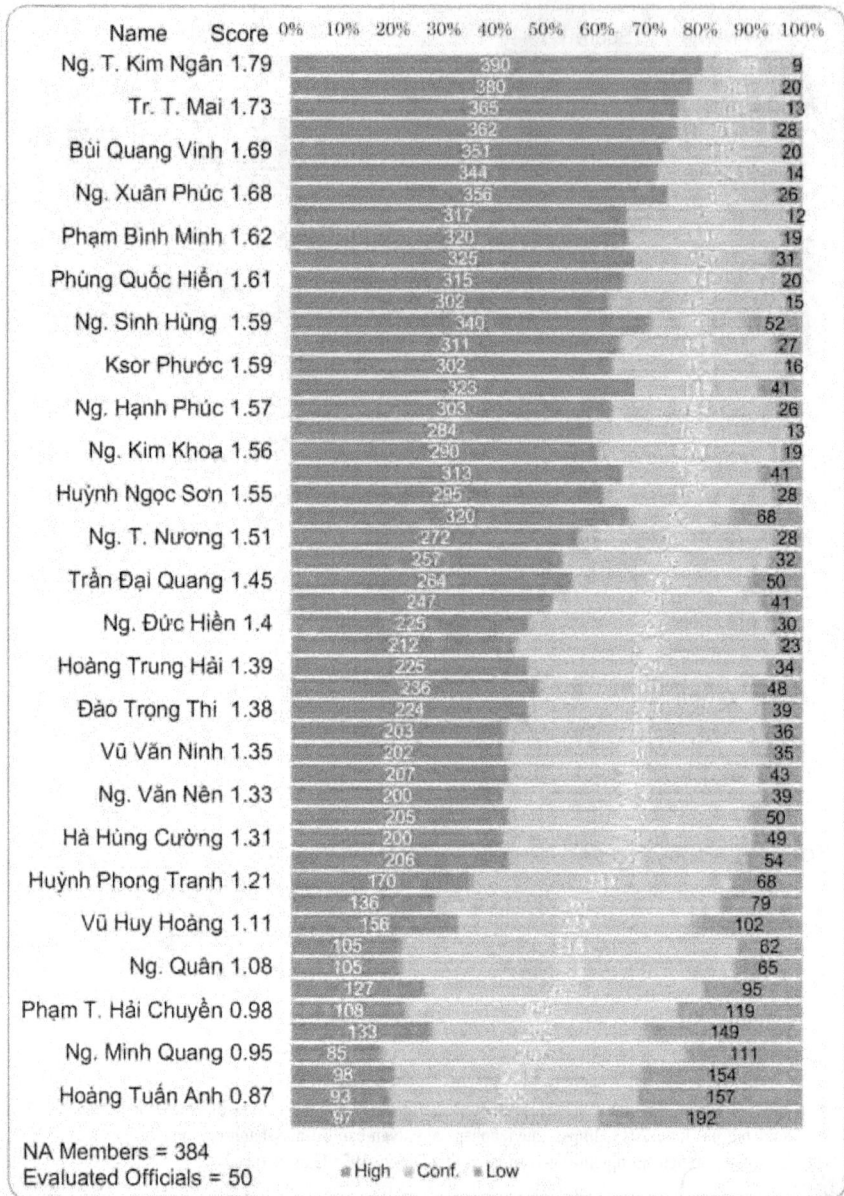

Name	Score	High	Low
Ng. T. Kim Ngân	1.79	390	9
		380	20
Tr. T. Mai	1.73	365	13
		362	28
Bùi Quang Vinh	1.69	351	20
		344	14
Ng. Xuân Phúc	1.68	356	26
		317	12
Phạm Bình Minh	1.62	320	19
		325	31
Phùng Quốc Hiển	1.61	315	20
		302	15
Ng. Sinh Hùng	1.59	349	52
		311	27
Ksor Phước	1.59	302	16
		323	41
Ng. Hạnh Phúc	1.57	303	26
		284	13
Ng. Kim Khoa	1.56	290	19
		313	41
Huỳnh Ngọc Sơn	1.55	295	28
		320	68
Ng. T. Nương	1.51	272	28
		257	32
Trần Đại Quang	1.45	264	50
		247	41
Ng. Đức Hiền	1.4	225	30
		212	23
Hoàng Trung Hải	1.39	225	34
		236	48
Đào Trọng Thi	1.38	224	39
		203	36
Vũ Văn Ninh	1.35	202	35
		207	43
Ng. Văn Nên	1.33	200	39
		205	50
Hà Hùng Cường	1.31	200	49
		206	54
Huỳnh Phong Tranh	1.21	170	68
		136	79
Vũ Huy Hoàng	1.11	156	102
		105	82
Ng. Quân	1.08	105	65
		127	95
Phạm T. Hải Chuyền	0.98	108	119
		133	149
Ng. Minh Quang	0.95	85	111
		98	154
Hoàng Tuấn Anh	0.87	93	157
		97	192

NA Members = 384
Evaluated Officials = 50   ▪ High   ▪ Conf.   ▪ Low

Source: Vietnam Government Portal, "Quốc hội công bố kết quả lấy phiếu tín nhiệm" [National Assembly announces results of confidence votes], 15 November 2014, https://baochinhphu.vn/quoc-hoi-cong-bo-ket-qua-lay-phieu-tin-nhiem-102174169.htm (accessed 17 July 2024).

Figure 5.10
Result of the 2018 Vote of Confidence

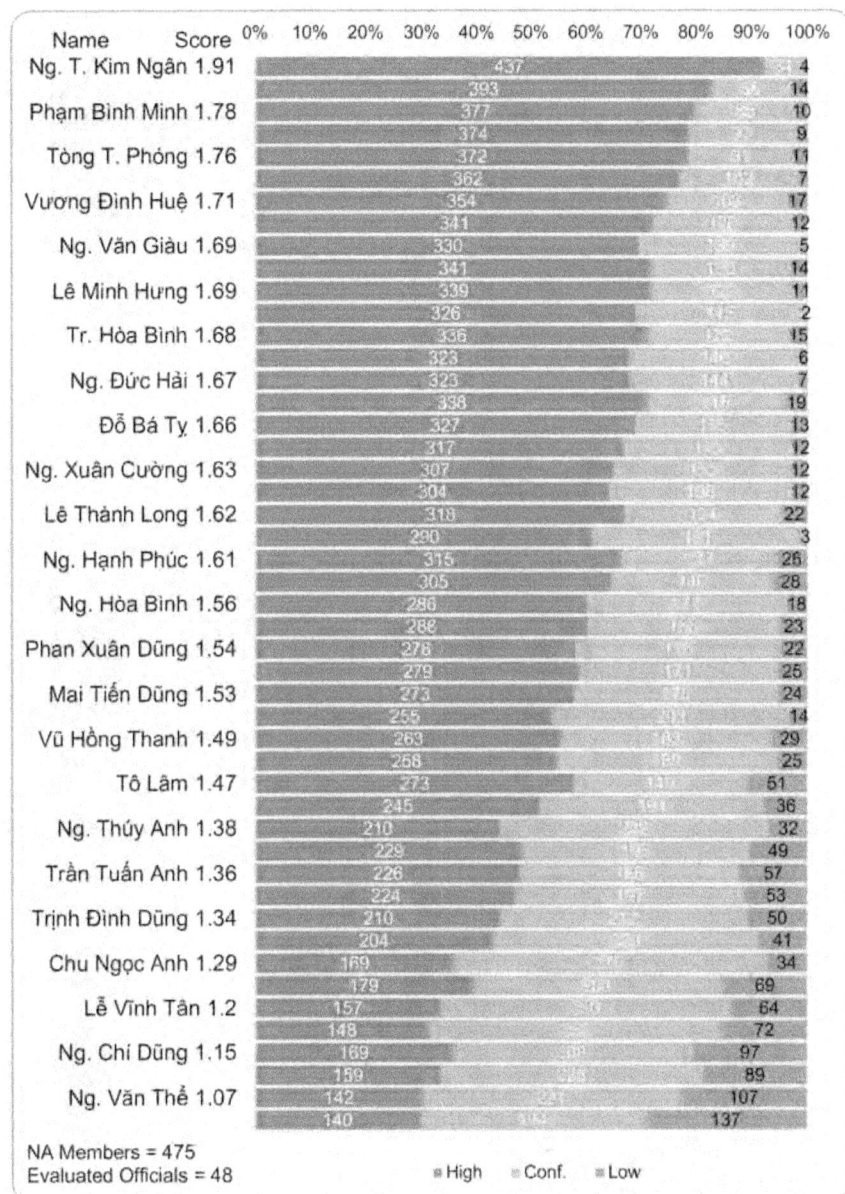

Name	Score
Ng. T. Kim Ngân	1.91
Phạm Bình Minh	1.78
Tòng T. Phóng	1.76
Vương Đình Huệ	1.71
Ng. Văn Giàu	1.69
Lê Minh Hưng	1.69
Tr. Hòa Bình	1.68
Ng. Đức Hải	1.67
Đỗ Bá Tỵ	1.66
Ng. Xuân Cường	1.63
Lê Thành Long	1.62
Ng. Hạnh Phúc	1.61
Ng. Hòa Bình	1.56
Phan Xuân Dũng	1.54
Mai Tiến Dũng	1.53
Vũ Hồng Thanh	1.49
Tô Lâm	1.47
Ng. Thúy Anh	1.38
Trần Tuấn Anh	1.36
Trịnh Đình Dũng	1.34
Chu Ngọc Anh	1.29
Lê Vĩnh Tân	1.2
Ng. Chí Dũng	1.15
Ng. Văn Thể	1.07

NA Members = 475
Evaluated Officials = 48

■ High   ■ Conf.   ■ Low

Source: Vietnam Government Portal, "Quốc hội công bố kết quả lấy phiếu tín nhiệm 48 chức danh" [National Assembly announces results of confidence votes for 48 positions], 25 October 2018, https://baochinhphu.vn/quoc-hoi-cong-bo-ket-qua-lay-phieu-tin-nhiem-48-chuc-danh-102246771.htm (accessed 17 July 2024).

Figure 5.11
Result of the 2023 Vote of Confidence

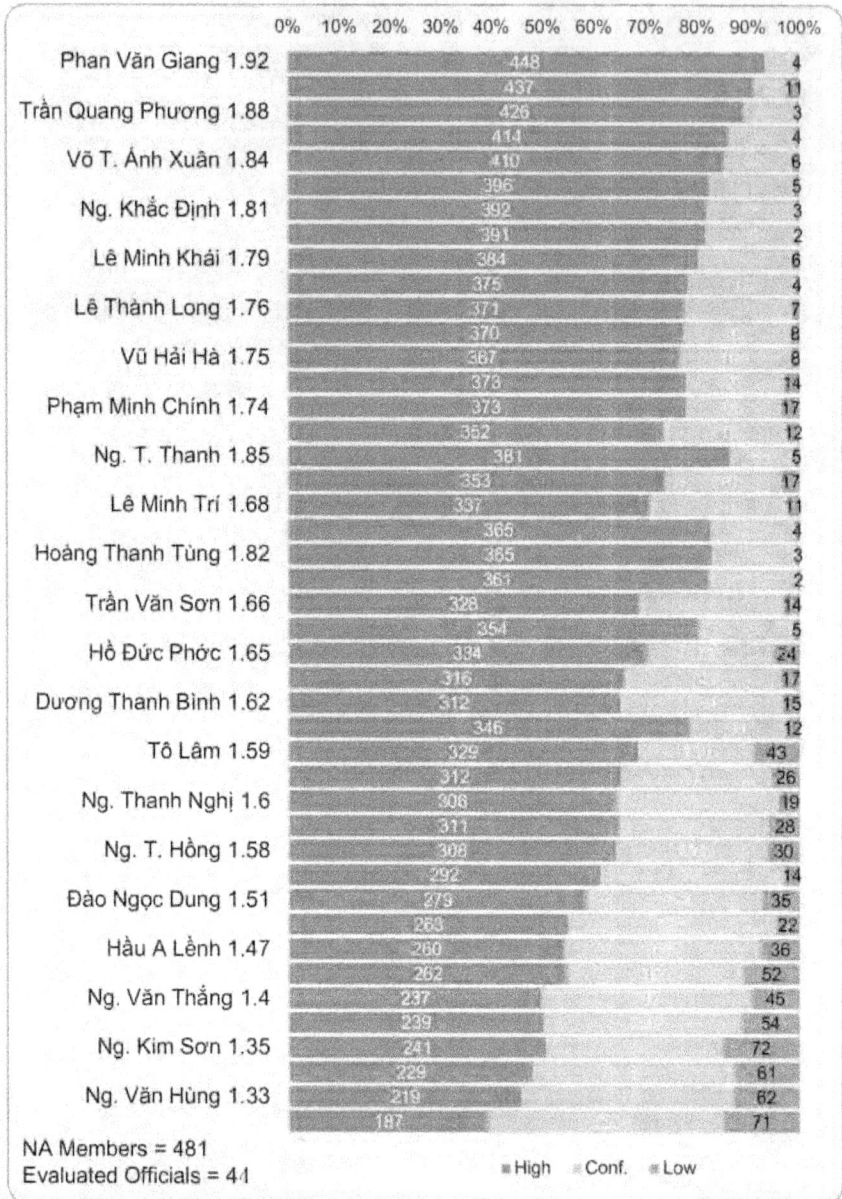

Phan Văn Giang 1.92	448	4
	437	11
Trần Quang Phương 1.88	426	3
	414	4
Võ T. Ánh Xuân 1.84	410	6
	396	5
Ng. Khắc Định 1.81	392	3
	391	2
Lê Minh Khái 1.79	384	6
	375	4
Lê Thành Long 1.76	371	7
	370	8
Vũ Hải Hà 1.75	367	8
	373	14
Phạm Minh Chính 1.74	373	17
	362	12
Ng. T. Thanh 1.85	381	5
	353	17
Lê Minh Trí 1.68	337	11
	365	4
Hoàng Thanh Tùng 1.82	365	3
	361	2
Trần Văn Sơn 1.66	328	14
	354	5
Hồ Đức Phớc 1.65	334	24
	316	17
Dương Thanh Bình 1.62	312	15
	346	12
Tô Lâm 1.59	329	43
	312	26
Ng. Thanh Nghị 1.6	308	19
	311	28
Ng. T. Hồng 1.58	308	30
	292	14
Đào Ngọc Dung 1.51	279	35
	263	22
Hầu A Lềnh 1.47	260	36
	262	52
Ng. Văn Thắng 1.4	237	45
	239	54
Ng. Kim Sơn 1.35	241	72
	229	61
Ng. Văn Hùng 1.33	219	62
	187	71

NA Members = 481
Evaluated Officials = 44

■ High   ≡ Conf.   ≋ Low

Source: Vietnam Government Portal, "Tiến hành lấy phiếu tín nhiệm 44 nhân sự do Quốc hội bầu, phê chuẩn" [Conducting confidence votes for 44 personnel elected and approved by the National Assembly], 25 October 2023, https://xaydungchinhsach.chinhphu.vn/tien-hanh-lay-phieu-tin-nhiem-44-nhan-su-do-quoc-hoi-bau-phe-chuan-119231025103632492.htm (accessed 17 July 2024).

Table 5.4
Votes of Confidence Score Comparison

	2013	2014	2018	2023
Highest Score	1.73	1.79	1.91	1.92
Lowest Score	0.75	0.80	1	1.24
Average Score	1.33	1.40	1.52	1.64
Pres. Bloc Avg.	1.57	1.67	1.67	1.84
NA Bloc Avg.	1.54	1.56	1.64	1.74
Gov. Bloc Avg.	1.17	1.29	1.44	1.56
Court Bloc Avg.	1.35	1.25	1.45	1.61

The criteria for confidence voting are stipulated in Decree 35/2012/ QH13, issued by the National Assembly one year before the first confidence vote. Officials are appraised based on *Tài* (performance) and *Đức* (virtue), which are concepts deeply entrenched in Vietnamese culture. However, these criteria are somewhat nebulous as measures of official evaluation. The extent to which National Assembly members have access to information about the evaluated officials that is not publicly available, and the degree to which their votes are cast autonomously or subject to external influence, may also have a significant impact.

According to Decree 35/2012/QH13, an official who receives a majority of "low confidence" votes is encouraged to resign. Although resignation is not mandatory, if two thirds of the votes read "low confidence" or if there is a majority of "low confidence" for an official two years in a row, a second vote of confidence round will be held for the person in question. If in the second round the majority of votes are again "low confidence", the person or the organization that nominated the official will be responsible for submitting the necessary documents to the National Assembly to consider the removal of the said official. No official has failed a vote of confidence as of April 2024. In some instances, the percentage of "low confidence" votes were as high as 43 per cent, as was the case with Governor of the State Bank of Vietnam Nguyen Van Binh in 2013. The governor, however, made a "spectacular comeback" in the 2014 National Assembly vote of confidence with more than 67 per cent of votes declaring "high confidence".[85]

The vote of confidence can be used as a tool of signalling, as exemplified in the case of Prime Minister Nguyen Tan Dung, who received 160 "low confidence" votes, amounting to 32 per cent of the total votes, in 2013.[86] Facing an overwhelming disapproval of his leadership, Dung then stepped down as prime minister in April 2016. Table 5.5 details the subsequent career trajectories of officials who received the lowest confidence scores in the 2013, 2014 and 2018 votes of confidence. Officials who received low scores during the 2023 vote of confidence remain in office as of April 2024 and have therefore not been included.

In Vietnamese, the phrase *hạ cánh an toàn* (safe landing) metaphorically means an untroubled retirement. Most government officials exploit their position to some extent, and depending on the severity of the abuse, such actions are sometimes even openly tolerated. Nonetheless, these transgressions are fundamentally breaches of the law and may result in disciplinary action and even prosecution years later, if political support wanes and sufficient evidence comes to light.

The five levels of discipline for managerial government officials, from the lightest to the most severe, are as follows: reprimand, warning, demotion, dismissal and termination of employment (Decree 112/2020/ NĐ-CP). The first three categories are self-explanatory. However, it is important to differentiate between dismissal and termination of employment. Dismissal entails the removal of an individual from their managerial role, relegating them to a non-managerial position within the government. Conversely, termination of employment means the complete cessation of the individual's governmental employment, thereby revoking their status as a government official. The term "relief of duty" denotes the uneventful conclusion of an official's tenure, typically involving a transfer to a less influential position or retirement.

Most officials who received low scores demonstrated minimal improvement in their subsequent evaluations between 2013 and 2014. In the 2013 vote of confidence, three out of the five officials rated lowest

Table 5.5
Career Trajectories of Lowest Scored Officials

2013			2014			2018		
Name Position	Conf. Score	Career	Name Position	Conf. Score	Career	Name Position	Conf. Score	Career
Ng. Văn Bình[i] State Bank Gov	0.75	Warning Nov 2020	Ng. Thị Kim Tiến Minister	0.80	Warning, Dismissed Nov 2021	Phùng Xuân Nhạ[ii] Minister	1.01	Warning, Oct 2022
Phạm Vũ Luận Minister	*0.82*	*Relieved Apr 2016*	*Hoàng Tuấn Anh Minister*	*0.87*	*Relieved Apr 2016*	Ng. Văn Thể Minister	1.07	Incumbent
Ng. Thị Kim Tiến[iii] Minister	0.92	Warning Dismissed Nov 2021	*Ng. Thái Bình Minister*	*0.88*	*Relieved Apr 2016*	Ng. Chí Dũng Minister	1.15	Incumbent
Hoàng Tuấn Anh Minister	*0.95*	*Relieved Apr 2016*	Ng. Minh Quang Minister	0.95	Warning Aug 2017	*Phạm Hồng Hà Minister*	*1.15*	*Relieved April 2021*
Ng. Minh Quang[iv] Minister	0.96	Warning Aug 2017	*Phạm Vũ Luận Minister*	*0.97*	*Relieved Apr 2016*	*Ng. Ngọc Thiện Minister*	*1.16*	*Relieved April 2021*

As of May 2024. Officials subject to disciplinary measures are marked in grey. Uneventfully retired officials are marked in italics.

Sources: (i) Vietnam Government Portal, "Bộ Chính trị kỷ luật cảnh cáo đồng chí Nguyễn Văn Bình" [The Politburo warns Comrade Nguyen Van Binh], 6 November 2020, https://baochinhphu.vn/bo-chinh-tri-ky-luat-canh-cao-dong-chi-nguyen-van-binh-102282236.htm (accessed 17 July 2024); (ii) Thanh Nien, "Cảnh cáo nguyên Bộ trưởng Bộ GD-ĐT Phùng Xuân Nhạ" [Warning for former Minister of Education and Training Phung Xuan Nha], 24 March 2023, https://thanhnien.vn/canh-cao-nguyen-bo-truong-bo-gd-dt-phung-xuan-nha-1851514026.htm (accessed 17 July 2024); (iii) Thanh Tra, "Nguyên Bộ trưởng Y tế Nguyễn Thị Kim Tiến bị kỷ luật cảnh cáo, miễn nhiệm chức vụ" [Former Minister of Health Nguyen Thi Kim Tien warned and removed from office], 19 November 2021, https://thanhtra.com.vn/chinh-tri/doi-noi/nguyen-bo-truong-y-te-nguyen-thi-kim-tien-bi-ky-luat-canh-cao-mien-nhiem-chuc-vu-191105.html (accessed 17 July 2024); (iv) Prime Minister of the Socialist Republic of Vietnam, "Quyết định số 1199/QĐ-TTg về việc thi hành kỷ luật với ông Nguyễn Quang Minh" [Decision No. 1199/QĐ-TTg on disciplinary action against Mr Nguyen Quang Minh], 16 August 2017, https://datafiles.chinhphu.vn/cpp/files/vbpq/2017/08/1199.signed.pdf (accessed 17 July 2024).

were later disciplined, as were two out of five from the 2014 vote. These figures could increase, as disciplinary actions for transgressions during office often occur years after an official's transfer or retirement. This delay is because investigations usually take a long time, and an official may lose political backing only years after their retirement. Some officials who initially received high evaluations were later disciplined and even prosecuted. One such case is Transport Minister Dinh La Thang, which was detailed earlier in this book.

While the results of the votes of confidence may have some correlation with the future political careers of officials, negative votes alone usually do not directly result in an official's reprimand or dismissal. Nevertheless, the secret ballot allows many members of the National Assembly to express dissatisfaction with high-ranking officials and as such primarily serves as a means of publicly naming and shaming officials who make mistakes or exhibit questionable attitudes.

Enhancement of Decision-Making Functionality

Although recognized as the "the highest representative body of the People and the highest state power body of the Socialist Republic of Vietnam", the functionality of the National Assembly is often overlapped and compromised by the institutionalized leadership of the CPV, which is the "force leading the State and society". Traditionally, the decision-making mechanism of the CPV differs to that of other communist regimes in that, since the death of Ho Chi Minh in 1969, no individual has stood out as the paramount leader of the Party and the State. One could argue that Le Duan was the top decision-maker from the 1960s until his death in 1986, and Nguyen Phu Trong has been the top decision-maker from 2011 in Hanoi, but their influence and prominence was not on the same level as Deng Xiaoping in China or Tito in Yugoslavia, for example. Rather, most scholars studying modern Vietnam's politics agree that the CPV has adopted a collective leadership system.[87, 88, 89] This collective leadership is described in the official guideline of the political system of Vietnam as follows:

> The Party is firmly organized and unanimous in ideological views and actions. It takes democratic centralism as its fundamental organizational basis, practicing criticism, self-criticism, and strict discipline, pursuing collective leadership and individual responsibility, and promoting comradeship and solidarity in line with the Party's political programs and statutes.[90]

Historically, the majority of the most important decisions in Vietnam under communist rule have been made during the National Congresses of the CPV, which are usually held a few months before the National Assembly elections. During this period, the Central Committee of the CPV elects the Politburo, where most decision-making power is concentrated. As most of the decisions or policies approved by the National Assembly are usually decided by the innermost circle of the CPV beforehand and the vast majority of the membership of the National Assembly is also members of the CPV, the decision-making functionality of the National Assembly in reality is compromised.

Nevertheless, the decision-making functionality of the National Assembly has seen some improvements, particularly from 1992 as the 1992 Election Law provided the National Assembly with substantially improved and detailed powers. Specifically, the powers that were vested in the National Council from 1980 to 1992 were restored to the National Assembly and its Standing Committee. The roles and powers of the Standing Committee, the Chairman and the delegates of the National Assembly are also delineated in this law, which established a foundation for the robust activities of the National Assembly post-*Doi Moi*.

A significantly larger proportion of the National Assembly's working time was spent on the examination and discussion of new laws with 60 per cent of the fifth session of the Fourteenth National Assembly being devoted to law making with several important laws being examined and approved, which included the Law on Prosecution, the Law on Cyber Security and the Law on National Defence.[91]

While the National Assembly generally performs its functions in alignment with the policies dictated by the National Congress of the CPV, there are instances where it can delay or even reject decisions made previously during the National Congress. Two notable examples include the National Assembly's rejection of nominations for State Bank Governor Cao Sy Kiem in 1997 and Minister of Public Security Le Minh Huong in 2002, both of whom had held their respective positions prior to dismissal and had been previously approved by the Politburo. The dismissals of Kiem and Huong were allegedly prompted by major scandals that emerged during their tenures.

Kiem served as the State Bank Governor during the Epco-Minh Phung case, in which government officials and leading entrepreneurs created ghost companies to secure and embezzle loans amounting to hundreds of millions of US dollars from state-owned banks. Among the seventy-seven defendants, six individuals, including some government officials, were sentenced to death, and another six received life imprisonment for corruption and financial fraud charges. Occurring during the 1997 Asian financial crisis, this case was particularly detrimental to Vietnam's financial stability as a newly liberalizing economy, with most of the losses proving irrecoverable.[92, 93]

Similarly, Huong was dismissed in 2002 due to his gross incompetence or possible involvement with Nam Cam's syndicate, one of the most powerful criminal organizations in Vietnam at the time. Known for establishing and managing a vast criminal empire, Nam Cam was regarded as one of the most dominant crime lords in Vietnam in the 1990s. He was reputed to have the power to order hits on rivals and investigators with impunity. Even state-owned media conceded that Nam Cam likely received support from influential politicians and top police officials.[94] Many of the 150 defendants who were tried along with Nam Cam were high-ranking government officials and CPV members.[95]

An instance worth noting that illustrates the deterrent role of the National Assembly is the postponement and eventual withdrawal of the Demonstration Act, which was originally scheduled to be passed in late 2016. As the right to protest is recognized as a constitutional right of the people and there are no regulations prohibiting protests in Vietnam, law enforcement has no legal basis to hinder or stop peaceful demonstrations. To address the increasing number of demonstrations nationwide, the adoption of a new demonstration act was initiated as early as 2014. However, this law was controversial and faced public objections. Although the government's official stance was that the approval of a demonstration law would bring about "positive changes" in society, a member of the National Assembly asserted that "the majority of the population would not support this law".[96] Consequently, as of 2018, the law had not been submitted to the National Assembly for approval, with the official explanation being that the government had not yet completed the draft of the law. No further plans have been set for the resubmission of the draft before 2026.[97] This serves as a prime example of how a decision, although beneficial for and backed by the ruling regime, is rejected by popular opinion through the National Assembly even before its official submission. This demonstrates that the National Assembly can be expected to fulfil its functions in lawmaking.

Two other significant decisions made by the National Assembly of Vietnam were the postponement of the highly unpopular Special Economic Zone Act, originally scheduled for approval in June 2018, and the veto of the costly North–South High-Speed Railway Project in 2010. A notable 85 per cent of the National Assembly members voted to postpone the Special Economic Zone Act,[98] while 41 per cent voted against the North–South High-Speed Railway Project.[99] However, the eventual outcomes of these two projects have diverged. After several adjustments, the government has demonstrated its commitment to advancing the North–South High-Speed Railway Project and will submit another draft to the National Assembly in 2024,[100] whereas there appears to be little prospect that the Special Economic Zone Act will pass in the foreseeable future. Nonetheless, a Management Board for the Van Don Special Economic Zone, a zone outlined in the failed draft of the Special Economic Zone Act of 2018, was established without the approval of the National Assembly.[101] Another similarly unpopular law, the Law on Cyber Security, while initially rejected, was conversely approved by more than 86 per cent of the National Assembly.[102] Although the National Assembly, representing the will of the people, can reject or delay widely unpopular laws or drafts, it appears that when the government is determined to advance certain projects, it can find ways to proceed one way or another.

An illustration of the compromised role of the National Assembly is the highly debated zero-tolerance alcohol policy, which is insisted upon by the Ministry of Public Security. In March 2024, the Ministry of Public Security submitted an explanatory report on the draft Law on Road Traffic Order and Safety to the Government. In this report, the Ministry proposes that drivers must be completely sober, having consumed no alcoholic beverages while operating vehicles. While most Vietnamese citizens and National Assembly delegates agree that driving under the influence of alcohol should be severely punished, many also believe that a zero-tolerance alcohol policy is impractical and that the current minimum threshold for blood alcohol content should be maintained. The public also favours keeping the current minimum threshold.[103]

The Ministry of Public Security has been adamant about setting the zero-tolerance alcohol policy for health and safety reasons. Nevertheless, there is allegedly another motive for their determination: 85 per cent of the fines collected in traffic violations go directly into the Ministry's coffer,[104] and given the drinking culture in Vietnam, this can accumulate into a very significant amount. Driving under the influence of alcohol, drivers face fines up to $1,600, which is four times the average monthly salary in Vietnam. Furthermore, they may have their driving licenses suspended for up to twenty-four months, which effectively terminates the livelihood of people such as taxi drivers or food delivery workers. As such, offenders very easily yield to police officers who solicit bribes to overlook such violations, a practice widely tolerated within the Ministry of Public Security.

The examples demonstrate that after *Doi Moi*, the National Assembly has shown its legislative capacity in many instances, ranging from postponing unpopular laws to outright rejecting questionable nominations made by the innermost leadership circle of the CPV. In most cases, the National Assembly was able to perform its duties effectively thanks to overwhelming popular support, as the laws or nominations in question faced significant public opposition. Nevertheless, there have been instances where initial rejections were later overturned by the Assembly itself or circumvented by the government.

Given that the majority of its members are affiliated with the CPV, it is improbable that the National Assembly would pass laws undermining the CPV's authority. Since this situation is unlikely to change in the foreseeable future, despite recent enhancements in the National Assembly's functionality, it might be more aptly characterized as a conduit for the CPV leadership to formalize and communicate its decisions to the public, rather than the highest legislative body of state authority in Vietnam.

Debate Sessions at the National Assembly

According to Article 32 of the Law on the Organization of the National Assembly, all members of the National Assembly are given the right to question the state president, the chairperson of the National Assembly, the prime minister, ministers and other members of the cabinet, the chief justice of the Supreme People's Court, the prosecutor general of the Supreme People's Procuracy and the auditor general of the State Audit Office. Officials who are questioned are obliged to answer the questions during the working sessions of the National Assembly or during the working sessions of the Standing Committee of the National Assembly. In special cases, written answers are permitted by the National Assembly or the Standing Committee of the National Assembly. If those who have posed the questions are not satisfied with the answers, they can pursue the issue further by posing another question during the working sessions of either the National Assembly or its Standing Committee.

While the right of delegates to engage in queries has been acknowledged since the enactment of the 1960 Law on the Organization of the National Assembly, subsequent laws and legal documents have provided more detailed provisions regarding the query session. One particular improvement is that in a twenty-day working session, three days are now to be devoted solely to debating and fielding questions. Additionally, owing to the substantial volume of queries submitted by delegates, the duration allotted for each query session has been significantly constrained. In 2002, delegates were afforded a maximum of three minutes to pose questions, while responding ministers were granted fifteen minutes to address those inquiries.[105] By 2015, these time limits were reduced to two minutes for questioning and five minutes for responses.[106] Most recently, delegates are granted only one minute for posing a question, with responses required immediately and permitted up to three minutes in duration.[107] This adjustment was implemented in response to the escalating number of questions posed and aimed at curbing the potential for queried officials to evade direct responses.

A substantial portion of debate sessions has been designated for live broadcasting. The live broadcasts have shown that members of the National Assembly are increasingly vocal in expressing their opinions, frequently engaging in open criticism of officials. Since the early 1990s, query sessions have been televised live during daytime hours, with notable segments replayed during evening prime time. As evidenced by Salomon's comparative analysis of parliamentary question periods, these platforms have fostered political awareness and engagement among Vietnamese citizens.[108] Amidst pressing contemporary issues such as corruption in construction projects or academic dishonesty in university examinations, query sessions have emerged as essential viewing. According to a survey conducted by the United Nations Development Programme in 2009, 60 per cent of Vietnamese citizens reported watching portions of the query sessions, while an additional 24 per cent claimed to view the broadcasts in their entirety.[109]

Recently, members of the National Assembly have been very active in using their questioning privilege. For example, during the debate session with the minister of education in the fifth session of the Fourteenth National Assembly, overwhelmed by the exceedingly high number of requests for time to ask questions, the computer handling the requests malfunctioned.[110] Sensitive topics are not to be avoided[111] and members of the cabinet are also requested to answer their questions without beating around the bush.[112] A few examples of the most severe criticisms made thus far are the neglect of the development of rail transportation, low quality education and hospitals operating over capacity; these were directed towards the transport minister, the education minister and the health minister, respectively. Members of the National Assembly have also on several occasions openly expressed dissatisfaction with the answers provided by the cabinet members. For example, during the sixth session of the Fifteenth National Assembly in November 2023, one delegate highlighted the fact that anti-corruption officials are also prone to corruption themselves as evident in the fact that in just the first six months of 2023 alone, thirty anti-corruption officials were disciplined, and twenty-six were criminally prosecuted. He criticized the chief inspector's response—that he only follows the directives of the Party and the State—as irresponsible and demanded that the inspector general take responsibility for the wrongful actions of his subordinates. During the same session, the state bank governor was also bombarded with questions regarding his responsibility in the Saigon Commercial Bank incident, which caused a loss of roughly one tenth of Vietnam's GDP in 2022.[113, 114]

This illustrates that delegates can be forthright in criticizing the leadership. Malesky and Schuler analysed the 2007 National Assembly's debate session and discovered that some delegates did not agree with the central leadership's views.[115] A significant majority of these delegates are local government and party officials, whose interests may diverge from those of the central leadership. Moreover, many delegates who work in sectors such as private business, which do not depend on central authorities for success, exhibit greater responsiveness to their constituents.[116] Notably, full-time delegates nominated at the local level show the highest levels of responsiveness. These delegates are most likely to challenge the government and raise issues of local concern. Non-party members, southern delegates and those from provinces not benefitting from central transfers—who are expected to be the most independent from the CPV—are more active and critical. Conversely, delegates closely associated with the central CPV leadership are much less likely to voice opinions.[117] However, active and critical delegates are overwhelmingly outnumbered by those dependent on the regime. The silent majority are relied upon to block contentious initiatives or facilitate votes crucial to CPV elites.[118]

Schuler contends that the primary role of the National Assembly is for the CPV to project strength to the public. He argues that critical behaviour exhibited by delegates in the legislature reflects internal power struggles within the regime rather than genuine citizen feedback. Schuler's analysis counters a growing scholarly trend that views democratic institutions within single-party systems, such as China and Vietnam, as beneficial for citizens or regime performance.[119] Furthermore, his argument suggests that quasi-democratic institutions have limitations in achieving genuinely "consultative authoritarianism", in which an authoritarian regime maintains strict control over the government and society while allowing for some degree of consultation or input from various stakeholders.[120] Despite appearing to be a robust legislative body through the debate sessions, the National Assembly primarily serves to communicate the regime's preferences and undermine rivals rather than genuinely reflect citizen views.

Duong Trung Quoc, a veteran delegate, alleged that although some CPV members in the National Assembly are quite straightforward in expressing their opinions, the majority are unable to do so due to limitations imposed by the Party. He contends that conflicts of interest sometimes arise in serving their dual roles as CPV members and National Assembly delegates.[121]

Ministers who are unable to persuasively address questions or complaints from delegates are more likely to receive a negative vote of confidence. However, this is not solely based on their performance during the debate sessions, but also on their reputation and charisma. Nevertheless, failing to persuasively answer the questions or having their bad governance exposed does not necessarily result in an apology or a resignation from a cabinet member. For example, in 2017, despite rumours that Minister of Health Nguyen Thi Kim Tien would resign amidst a maelstrom of scandals, she remained stalwart and refused to step down.[122] Having said that in Vietnam, resignation, as a form of apology and taking responsibility for mistakes, rarely comes, no matter how severe such mistakes are. As long as they are not formally dismissed, most officials opt to "stay and correct their mistakes". Furthermore, while minister-level officials have been regular targets of criticism, the highest-level officials of the Politburo are rarely openly criticized at the National Assembly. As such it is unlikely that criticism from members of the National Assembly will directly lead to sustained political changes.

More Communication with the Press and Voters

The activities of the National Assembly have been increasingly reported by domestic media. Forty per cent of the total working time of the fifth session of the Fourteenth National Assembly was broadcast live on the Vietnam Television network.[123] Furthermore, the complete record of the working session of the 10th National Assembly is open to the public and can be easily accessed through the official website of the Government of Vietnam.

According to Article 93 of the Law on the Organization of the National Assembly, representatives from press agencies and even common citizens can attend open working sessions of the National Assembly. Under Article 41 of the Press Law of Vietnam, the spokespersons of the National Assembly must "hold regular or irregular press conferences to provide information to the press agencies".[124] Under Article 48 of the Law on the Organization of the National Assembly, the person in charge of disseminating information to the press is the secretary general of the National Assembly (not to be confused with the general secretary of the CPV).

As a part of its legitimacy-enhancing strategies, top leaders of the CPV have been encouraging members of the National Assembly to be more active in engaging with the media. For example, the chairwoman of the National Assembly of Vietnam asked members of the National Assembly to "walk a mile on reporters' shoes" and declared that refusing to answer questions from journalists can be considered an ugly action. She further stressed that members of the National Assembly are obliged to answer requests for interviews and that failing to do so might result in a warning.[125]

One of the more outspoken members of the National Assembly is historian Duong Trung Quoc. He has been noted for openly criticizing government policies such as bauxite mining in the Western Highlands of Vietnam, the handling of the territorial dispute in South China Sea, corruption in the government and resignation-culture or rather the lack thereof in Vietnam.[126] Quoc also stated that he would prefer that the vote of each member of the National Assembly on important issues be publicized and said that he has always been honest in providing the media and voters with information about his own decisions in the National Assembly.[127] Quoc's comments enjoyed wide coverage by domestic media.

According to Article 27 of the Law on the Organization of the National Assembly, delegates are responsible for maintaining close contact with voters to understand their views and wishes, and accurately conveying their opinions to the National Assembly and relevant authorities. Article 28 stipulates that delegates must hold meetings with voters as required by law. Upon receiving complaints or accusations from voters, they must thoroughly investigate the issues, report to the appropriate authority and keep the claimants informed. The Law on the Organization of the National Assembly further grants delegates the privilege to request the related authority to review the case should they consider the resolution unacceptable or illegal and may even submit the case to the highest-level official of the authority in question.

In one of the more noticeable cases recently, former residents of the Thu Thiem elite zone in Ho Chi Minh City, whose households were relocated in preparation for the construction of an international financial and commercial centre, claimed that they were not fairly compensated for their lands. The case was investigated by a team assigned by the National Assembly[128] and, consequently, the prime minister stepped in and ordered a thorough investigation on the faulty relocation and compensation process.[129]

Several members of the National Assembly have admitted that overall, the National Assembly has not been able to fulfil its responsibility as the representative of the people. Nguyen Khac Dinh, the head of the Legal Committee of the National Assembly, argued that due to inconsistencies in the policies of the government, there has been an increase in the number of large groups of complainants whose concerns are chiefly related to land confiscation, relocation and compensation. Another fellow member of the National Assembly, Nguyen Minh Son, added that pursuing prolonged legal cases has cost many people their entire fortunes.[130]

In general, members of the National Assembly have been enjoying more liberal contact with the press and are encouraged to be more active in hearing from the voters. Although this has not been directly translated into any major changes, in combination with the aforementioned improvements in the functionality of the National Assembly, a number of interesting phenomenon can be observed: shortcomings in the functionality of the National Assembly are admitted by its members and are now sometimes exposed to the press; debate sessions between the members of the National Assembly and members of the cabinet, which are widely covered, have become more fierce; an inability to deal with questions and criticism may lead to a negative vote of confidence session, which in turn would be publicized by the media.

This does not change the fact that media within Vietnam's borders is either monopolized or subjected to strict CPV monitoring and that news coverage concerning political matters necessitates government approval. Insights from interviews with reporters reveal that news, particularly related to political subjects, must receive clearance from the Ministry of Information and Communications before publication. The Central Propaganda Department of the CPV and the Ministry of Public Security also play significant roles in guiding and censoring news outlets. News coverage of the National Assembly is regarded as a top priority and is consequently subjected to thorough scrutiny. Generally, unfavourable news stories have minimal chances of being published. In rare instances when such publications proceed, both reporters and news outlets may face official and unofficial consequences. One reporter who had worked for *VnExpress* said that:

> You must realize that most of the news outlets here are pretty much controlled by the government. You might think it's just papers like Nhan Dan or The Communist Reviews that are directly influenced by the Party, but honestly, we all speak their language. We can't say stuff that doesn't match what the big shots want.
>
> You know those recent corruption scandals in the news? Well, I'm pretty sure the journalists who dug them up got the green light from the higher-ups before they could go on with their investigations. When it comes to people like Nguyen Phu Trong or Pham Nhat Vuong, it's like they're in a no-touch zone.

Personal communication, 10 October 2022

A reporter who worked for Forbes Vietnam alleged:

> If you want to do (publishing) business in Vietnam, you need to obtain a publishing license, which essentially puts you under the umbrella of a

state-owned news agency. Every article we publish has to undergo state scrutiny, and my bosses regularly meet with the C48, the economic police department's anti-corruption section for guidance. I don't know why it must be the economic police. Of course, we are also being monitored by the Ministry of Information and Communication. We also have emergency meetings when, for example, scandals involving high-ranking officials come to light.

Personal communication, 21 February 2023

Consequently, while Vietnamese news outlets have recently enjoyed increased leeway in covering the National Assembly, they remain under the firm control and censorship mechanisms of the CPV. It can be asserted that the CPV employs news coverage as an instrument to enhance the public's perception of the National Assembly, even though little substantial change has taken place.

Conclusion

From the inaugural National Assembly Election in 1946 to the present, elections for the National Assembly have been conducted periodically in North Vietnam until 1975 and in a newly unified Vietnam from 1976. Throughout the tumultuous Vietnam War era, the CPV had gone great length to ensure the continuity of elections, even amidst the most devastating circumstances. Those elections had implausibly high voter turnouts, with reported figures exceeding 97 per cent in consecutive elections from 1960 to 1975. These inflated statistics, a recurring phenomenon, serve the singular purpose of legitimizing CPV leadership decisions under the guise of democratic mandate.

However, during wartime, the imperative for such façades may seem less pressing, as the centralization of power can be justified. As alternative sources of legitimacy wane, particularly in the contemporary era, democratic legitimacy has become more vital for the authority of the CPV. The Party has spared no effort in propagating the National Assembly as the quintessential embodiment of the Vietnamese people's will. Yet, in reality, the CPV exercises firm control over electoral processes. Despite the introduction of ostensibly sophisticated mechanisms and regulations to uphold electoral integrity on paper, over 90 per cent of National Assembly seats consistently remain in the hands of CPV members, while non-CPV representatives are also selected and nominated by the CPV and its affiliated organizations.

There have been several changes in the functionality of the National Assembly recently, including the introduction of the vote of confidence system, a more significant law-making role and better communication with the media. While these changes could improve the performance of the National Assembly, as things stand, their effectiveness is hindered by behind-the-scenes decisions of the CPV and their main purpose is to serve as tools for bargaining and appeasement. As the National Assembly has the legal authority to challenge the party's supremacy, the CPV is cautious about relinquishing any control over it.

This chapter elucidates the dubious nature of elections and the compromised authority of the National Assembly. Yet, the extent to which ordinary voters are aware of these issues is a completely different question that will be answered empirically in the next chapter.

Notes

1. Ministry of Home Affairs, "Họp báo về công tác bầu cử đại biểu Quốc hội khóa XV" [Press conference on the election of the Fifteenth National Assembly delegates], 2021, https://moha.gov.vn/tin-tuc---su-kien/tin-hoat-dong-cua-bo-noi-vu/hop-bao-ve-cong-tac-bau-cu-dai-bieu-quoc-hoi-khoa--d610-t53925.html (accessed 10 July 2024).
2. Ministry of Home Affairs, "Bổ sung kinh phí bầu cử đại biểu Quốc hội và đại biểu HĐND các cấp" [Additional funding for the election of National Assembly delegates and people's councils at all levels], 2021, https://vpcp.chinhphu.vn/bo-sung-kinh-phi-bau-cu-dai-bieu-quoc-hoi-va-dai-bieu-hdnd-cac-cap-11526117.htm (accessed 10 July 2024).
3. Government Portal, "Nghị Định 1927/BTC" [Decision No. 1927/BTC], https://datafiles.chinhphu.vn/cpp/files/vbpq/2020/12/1927-btc.pdf (accessed 10 July 2024).
4. Government Portal, "Nghị Định 1169/NQ-UBTVQH14" [Decision No. 1169/NQ-UBTVQH14], https://datafiles.chinhphu.vn/cpp/files/vbpq/2021/01/1169.signed.pdf (accessed 10 July 2024).
5. World Bank, "GDP per capita (current US$) – Vietnam", https://data.worldbank.org/indicator/NY.GDP.PCAP.CD?locations=VN (accessed 10 July 2024).
6. Jennifer Gandhi and Adam Przeworski, "Authoritarian Institutions and the Survival of Autocrats", *Comparative Political Studies* 40, no. 11 (2007): 1279–301.

7. Steven Levitsky and Lucan A. Way, *Competitive Authoritarianism: Hybrid Regimes after the Cold War* (Cambridge: Cambridge University Press, 2012), pp. 6–7.

8. Larry Diamond, "Thinking about Hybrid Regimes", *Journal of Democracy* 13, no. 2 (2002): 21–35.

9. Andreas Schedler, "Without Democracy: The Menu of Manipulation", *Journal of Democracy* 13, no. 2 (2002): 36–50.

10. Philippe C. Schmitter, "The Impact and Meaning of 'Non-Competitive, Non-Free and Insignificant' Elections in Authoritarian Portugal, 1933–74", in *Elections Without Choice*, edited by Guy Hermet, Richard Rose, and Alain Rouquié (London: Palgrave Macmillan, 1978), pp. 145–68.

11. Juan J. Linz, "Non-Competitive Elections in Europe", in *Elections Without Choice*, pp. 36–65.

12. Ellen Lust, "Competitive Clientelism in the Middle East", *Journal of Democracy* 20, no. 3 (2009): 122–35.

13. Jennifer Gandhi, *Political Institutions under Dictatorship* (Cambridge, UK: Cambridge University Press, 2008).

14. Andrew J. Nathan, "Authoritarian Resilience", *Journal of Democracy* 14, no. 1 (2003): 6–17.

15. Melanie Manion, "The Electoral Connection in the Chinese Countryside", *American Political Science Review* 90, no. 4 (1996): 736–48.

16. Andreas Schedler, "The Contingent Power of Authoritarian Elections", in *Democratization by Elections: A New Mode of Transition*, edited by Staffan I. Lindberg (Baltimore, MD: The Johns Hopkins University Press, 2009), pp. 291–313.

17. Gandhi and Przeworski, "Authoritarian Institutions and the Survival of Autocrats".

18. Luu Minh Han, *Lịch sử Quốc hội Việt Nam* [The history of the National Assembly of Vietnam] (Hanoi: National Political Publishing House, 2016).

19. Fumio Goto, "ドイモイ下における国会の変容" [Changes in the National Assembly of Vietnam under *Doi Moi*], in 社会主義ベトナムとドイモイ, edited by Fumio Goto, Eiichi Imagawa, and Hidekuni Takeshita (Chiba: Institute of Developing Economies, 1994), pp. 117–34.

20. Fumio Goto, "ドイモイにおける国会と人民評議会の変容" [Changes in the National Assembly of Vietnam and People's Committees under *Doi Moi*], IDE-JETRO, 2014, https://www.ide.go.jp/library/Japanese/Publish/Reports/InterimReport/2013/pdf/C13_ch2.pdf (accessed 10 July 2024).

21. Edmund Malesky and Paul Schuler, "Why Do Single-Party Regimes Hold Elections? An Analysis of Candidate Data in Vietnam's 2007 National Assembly Contest", presented at APSA Annual Meeting, Boston, MA, 28 August 2008, https://www.researchgate.net/publication/228869053_Why_do_Single-Party_Regimes_Hold_Elections_An_Analysis_of_Candidate_Data_in_Vietnam's_2007_National_Assembly_Contest (accessed 10 July 2024).

22. Edmund Malesky and Paul Schuler, "Nodding or Needling: Analyzing Delegate Responsiveness in an Authoritarian Parliament", *American Political Science Review* 104, no. 3 (2010): 482–502.

23. Edmund Malesky and Paul Schuler, "Paint-by-Numbers Democracy: The Stakes, Structure, and Results of the 2007 Vietnamese National Assembly Election", *Journal of Vietnamese Studies* 4, no. 1 (2009): 1–48.

24. Edmund Malesky, Paul Schuler, and Anh Tran, "The Adverse Effects of Sunshine: A Field Experiment on Legislative Transparency in an Authoritarian Assembly", *American Political Science Review* 106, no. 4 (2012): 762–86.

25. Edmund Malesky, Paul Schuler, and Anh Tran, "Vietnam: Familiar Patterns and New Developments ahead of the Eleventh Party Congress", *Southeast Asian Affairs* (2011): 339–63.

26. Malesky and Schuler, "Why Do Single-Party Regimes Hold Elections? An Analysis of Candidate Data in Vietnam's 2007 National Assembly Contest".

27. Fumio Ishizuka, "ドイモイ期ベトナムにおける国会の刷新と政治的機能" [Changes and political functionality of the National Assembly of Vietnam during *Doi Moi*], in 独裁体制における議会と正当性：中国、ラオス、ベトナム、カンボジア [National Assembly in dictatorships and legitimacy: China, Laos, Vietnam, Cambodia], edited by Norihiko Yamada (Tokyo: Nihonbōekishinkōkikō Ajiakeizaikenkyūjo, 2015).

28. Edmund J. Malesky, "Understanding the Confidence Vote in the Vietnamese National Assembly: An Update on 'Adverse Effects of Sunshine'", in *Politics in Contemporary Vietnam*, edited by Jonathan London (London: Palgrave Macmillan, 2014), pp. 84–99.

29. Ibid.

30. Asako Nakano, ベトナムの人権 多元的民主化の可能性 [Human rights in Vietnam: the possibility of pluralist democracy] (Tokyo: Fukumura Publisher, 2009).

31. Benedict J. Kerkvliet, "Democracy and Vietnam", in *Routledge Handbook on Southeast Asian Democratization*, edited by William Case (London: Routledge, 2015), pp. 426–41.

32. Zachary Abuza, *Renovating Politics in Contemporary Vietnam* (London: Lynne Rienner Publishers, 2001).

33. Ibid.

34. Carlyle A. Thayer, "Recent Political Developments: Constitutional Change and the 1992 Elections", in *Vietnam and the Rule of Law*, edited by Carlyle A. Thayer and David G. Marr (Canberra: Department of Political and Social Change, Research School of Pacific Studies, The Australian National University, 1993), p. 5.

35. Malesky and Schuler, "Why Do Single-Party Regimes Hold Elections? An Analysis of Candidate Data in Vietnam's 2007 National Assembly Contest".

36. David Koh, *Wards of Hanoi* (Singapore: Institute of Southeast Asian Studies, 2006).

37. Thayer, "Recent Political Developments: Constitutional Change and the 1992 Elections", p. 189.

38. Malesky and Schuler, "Why Do Single-Party Regimes Hold Elections? An Analysis of Candidate Data in Vietnam's 2007 National Assembly Contest".

39. *Đảng cử, dân bầu* [in Vietnamese].

40. Nguyen Minh, "Mũi công kích nguy hiểm vào nguyên tắc Đảng lãnh đạo bầu cử" [A dangerous criticism against the party's organization of elections principle], *Quân Đội Nhân Dân*, 25 April 2016, https://www.qdnd.vn/phong-chong-dien-bien-hoa-binh/ mui-cong-kich-nguy-hiem-vao-nguyen-tac-dang-lanh-dao-bau-cu-472643 (accessed 10 July 2024).

41. *Bầu cử đại biểu Quốc hội và đại biểu hội đồng nhân dân các cấp* [in Vietnamese]. The official name given to the quinquennial legislative elections in Vietnam could be translated word-by-word into English as Election of Representatives to the National Assembly and Representatives to the people's councils of various levels. As the name suggests, in addition to the National Assembly election, people's council elections are also held. The term various levels is defined by Article 4 of the Law on Organization of the People's Council and the People's Committee as follows:

    – Provinces and cities directly under the Central Government (hereinafter referred to as provincial level);

    – Rural and urban districts, provincial towns and provincial cities (hereinafter referred to as district level);

    – Communes, urban wards and district townships (hereinafter referred to as commune level).

42. In this book, the terms the 2016 election or the 2021 election are used to refer to the 2016 National Assembly Election and the 2021 National Assembly Election, respectively. The terms 2016 legislative elections and 2021 legislative elections are used to refer to the 2016 and 2021 National Assembly and people's councils elections as a whole.

43. The National Assembly is granted the powers to draw up new constitutions and laws and to make amendments to existing ones; to examine reports by the president of Vietnam, the National Assembly's Standing Committee, the Supreme People's Court and the government; to make plans for national-level and major socioeconomic development; to make decisions on important matters, such as national financial policies, taxes, central and local budgets, and national debts, and to allocate funds to development projects; and to make decisions on matters related to ethnic minorities and religions. The 2013 Constitution of Vietnam stipulates that the National Assembly can also directly regulate the organization and operation of itself, the State President Office, the Supreme People's Court, the Supreme People's Procuracy, the National Council of Election and other government agencies (2013 Constitution of Vietnam, Article 70).

  Furthermore, the National Assembly holds the power to execute the appointment, suspension and revocation of the most important political positions in Vietnam, including the post of state president and vice president, the chairman and vice chairman of the National Assembly, members of the Standing Committees and its subcommittees, the prime minister, deputy prime ministers, and minister and minister-level position as well as the heads of the Supreme People's Procuracy and the Supreme People's Court. Moreover, the National Assembly also boasts complete control over the armed forces and police apparatus (2013 Constitution of Vietnam, Article 74).

44. It should be noted that in addition to National Assembly elections, legislative elections for deputies to lower-level people's councils are also governed by the Election Law. The latest version of this law took effect in 2015. However, this book focuses on the National Assembly, and any reference to a legislative election pertains to the National Assembly election unless otherwise specified.

45. Hereinafter referred to as the 2015 Election Law or just Election Law.

46. An unofficial translation of the Law on the Organization of the National Assembly can be accessed at http://www.economica.vn/Portals/0/Documents/572014QH13267269.pdf. The candidate must fulfil the requirements listed on the next page.

    1. To be loyal to the Fatherland, the People and the Constitution, to strive to carry out the renewal cause for the goal of a prosperous people and a strong, democratic, equitable and civilized country.

    2. To possess moral qualities, to be diligent, thrifty, incorruptible, public-spirited and selfless, exemplary in the observance of law; to have the spirit and be determined to control corruption, waste and all manifestations of bureaucracy, imperiousness and authoritarianism, and other illegal acts.

    3. To possess educational and professional qualifications, to have full capacity, health, work experience and prestige to perform the tasks of a National Assembly deputy.

    4. To keep close ties with the people, to listen to opinions of the people, to gain confidence of the people.

    5. To have the conditions to participate in the activities of the National Assembly.

47. First-tier administrative units of Vietnam include five centrally direct-controlled municipalities (Hanoi, Ho Chi Minh City, Can Tho, Da Nang and Hai Phong) and fifty-eight provinces.

48. Neither the 2015 Law of the Election of Deputies to the People's Councils nor the Law on the Organization of the National Assembly explicitly mentions what the "special characteristics" are that contribute to the number of representatives elected in each administrative unit. Article 9 of the 2015 Election Law mentions that the location of the administrative unit and its population are considered when the number of representatives is calculated.

49. *Hiệp thương* [in Vietnamese].

50. However, there is currently no law or legal document that clearly indicates how the voters are supposed to submit their inquiries.

51. If the inquiries are related to the candidate's workplace, it is the responsibility of the organization they work for to conduct investigations and report to the corresponding standing board of the Vietnam Fatherland Front. In cases where the nominee is the

head of the organization, the head of the immediate superior organization is accountable for responding to the voters' queries.

Concerning matters regarding the candidate's place of residence, the nominating organization must collaborate with the people's committees at the hamlet level to investigate and report to the standing board of the Vietnam Fatherland Front that organized the consultative conference. The provincial election council is required to coordinate with the organization directly responsible for the candidate or the township-level people's committee of the candidate's residence to address issues concerning the candidate and provide written responses to the provincial standing board of the Fatherland Front Committee.

52. The lists must include such information as the person's full name, date of birth, sex, hometown, place of residence, ethnic group, religion, educational background, occupation, position and workplace. The names of the candidates are sorted in alphabetical order. Each candidate can only stand for election in one voting district. The number of candidates must exceed the number of elected representatives by at least two people. The National Election Council, however, can make exceptions to this rule. The final list of candidates must be publicized by the election teams at the polling location twenty days before the election day at the latest.

53. It should be noted that anonymous complaints are invalid.

54. Should the complaints be verified and it is sufficiently proven that the candidate is unfit for nomination, their name might be removed from the list. In the case that the complainants are not satisfied with the way the election committees handle their complaints, further complaints might be lodged to the National Election Council. The National Election Council's decision is final.

55. As a matter of fact, the candidates may not decide who are invited to their rallies. All of the participants would be invited by the organizers, namely the standing board of the Fatherland Front provincial committee and people's committee of the voting district. The law also does not clearly indicate from which kinds of organizations representatives would be invited.

56. According to Article 36, organizations that are capable of nominating candidates for election are political organizations, sociopolitical organizations, social organizations, People's Armed Force units, governmental agencies or local economic organizations.

57. Tran Van Tam, "Tổng tuyển cử bầu Quốc hội khóa I và việc hoàn thiện pháp luật về bầu cử ở nước ta" [The first National Assembly Election in Vietnam and the perfection of legal documents on elections], *Xây Dựng Đảng*, 2011, https://xaydungdang.org.vn/ly-luan-thuc-tien/tong-tuyen-cu-bau-quoc-hoi-khoa-i-va-viec-hoan-thien-phap-luat-ve-bau-cu-o-nuoc-ta-3254 (accessed 10 July 2024).

58. *Quốc Ngữ* is the modern writing system for the Vietnamese language, which employs the Latin script. This writing system was introduced into Vietnam in the sixteenth century and was made mandatory by the French colonial administration.

59. Candidates must be committed to the nation, its people and the constitution, and aim to promote prosperity, strength, democracy, justice and civilization. Candidates must also be Vietnamese citizens and demonstrate strong moral values, including industriousness, frugality, honesty, fairness and exemplary compliance with the law. Additionally, they must be determined in combating corruption, waste, bureaucracy, authoritarianism, nepotism and other legal violations. Candidates are required to have the necessary cultural and professional qualifications, capabilities, health, experience and reputation to effectively fulfil the responsibilities of a National Assembly delegate. Furthermore, they should maintain close relationships with the people, listen to their opinions, gain their trust and meet all requirements to participate in National Assembly activities.

60. Article 4 of the 2008 Law on Cadres and Civil Servants defines cadres or civil servants as individuals who hold positions or provide service in "agencies of the CPV, the State, socio-political organizations at the central level, in provinces and centrally run cities (below collectively referred to as provincial level), in districts, towns and provincial cities (below collectively referred to as district level), included in the payrolls and salaried from the state budget". Article 39 further notes that the following agencies are allowed to recruit civil servants:

1. The Supreme People's Court, the Supreme People's Procuracy and the State Audit may recruit, and decentralize the recruitment of, civil servants in agencies, organizations and units under their respective management.

2. The Office of the National Assembly and the Office of the President may recruit civil servants in agencies and units under their respective management.

3. Ministries, ministerial-level agencies and government-attached agencies may recruit, and decentralize the recruitment of, civil servants in agencies, organizations and units under their respective management.

4. Provincial-level Peoples' [sic] Committees may recruit, and decentralize the recruitment of, civil servants in agencies, organizations and units under their respective management.

5. Agencies of the CPV and sociopolitical organizations may recruit, and decentralize the recruitment of, civil servants in agencies, organizations and units under their respective management.

Unofficial translation of the 2008 Law on Cadres and Civil Servants is provided by the Ministry of Justice of Vietnam, http://moj.gov.vn/vbpq/en/lists/vn%20bn%20 php%20lut/view_detail.aspx?itemid=10505.

61. Translation provided by the Ministry of Justice of Vietnam at https://vanbanphapluat. co/law-on-the-people-s-public-security-forces.

62. To Lan Huong, "Dù có vào Đảng hay không tôi vẫn cống hiến hết mình cho Đất nước" [Whether I joined the Communist Party or not, I would be devoted entirely to the Fatherland], *Soha*, 5 September 2018, http://soha.vn/pgsbs-nguyen-lan-hieu-du-co-

vao-dang-hay-khong-toi-van-cong-hien-het-minh-cho-dat-nuoc-20180904070651571. htm (accessed 10 July 2024).

63. Mai Lam, "Tự ứng cử: Quyền và ý thức dân chủ cao nhất của công dân" [Self-nomination, the peak of a citizen's rights and democratic consciousness], Radio Free Asia, 10 February 2016, https://www.rfa.org/vietnamese/in_depth/independent-candidatesan-aggressive-enforcement-of-democracy-actions-02102016144805.html (accessed 10 July 2024).

64. Phuong Thao, "Chốt danh sách 154 người tự ứng cử đại biểu Quốc hội khoá mới" [List of independent candidates for National Assembly election finalized], *Dan Tri*, 30 March 2016, https://dantri.com.vn/chinh-tri/chot-danh-sach-154-nguoi-tu-ung-cu-dai-bieu-quoc-hoi-khoa-moi-20160330095626306.htm (accessed 10 July 2024).

65. Vo Hai, "11 người tự ứng cử Quốc hội lọt qua vòng cuối" [11 self-nominated candidates reached the final consultative conference], *VnExpress*, 26 April 2016, https://VnExpress.net/tin-tuc/thoi-su/11-nguoi-tu-ung-cu-quoc-hoi-lot-qua-vong-cuoi-3393717.html (accessed 10 July 2024).

66. BBC, "TS Nguyễn Quang A: nói gì về việc 'tôi bị loại?'" [Doctor Nguyễn Quang A: comments on my own disqualification], 10 April 2016, https://www.bbc.com/vietnamese/multimedia/2016/04/160410_nguyenquanga_voter_conference (accessed 10 July 2024).

67. *Quân Đội Nhân Dân*, "Từ nước ngoài về sau ngày lập danh sách cử tri, làm thế nào để được bầu cử?" [Returning from abroad after the voter list is established, how to vote?], 20 April 2021, https://www.qdnd.vn/bau-cu-dai-bieu-quoc-hoi-khoa-xv-va-dai-bieu-hdnd-cac-cap/hoi-dap-bau-cu/tu-nuoc-ngoai-ve-sau-ngay-lap-danh-sach-cu-tri-lam-the-nao-de-duoc-bau-cu-657312 (accessed 10 July 2024).

68. Vietnam News Agency, "Công tác bầu cử diễn ra sôi nổi, an toàn và đúng luật trên phạm vi cả nước" [Elections were carried out smoothly, safely and legally nationwide], 23 May 2016, http://quochoi.vn/tintuc/Pages/chinh-tri.aspx?ItemID=8164 (accessed 10 July 2024).

69. *Nhân Dân*, "Cử tri cả nước đi bầu cử đại biểu Quốc hội khóa XIV và đại biểu HĐND các cấp nhiệm kỳ 2016–2021" [Voters nationwide take part in the Fifteenth National Assembly Election and other legislative elections 2016–2021], 22 May 2016, http://www.nhandan.com.vn/chinhtri/tin-tuc-su-kien/item/29663902-cu-tri-ca-nuoc-di-bau-cu-dai-bieu-quoc-hoi-khoa-xiv-va-dai-bieu-hdnd-cac-cap-nhiem-ky-2016-2021.html (accessed 10 July 2024).

70. *Nhân Dân*, "Hơn 69 triệu cử tri cả nước đi bầu cử đại biểu Quốc hội khóa XIV và đại biểu HĐND các cấp nhiệm kỳ 2016–2021" [More than 69 million voters nationwide take part in the Fifteenth National Assembly Election and other legislative elections 2016–2021], 22 May 2016, https://nhandan.vn/hon-69-trieu-cu-tri-ca-nuoc-di-bau-cu-dai-bieu-quoc-hoi-khoa-xiv-va-dai-bieu-hdnd-cac-cap-nhiem-ky-2016-2021-post263602.html (accessed 10 July 2024).

71. Vo Hai, "11 người tự ứng cử quốc hội lọt qua vòng cuối?" [11 self-nominated candidates passed the last negotiation round], *VnExpress*, 26 April 2016, http://VnExpress.net/tin-tuc/thoi-su/11-nguoi-tu-ung-cu-quoc-hoi-lot-qua-vong-cuoi-3393717.html (accessed 10 July 2024).

72. Candidates can still be disqualified after being elected. For example, the cases of Nguyễn Thị Nguyệt Hường (for having two citizenships) and Trịnh Xuân Thanh (for being investigated for corruption charges) in the 2016 National Assembly Election.

73. Inter-Parliamentary Union, "Vietnam National Assembly", 2016, http://www.ipu.org/parline-e/reports/2349_E.htm (accessed 10 July 2024).

74. *VnExpress*, "Những gương mặt mới chiếm đa số trong quốc hội" [The majority of the newly elected membership of the National Assembly was elected for the first time], 9 June 2016, http://VnExpress.net/infographics/thoi-su/nhung-guong-mat-moi-chiem-da-so-trong-quoc-hoi-3417213.html (accessed 10 July 2024).

75. Vo Van Thanh, "496 đại biểu quốc hội trúng cử với tỷ lệ như thế nào?" [496 newly elected National Assembly members by popular vote margin], *VnExpress*, 10 June 2016, http://VnExpress.net/tin-tuc/thoi-su/496-dai-bieu-quoc-hoi-trung-cu-voi-ty-le-nhu-the-nao-3417578.html (accessed 10 July 2024).

76. Do Thoa, "Cả nước có hơn 69 triệu cử tri thực hiện quyền bầu cử" [69 million voters participated in the election nationwide], Communist Party of Vietnam Portal, 20 May 2021, https://daihoi13.dangcongsan.vn/bau-cu-dai-bieu-quoc-hoi-khoa-xv-va-dai-bieu-hdnd-cac-cap/tin-tuc/ca-nuoc-co-hon-69-trieu-cu-tri-thuc-hien-quyen-bau-cu-6301 (accessed 10 July 2024).

77. *Lao Dong*, "Chính thức công bố toàn bộ kết quả bầu cử đại biểu Quốc hội khóa XV" [Official announcement of the complete results of the Fifteenth National Assembly election], 10 June 2021, https://laodong.vn/thoi-su/chinh-thuc-cong-bo-toan-bo-ket-qua-bau-cu-dai-bieu-quoc-hoi-khoa-xv-919019.ldo (accessed 10 July 2024).

78. Tran Uyen, "4 người tự ứng cử trúng cử, tỷ lệ đại biểu quốc hội chuyên trách cao nhất từ trước đến nay" [4 self-nominated candidates elected. Percentage of specialized representatives reaches the highest level], National Election Council, 2021, https://hoidongbaucu.quochoi.vn/tintuc/pages/chi-tiet.aspx?ItemID=11723 (accessed 10 July 2024).

79. Bau Cu Quoc Hoi, "Danh sách đại biểu quốc hội" [List of elected National Assembly members], National Assembly Election, 2021, https://baucuquochoi.vn/dai-bieu/quoc-hoi-khoa-XV-37.vnp (accessed 10 July 2024).

80. *Lao Dong*, "Chính thức công bố toàn bộ kết quả bầu cử đại biểu Quốc hội khóa XV" [Officially announcing the complete results of the Fifteenth National Assembly election], 10 June 2021, https://laodong.vn/thoi-su/chinh-thuc-cong-bo-toan-bo-ket-qua-bau-cu-dai-bieu-quoc-hoi-khoa-xv-919019.ldo (accessed 10 July 2024).

81. Pham Quy Tho, "Việt Nam: 'Quốc hội cần đổi cách lập pháp'" [Vietnam: The National Assembly must change its method of law making], BBC, 9 June 2018, https://www.bbc.com/vietnamese/vietnam-44424223 (accessed 10 July 2024).

82. Anh Vu, "Vì sao Quốc hội Việt Nam không làm gì được cho dân?" [Why has the National Assembly of Vietnam not been very beneficial to the people?], Radio Free Asia, 14 November 2013, https://www.rfa.org/vietnamese/in_depth/y-nati-assem-cnt-help-11142013055115.html (accessed 10 July 2024).

83. BBC, "Quốc hội VN 'giám sát chưa thành công'" [The National Assembly of Vietnam has been 'not very successful in its monitoring function'], 17 May 2017, https://www.bbc.com/vietnamese/vietnam-39974085 (accessed 10 July 2024).

84. Cong Minh and Nguyen Minh, "Lật tẩy chiêu trò chia rẽ Đảng và Quốc hội" [Expose the deceptions to cause friction between the Party and the National Assembly], Dan Tri, 22 May 2018, https://dantri.com.vn/dien-dan/lat-tay-chieu-tro-chia-re-dang-va-quoc-hoi-20180522094952603.htm (accessed 10 July 2024).

85. Hoang Thuy and Viet Tuan, "'Cảm xúc đặc biệt' qua hai lần lấy phiếu tín nhiệm" ['Special feeling' after two votes of confidence], VnExpress, 22 October 2018, https://VnExpress.net/tin-tuc/thoi-su/cam-xuc-dac-biet-qua-hai-lan-lay-phieu-tin-nhiem-3827510.html (accessed 10 July 2024).

86. VnExpress, "Kết quả lấy phiếu tín nhiệm 2013" [The result of 2013 Vote of Confidence], 2013, https://VnExpress.net/su-kien/ket-qua-lay-phieu-tin-nhiem-2013 (accessed 10 July 2024).

87. Benedict J. Tria Kerkvliet, "An Approach for Analysing State-Society Relations in Vietnam", SOJOURN: Journal of Social Issues in Southeast Asia 33, no. 1 (2018): S156–S198.

88. Thai Quang Trung, Collective Leadership and Factionalism: An Essay on Ho Chi Minh's Legacy (Singapore: Institute of Southeast Asian Studies, 1985).

89. M. Shiraishi, "ベトナムの社会主義体制" [Vietnam – socialist regime], in 海域アジア現代東アジアと日本 (in Japanese), edited by 関根政美, 山本信人 (Tokyo: Keio University Press, 2005), pp. 175–200.

90. Government Portal, "Political System", 2018, http://www.chinhphu.vn/portal/page/portal/English/TheSocialistRepublicOfVietnam/AboutVietnam/AboutVietnam (accessed 10 July 2024).

91. Nhan Dan, "Quốc hội sẽ thông qua chín dự án luật" [The National Assembly will discuss nine new laws], 2018, http://www.nhandan.com.vn/chinhtri/item/37996602-quoc-hoi-se-thong-qua-chin-du-an-luat.html (accessed 10 July 2024).

92. Huy Thinh, "Epco – Minh Phụng qua hồi ức của Liên Khui Thìn" [Epco – Minh Phung through the memoir of Lien Khui Thin], Tien Phong, 30 June 2018, https://tienphong.vn/epco-minh-phung-qua-hoi-uc-cua-lien-khui-thin-post1064440.tpo (accessed 10 July 2024).

93. Minh Phung, "Epco: Bài học cuộc đời cựu Thống đốc Cao Sỹ Kiêm" [Epco: life lessons of former governor Cao Sy Kiem], VietNamNet, 17 July 2023, https://vietnamnet.vn/minh-phung-epco-bai-hoc-cuoc-doi-cuu-thong-doc-cao-sy-kiem-216514.html (accessed 10 July 2024).

94. Nguyen Cong Khe, "Qua vụ án Năm Cam, những câu hỏi bức xúc nhất sắp được trả lời" [Through the Nam Cam case, the most pressing questions are about to be answered], *Thanh Nien*, 15 August 2019, https://Thanh Nien.vn/qua-vu-an-nam-cam-nhung-cau-hoi-buc-xuc-nhat-sap-duoc-tra-loi-185419371.htm (accessed 10 July 2024).

95. BBC, "Vietnam's 'Trial of the Century'", 25 February 2003, http://news.bbc.co.uk/2/hi/asia-pacific/2794607.stm (accessed 10 July 2024).

96. Tien Dung, "Dự thảo Luật biểu tình: Luật biểu tình sẽ có tác dụng tích cực cho xã hội" [Draft of the Law on Demonstration: Law on Demonstration will be beneficial to the society], *VnExpress*, 17 November 2011, https://VnExpress.net/luat-bieu-tinh-se-co-tac-dung-tich-cuc-cho-xa-hoi-2211115.html (accessed 10 July 2024).

97. Ha Vu, "Chính phủ vẫn chưa chuẩn bị xong Luật Biểu tình" [The government has not completed the draft of the Law on Demonstration], *VnEconomy*, 19 May 2018, http://vneconomy.vn/chinh-phu-van-chua-chuan-bi-xong-luat-bieu-tinh-20180518203833331.htm (accessed 10 July 2024).

98. Ha Nhan, "Hơn 85% đại biểu Quốc hội đồng ý lùi Luật Đặc khu" [More than 85% of National Assembly members agree to postpone the Special Economic Zone law], *VnExpress*, 11 June 2018, https://vnexpress.net/hon-85-dai-bieu-quoc-hoi-dong-y-lui-luat-dac-khu-3761712.html (accessed 10 July 2024).

99. Ha Nhan, "Quốc hội bác dự án đường sắt cao tốc" [The National Assembly rejects the high-speed rail project], *Tien Phong*, 19 June 2010, https://tienphong.vn/quoc-hoi-bac-du-an-duong-sat-cao-toc-post504138.tpo (accessed 10 July 2024).

100. Chi Tue, "Sắp trình dự án đường sắt tốc độ cao Bắc-Nam" [The high-speed rail project from North to South is about to be submitted], *Tuoi Tre*, 7 March 2024, https://tuoitre.vn/sap-trinh-du-an-duong-sat-toc-do-cao-bac-nam-20240307101926773.htm (accessed 10 July 2024).

101. BBC, "Quốc hội thông qua Luật An ninh mạng" [The National Assembly passed the cybersecurity law], 23 May 2020, https://www.bbc.com/vietnamese/vietnam-52749462 (accessed 10 July 2024).

102. Chiem Binh, "86.86% đại biểu Quốc hội tán thành thông qua Luật An ninh mạng" [86.86% of the National Assembly approved the Law on Cyber Security], *Zing News*, 12 June 2018, https://news.zing.vn/86-86-dai-bieu-quoc-hoi-tan-thanh-thong-qua-luat-an-ninh-mang-post850229.html (accessed 10 July 2024).

103. Viet Dung, "Bộ Công an tiếp tục bảo lưu quan điểm quy định nồng độ cồn bằng 0" [The Ministry of Public Security continues to uphold the zero alcohol level regulation], *Lao Dong*, 3 August 2023, https://laodong.vn/phap-luat/bo-cong-an-tiep-tuc-bao-luu-quan-diem-quy-dinh-nong-do-con-bang-0-1333729.ldo (accessed 10 July 2024).

104. Communist Party of Vietnam, "Nghị quyết số 105/2023 QH15 về phân bổ ngân sách trung ương" [Resolution no. 105/2023 QH15 on central budget allocation],

December 2023, https://datafiles.chinhphu.vn/cpp/files/vbpq/2023/12/nq105-sao-y. signed.pdf (accessed 10 July 2024).

105. Communist Party of Vietnam, "Nghị quyết số 07/2002/NQ-QH11 về nội quy kỳ họp Quốc hội" [Resolution no. 07/2002/NQ-QH11 on the rules of the National Assembly meetings], December 2002.

106. Communist Party of Vietnam, "Nghị quyết số 102/2015/QH13 ban hành nội quy kỳ họp Quốc hội" [Resolution no. 102/2015/QH13 promulgating the rules of the National Assembly meetings], 24 November 2015.

107. Communist Party of Vietnam, "Nghị quyết số 71/2022/QH15 ban hành nội quy kỳ họp Quốc hội" [Resolution no. 71/2022/QH15 promulgating the rules of the National Assembly meetings], 15 November 2022.

108. Mathieu Salomon, "Power and Representation at the Vietnamese National Assembly: The Scope and Limits of Political *Doi Moi*", in *Vietnam's New Order*, edited by Stephanie Balme and Mark Sidel (New York: Palgrave MacMillan, 2007), pp. 198–216.

109. United Nations Development Programme (UNDP), Public Administration Performance Index Pilot Survey (Hanoi, Vietnam: UNDP, 2009).

110. Van Hieu, "Tuần làm việc thứ 3 QH: Bước đột phá trong hoạt động chất vấn" [Third working week in the National Assembly: a great leap in questioning session], Voice of Vietnam, 10 June 2018, https://vov.vn/chinh-tri/quoc-hoi/tuan-lam-viec-thu-3-qh-buoc-dot-pha-trong-hoat-dong-chat-van-772738.vov (accessed 10 July 2024).

111. It should be noted, however, that topics that may undermine the political power of the CPV, such as transition to a multi-party system, are rarely, if at all, touched. Some members of the National Assembly have mentioned Vietnam's political and economic reliance on China, however, so the red line of taboo topics is rather ambiguous.

112. Ngoc Thanh, "4 Bộ trưởng trả lời chất vấn: Không né tránh các vấn đề nóng" [Four ministers responded to questioning session: no avoidance on sensitive issues], Voice of Vietnam, 4 June 2018, https://vov.vn/chinh-tri/quoc-hoi/4-bo-truong-tra-loi-chat-van-khong-ne-tranh-cac-van-de-nong-770040.vov (accessed 10 July 2024).

113. YouTube, "Họp báo sau kỳ họp thứ 10, Quốc hội khóa XIV" [Press conference after the tenth session of the Fourteenth National Assembly], VTC1 – TIN TỨC, 19 November 2020, https://www.youtube.com/watch?v=CP1iM8FwTQg&ab_channel=VTC1-TINT%E1%BB%A8C (accessed 10 July 2024).

114. The SCB Bank scandal is one of the country's largest financial fraud cases in Vietnam. Truong My Lan, a real estate tycoon and chair of the Van Thinh Phat Holdings Group, was implicated in embezzling approximately $44 billion from the Saigon Commercial Bank, roughly one tenth of the country's GDP in 2022. This scandal not only highlighted significant corruption within the Vietnamese banking sector but also led to extensive legal consequences for those involved.

115. Edmund Malesky and Paul Schuler, "Nodding or Needling: Analyzing Delegate Responsiveness in an Authoritarian Parliament", *American Political Science Review* 104, no. 3 (2010): 482–502.

116. Ibid.

117. Ibid.

118. Ibid.

119. Paul Schuler, *United Front: Projecting Solidarity through Deliberation in Vietnam's Single-Party Legislature*, Studies of the Walter H. Shorenstein Asia-Pacific Research Center Series (Stanford: Stanford University Press, 2021).

120. Ibid.

121. BBC, "Quốc hội Việt Nam chính thức bãi nhiệm Bộ trưởng Nguyễn Thanh Long, Chủ tịch Hà Nội Chu Ngọc Anh" [Vietnam's National Assembly officially dismissed Minister Nguyen Thanh Long and Hanoi Chairman Chu Ngoc Anh], 7 June 2022, https://www.bbc.com/vietnamese/vietnam-61793526 (accessed 10 July 2024).

122. Xuan Hai, "Không ít đại biểu Quốc hội chưa hài lòng về trả lời chất vấn của Bộ trưởng GTVT" [A number of members of the National Assembly are unsatisfied with the performance of the minister of transport during questioning session], *Lao Dong*, 5 June 2018, https://laodong.vn/thoi-su/khong-it-dai-bieu-quoc-hoi-chua-hai-long-ve-tra-loi-chat-van-cua-bo-truong-gtvt-611044.ldo (accessed 10 July 2024).

123. VTV, "40% thời lượng của Kỳ họp thứ 5, Quốc hội khóa XIV sẽ được truyền hình trực tiếp" [40% of the fifth session, fourteenth National Assembly will be broadcast live], 19 May 2018, https://vtv.vn/trong-nuoc/40-thoi-luong-cua-ky-hop-thu-5-quoc-hoi-khoa-xiv-se-duoc-truyen-hinh-truc-tiep-20180519114155278.htm (accessed 10 July 2024).

124. Unofficial translation provided by the World Intellectual Property Organization at https://www.wipo.int/wipolex/en/text.jsp?file_id=447052.

125. Le Kien, "Khi Quốc hội phải nhắc giảm tiệc tùng, tăng trả lời báo chí" [The National Assembly must self-discipline to reduce wasteful parties and increase response to the press], *Tuoi Tre*, 21 October 2018, https://tuoitre.vn/khi-quoc-hoi-phai-nhac-giam-tiec-tung-tang-tra-loi-bao-chi-20181020213017205.htm (accessed 10 July 2024).

126. Nguyen Hue, "Những phát biểu thẳng thắn của ông Dương Trung Quốc tại Quốc hội" [Mr Duong Trung Quoc's frank statements at the National Assembly], *Giao Duc*, 19 February 2013, http://giaoduc.net.vn/Xa-hoi/Nhung-phat-bieu-thang-than-cua-ong-Duong-Trung-Quoc-tai-Quoc-hoi-post110564.gd (accessed 10 July 2024).

127. Vu Viet Tuan, "Ông Dương Trung Quốc: 'Nên công khai nút bấm của đại biểu Quốc hội'" [Mr Duong Trung Quoc: members of the National Assembly's votes should be publicized], *VnExpress*, 13 June 2018, https://VnExpress.net/tin-tuc/thoi-su/ong-duong-trung-quoc-nen-cong-khai-nut-bam-cua-dai-bieu-quoc-hoi-3762153.html (accessed 10 July 2024).

128. Tran Son and Pham Duy, "Bà Quyết Tâm: 'Còn làm đại biểu tôi sẽ giải quyết bằng được vụ Thủ Thiêm'" [Ms Quyet Tam: as long as I am a member of the National Assembly, I will try my best to resolve the Thu Thiem case], *VnExpress*, 9 May 2018, https://VnExpress.net/tin-tuc/thoi-su/ba-quyet-tam-con-lam-dai-bieu-toi-se-giai-quyet-bang-duoc-vu-thu-thiem-3747411.html (accessed 10 July 2024).

129. Hoang Thuy, "Vietnam PM Orders Inspection into 'Faulty' Planning of Thu Thiem Elite Zone", *VnExpress*, 15 May 2018, https://e.VnExpress.net/news/news/vietnam-pm-orders-inspection-into-faulty-planning-of-thu-thiem-elite-zone-3750256.html (accessed 10 July 2024).

130. Vo Hai, Hoang Thuy, and Anh Minh, "Đại biểu Quốc hội: Nhiều người dân phải bán hết tài sản đi khiếu nại" [Member of the National Assembly: many people had to sell all of their belongings to fund their legal cases], *VnExpress*, 7 November 2017, https://VnExpress.net/dai-bieu-quoc-hoi-nhieu-nguoi-dan-phai-ban-het-tai-san-di-khieu-nai-3666861.html (accessed 10 July 2024).

6

Survey on Voters' Perceptions of Democracy and Elections

I don't know about elections in the West. Here (elections are) more or less for show. All of them are blue candidates and red candidates. But even if we had real elections, would we really have any better options than the Party?

Senior CPV member,
personal communication, 4 July 2021

To assess the level of political interest and perception of the political landscape and elections in Vietnam among its citizens, the author conducted two surveys in the weeks following the 2016 and 2021 National Assembly elections. Since people are typically more enthusiastic about politics-related issues during elections, the author expected that they would be more inclined to respond to the surveys. The author directly contacted respondents through social media and requested their participation in the survey, also asking them to refer any political enthusiasts who might be interested. The 2016 survey recorded a total of 988 valid responses while the 2021 survey recorded 385 valid responses.

Convenience sampling, a type of non-probability sampling, was utilized. In non-probability sampling, respondents are not selected in proportion to the population. Although simple random sampling is preferred, convenience sampling was chosen because there were no other feasible options. The author initially planned to acquire a list of voters of a voting district (Cau Giay District, Hanoi) using his personal connection but that was impossible given the sensitive nature of the survey.

Some limitations of this sampling method could potentially undermine the credibility of the survey. The reliance on social networks as the primary means of conducting the survey created a disproportionate impact on the outcomes, as only individuals with a social network account could be reached. In 2016, most social network users were forty years old or younger, meaning that a significant portion of the population, primarily people who were over sixty, could not be adequately included. Considering that younger individuals tend to be more open-minded, this may affect the results of the survey as a whole. Respondents are divided into two age groups: between eighteen and thirty, and over thirty. The age thirty was chosen because *Doi Moi* was initiated thirty years before the 2016 election. Respondents under eighteen, who are not legally allowed to vote, were excluded. As of June 2016, out of 988 respondents, 828 (84 per cent) were between eighteen and thirty, while 160 (16 per cent) were over thirty.

Another limitation of the survey was the underrepresentation of people living in rural areas. In 2016, approximately 64.5 per cent of the Vietnamese population resided in rural areas.[1] However, internet access in rural areas is significantly lower compared to urban areas. As a result, out of 988 respondents, only 38 (4 per cent) were from rural areas. 741 (75 per cent) were from urban areas and 209 (21 per cent) were living outside of Vietnam. To mitigate these issues, the responses of each age group and location group are analysed and compared individually.

2016 Survey on Voters' Perceptions of Democracy and Elections

The 2016 survey aimed to gain insights into Vietnamese perspectives on democracy and elections within the country. The first part of the survey sought to assess respondents' engagement and perceptions of elections in Vietnam in general, with a specific focus on the 2016 legislative election. The second section aimed to evaluate respondents' perspectives on Vietnam's current political situation and the importance of democracy in the legitimacy of the CPV. The questionnaire explored the criteria Vietnamese people use to define democracy, their preferences for democracy compared to other political systems and their perception of the effectiveness of the single-party political framework. The survey allowed respondents to express their opinions on democracy as a source of legitimacy for the CPV, starting with questions about their understanding of democracy and their assessment of whether the current political environment in Vietnam can be considered democratic. It further examined respondents' views on the relevance of democracy to the legitimacy of the CPV by inquiring about their opinions on the relationship between democracy, economic development and international influence. Additionally, respondents were asked about their personal sentiments towards democracy or the absence of democracy in Vietnam.

Criteria for Democracy

Figure 6.1 shows the response to the question "which dimension(s) are necessary for a country to be considered a democracy?" Regardless of age and locality, nearly nine out of ten respondents stated that they prioritize government accountability and responsiveness. This was followed by conditions such as free and fair elections and the protection of human rights. Some respondents additionally mentioned that they selected these conditions based on what they believed was lacking the most in Vietnam.

Figure 6.1
Vietnamese Voters' Criteria for Democracy (2016)

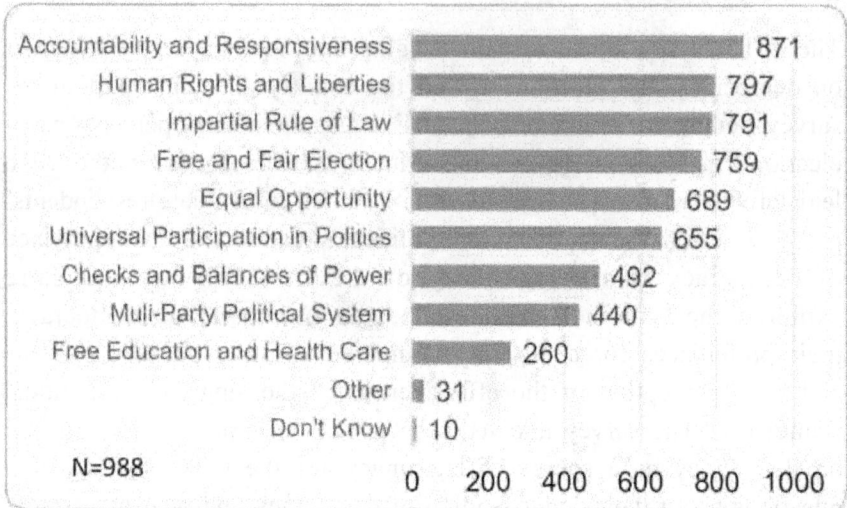

During the 2016 National Assembly Election, a marine life disaster occurred, severely impacting the livelihoods of individuals residing along the coast of central Vietnam. This disaster was allegedly caused by the illegal release of industrial waste into the ocean by a Taiwanese corporation called Formosa Plastics. The government was criticized for its slow response and perceived irresponsibility, and there were even accusations of accepting bribes to conceal information from the public. Against this backdrop, it is understandable that government transparency and responsiveness were prioritized by Vietnamese voters. Furthermore, protests were organized both within Vietnam and abroad in response to the crisis. The government's crackdown on peaceful demonstrations only fuelled further scepticism, leading more people to emphasize the importance of human rights, particularly the freedoms of assembly and expression.

Some respondents drew connections between their answers and the aforementioned Formosa disaster. Considering the timing of the survey, which was conducted close to the election, it is understandable that most respondents emphasized the importance of free and fair elections in a democratic system.

More than half of the respondents expressed the belief that equal opportunity, protection against poverty and the reduction of income inequality are essential elements of a functioning democracy. However, the respondents' views on checks and balances of power and a multiparty political system were divided. In both cases, more than half of the respondents believed that these aspects are not crucial for a country to be considered democratic, while the remaining respondents believed that they are integral to a functional pluralistic democracy.

In Vietnamese politics, discussions about a multiparty political system and pluralism are deemed taboo. Following the unification of Vietnam in 1976, the CPV disbanded and absorbed two of its satellite parties, effectively becoming the sole legal party in the country. Although there have been suggestions and efforts aimed at moving towards a more democratic system from within the Party, such attempts have been met with harsh rejection and punishment. During an official trip to India, Nguyen Phu Trong responded to a reporter by stating, "Vietnam does not need a multi-party-political system."[2]

While some respondents expressed support for a multiparty political system, they also believed that even if such a system were permitted, there would be no viable alternative to the CPV. One senior voter stated:

> A multi-party-political system introduced in Vietnam now would be total chaos. The best system for us is a single party system, but the Party must be transparent and responsible.

> Personal communication, 21 June 2016

Some respondents who did not consider checks and balances of power and a multiparty political system essential to democracy added that they believed a multiparty system often involves cumbersome political processes and that a transparent and strong central government controlled by a single party would be more efficient and beneficial. Some respondents pointed out that the CPV has absolute control over the police apparatus and the PAV and argued that democracy cannot be achieved without transferring control of law enforcement and military forces back to the people. Citing the United States electoral system as an example, some respondents believed that people should be able to directly elect the head of state or head of government. Some respondents argued that without the general population reaching a certain level of intellectual capacity, true democracy would be unattainable.

As discussed earlier in this book, the model of democracy espoused by the CPV is democratic centralism, which significantly differs from modern Western democracy. Democratic centralism prioritizes centralized leadership over a democratic decision-making process and does not include factors such as human rights or the rule of law. Although pluralism and a multiparty system are viewed as non-essential or even harmful to democracy from the CPV's perspective, more than half of the respondents favoured these elements, perhaps influenced by Western democratic models. Nonetheless, the consensus among respondents indicates that accountability and responsiveness received higher ratings compared to other criteria that are considered vital to democracy in Western societies. This may be partly due to the centuries-long influence of Chinese statecraft theory, which emphasizes the importance of a wise ruler and a non-corrupt bureaucracy. A comparative study conducted in parallel with other Sinicized societies such as China, Korea, Taiwan or Japan could prove useful.

Rating the State of Democracy in Vietnam from One to Ten (2016)

Respondents were asked to rate the current state of democracy in Vietnam using a scale of one to ten, where one represents an absolute totalitarian society, and ten represents an ideal democratic system in which citizens can fully exercise their rights.

As illustrated by Figure 6.2, only 3 per cent of respondents assigned a score of eight to ten points. Most respondents gave a score between one and five points. The average score given by the 988 respondents was 3.57, which is quite close to the score of 3.38 given by The Economist Intelligence Unit's Democracy Index in 2016.[3] This similarity indicates that despite the CPV's efforts to use propaganda to bolster its democratic legitimacy, Vietnamese citizens generally hold

Figure 6.2
Assessing Vietnamese Democracy on a Scale of 10 (2016)

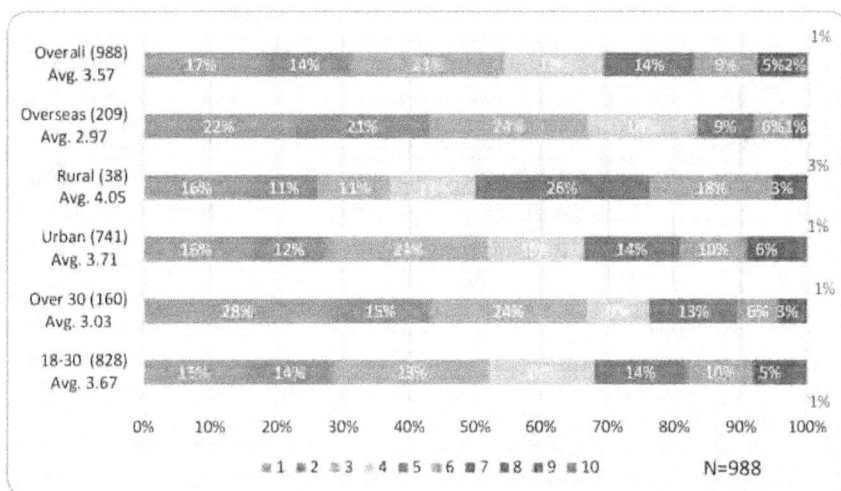

a realistic, and perhaps even pessimistic, view of democracy in their country. This sentiment is particularly pronounced among overseas individuals and those over thirty years of age.

Overall low scores show that scepticism is high across all age and locality groups. Overseas Vietnamese gave the lowest score (2.97), followed by people over 30 (3.03). As most overseas Vietnamese are living in more democratic countries like the United States, Japan, France and Australia, it is understandable that they are exposed to less restricted information and are able to compare Vietnam to those countries, thus explaining the lower score. Furthermore, Vietnamese living overseas are less likely to be harassed for their unfavourable opinions about the ruling regime and are, therefore, more open to sharing their views. Another element that, in hindsight, should be considered in this book is the background of these Vietnamese expatriates, as it can significantly influence their political leanings. For instance, individuals from families of Vietnamese War refugees are expected to be much more critical of the government.

Older voters who experienced the Subsidy Period are expected to give higher scores, as living conditions have improved significantly compared to a few decades ago. Surprisingly, overall, they disapprove of the current political situation in Vietnam. Explaining the low score, some of the respondents in this age group said that they are pessimistic of the direction that the country is leading, and they have no illusions of the reality of democracy in Vietnam. Many among them, while tolerant of CPV rule, are disillusioned with its performance, particularly regarding nepotism, corruption within the government and the distribution of wealth. Individuals over thirty are also less likely to respond to the author's request for surveys and interviews, citing fear of discussing sensitive topics such as democracy, which they believe could bring negative consequences for them and their families. The most optimistic group are rural voters, who gave an average score of 4.05.

This indicates that despite the CPV's efforts to employ propaganda in promoting its own interpretation of democracy to the populace, the outcomes are not as they might have anticipated. While some respondents embrace the concepts of democratic centralism and socialist democracy advocated by the CPV, assigning high scores to Vietnamese democracy, the majority reject these notions. Remarkably, despite the historically tense relationship between the two countries and Vietnamese nationalism, respondents seem to hold the United States in high regard in terms of governance and its role in international politics. Many respondents view the United States as a prime example of a pluralistic democracy, followed by European countries. Many respondents point to North Korea and "Arab countries" as examples of absolute totalitarian regimes.

Rural dwellers, despite being the group with lowest income, exhibit greater tolerance for the state of democracy in Vietnam, perhaps partly due to their limited access to unrestricted information when compared to other groups. Some younger voters' express optimism, believing that the current situation can be improved through democratic processes. Therefore, while the support for democracy might not be overwhelming, it would be incorrect to entirely dismiss it as a source of the CPV's legitimacy.

The Link between Democracy and Economic Development

The relationship between democracy and economic growth has long been a subject of debate among scholars and policymakers. Empirical evidence suggests that the process of democratization initially leads to a decline in GDP, followed by long-term growth that can be volatile but expected.[4] A meta-analysis conducted in 2008 found that democracy has significant indirect effects on economic growth, including higher accumulation of human capital, lower inflation rates, reduced political instability and increased economic freedom.[5] However, there are cases of countries experiencing significant economic growth without proper democracy, and Vietnam is one such example.

The author was mildly surprised to find that only a few respondents outright rejected the notion that democracy has a positive impact on economic development, as shown in Figure 6.3. This is notable because until the 2016 National Assembly Election, Vietnam had

Figure 6.3
Perceived Relationship between Democracy and Economic Development

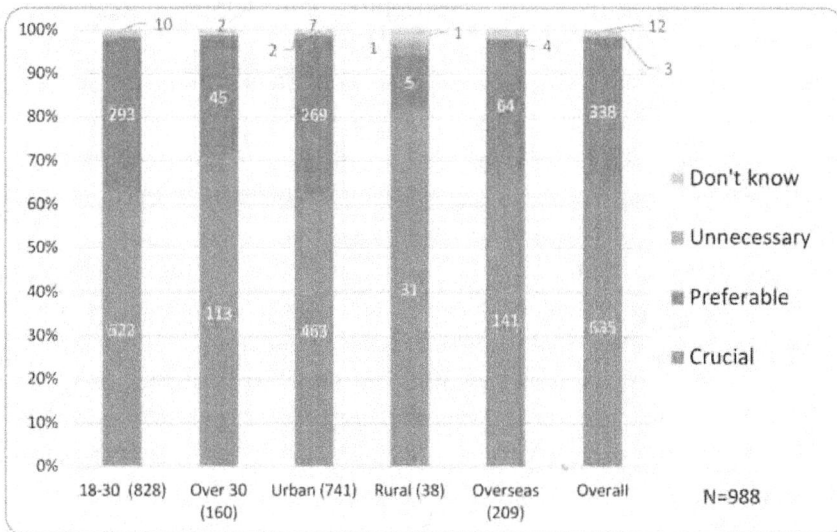

achieved nearly three decades of remarkable economic progress under a non-democratic system. Around two-thirds of respondents believed that a democratic and stable political environment is essential for economic development and international influence. It was expected that more respondents, especially those born during the period of rapid development, would have a more favourable view of the CPV dictatorship. Since the introduction of *Doi Moi* in 1986, Vietnam has benefitted from economic success, and despite the impacts of the Asian financial crisis and the 2007–8 financial crisis, has been one of the fastest growing economies in the twenty-first century.[6] It is also projected to become one of the top twenty economies in the world by 2050.[7]

Despite the economic success achieved under the rule of the CPV, some respondents expressed clear cynicism regarding the influence of the current political regime on economic growth. They pointed to corruption scandals that emerged during the first half of the 2010s and the CPV's lack of transparency in addressing those scandals as reasons for their pessimism. While top party leaders have acknowledged on multiple occasions that widespread corruption remains a problem,[8, 9] reports from the Government Inspectorate of Vietnam maintain that corruption is primarily limited to local-level authorities, with minimal cases of central-level corruption.[10] This consistent denial has severely undermined public trust. This narrative, however, has changed after the initiation of the Blazing Furnace Anti-Corruption Campaign by Nguyen Phu Trong, as even high-ranking officials have been exposed and prosecuted for corruption-related charges.

Support for democracy remains high across all groups. More than 64 per cent of respondents consider democracy crucial to economic development while 33 per cent stated that democracy would facilitate economic development better than dictatorship but believed that democracy is not the most crucial factor for economic gains. Less than 1 per cent outright dismiss the relationship between democracy and economic development.

When asked to elaborate on their answers, respondents cited China and Singapore as examples of successful economies without proper democracy. Few also mentioned authoritarian developmental states in East and Southeast Asia, such as South Korea or Malaysia, and argued that following the models of these countries would be more beneficial for Vietnam than blindly adopting Western democracy.

Despite the significant economic development achieved under the authoritarian rule of the CPV, most respondents expressed a preference for democracy. One interpretation is that, despite decades of rapid economic growth, the CPV was facing several issues, including corruption scandals, bad governance and social inequality. While overall standard of living has improved, so has income disparity. Many respondents believe that they are the victims of a system riddled with corruption, nepotism and red-tape bureaucracy.

Another explanation is that many respondents, who have experienced significant improvements in their standard of living over the past three decades due to *Doi Moi*, may have confused economic freedom with political liberty. Additionally, Vietnamese respondents may hold Western democracies in high regard for their socioeconomic development and attribute this growth to their political system. The respondents' support for democracy reflects their disapproval of the CPV's governance. They believe that a more democratic and transparent system would result in better governance, faster growth and greater equality.

Satisfaction with Vietnam's Current Political System

Respondents are asked to answer the question: "How satisfied are you with the current political system in Vietnam?". This question aimed to capture respondents' subjective feelings, for example, even when a respondent feels that Vietnam is non-democratic, they can express their approval for the CPV.

A significant majority expressed dissatisfaction with the current state of Vietnamese politics, as shown in Figure 6.4. Three out of every five respondents answered "very unsatisfactory" or "unsatisfactory". Twenty-one per cent of respondents chose a neutral answer, and only 5 per cent indicated they were either "happy" or "very happy" with

Figure 6.4
Vietnamese Voters' Assessment of the Ruling Regime

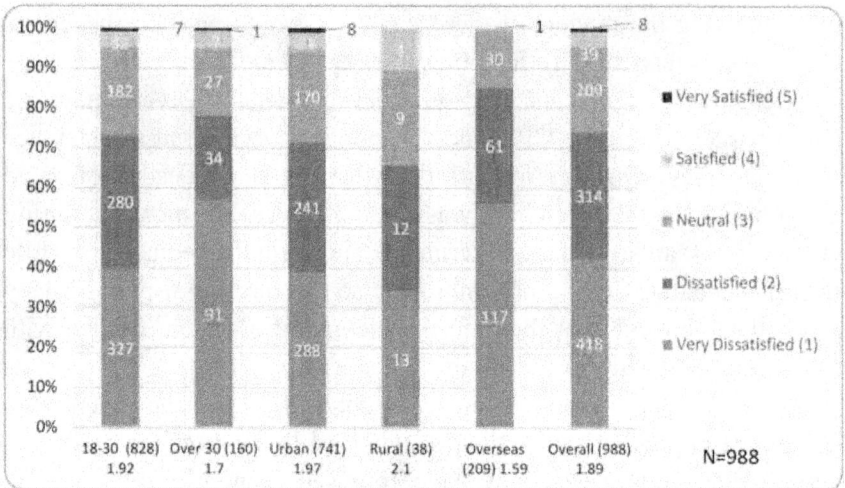

the ruling communist regime. Notably, overseas respondents and those over thirty years old are the most dissatisfied with the CPV's rule, while rural voters are the most tolerant. Most of the respondents who chose "very satisfactory", also expressed the belief that democracy was unnecessary for economic growth in the fifth question.

In 2016, Vietnam had 2.8 million government employees[11] and 4.4 million party members, constituting 2.5 per cent and 4.1 per cent of the population, respectively.[12] These individuals generally support the CPV due to their political alignments and personal interests. However, not all of them do so unequivocally. Many are indifferent or even disapproving of the CPV's rule but maintain their party membership or government positions due to the perceived benefits for their careers and social standing.

Excluding the "very unsatisfactory" or "unsatisfactory" responses, only 26 per cent of respondents actively supported or were neutral towards the CPV's rule. To put this into perspective, the lowest job approval rating recorded for a US president was 22 per cent, registered by Harry Truman in February 1952.[13]

In a multiparty system, each political party typically has a loyal voter base that seldom switches sides. For example, in the United States, voters affiliated with the Democratic Party rarely vote for the Republican Party and vice versa.[14] In Vietnam, however, with only one legal political party, the divide exists not between different political parties but between CPV supporters and the silent majority, who has remained tolerant and indifferent to the CPV's rule, offering no resistance. The few who genuinely aim to challenge the CPV's rule lack a legal framework to do so, in addition to lacking organizational and financial support. Consequently, as long as the Party retains its support base and keeps the masses silent while marginalizing dissidents, its authority remains relatively unchallenged, despite low approval ratings.

Moreover, there is no opposition with the capacity to challenge the CPV's rule. Most respondents exhibited either a lack of knowledge or expressed disdain when asked about overseas-based political parties like Viet Tan or Viet Nam Quoc Dan Dang. To them, these groups lack legitimacy and are not even worthy of consideration as a legal opposition. Furthermore, these parties also do not cooperate well with one another in addition to having infightings and have failed to organize effective resistance against the CPV.

Needed Improvements

If a respondent thought that Vietnam lacks, for example, a multiparty system but did not think a multiparty system is needed for the betterment of the current political situation, or could even worsen it, they could reflect their opinion here. While most respondents believed Vietnam lacks free and fair elections in the previous question, only six out of ten responded that free and fair elections should be considered a needed improvement, as shown in Figure 6.5.

Moreover, only half of the respondents considered universal participation in elections and political discussions a priority improvement. Respondents considered universal free education and healthcare luxuries and thus placed them at the bottom of the list

Figure 6.5
Improvements Needed According to Voters

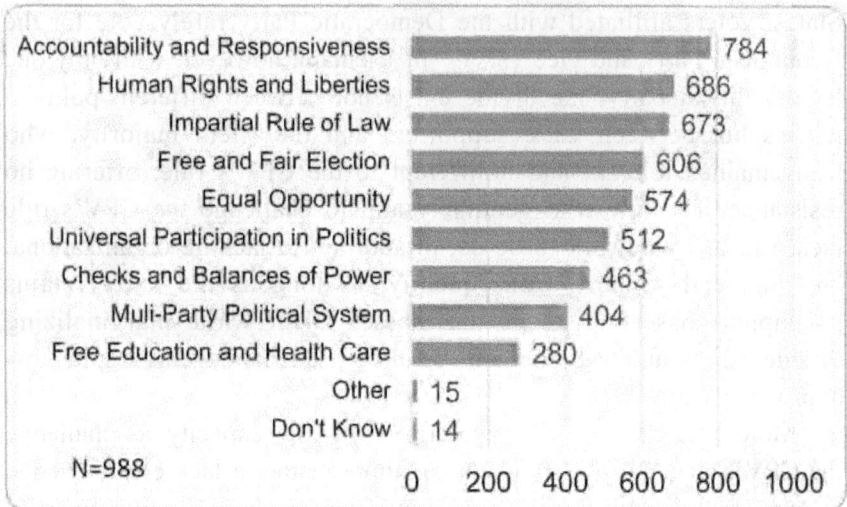

Improvement	Value
Accountability and Responsiveness	784
Human Rights and Liberties	686
Impartial Rule of Law	673
Free and Fair Election	606
Equal Opportunity	574
Universal Participation in Politics	512
Checks and Balances of Power	463
Muli-Party Political System	404
Free Education and Health Care	280
Other	15
Don't Know	14

N=988

0   200   400   600   800   1000

of needed improvements, followed by a multiparty political system as only four out of ten Vietnamese believed a multiparty political system would enhance the current political situation.

Almost seven out of ten surveyed respondents agreed that Vietnam lacked protection of human rights, freedom, equality before the rule of law, and deemed these areas in need of significant improvement. Although Vietnam lacked an effective mechanism to separate and balance power, only 463 respondents felt that improvements in this regard were necessary. Other responses called for better state management and the rule of law, a more transparent government recruitment process and remedies for widespread nepotism. Respondents also suggested that the CPV should acknowledge its flaws and genuinely seek ways to address them.

Paradoxically, while the majority of respondents said that they highly value democracy and express disapproval of the current political system in Vietnam, they believe that what the CPV needs most is improved performance rather than a drastic change such as implementing a multiparty system. The response to this question reveals that, to the average Vietnamese, democracy does not necessarily mean Western democracy or democratic centralism. Instead, it signifies a functional and accountable political system that prioritizes transparency and is free from corruption.

2016 National Assembly Election Participation

The voter turnout for the 2016 legislative election in Vietnam was reported as 98.77 per cent. This high turnout did not come as a surprise because previous legislative elections have also consistently reported exceedingly high voter turnouts, as shown in Figure 5.3. It is important to note that abstaining from voting is not considered a violation of the law in Vietnam and is therefore not subject to fines or legal charges. As a result, an unusually high voter turnout could potentially raise concerns about the integrity of the election.

Official statistics contradict the respondents' reports, as illustrated in Figure 6.6. Only 29 per cent of the respondents reported actually went to a polling location and voted, with an additional 25 per cent stating that they asked someone else to vote on their behalf. This means

Figure 6.6
Participation in the 2016 Legislative Election

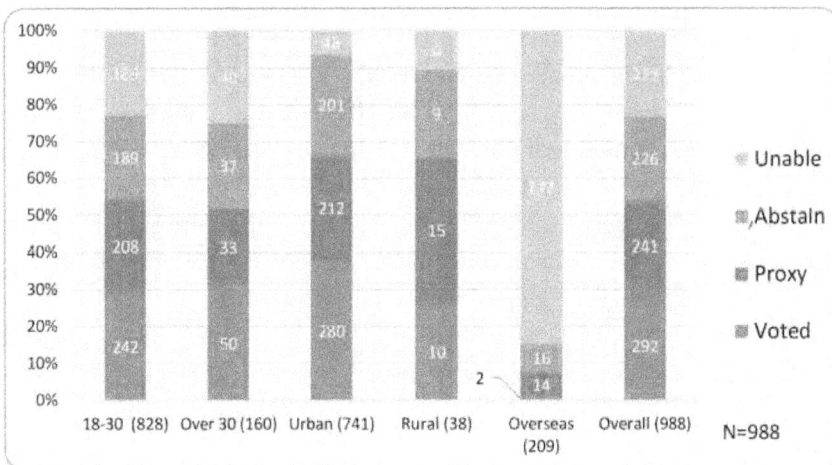

that the overall voter turnout was only around 54 per cent, 45 per cent lower than the official number. It should be noted that according to Article 69 of the 2015 Election Law, asking someone else to vote on one's behalf is a violation. Nevertheless, the Election Law does not prescribe a penalty for proxy voting. State-owned news agencies admitted that "it could be asserted that [voter turnout] was not 99 per cent, but much lower", and also warned against unlawful voting.[15]

Twenty-two per cent said that they deliberately abstained from voting, with most explaining that they did so because they were either busy or thought that voting is meaningless. More than a dozen people who reported that they did vote clarified that they either left the ballot blank or crossed out all candidates' names to express dissatisfaction with the political system. Two people specifically alleged that they were forced to vote by local authorities, and abstention would have possibly resulted in their families being warned.

Eighteen per cent of the respondents, most of whom lived overseas, answered that they could not access the voting site. Although the Constitution of Vietnam guarantees the right to vote for any Vietnamese citizen over eighteen years old, it seems that Vietnamese who were living abroad at the time of the election were not guaranteed that right. The author of this survey contacted the Embassy of Vietnam in Tokyo to inquire about the voting location but was told that voting in Japan was not possible, and as such, he was not able to legally cast his vote. Therefore, people who were living in Japan at that time were denied the right to vote. A vote registered under the author's name was later cast by a family member who was residing in Hanoi. The same situation was reported by Vietnamese who lived in other countries as well. All overseas respondents elaborated that they were not informed about the election and voting method by the corresponding Vietnamese embassy or the consul-general in the country they were living in.

It should be noted that the election was held on a normal Sunday, not amidst a long national holiday, so many people could not return to their hometown to vote. Many respondents said that the paperwork needed to vote as a temporary resident combined with the bureaucratic voter registration system discouraged them from voting. Some respondents who were not able to vote were living in Vietnam at the time of the election but were not informed of the election by the authorities or could not reach the voting location.

Additionally, approximately 5 per cent of respondents responded that they could not vote for reasons other than accessibility to polling places. Most of the people who were unable to vote said that they could not do so due to procedural issues, for example, they were not allowed to register to vote in their temporary residence or they were not issued a voter identification card. They lay the blame on the organizers, namely the local electoral council and the Fatherland Front.

Overseas voters were included in the survey because they are eligible to vote on paper. However, 20 per cent of the survey respondents are currently living overseas, while Vietnamese expatriates constitute only 5 per cent of the total population. There are two reasons for this discrepancy. First, domestic Vietnamese often hesitate to participate in surveys on sensitive issues, while overseas Vietnamese are usually more open-minded about discussing such topics with people they are not familiar with, as they are less likely to be harassed if their unfavourable opinions are leaked to the authorities. Secondly, the author, being an expatriate himself, has access to a significant expatriate community willing to answer his questions.

If we exclude the overseas voters the picture changes slightly as represented in Figure 6.7. The combined percentage of direct and proxy voting rises to 66 per cent. However, political apathy remains high, with more than 30 per cent of respondents across all categories not voting either directly or via proxy. Only less than 7 per cent of voters were unable to vote due to logistical or procedural issues. This indicates that while Vietnamese embassies and consulates have not been performing their electoral functions, the organization of domestic elections in urban and suburban areas has been adequate.

Nevertheless, the actual number of votes cast may be higher than reported in this survey because some individuals who did not vote themselves mentioned that their family members might have voted on their behalf without their knowledge. Electoral officials report going

Figure 6.7
2016 Election Participation (Overseas Voters Excluded)

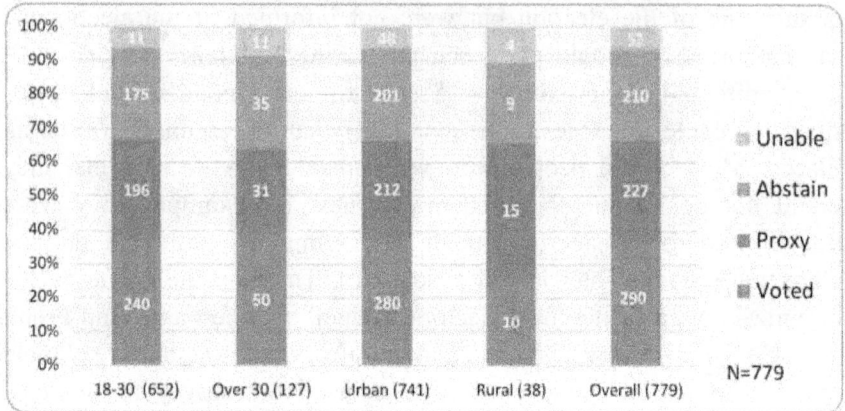

door to door on election day to encourage citizens to vote. Furthermore, it is quite common for a family representative to vote for absent members. Officials openly accept and even encourage the practice of proxy voting despite its questionable legality, as they must ensure that the voter turnout within their district meets a certain quota. As such, in northern cities and provinces where political support for the CPV is high and elections are well organized, a high voter turnout can be expected. However, an overall nationwide voter turnout of more than 99 per cent is simply impossible to achieve, even when proxy voting is accounted for.

According to the 2018 PAPI Report,[16] of the 14,408 respondents surveyed, 69 per cent participated directly in the 2016 National Assembly Election. PAPI's findings are considerably higher than those of the author's survey, but still fall short of the official number reported by the Vietnamese authorities. PAPI attributes the difference between its findings and the government's to the practice of proxy voting.

According to PAPI, 42 per cent of the surveyed voters were invited to attend voter meetings; among them, 30 per cent participated. PAPI also suggests that there is a significant gap between party members and non-members. Specifically, 81 per cent of surveyed party members reported being invited to voter meetings for candidates in the 2016 National Assembly Election, while only 30 per cent of non-CPV members reported the same. Interviewed party members and government officials also revealed similar results, indicating that individuals considered loyal to the CPV and with higher social status are more likely to be invited to these meetings. These voters are sometimes referred to as "professional voters",[17] a phenomenon acknowledged by state media.[18]

Vietnam's exceptionally high voter turnout does not necessarily indicate a healthy election; instead, it suggests possible fraudulent practices during voter registration, voting, vote counting, reporting stages or press coverage. To defend the elections' legitimacy, state media acknowledges the discrepancy between real and reported voter turnout but attributes it to proxy voting rather than fraud.

Selection Criteria for National Assembly Representatives (2016)

Overall, most voters express apathy to the candidates they are allowed to choose from, as in Vietnam, there is only one legal political party. Additionally, independent candidates must be approved by the pro-communist Fatherland Front. As a result, a candidate's political leaning is not as important to Vietnamese voters as it is in countries with a functional multiparty system. The three most important criteria for Vietnamese voters were a candidate's professional background, academic background and the policies promised by the candidates, as illustrated in Figure 6.8.

Surprisingly, over one-third of the respondents said that they would prefer a non-communist candidate while only 5 per cent said that they preferred party members over independent candidates. This result contradicts the outcome of the elections, in which only 21 non-communist candidates were elected out of 496 seats in the National Assembly.

According to the 2018 PAPI Report, voters in Vietnam tend to vote for candidates who promise to eradicate poverty over other priorities such as environmental protection or economic growth.

Figure 6.8
Criteria for Choosing Representatives (2016)

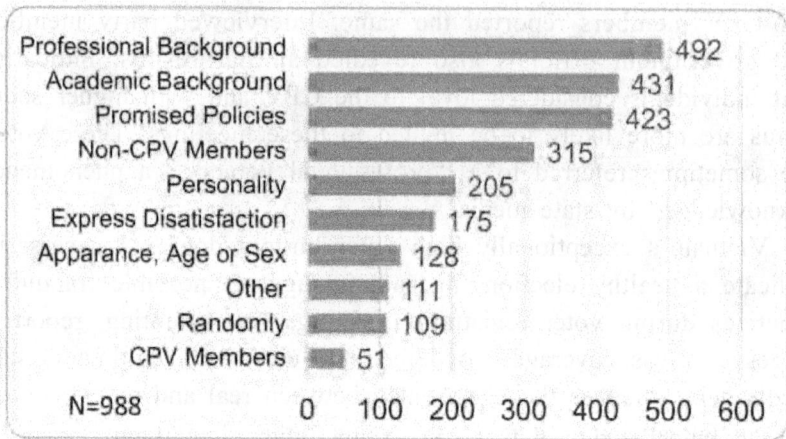

Criteria	Value
Professional Background	492
Academic Background	431
Promised Policies	423
Non-CPV Members	315
Personality	205
Express Disatisfaction	175
Apparance, Age or Sex	128
Other	111
Randomly	109
CPV Members	51

N=988   0   100   200   300   400   500   600

Only one-fifth of the respondents considered the personality of the candidate important, reasoning that they did not know the candidates personally. In general, candidates are not encouraged to individually carry out election campaigns. In Vietnam, the only thing that resembled election campaigning were the meetings held through the cooperation between the Fatherland Front and local authorities.

The number of voters who would cast a donkey vote or choose representatives based on looks was at more than 10 per cent. This represents the indifference of a sizable proportion of Vietnamese voters to the current political environment of the country. Furthermore, 175 respondents indicated that they would vote to express dissatisfaction with the election and the political system. This number could be higher as many people who chose "other" further explained that they would not vote due to the perceived meaningless nature of the election. Several respondents who chose "other" also said that they received instructions on who to vote for from their family members or the local authority. Other criteria listed by respondents were the candidate's social influence, age and gender. Voters who listed these criteria tended to prefer younger or female candidates with considerable social influence.

Many voters did not know anything about the candidates, except for the information provided by the election councils on the day of the election in the form of pamphlets and hanging panels at the voting venue. An example of the candidates' publicized information is shown in Figure 6.9.

There has been a significant shift in the composition of the National Assembly in Vietnam. Prior to *Doi Moi*, many members of the National Assembly were farmers and workers, representing the predominantly agricultural Vietnamese society and the leading role of the working

Figure 6.9
A List of Candidates for the 2016 National Assembly Election

Personal information of the candidates from left to right includes their name, date of birth, sex, current address, hometown, ethnic group, religion, educational and professional level (general educational level, professional level, degree, political theory level, foreign language level), place of work, position, political affiliation, experience as a member of the National Assembly and experience as a member of a local people's council. All five candidates were members of the CPV and were working for the government or state-owned company at the time of the election. Two of the candidates were nominated for the first time. Candidates' addresses are cropped out.

Source: the author.

class. Table 6.1 shows the percentage of delegates from the First National Assembly to the Ninth National Assembly, categorized by occupation. However, due to inconsistencies in reporting methods on the National Assembly website, such as omitting certain social classes in some years while dividing one class into smaller subclasses in other years, the percentages do not always add up to 100 per cent.

Table 6.1
Composition of the First to Ninth National Assembly by Social Class

	First (1946)	Second (1960)	Third (1964)	Fourth (1971)	Fifth (1975)	Sixth (1976)	Seventh (1981)	Eighth (1987)	Ninth (1992)
Intelligentsia	61	28.4	26.8	17.1	22	19.9	22.2	24.9	N/A
Workers	0.6	13.8	12.4	22.3	21	16.2	20.2	20	4.5
Peasants	22	12.9	12.4	21.4	22	20.3	18.6	21	14.7
Political cadres	N/A	35.2	19.2	25.5	23	28.6	24.4	20.2	31.3

Source: National Assembly of the Socialist Republic of Vietnam, "Thông tin đại biểu quốc hội" [Information of national assembly deputies], https://dbqh.quochoi.vn/default.aspx (accessed 17 July 2024).

In the Ninth National Assembly, the category "farmers" (*nông dân*) was renamed to "agriculture" (*nông nghiệp*), "workers" (*công nhân*) were renamed to "industries" (*công nghiệp*) and "political cadres" (*cán bộ chính trị*) were renamed to "government administration" (*quản lý nhà nước*). From the Tenth National Assembly onwards, the percentage of farmer and worker delegates ceased to be reported altogether. The composition of the National Assembly has since been categorized by ethnicity, age, political alignment and educational level. This reflects the CPV's awareness of the gap between its socialist ideological theory and reality, as an increasing number of National Assembly seats have been occupied by the intelligentsia, bourgeoisie and government officials, while farmers and workers are marginalized.

The majority of the Fourteenth National Assembly are government officials, university professors, religious leaders and even industrialists and entrepreneurs, most of whom are highly educated. Out of the

496 newly elected representatives, only five do not hold a bachelor's degree. As many as 185 representatives have a master's degree while 129 have a doctorate degree.[19] Only one of them is listed as a farmer on the official website of the National Assembly, and there are no registered factory workers.[20] About five seats in the National Assembly of Vietnam are specifically reserved for religious leaders of Buddhism and Catholicism, the two religions with the most followers in Vietnam not counting folk religions.

Ninety-six per cent of the National Assembly's delegates are also members of the CPV, whose political charter clearly indicates that they are "the vanguard of the Vietnamese working class, the loyal representative of the interests of the working class and the working people, and the whole Vietnamese people". Nevertheless, the composition of the National Assembly after *Doi Moi* shows that it no longer represents the working class. Interestingly enough, most of the respondents did not seem to notice this change, nor did they complain about it.

In general, since there are virtually no alternative options besides the CPV, voters' criteria for selecting representatives are considerably less partisan than those in the West. However, there is a division between party members and non-party members, with the former receiving more support from voters in the 2016 National Assembly Election. Nonetheless, the election's outcome tells a different story, as only twenty-one out of five hundred elected representatives are non-CPV members, and even those so-called independent candidates were nominated and approved by the CPV-controlled Fatherland Front.

Paradoxically, while Vietnamese voters claim to prioritize candidates' professional or academic backgrounds as their main selection criteria, they possess limited knowledge about the candidates. Ordinary voters are rarely invited to the campaign meetings organized by the authorities which are reserved for "professional voters", and they can only access general information provided by the authorities. Most respondents cannot even recall the names of candidates in their voting district, including the candidates they voted for.

Voters' Perception of the Significance of Their Votes

As shown in Figure 6.10, most respondents expressed pessimism regarding the significance of their votes, with 61 per cent saying that they do not think that their vote mattered at all. Most attributed the current dictatorial political system to their cynicism, explaining that voting for candidates nominated by only one political party was pointless. This echoes the apathy and indifference expressed in the previous answers. Others also pointed out that poor management of the election process by local committees further eroded their trust in the fairness of the election. Some added that they believe that elections are meaningful, but only in democratic countries.

One fourth of the respondents believed that individually their votes were irrelevant, but collectively they could make some meaningful change to the political environment of Vietnam. Some clarified this notion, further noting that among a list of candidates provided by the Fatherland Front, they had hoped to find somebody worth voting

Figure 6.10
Perception on the Significance of Votes

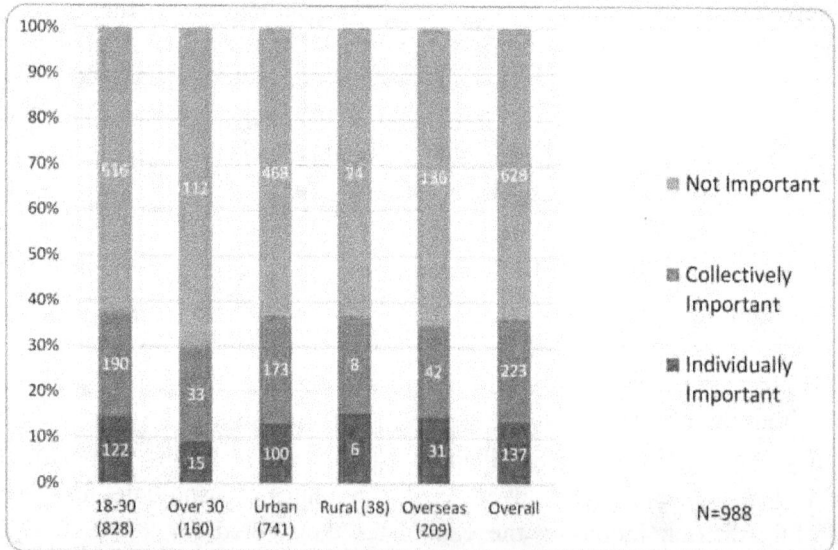

N=988

for. Around 15 per cent maintained that their votes were important to the election. However, most of those added that this importance was not because a single vote could have any impact, but rather it was meaningful because they had carried out their rights and responsibilities to the country.

Only a few respondents believed that their votes really counted towards the outcome of the election. Some respondents outright stated that the result of the election was preordained, and the election was held to legitimize the representatives chosen by the CPV. Older voters mentioned that previously, the number of elected officials matched the number of candidates available, meaning every candidate was predestined for election, and this renders voting merely symbolic. They added that the recent changes make voting looks more legitimate, but that does not change the fact that the outcomes of the election were decided even before the votes were cast. The over thirty age group is the most sceptical group as 60 per cent outright said that their vote has no meaning.

One respondent who had been a member of the CPV for thirty years at the time of the 2016 election, remarked:

> They've recently changed the process for selecting representatives. In the old days, there weren't any options. Now, not only in the National Assembly election but also within government agencies, they hold votes to choose leaders. It appears more democratic now, but it's essentially a choice between red candidates and blue candidates. They introduce blue candidates, who have no chance of being elected, to lend an appearance of legitimacy to the voting and elections. At my workplace, it's sometimes like this: they instruct all employees to vote to choose the head of the department from among the deputies, but we all know who would be selected. In the National Assembly election, it's undoubtedly the same.

Personal communication, 21 June 2016

Overall, more than 60 per cent of respondents believed that the elections have little meaning. Democracy, although unfamiliar to the average Vietnamese voters, is their preferred form of governance. While this makes it possible for the CPV to buttress their legitimacy through improvements in elections and democratic practices, the majority voters have no illusion about elections in Vietnam and in general, harbour strong suspicions that the results of the election were fraudulent and prearranged. The election itself was considered by most voters to be nothing more than a masquerade of democracy given the current political situation in Vietnam.

Voters' Attention to the Results of the 2016 Election

Voters' attention was surveyed before the announcement of the results of the National Assembly election. Despite almost no time having passed since the voting, more than half of the respondents said they are not interested in the outcome of the election, as shown in Figure 6.11. This result is logical, given that the majority had already said that they did not think that their vote would have any meaningful consequence. When questioned about their indifference, the respondents confirmed that their lack of faith in the organization of a fair and meaningful election naturally led to their apathy to the

Figure 6.11
Voters' Attention to the Results of the 2016 Election

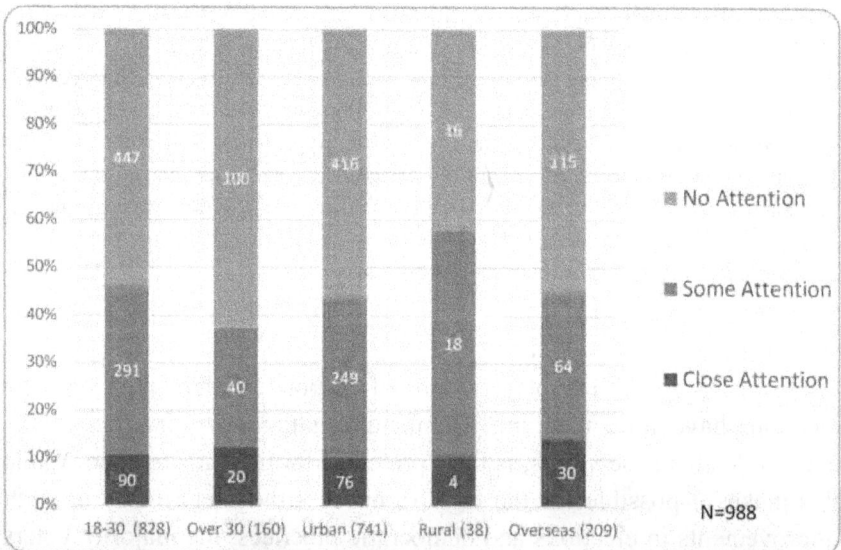

N=988

results. This echoes the sentiment that the election was fraudulent and just for show.

One-third of the respondents indicated that they would pay some attention to the results, with some reasoning that despite their distrust, they wanted to confirm their expectation that the results were fraudulent. While almost no respondents expressed strong support for any particular candidate, some revealed that they cared about independent candidates in general. Those respondents reported that they would not actively seek out information about the elections; however, if they happen to come across news about it, they would spend some time reading it.

Twelve per cent of the respondents stated that they would closely follow the outcome of the election. This number largely overlaps with the 17 per cent who believed that their votes held some relevance. Again, voters over age thirty expressed their strong apathy reasoning that the result of the election is already decided regardless of their vote. Overall, the responses to this question suggest that Vietnamese voters appear indifferent to election results due to a deep distrust of the electoral process.

Impact of the 2016 National Assembly Election on the Current Political Situation of Vietnam

As illustrated in Figure 6.12, the responses to this topic were consistent with those of the previous questions, indicating that Vietnamese voters have little faith in the electoral system. More than half of the respondents outright rejected the possibility of the election bringing about any changes to Vietnam's current political environment. Many of these respondents reiterated the argument that the members of the National Assembly were preordained and that the election was merely a facade organized by the CPV to legitimize its control over the assembly. However, 18 per cent of the respondents believed that despite the fraudulent nature of the election, minor changes could still occur with the election of a new generation of representatives.

Figure 6.12
Expected Impact of 2016 Legislative Election

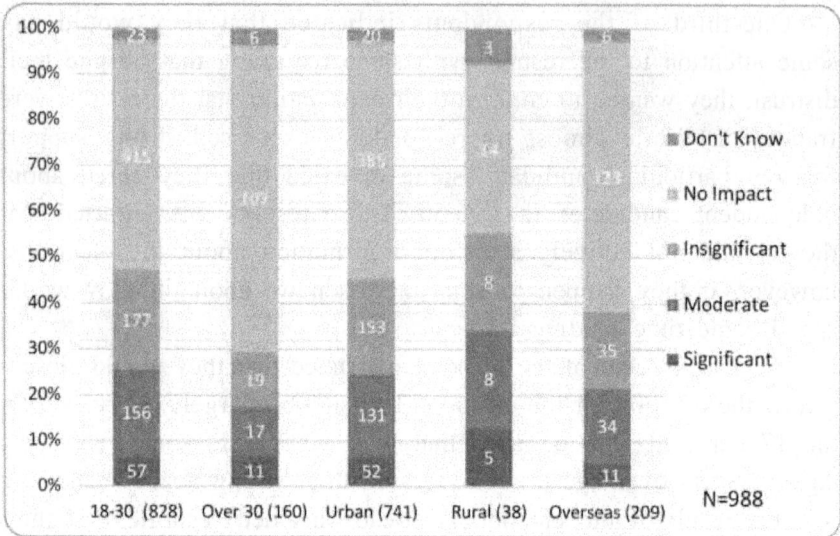

Approximately one in five respondents believed that gradual and noticeable changes would take place as some respondents highlighted the passing of Decision 262-QĐ/TW in 2014 that allowed for open scrutiny of top government officials, the CPV and the National Assembly through votes of confidence.

Seven per cent firmly believed that significant impact would result, potentially altering the political scene of Vietnam. Three per cent were unsure about what impact, if any, the election might have. In general, the Vietnamese were shown to have a realistic perception of the improvements that the election might bring to the political situation in their country, as nearly three in four respondents expressed pessimism about changes. However, one-fourth of the respondents still expected the election to bring about something new. People over age thirty are the most sceptical, with fewer than one in five respondents believing in improvements from the election. In terms of respondents' locations, rural voters are the most optimistic, while overseas voters tend to be more pessimistic. It should be noted that at least a dozen people who believed that there would be noticeable or significant changes further explained that the changes they were expecting were not improvements but rather a deterioration in the political landscape.

Survey on Voters' Perceptions of the 2021 National Assembly Election

There are several changes between the 2016 and the 2021 survey. To specifically address the National Assembly Election, questions about voters' perceptions of the general state of democracy in Vietnam were excluded. Instead, several questions were introduced to delve deeper into respondents' views and involvement in the 2021 legislative elections, allowing for a comparison between the 2016 and 2021 elections. The respondents' ages were inquired but not their locations. Given that five years had passed since the 2016 National Assembly Election, the author divided the two age groups at the age of thirty-five, rather than thirty.

Respondents' political alignment (i.e., if they are members of the CPV or not) were asked. In hindsight, this is a very important question as it would help to define the respondents' political leaning. In democracies, voters affiliated with a political party are more likely to vote for candidates from the same party. Since there is only one *de facto* legal political party in Vietnam, it is impossible to compare the voting tendency based on partisan preference. This question's main purpose is to separate CPV members and non-members, and respondents' answers in the next questions will be analysed based on their political leaning. The term "full member" means that the respondent is currently a member of the CPV. The CPV encompasses numerous sub-organizations, including the Ho Chi Minh Young Pioneer Organization and the Ho Chi Minh Communist Youth Union, which collectively represent most children and youth in Vietnam. There are also prospective members who are undergoing political training courses to become eligible for full membership. These individuals are not considered full members.

As of early 2021, roughly 5.2 per cent of Vietnam's total population are members of the CPV. However, in the survey, 34 per cent of respondents said they are currently a member of the CPV, which is more than six times the percentage of CPV members in the total population. Therefore, the survey results may be disproportionately in favour of the CPV. For this reason, the responses of non-members and members of the CPV will be analysed separately in some questions.

CPV membership is lifelong, and members usually keep their membership until their death. The annual total number of people who left the Party or were dismissed is difficult to estimate since the CPV does not publicize such statistics. Data can only be found on a case-by-case basis. For example, between 2015 and 2020, out of the 37,000 CPV members in Tay Ninh District, 424 members (1.14 per cent) were dismissed and 238 left voluntarily (0.65 per cent).[21] Members are usually dismissed for serious violations of the laws or the CPV Charter.[22] Five respondents said they were former CPV members who had left the organization voluntarily. However, since their views on the CPV were no more negative than those of regular non-members, their responses were analysed as if they were regular non-members.

In the 2016 survey, many CPV members outright refused to respond after reading the first few questions, reasoning that democracy is a sensitive topic and the survey is biased against the CPV. More CPV members agreed to take part in the 2021 survey, perhaps because democracy related questions were removed, and the questionnaire sounds more neutral to them.

The professions of the respondents have been surveyed. As shown in Figure 6.13, most non-government workers are also not CPV members, while almost two-thirds of current government employees are CPV members. Government workers who are not members of the CPV are typically junior employees, and most of them plan to obtain CPV membership in the future. Out of nearly one hundred respondents who have retired or left their public sector jobs, only five have relinquished their CPV membership.

Figure 6.13
2021 Survey Respondents' Occupations and CPV Membership

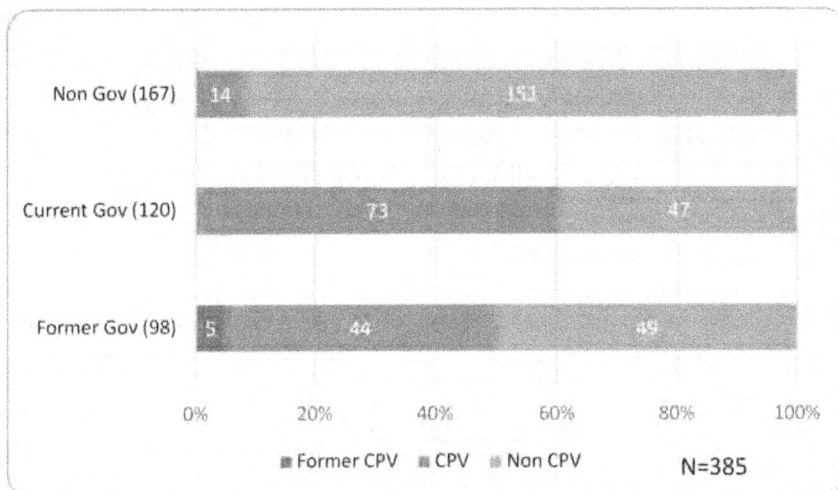

2021 National Assembly Election Participation

According to official reports from the National Assembly Office, voter turnout for the 2021 legislative election was 99.6 per cent, with virtually no illegal votes or election fraud recorded.[23] This extremely high voter turnout is consistent with the voter turnout of previous elections reported by official sources, as presented in Figure 5.3.

In the 2021 survey, the percentage of proxy voting remained high, at 17 per cent overall; the percentage of voters who voted directly unexpectedly increased to 57 per cent. Overall, 75 per cent of respondents voted, either directly or through another person.

Perhaps the most crucial factor is the more proactive approach of the government. This is reflected in the answers to the fifth question, where 85.4 per cent of respondents believed that the public information campaigns for the National Assembly election were either "very good" or "adequate". Respondents reported that officials would go door to door to remind people to vote during the week before the election. Preparation took place weeks, even months before the election day, with flyers and guidelines being distributed to each household. One organizer mentioned that the 2021 Election was the busiest for her. Local People's Councils and members of the Communist Youth Union were all employed to prepare for the National Assembly election. Furthermore, a representative of each family is asked to vote instead of the absent members.

The CPV recognizes the importance of democratic legitimacy and has been making subtle yet significant changes to the National Assembly elections to make them appear more legitimate to its voters, such as adding candidates to the ballot over that of the number of elected representatives. The unrealistically high voter turnout has been a subject of debate. Since admitting to falsifying statistics is out of the question, one way to address this issue is by increasing voter participation through its grassroots organizations.

In May and June 2021, the CPV seemed to enjoy widespread popular support due to its perceived successful handling of the COVID-19 pandemic, which may have led to higher voter turnout. Positive perception of the CPV is also reflected in the next questions. Spikes in approval ratings are not rare; for example, George W. Bush, despite his unremarkable presidency prior to September 2001, received an approval rating of 90 per cent thanks to his response to the September 11 attacks. The CPV's propaganda agencies had spared no effort to capitalize on the Party's initial successes against COVID-19 to improve the Party's popular support before the election day. As shown in Figure 6.14, the total number of COVID-19 cases reported by local authorities in Vietnam surged in July 2021, shortly after the National Assembly election, which was held on May 23rd, with results announced on June 11th.

Eighty-five per cent of CPV members participated in the voting process directly, nearly doubling the voter turnout compared to non-members, which stood at only 43 per cent, as illustrated by Figure 6.15. The percentage of voters who asked someone else to vote on their behalf, were unable to vote or chose not to vote is also significantly higher among non-members than among CPV members. In terms of age, voter turnout for the over thirty-five group is nearly 20 per

Figure 6.14
Total COVID-19 Cases in Vietnam and the 2021 NA Election

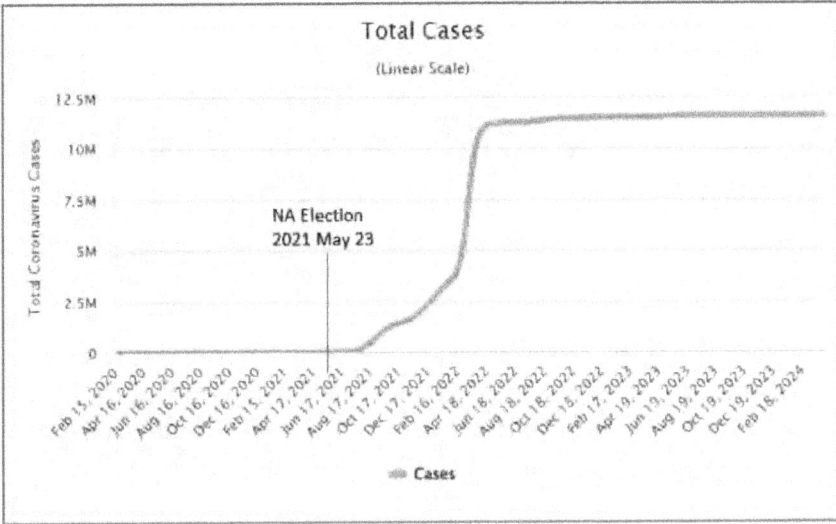

Source: Worldometer, "Vietnam Coronavirus Cases", https://www.worldometers.info/coronavirus/country/
viet-nam/ (accessed 17 July 2024).

Figure 6.15
Participation in the 2021 National Assembly Election

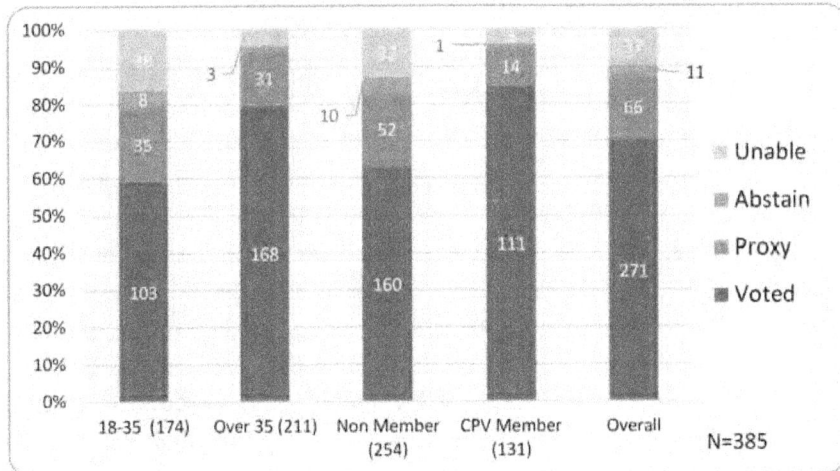

cent higher than that of the eighteen to thirty-five group. Political participation being lower among young people is consistent with the findings of the 2016 survey.

Ten per cent of the respondents were unable to vote, with 8 per cent of them residing overseas at the time of the election and 2 per cent encountering issues related to voter registration, logistics or transportation. Similar to the situation in 2016, Vietnamese citizens who were not residing in Vietnam at the time of the election were not able to vote. For instance, when enquiries were made regarding voting in Japan, the Embassy of the Socialist Republic of Vietnam simply replied that they did not have the capability to do so. As of December 2020, the number of Vietnamese nationals in Japan was 448,053 people,[24] most of whom were unable to return to Vietnam by the time of the National Assembly election due to the COVID-19 pandemic outbreak and the subsequent restrictions on international travel, and thus were unable to vote. In the 2016 survey, the proportion of overseas respondents was disproportionately higher than that of Vietnamese expatriates relative to the country's population. Drawing from this experience, efforts were made to limit the number of respondents living outside of Vietnam in the 2021 survey.

In 2020, it was estimated by MOFA that there were 5.3 million Vietnamese citizens overseas.[25] Similar to the 2016 election, official statistics by the Vietnamese government are ambiguous on whether overseas Vietnamese are accounted for. PAPI (2022) reports a voter turnout for the National Assembly election at 63 per cent, excluding proxy voting.[26]

The author himself was not in Vietnam but was registered as a legal voter and his vote was cast by his father. Respondents also confirmed that this illegal practice is widespread and openly allowed by election officials. In certain voting districts, especially in crowded residential areas in Hanoi, one person voting for the whole family is even encouraged as a measure to slow down the spread of COVID-19.

Interestingly enough, among CPV members surveyed, 10 per cent asked somebody to vote for them while fully aware that such action is a violation of the Election Law and almost 3 per cent deliberately abstained from voting with the most common explanation being that they were either apathetic towards or sceptical about the election and felt that voting was meaningless. This demonstrates that although they constitute the group most supportive of the ruling regime, with many individuals serving as electoral officials, not all CPV members view the legislative elections favourably.

Selection Criteria for National Assembly Representatives (2021)

The criteria for selecting representatives do not differ significantly between CPV members and non-members, except for the political alignment of the candidate as almost no CPV member prefers a self-nominated candidate. As shown in Figure 6.16, similar to the 2016 survey, the majority of voters consider the academic and professional backgrounds of the candidates as the most important criteria, followed by their political theoretical background. While academic and professional backgrounds are self-explanatory, political theoretical background requires clarification.

Figure 6.16
Representative Selection Criteria (2021)

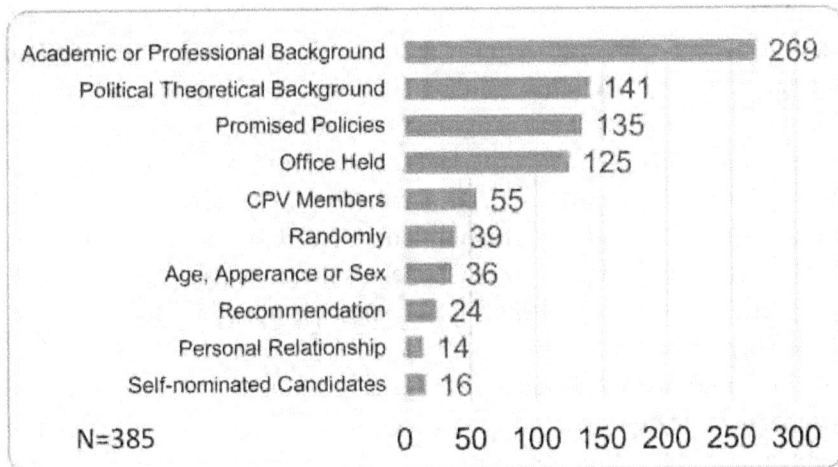

Criteria	Value
Academic or Professional Background	269
Political Theoretical Background	141
Promised Policies	135
Office Held	125
CPV Members	55
Randomly	39
Age, Apperance or Sex	36
Recommendation	24
Personal Relationship	14
Self-nominated Candidates	16

N=385

According to Order 12/TC-TTVH by the Central Propaganda Department of the Communist Party of Vietnam, there are three levels of political theory education: elementary, intermediate and advanced. People who have graduated from Vietnamese universities, colleges and military academies are considered at the elementary political theory level. Those who graduated from Vietnamese universities and colleges with a major in political science, economics or humanities, those who received special political theories training at CPV training centres, and those who hold a master's or doctoral degree from a Vietnamese or socialist country's university are considered at the intermediate level. People who hold a bachelor's, master's or doctoral degree on Marxism-Leninism and Ho Chi Minh Thought, or who have completed cadre training at military academies, are considered at the advanced political theory level.

In short, a candidate's political theoretical background indicates their level of proficiency in the official state ideology. Those who are more proficient in political theory are considered more loyal to the CPV and have a better chance of career advancement. High level of political theory education is considered mandatory for advancement in many cases. As illustrated in Figure 6.17, the political theoretical background of each candidate is listed in their profile, which is made public before the National Assembly election.

Many respondents mistook this for the leadership skills, management capacities and expertise of the candidate. Perhaps this could explain the fact that even though a candidate's political theory level is closely linked to that candidate's alignment to the CPV, 139 respondents chose this as one of their criteria for choosing a representative while only 55 said that they prioritize candidates nominated by the CPV. In contrast, only sixteen respondents listed self-nomination (i.e., not nominated by the CPV) as one of their criteria. PAPI (2022) also reports that respondents prefer party members as their National Assembly representative.[27]

The third and the fourth most chosen criteria are policies promised by the candidates and the office that they held, respectively. The percentages of responses that chose the policies promised by the

Figure 6.17

A List of Candidates for the 2021 National Assembly Election

ÚY BAN BẦU CỬ
THÀNH PHỐ HÀ NỘI

CỘNG HÒA XÃ HỘI CHỦ NGHĨA VIỆT NAM
Độc lập - Tự do - Hạnh phúc

DANH SÁCH CHÍNH THỨC
NHỮNG NGƯỜI ỨNG CỬ ĐẠI BIỂU QUỐC HỘI KHÓA XV Ở ĐƠN VỊ BẦU CỬ SỐ 03
GỒM QUẬN CẦU GIẤY, QUẬN NAM TỪ LIÊM VÀ QUẬN THANH XUÂN

Personal information listed is identical to that of the 2016 list of candidates. All five candidates were members of the CPV and were working for the government or state-owned company at the time of the election. Three of the candidates were nominated for the first time. Only one candidate of the 2016 election was nominated again. Candidates' addresses are cropped out.

Source: the author.

candidates as one of the criteria do not differ greatly between the 2016 survey (42.1 per cent) and the 2021 survey (35 per cent). Roughly one in three respondents chose "current position and office held by the candidate" as one of their preferred criteria. The percentage of people who voted randomly also remains more or less the same with 10.1 per cent choosing this option in the 2016 survey and 9.3 per cent in the 2021 survey, respectively. Nine per cent voted based on the candidates' age, appearance or sex in comparison with 12.7 per cent in the 2016 survey.

Overall, the results of the 2021 survey remained consistent to that of the 2016 survey except for criteria related to political matters, which showed an increase in the support of voters to the CPV. The high number of CPV members responding to the 2021 survey is one reason that explains this discrepancy. Nevertheless, non-CPV voters also expressed favourable views towards the CPV. When asked about their preference for CPV members over independent candidates, one voter responded that she is optimistic about the leadership of the CPV because she believes they have handled the pandemic very well and that the Party's leadership would be beneficial to the country. While some voters also share this view, it should be noted that only 14 per cent of voters, both CPV members and non-members, explicitly expressed support for communist candidates, compared to 5 per cent who preferred independent candidates. This indicates that, unlike elections in the West, Vietnamese voters do not consider the political alignment of candidates as important as other qualities.

Perception of the Public Information Campaign

As shown in Figure 6.18, 93 per cent of the respondents reported that public information campaigns for the 2021 National Assembly Election were carried out. More than half of the respondents thought that those campaigns were "very good", while 31 per cent viewed

Figure 6.18
Evaluation of Election Public Information Campaign

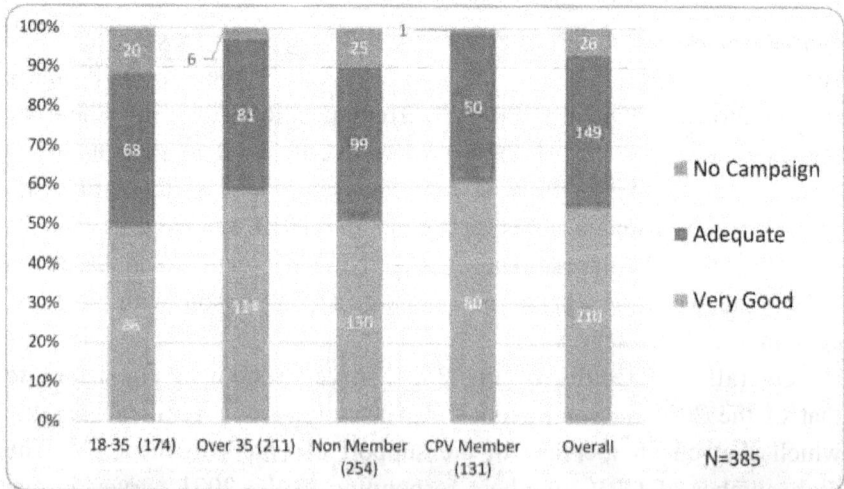

them as "adequate". Only 8 per cent responded that the campaigns were ineffective. Only 3 per cent were unsure whether any campaigns were carried out or not, and 4 per cent thought that there were no campaigns.

Among CPV members, more than 90 per cent thought that the public information campaigns were successful and only 7 per cent judged that they were ineffective. All CPV members were aware that public information campaigns were carried out in their voting district and only one person expressed an entirely apathetic attitude towards those campaigns. While most non-member respondents shared the same view, 8 per cent reported that they were not informed that those campaigns were carried out in their voting district and 4 per cent expressed apathy towards those campaigns. These results are expected as CPV members are usually asked to participate in the preparation for the elections.

Interviews with an election organizer revealed that much more effort was put into preparing for the 2021 National Assembly Election, including the public information campaigns, in comparison to 2016, despite the COVID-19 pandemic. Organizers learned from their past experiences and created flyers, maps and voting manuals, which were distributed to every household in the district. Figure 6.20 shows a map to a voting venue in the Cau Giay Voting District. Some voters reported that organizers visited each household to encourage people to vote. In certain districts, organizers also provided advice to voters on who to vote for.

Figure 6.19 shows a pamphlet with information regarding the 2021 People's Councils and National Assembly election issued to voters of Cau Giay District, Hanoi. The information includes time and date of the election and voters' rights and responsibilities. The front-page features people from all walks of life voting. To emphasize the inclusiveness and democratic nature of the National Assembly elections, it is customary for the following people to be illustrated in such documents: a police officer, a woman in *áo dài*, a factory worker, a coast guard or a soldier, an old man or woman, a person from an ethnic minority group and a monk.

Figure 6.19
A Pamphlet of 2021 Legislative Elections

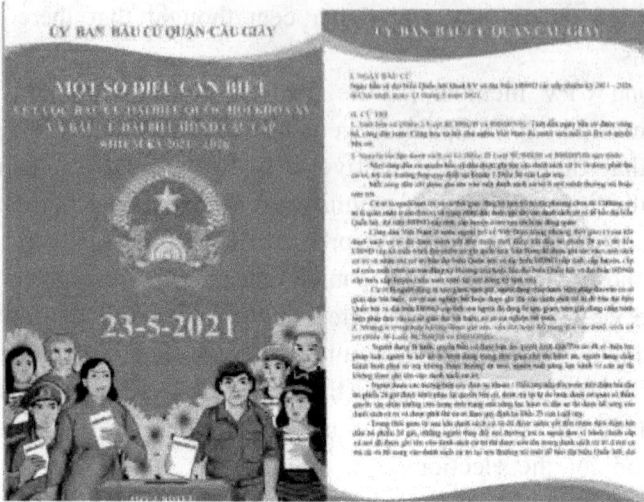

Source: the author.

Figure 6.20
A Map to the Voting Venue

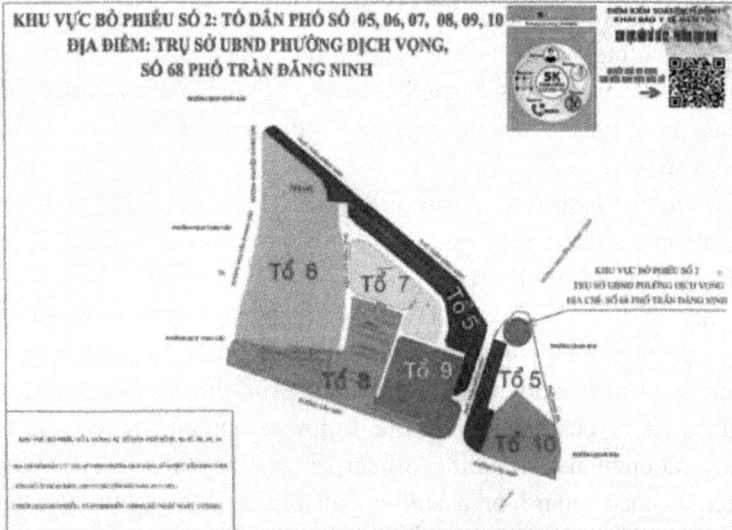

Source: the author.

Figure 6.21 shows an unfilled voter registration card for the 2021 legislative elections. The back of the registration card reads "To maintain social distance amidst the COVID-19 pandemic, please go to the polling location between 9 a.m. and 10 a.m. on May 23 2021. This is not mandatory, and you can go to the polling location at any time between 7 a.m. and 7 p.m. on May 23 2021 that your schedule allows." Although votes cast by any other than the voter themselves are considered to be invalid, election organizers encouraged one person to vote for the whole family to prevent the spread of the pandemic.

It should be noted that those materials are collected in Hanoi, the capital city of Vietnam and the seat of power of the CPV. Election

Figure 6.21
An Unfilled Voter Registration Card

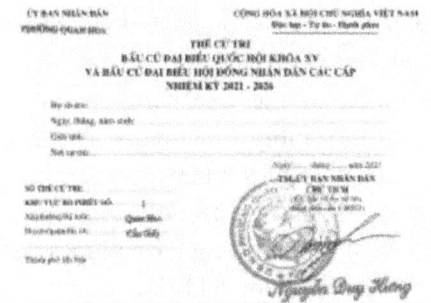

Source: the author.

preparation and organization in more remote areas may not be as sophisticated or adequate.

2021 National Assembly Election's Transparency

While there have been conflicting views regarding the transparency and accountability of legislative elections in Vietnam, the government has always maintained that they are free and fair. As mentioned earlier, the National Assembly's Standing Committee oversees the overall process of the legislative elections. The National Assembly has also appointed the National Election Council, whose main responsibility is to organize, maintain security and monitor the legislative elections. The Fatherland Front local committees, under the direction of the Fatherland Front Central Committee, are also responsible for monitoring the election process, including vote counting. As these organizations are under either direct or indirect control of the CPV, the transparency and accountability of legislative elections in Vietnam are not monitored as a whole by any third-party organizations, and as such can only be observed on a case-by-case basis.

Voters' perception of the transparency and accountability of the May 2021 National Assembly Election is shown in Figure 6.22. Non-CPV members' perception of the transparency and accountability of the May 2021 National Assembly Election is generally favourable. Forty-six per cent thought that the election was transparent and accountable, although 26 per cent of them added that small improvements could have been made. Among CPV members, the perception of the election was overwhelmingly positive. Sixty-one per cent thought that the 2021 election was transparent and accountable, while 31 per cent viewed that minor adjustments could have been made. Roughly one in five non-CPV members thought that certain stages or the whole election could be fraudulent, while this number among CPV members was only one in twenty. Eighteen per cent of non-CPV members chose the option "I do not know", while only three per cent of CPV members did so.

Overall, the election was positively perceived as almost three in four respondents thought that the election was either free and fair

Figure 6.22
2021 National Assembly Election's Transparency

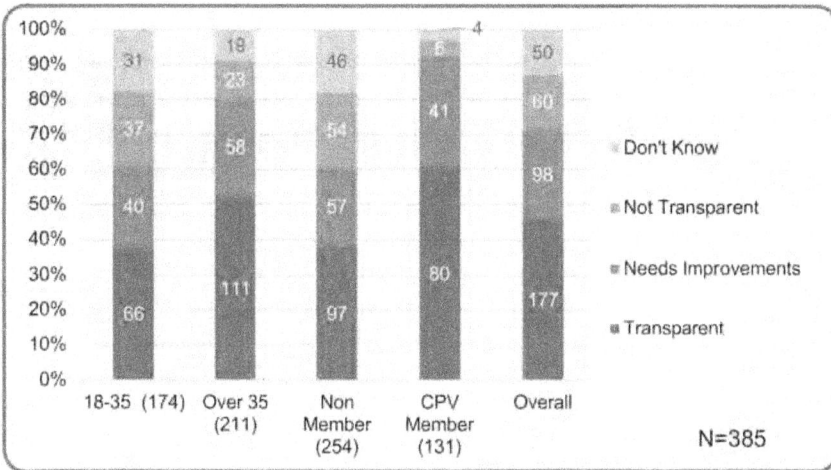

or needing minor improvements, while one in four respondents were sceptical about the transparency of the election.

Most people who had expressed their satisfaction by saying that the election was free and fair in the previous question also responded that they could not think of any particular stage of the election that needs significant improvement. In total, 278 respondents chose the answer "no stage in particular", matching the number of respondents who had chosen the answers "the election was transparent and accountable" and "election was transparent and accountable but some small adjustments could be made" in the previous question.

Among respondents who were unsatisfactory with the transparency and accountability of the election, the stages that needed improvement the most were the voter meetings and candidate's electoral campaign, followed by vote counting and results announcement. The nomination and self-nomination as well as candidate screening processes were also thought to be not transparent enough. Less than 10 per cent of the 385 respondents thought that the voter registration and voting processes were not transparent. Respondents also considered the public information campaign successful, which is consistent with the answers provided in the fourth question. The voters raised a few of the issues with each stage of the election as illustrated in Figure 6.23.

The voter meetings and election campaign were believed to be not adequately publicized. Most non-CPV members have never attended any voter meetings and, as a result, have never seen a candidate in person and possess limited knowledge about the candidates and their policies. In contrast, more than half of the interviewed party members have attended at least one voter meeting. Some of them acknowledged that they are frequently invited to such meetings and could be considered a "professional voter". Beyond these gatherings, candidates have very limited opportunities for election campaigning. Furthermore, their information provided to the public must be reviewed and approved by the authorities.

Respondents also reported that the vote counting and result announcement stages lack transparency. In theory, the local election council is responsible for vote counting, and candidates or their representatives, the nominating office's representative and news reporters are allowed to be present during the vote counting process. Additionally,

Figure 6.23
Needed Improvements for the National Assembly Elections

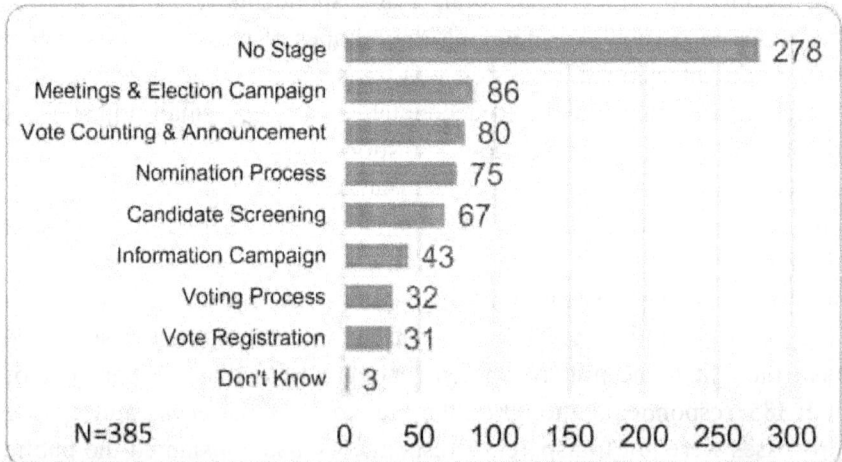

Category	Value
No Stage	278
Meetings & Election Campaign	86
Vote Counting & Announcement	80
Nomination Process	75
Candidate Screening	67
Information Campaign	43
Voting Process	32
Vote Registration	31
Don't Know	3

N=385

two literate and trustworthy voters are invited as witnesses. Ordinary voters are not permitted to be present during the vote counting process. Since all of the individuals mentioned above are affiliated with the CPV or must be approved by the authorities beforehand, there is no third party present during the vote counting. Undesirable candidates are almost always removed during the second consultative conference and as such cannot monitor the vote counting process. Respondents who were directly involved in vote counting reported that there was no fraudulent activity in their district, but the results were as expected. Some respondents mentioned that rarely minor unexpected results can occur, but it is nearly impossible for high-ranking party officials, such as those in the Politburo, to lose the election.

As the nomination and candidate screening processes are often used to get rid of undesirable self-nominated candidates, they also received some criticism. People who acknowledge those stages are not fair and transparent enough suggest that more independent candidates should be allowed to participate in the election.

Most Vietnamese voters are apathetic towards elections and have limited knowledge of the voting process. This may be one of the reasons explaining their apathy towards voting, even though support for the ruling party reached its peak during this period.

Number of Unsuccessful Candidates Voted for

In the 2021 National Assembly Election, 184 voting districts were allocated across five municipalities and fifty-eight provinces. Both Hanoi and Ho Chi Minh City were subdivided into ten voting districts, while other municipalities and provinces typically comprised two or three voting districts each. Among these 184 voting districts, 132 had a 5/3 candidate-to-seat ratio, while 52 had a 4/2 candidate-to-seat ratio.[28] In districts with a 5/3 ratio, voters were expected to select up to three candidates, while in districts with a 4/2 ratio, they were to choose fewer than two candidates by crossing out the names of unwanted candidates. Ballots featuring more crossed-out names than the maximum allowable delegates were considered invalid, as were ballots with no crossed-out names. Additionally, voters were prohibited from inscribing any additional information on the ballot card (2015 Election Law, Article 74).

While the survey was carried out right after the results of the National Assembly were announced, a significant proportion of the respondent's showed apathy to those results, as shown in Figure 6.24. Forty-five per cent of respondents said that they did not care about the results of the National Assembly election or did not even bother to remember the name of the candidates they had voted for. Far fewer respondents who are CPV members chose the same option, at 26 per cent. An observation can be made when the results of the 2016 survey are also taken into consideration: voters participate more actively in elections when support for the ruling regime is high and are more likely to abstain from voting when support for the ruling regime wanes. In other words, although many have little interest in who they vote for, they go to vote to show support for the ruling regime.

Figure 6.24
Unsuccessful Candidates Voted for by Respondents

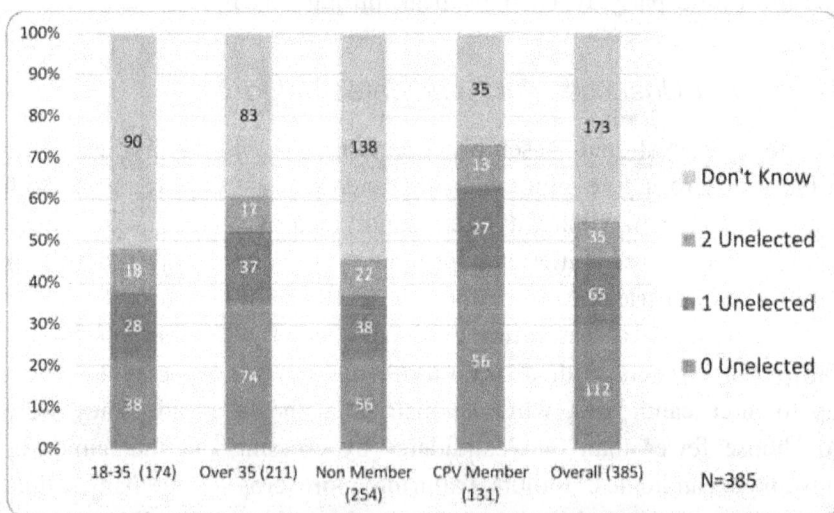

N=385

The responses to this question are consistent with the 2016 survey, in which 55 per cent of the respondents said that they would pay no attention to the results of the National Assembly election. The responses in the 2021 survey imply that despite having a relatively favourable view towards the ruling CPV, many voters did not have strong feelings towards the National Assembly election or any candidates in particular. Many openly stated that while they support the government in general, they do not feel that there is much difference between one candidate and another. Non-CPV member respondents seemed to be much more apathetic to the National Assembly election than CPV members.

Despite voters' apathy, the results of the 2021 Election were far from random. If we assume that each candidate has an equal likelihood of being elected, disregarding their individual strengths and support, then in the 2021 National Assembly Election, each voter has approximately a 12 per cent chance of selecting all the successful candidates within their district[29]—for instance, choosing two winning candidates in a 4/2 district and three winning candidates in a 5/3 district. Among those voters who recall their choices and monitored the election outcomes, young people and non-CPV members are the least likely to select all winning candidates, whereas CPV members are significantly more likely to do so. Even after excluding individuals who do not remember who they voted for, about 40 per cent of CPV members successfully chose all the winning candidates, a rate four times higher than the expected random selection rate. Non-CPV members are also twice as likely to select all winning candidates compared to the aforementioned probability. This suggests that, although all candidates must be approved by the CPV in one way or another, some are more appealing to voters than others. Explaining this phenomenon, some CPV voters said that by looking at the profile of the candidates, they can tell which ones are earmarked for office and which ones are just placeholders.

The publicly available information about candidates provided by local election councils includes their name, date of birth, gender, current address, hometown, ethnic group, religion, educational and professional qualifications, workplace, position, political affiliation, experience in the National Assembly and experience in local People's Councils. However, there is also an unmentioned criterion that is crucial to the success of candidates in the National Assembly election, as well as in local council level elections. This criterion is the rank of the candidate within the hierarchy of the CPV. Figure 6.25 illustrates the hierarchy within the CPV and provides an estimate of the membership at each rank.

Figure 6.25
CPV Hierarchy and Membership Distribution

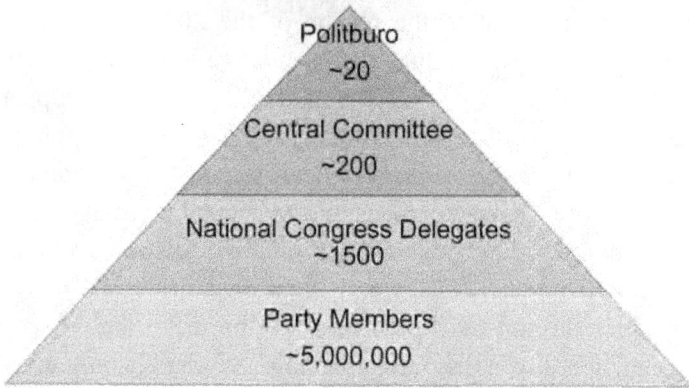

Among the approximately five million members of the CPV, every five years, up to 1,500 individuals in managerial positions are invited to the National Congress. At this congress, around 200 members are elected to the Central Committee, which, as the name suggests, forms the core leadership circle of the CPV. Of these 200 Central Committee members, approximately 175 are full members, and 25 are alternate members, maintaining a ratio of seven full members for every alternate member. The twenty-five alternate members, colloquially referred to as the "red seeds",[30] are typically promising leaders under the age of forty-five. Although ineligible for selection to the Politburo, they are anticipated to ascend to the top leadership positions in the future. Of the Central Committee members, up to twenty are usually selected for the Politburo, where most of the decision-making power is concentrated. Membership in this elite body is so selective that even holding a ministerial position does not ensure inclusion. Table 6.2 illustrates the success rates of candidates categorized by their position within the CPV.

Table 6.2
CPV Ranks and Election Success Rate

	2021		2016	
	Number	Percentage	Number	Percentage
Candidates by Nomination				
Total Candidates	868	100%	870	100%
Centrally Nominated	203	23.39%	197	22.64%
Locally Nominated	665	76.61%	673	77.36%
CPV Central Committee	102	11.75%	100	11.49%
Politburo	17	1.61%	19	2.18%
Success Rate				
Elected Delegates	499	57.49%	496	57.01%
Centrally Nominated	194	95.57%	182	92.39%
Locally Nominated	301	45.26%	314	46.66%
CPV Central Committee	101	99.02%	100	100.00%
Politburo	17	100.00%	19	100.00%

Centrally nominated candidates are significantly more likely to be elected than locally nominated ones, as evidenced in the 2016 and 2021 National Assembly elections. In both instances, over 90 per cent of centrally nominated candidates secured election, while fewer than half of the locally nominated candidates achieved similar success. Research on the 1992 and 2007 elections suggest that upsets are possible.[31, 32] This is also the case in the 2016 and 2021 elections. For example, in the 2016 National Assembly Election, fifteen centrally nominated candidates were not elected,[33] and in the 2021 election, this figure was nine.[34] Ho Chi Minh City presents a challenging environment for centrally nominated candidates; in 2016, seven out of fourteen failed to win seats, and in 2021, six out of thirteen suffered defeats. Except for the case of Hanoi in 2016, where four out of thirteen centrally nominated candidates were unsuccessful, all other unsuccessful candidates competed for seats in districts in southern provinces. This trend underscores the potential influence of geographic location on voters' political preferences.

Although the CPV does not officially recognize "blue" and "red" candidates, voters appear to be able to distinguish between them in their own way. In northern provinces, being a "red" candidate almost always secures a seat; however, this is not the case in the South. In locations such as Ho Chi Minh City, being centrally nominated seems to adversely affect election prospects. For instance, the election rates for centrally nominated candidates in the 2016 and 2021 National Assembly elections were only 50 per cent and 46 per cent, respectively, both of which are lower than the overall election probabilities, which stood at approximately 57 per cent. While this excludes the possibility of a completely orchestrated election, perhaps from the perspective of the CPV, the rejection of centrally nominated candidates by voters may be considered a manageable risk. Furthermore, the rejection of centrally nominated candidates can be used to propagate the notion that the National Assembly elections are democratic and free from fraud.

While being centrally nominated does not always secure a seat in the National Assembly, membership in the Central Committee of the CPV always guarantees election if nominated. Typically, about half of the two hundred Central Committee members are nominated for the National Assembly elections. Among the total of 202 Central Committee members nominated during the 2016 and 2021 elections, only one failed. Tran Van Nam, Binh Duong Province's Party Committee Secretary, initially won over 81 per cent of the vote;[35] however, his delegate status was revoked by the National Election Council due to violations of the CPV's code of conduct. Interestingly, Nam's disqualification as a National Assembly delegate stemmed from infractions committed as a CPV member, illustrating the overlapping roles of the CPV and the National Assembly, despite their nominal independence. Nam was subsequently arrested in July 2021 and sentenced to seven years in prison for violating regulations on managing and using state assets, resulting in significant losses.[36]

All nineteen members of the 2016 Politburo were also delegates of the National Assembly, while seventeen of the eighteen 2021 Politburo members held the same role. Tran Van Nen, Ho Chi Minh City's Party Committee Secretary and a 2016 National Assembly delegate, although elected as a Politburo member, did not seek re-election to the 2021 National Assembly. It can be concluded that while centrally nominated candidates have the backing of the CPV and are often seen as preferred candidates, they are not guaranteed seats in the National Assembly. The distribution of voting districts plays a crucial role in determining a candidate's success as it affects opposition strength, candidate-to-seat ratio, and critically, political inclinations of the voters.

Although membership in the Central Committee of the CPV almost always ensures election, there are rare instances where delegate status can be revoked. Similarly, being a member of the Politburo, which is the most elite decision-making body of the CPV, typically secures a seat in the National Assembly; however, even those top leaders can be removed. As of May 2024, only thirteen out of the eighteen Politburo members elected to the National Assembly in May 2021 still retain their seats. The five dismissed officials and their previous positions include Nguyen Xuan Phuc, State President until January 2023; Vo Van Thuong, State President until March 2023; Vuong Dinh Hue, National Assembly Chairman until May 2023; Pham Binh Minh, Deputy Prime Minister until December 2022; and Tran Tuan Anh, Head of the Central Economic Committee of the CPV until January 2024.

Expected Impact of the Election on Democracy

As illustrated in Figure 6.26, to some respondents a more liberal and democratic political system is considered to be positive, while to others retaining the status quo of the political system while voting in better candidates is considered to be an improvement. Furthermore, opinion among people who support more liberal changes differs. For example, some called for an immediate push for a multiparty system, while others wanted the system to democratize gradually.

Figure 6.26
Expected Impact of the 2021 Election on Democracy

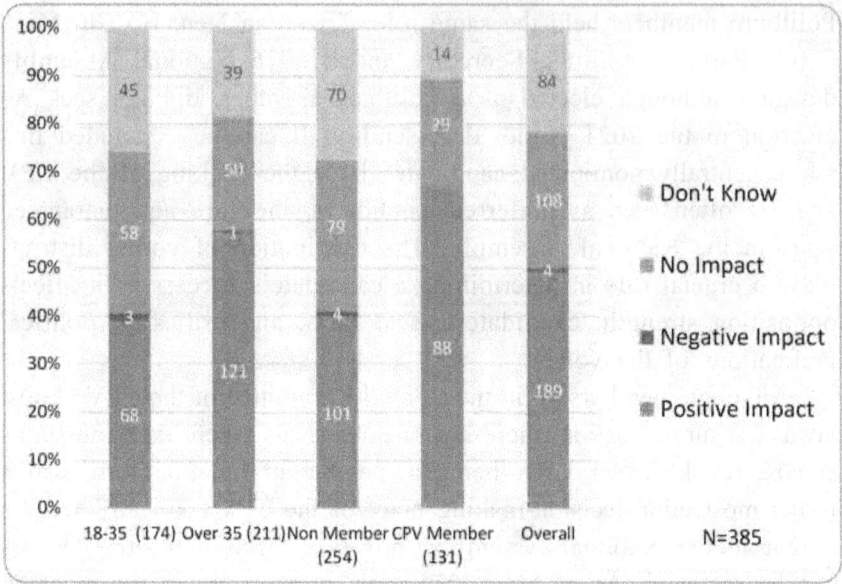

Although overall one in every two respondents believed that the 2021 National Assembly Election would bring about positive change to the current situation of democracy in Vietnam, the difference between CPV members and non-CPV member respondents on this issue is clear. While 67 per cent of CPV member respondents thought that the 2021 National Assembly Election would improve democracy in Vietnam, only 40 per cent of non-CPV members thought so. Thirty-one per cent of non-CPV members said that there would be no significant change in the situation of democracy in Vietnam while only 22 per cent of CPV members gave the same answer. Nevertheless, even among non-CPV members, the number of respondents who held a negative view towards the expected impact of the 2021 National Assembly Election is quite insignificant.

Overall, respondents expressed optimism regarding the potential changes that the 2021 National Assembly Election could bring. They believed that Vietnam has been successful in combating the COVID-19 pandemic and addressing issues of corruption. This illustrates that the government's immediate performance can significantly shape the perception of an average voter. The CPV is aware of this and has actively utilized state-controlled media to portray a positive image of its efforts, particularly in the lead-up to the National Assembly election. According to one reporter, the CPV even goes so far as to establish a quota for negative news and strictly prohibit news that appears critical of the political system.

Rating the State of Democracy in Vietnam from One to Ten (2021)

The final question mirrored its counterpart in the 2016 survey. This question aims to evaluate respondents' overall perception on the current situation of democracy in Vietnam. Prior to answering this question, the scale of one to ten is explained to respondents as follows: ten means a perfect political system where citizens can fully execute the power of the State directly and indirectly through the National Assembly, while one means an absolute totalitarian system where citizens are completely powerless to express their opinions and execute their political rights. Overall, as shown in Figure 6.27, CPV members seemed to hold a more positive view towards the current situation of democracy in Vietnam than non-CPV members did, although not significantly so. Non-CPV members gave an average score of 6.85 while CPV members' average score was 7.53. The average score given by all the respondents was 7.09. Given that in 2016, the average score given by voters was only 3.57, it seems that perception of voters on the situation of democracy in Vietnam had greatly improved during those five years. In comparison, the score given to Vietnam by the Economist Intelligence Unit in their 2020 Democracy Index was 2.94.[37] Interviews with voters after the election revealed that most of them think that the 2021 election was more orderly and accountable than the 2016 election, as more effort has been put into the preparation for the election in the context of a global pandemic.

Figure 6.27
Vietnamese Democracy on the Scale of 10 (2021)

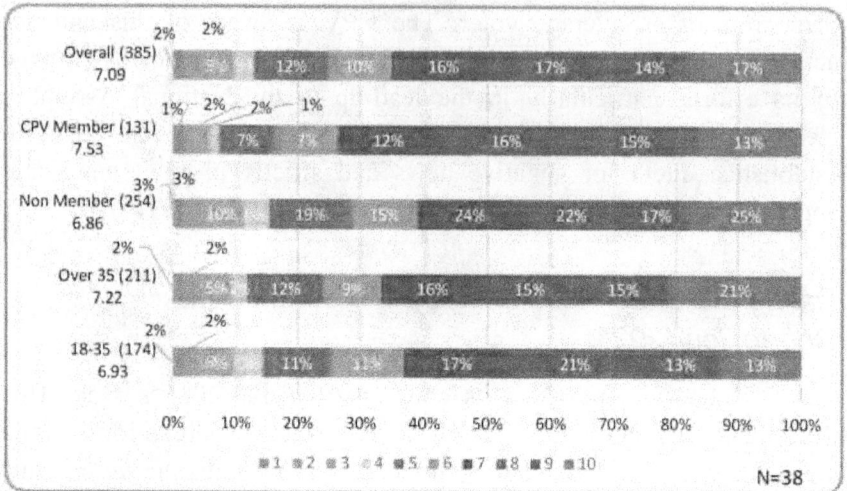

Nevertheless, the perception of democracy in Vietnam being greatly improved between 2016 and 2021 without any substantial change in the political system shows how fickle public opinion could be. Interviews with voters suggest that many, if not most of the voters, are confused between freedom and performance. Between May 2016 and June 2021, Vietnam enjoyed a period of fast economic growth with the GDP Annual Growth Rate averaging more than 6 per cent.[38] Furthermore, prior to July 2021, Vietnam had been widely praised as one of the most competent countries in dealing with the COVID-19 pandemic.[39] Success in combating the pandemic was attributed to the early detection and containment strategy employed by the government. From July 2021, however, the number of COVID cases in Vietnam sharply increased which many Vietnamese believed that it has exposed the loopholes in the government's strategy.

Nevertheless, the most significant accomplishment of the government during this period was the anti-corruption campaign spearheaded by Nguyen Phu Trong. The campaign has resulted in the arrest of many high-ranking party members and government officials on corruption charges and has been well-received by ordinary Vietnamese. This effort has been reflected in improved ratings given to Vietnam by non-governmental organizations such as Transparency International. As suggested by the earlier findings in this book, accountability and responsibility on the part of the government are the most critical areas that need improvement, according to Vietnamese voters. Therefore, many view the anti-corruption campaign as a demonstration of a more transparent government, which has translated into a more favourable perception.

Public approval can also be improved through superficial appeasement, "bread and circuses". For instance, the Vietnamese national football team's successive victories against Southeast Asian rivals and the positive outcomes in the SEA Games may have contributed to a positive public perception.

Understanding the Mindset of Vietnamese Voters

At this point in the book, readers may have noticed various discrepancies and shortcomings in the two surveys. Some of these issues arise from the inherent risks to both researchers and respondents when conducting sensitive surveys within Vietnamese borders, as well as the flaws associated with the convenience sampling method. However, in hindsight, many of these shortcomings were the result of the author's oversight and lack of understanding of the mindset of Vietnamese voters. This section discusses the discrepancies and shortcomings of the two surveys and suggests improvements for further research, particularly concerning the upcoming 2026 legislative elections so that the same discrepancies can be mitigated or otherwise avoided.

Few surveys have been conducted in Vietnam regarding legislative elections, most notably the PAPI survey, which has been discussed in this book. Large-scale surveys on sensitive subjects, such as citizens' perceptions of political issues, require government approval regarding their content and reporting, which may compromise their integrity. Without official approval, efforts to conduct such surveys may be hindered by law enforcement through both official and unofficial means. Additionally, respondents often hesitate to respond to surveys unauthorized by the government and are unlikely to answer truthfully to researchers they do not know personally or are introduced to them by people they know. Therefore, while convenience sampling may not be the most accurate sampling method, it is the most feasible for gathering enough responses. To address the inherent shortcomings of convenience sampling, improvements can be made in the timing, design of the survey and data analysis.

The results of legislative elections in Vietnam are typically announced two weeks after the elections. During this period, political enthusiasm is higher than usual, and voters are more willing to respond to survey requests. However, this enthusiasm tends to wane quickly. The 2016 survey, conducted immediately after the National Assembly election, received a much higher response rate compared to the 2021 survey, which was conducted after the announcement of the results. It seems that, after only two weeks, voters had lost much interest in the elections and showed little inclination to respond to the survey. Most of the voters surveyed also expressed little interest in the election results. Therefore, conducting the survey immediately after the election seems to attract respondents who are otherwise apathetic to politics. Nevertheless, by doing so, researchers may lose the opportunity to study respondents' perceptions of the election outcomes.

Another reason for the lower response rate in the 2021 survey may be the ongoing anti-corruption campaign led by Nguyen Phu Trong. While the media primarily focused on high-ranking officials, minor violations such as police officers accepting bribes to overlook traffic infractions or tax evasion were also subject to punishment. Many voters refused to participate in the survey because they were uncertain about the potential risks associated with their involvement.

Questions regarding the address or name of respondents were not asked because many would refuse to participate in a sensitive survey if there was a risk that their personal information might be compromised. Nevertheless, information regarding the respondents' voting district and affiliation with the CPV should be collected as it would help to classify respondents better, thereby alleviating the shortcomings of the convenience sampling method.

This information is crucial because the location of a voting district (e.g., in the North or the South, urban area or rural area) may affect voters' political leanings. While being centrally nominated is generally advantageous for a candidate, this is not the case in southern provinces, especially in Ho Chi Minh City, as half of the centrally nominated candidates assigned to Ho Chi Minh City failed to win seats. Respondents from the South or those with roots in the South also seem to be much more critical of the ruling regime. In contrast, respondents from Central-Northern and Northern provinces appear to be more tolerant of communist rule. Furthermore, it appears that rural dwellers are more tolerant than their urban counterparts. These observations on voters' locations and their political leanings, however, warrant more research. The voting district being in urban or rural areas may affect the election's organization and campaign, press coverage, vote counting and results announcement. Some respondents reported that due to the remoteness of their location, they had to travel great lengths to vote. This also applies to people living overseas and people who are not residing in their assigned voting district at the time of the election. As such, the location of the voters may affect not only their political leanings but also their ability to vote and overall voter turnout.

Overseas Vietnamese citizens are another topic that should be treated with care. Overseas Vietnamese account for roughly 5 per cent of the total population of Vietnam in 2021. Only Vietnamese citizens who are eligible to vote are invited to participate in the surveys. Overseas Vietnamese expatriates have diverse backgrounds, which can be classified by their reasons for travelling abroad such as those who left Vietnam for political or economic reasons after the fall of Saigon and Vietnamese workers, students and family members of foreigners who travelled overseas after the country opened up.

The host country of these expatriates can also affect their political leanings. For example, expatriates in socialist or former socialist countries like China or Russia may have different views towards the CPV compared to Vietnamese living in the United States or Europe. Factors such as the length of time these expatriates have been living overseas, the frequency of their visits to Vietnam, and the channels through which they access information about political developments in Vietnam also contribute to their perceptions. While overseas Vietnamese generally tend to be more critical of the ruling regime, those factors may also influence their political view.

The second important aspect to consider is the respondents' affiliation with the CPV. While this primarily pertains to whether a voter is a member of the CPV, the issue of whether this affiliation should encompass their immediate family also requires examination. It is not uncommon for children to follow their parents' career paths in Vietnam. Despite recent declines in the attractiveness of state-sector employment, such positions continue to be highly coveted due to their stability, social position and various official and unofficial advantages. As previously discussed, nepotism is widespread in Vietnam, with an unwritten rule ensuring that children of government officials often secure positions within their parents' organizations. Consequently, it is frequent for households to include multiple CPV members, and children of CPV affiliates are likely to be influenced by their parents' political alignment. The respondents' age, education level and gender may also provide insightful information into the perceptions of Vietnamese voters.

Given the sensitive political environment during the 2021 National Assembly Election, questions regarding the political system of the country were omitted from the survey, and the focus was solely on the election itself. During the data collection for the 2016 survey, some voters outright refused to respond to the survey after reviewing the list of questions, citing sensitivity.

While not all criticism of the CPV leads to punishment, Article 88 (Conducting propaganda against the Socialist Republic of Vietnam), Article 117 (Making, storing, spreading information, materials, items for the purpose of opposing the State of Socialist Republic of Vietnam) and Article 331 (Abusing democratic freedoms to infringe upon the interests of the State, lawful rights and interests of organizations and/or citizens) of the 2015 Criminal Code are frequently employed against dissidents who openly express their opinions. Investigation and enforcement are entrusted to the police apparatus, and interpretation of such laws falls within the purview of the courts, both of which are under the influence, if not direct control, of the CPV. Consequently, involving in surveys on subjects such as democracy poses risks to not only researchers but also respondents.

Despite their flaws, the 2016 and 2021 surveys have provided intriguing perspectives and insights on the perceptions of Vietnamese voters.

Notes

1. General Statistics Office of Vietnam, "Thông cáo báo chí về kết quả chính thức Tổng điều tra nông thôn, nông nghiệp và thủy sản năm 2016" [Press release on official results of the 2016 Rural, Agricultural, and Fishery Census], 2019, https://www.gso.gov.vn/su-kien/2019/04/thong-cao-bao-chi-ve-ket-qua-chinh-thuc-tong-dieu-tra-nong-thon-nong-nghiep-va-thuy-san-nam-2016/ (accessed 17 July 2024).

2. *Communist Party of Vietnam Online Newspaper*, "Chủ tịch Quốc hội Nguyễn Phú Trọng trả lời phỏng vấn báo Express Ấn Độ" [President Nguyen Phu Trong's interview with the Indian Express], 27 January 2010, https://dangcongsan.vn/thoi-su/chu-tich-quoc-hoi-nguyen-phu-trong-tra-loi-phong-van-bao-express-an-do-8846.html (accessed 17 July 2024).

3. The Economist Intelligence Unit, "Democracy Index 2016", 2016, https://www.eiu.com/public/topical_report.aspx?campaignid=DemocracyIndex2016 (accessed 17 July 2024).

4. Daron Acemoglu, "Democracy Does Boost Economic Growth", World Economic Forum, 8 May 2014, https://www.weforum.org/agenda/2014/05/democracy-boost-economic-growth/ (accessed 17 July 2024).

5. Hristos Doucouliagos and Mehmet Ali Ulubaşoğlu, "Democracy and Economic Growth: A Meta-Analysis", *American Journal of Political Science* 52, no. 1 (2008): 61–83, https://doi.org/10.1111/j.1540-5907.2007.00299.x.

6. Salvatore Babones, "Vietnam's GDP Is Just 11 Years behind China, and Growing Rapidly", *Forbes*, 9 November 2017, https://www.forbes.com/sites/salvatorebabones/2017/11/09/vietnam-is-following-in-chinas-footsteps-in-gdp-growth-at-least (accessed 17 July 2024).

7. PricewaterhouseCoopers (PwC), "The Long View: How Will the Global Economic Order Change by 2050?" February 2017, https://www.pwc.com/gx/en/research-insights/economy/the-world-in-2050.html (accessed 17 July 2024).

8. Nguyen Cuong, "Chủ tịch nước: 'Người trong cuộc mới thấy chống tham nhũng cam go, quyết liệt'" [President of Vietnam: only insiders could understand the ongoing fierce fight against corruption], Infonet, 7 July 2017, https://infonet.vietnamnet.vn/chu-tich-nuoc-nguoi-trong-cuoc-moi-thay-chong-tham-nhung-cam-go-quyet-liet-82771.html (accessed 17 July 2024).

9. Voice of Vietnam, "Toàn văn phát biểu của Tổng Bí thư tại Hội nghị của Chính phủ" [Complete transcript of the general secretary of the Communist Party of Vietnam's speech at the government's conference on December 28th, 2017], 28 December 2017, https://vov.vn/chinh-tri/dang/toan-van-phat-bieu-cua-tong-bi-thu-tai-hoi-nghi-cua-chinh-phu-712527.vov (accessed 17 July 2024).

10. *An ninh Thủ đô*, "Chính phủ báo cáo Quốc hội về công tác phòng chống tham nhũng" [The cabinet's report to the National Assembly on corruption prevention], 6 November 2017, http://anninhthudo.vn/chinh-tri-xa-hoi/chinh-phu-bao-cao-quoc-hoi-ve-cong-tac-phong-chong-tham-nhung/747095.antd (accessed 17 July 2024).

11. *VietNamNet*, "Bỏ biên chế để giảm gánh nặng 11 triệu người ăn lương nhà nước" [Reduce the burden on the state budget by reducing the 11 million people on the state payroll], 9 June 2016, http://vietnamnet.vn/vn/thoi-su/chinh-tri/bo-bien-che-de-giam-ganh-nang-11-trieu-nguoi-an-luong-309270.html (accessed 17 July 2024).

12. Nguyen Thi Mai Anh, "Nâng cao chất lượng đảng viên – Vấn đề cốt lõi để xây dựng Đảng trong sạch, vững mạnh trong tình hình hiện nay" [Improving party members' quality – the core issue in building a strong and transparent party in the current situation], *Communist Review*, 2016, http://www.tapchicongsan.org.vn/Home/ Nghiencuu-Traodoi/2016/40378/Nang-cao-chat-luong-dang-vien-Van-de-cot-loi-de. aspx (accessed 17 July 2024).

13. Michael J. Jeffrey, "Who Had the Lowest Gallup Presidential Job Approval Rating?" Gallup, 26 December 2019, https://news.gallup.com/poll/272765/lowest-gallup-presidential-job-approval-rating.aspx (accessed 17 July 2024).

14. Pew Research Center, "Voters Rarely Switch Parties, But Recent Shifts Further Educational, Racial Divergence", 4 August 2020, https://www.pewresearch.org/ politics/2020/08/04/voters-rarely-switch-parties-but-recent-shifts-further-educational-racial-divergence/ (accessed 17 July 2024).

15. Nguyen An, "Cử tri bỏ phiếu thay người khác là vi phạm Luật Bầu cử" [Voting in Other People's Stead Is a Violation of Election Law], Voice of Vietnam, 6 May 2016, http://vov.vn/chinh-tri/quoc-hoi/cu-tri-bo-phieu-thay-nguoi-khac-la-vi-pham-luat-bau-cu-507842.vov (accessed 17 July 2024).

16. PAPI, "2017 Annual Report", 2018, https://papi.org.vn/eng/bao-cao/?year-report=2017 (accessed 17 July 2024).

17. *Cử tri chuyên nghiệp* [in Vietnamese].

18. Trong Phu, "Tình trạng 'đại cử tri, cử tri chuyên nghiệp, đại biểu cử tri' còn phổ biến" [The Prevalence of 'Grand Electors, Professional Voters, and Delegate Voters'], *Tuoi Tre Online*, 12 July 2023, https://tuoitre.vn/tinh-trang-dai-cu-tri-cu-tri-chuyen-nghiep-dai-bieu-cu-tri-con-pho-bien-2023071209565672.htm (accessed 6 December 2024).

19. Vietnam News Agency, "Danh sách 494 đại biểu quốc hội khóa XIV, nhiệm kỳ 2016–2021" [The list of 494 members of the Fourteenth National Assembly, 2016–2021], 2016, https://infographics.vn/dai-bieu-quoc-hoi.vna (accessed 17 July 2024).

20. National Assembly of the Socialist Republic of Vietnam Portal, "Thông tin đại biểu khóa 14" [Profiles of the members of the Fourteenth National Assembly], 2016, http://dbqh.na.gov.vn/XIV/Daibieu.aspx (accessed 17 July 2024).

21. Nguyen Thi Yen Mai, "Tây Ninh xây dựng Đề án khắc phục tình trạng đảng viên bỏ sinh hoạt đảng" [Tay Ninh district to propose solution for CPV members who do not attend regular local party cell meetings], *Xây Dựng Đảng*, 12 September 2021, https://www.xaydungdang.org.vn/co-so-dang/tay-ninh-xay-dung-de-an-khac-phuc-tinh-trang-dang-vien-bo-sinh-hoat-dang-15663 (accessed 17 July 2024).

22. In additional to the Charter of the CPV, there are several decisions about this. See Decision 102-QĐ/TW, Decision 09-QĐ/VPTW and Decision 29-QĐ/TWV.

23. Bui Lan and Bui Hung, "Công tác bầu cử đại biểu quốc hội khóa XV và đại biểu HĐND các cấp nhiệm kỳ 2021-2026 thành công tốt đẹp" [The elections of deputies to National Assembly and of deputies to People's Councils were successfully completed], National Assembly of Vietnam Portal, 2021, https://quochoi.vn/tintuc/pages/tin-hoat-dong-cua-quoc-hoi.aspx?ItemID=56950 (accessed 17 July 2024).

24. Statistics of Japan, "在留外国人統計" [Statistics on foreigners in Japan], 2022, https://www.e-stat.go.jp/stat-search/files?page=1&layout=datalist&toukei=00250012&tstat=000001018034 (accessed 17 July 2024).

25. Dang Minh Khoi, "Cộng đồng người Việt Nam ở nước ngoài ngày càng lớn mạnh và gắn bó với quê hương" [Vietnamese diaspora communities are growing larger and their ties with Vietnam are becoming stronger], *Quân Đội Nhân Dân*, 24 November 2020, https://www.qdnd.vn/xa-hoi/cac-van-de/cong-dong-nguoi-viet-nam-o-nuoc-ngoai-ngay-cang-lon-manh-va-gan-bo-voi-que-huong-644730 (accessed 17 July 2024).

26. PAPI, "2021 Annual Report", 2022, https://papi.org.vn/eng/bao-cao/?year-report=2021 (accessed 17 July 2024).

27. Ibid.

28. *Communist Party of Vietnam Online Newspaper*, "Công bố danh sách chính thức 868 người ứng cử đại biểu Quốc hội khóa XV" [Official list of 868 candidates for the Fifteenth National Assembly], 27 April 2021, https://dangcongsan.vn/thoi-su/cong-bo-danh-sach-chinh-thuc-868-nguoi-ung-cu-dai-bieu-quoc-hoi-khoa-xv-579373.html (accessed 17 July 2024).

29. Probability of Selecting All Winning Candidates:

    1. 4/2 Districts. The probability P_{4,2} is:
       P_{4,2} = 1/6
    2. 5/3 Districts. The probability P_{5,3} is:
       P_{5,3} = 1/10

       Overall Probability Calculation: P_{total} = (52/184 * 1/6) + (132/184 * 1/10)
       The overall probability that a random voter in the election chooses all the candidates who eventually get elected, considering the distribution of different types of districts, is approximately 11.88 per cent.

30. *Hạt giống đỏ* [in Vietnamese].

31. Carlyle A. Thayer, "Recent Political Developments: Constitutional Change and the 1992 Elections", in *Vietnam and the Rule of Law: Political and Social Change Monograph no. 19*, edited by Carlyle A. Thayer and David G. Marr (Canberra: Department of Political and Social Change, Research School of Pacific Studies, The Australian National University, 1993).

32. Edmund Malesky and Paul Schuler, "Why Do Single-Party Regimes Hold Elections? An Analysis of Candidate Data in Vietnam's 2007 National Assembly Contest", presented at APSA Annual Meeting, Boston, MA, August 2008.

33. Vietnam Government Portal, "Công bố danh sách 496 đại biểu Quốc hội khóa XIV" [Official list of 496 deputies of the Fourteenth National Assembly], 10 June 2016, https://baochinhphu.vn/cong-bo-danh-sach-496-dai-bieu-quoc-hoi-khoa-xiv-102203984.htm (accessed 17 July 2024).

34. *Dan Tri*, "9 nhân sự Trung ương giới thiệu không trúng cử đại biểu Quốc hội" [9 central personnel nominated but not elected as National Assembly deputies], 15 July 2021, https://dantri.com.vn/xa-hoi/9-nhan-su-trung-uong-gioi-thieu-khong-trung-cu-dai-bieu-quoc-hoi-20210715105804036.htm (accessed 17 July 2024).

35. Voice of Vietnam, "101 ủy viên Trung ương Đảng trúng cử đại biểu Quốc hội khóa XV" [101 Central Committee members elected as deputies of the Fifteenth National Assembly], 12 June 2021, https://vov.vn/chinh-tri/101-uy-vien-trung-uong-dang-trung-cu-dai-bieu-quoc-hoi-khoa-xv-865300.vov (accessed 17 July 2024).

36. *Người Lao Động*, "Cùng đồng phạm gây thiệt hại 761 tỉ đồng, cựu Bí thư Bình Dương Trần Văn Nam lĩnh án 7 năm tù" [Along with accomplices causing damage of 761 billion VND, former Secretary of Binh Duong Tran Van Nam sentenced to 7 years in prison], 30 August 2022, https://nld.com.vn/phap-luat/cung-dong-pham-gay-thiet-hai-761-ti-dong-cuu-bi-thu-binh-duong-tran-van-nam-linh-an-7-nam-tu-20220830175711272.htm (accessed 17 July 2024).

37. The Economist Intelligence Unit, "Democracy Index 2022: Frontline Democracy and the Battle for Ukraine", 2023, https://pages.eiu.com/rs/753-RIQ-438/images/DI-final-version-report.pdf (accessed 17 July 2024).

38. World Bank, "GDP Growth (Annual %) – Vietnam", 2022, https://data.worldbank.org/indicator/NY.GDP.MKTP.KD.ZG?locations=VN (accessed 17 July 2024).

39. Todd Pollack, Guy Thwaites, Maia Rabaa, Marc Choisy, Rogier van Doorn, and Duong H. Luong, "Emerging COVID-19 Success Story: Vietnam's Commitment to Containment", 2020, https://ourworldindata.org/covid-exemplar-vietnam (accessed 17 July 2024).

7

Of the People, By the People, For the People

In mid-March 2024, during a private conversation, the author's sixty-seven-year-old uncle, a longstanding member of the CPV who fought for the North during the Vietnam War, predicted that the then State President Vo Van Thuong would be dismissed. When asked for the reason behind his prediction, he ascribed it to the sudden cancellation of the visit by the King of the Netherlands. The author's uncle further explained that State President Thuong had extended the invitation to King Willem-Alexander to visit Vietnam, and as the head of state, the responsibility to receive the Dutch monarch would naturally fall to Mr Thuong. However, the visit was quietly cancelled at the last minute, causing great confusion. This can only mean that Mr Thuong's status as head of state is somewhat compromised, and he may no longer be able to fulfil his duties. The reason, according to the author's uncle, was President Thuong's involvement with Phuc Son group, a construction entity under investigation for corruption and fraud.

Reports regarding the official visit of the King of the Netherlands were initially covered by the state-controlled media; however, it appears that most of these reports have since been removed. The abrupt cancellation of the visit, which occurred at the eleventh hour, received minimal coverage from domestic media outlets. Nonetheless, foreign media extensively reported on the cancellation. BBC highlighted that the stated reason for the cancellation was "internal affairs" and suggested the possibility of Mr Thuong's involvement in a corruption scandal.[1] The rumour that Mr Thuong allegedly received 60 billion VND from the Phuc Son group, purportedly to construct a worship house for his clan, was also reported by VOA.[2] This information, as my uncle explained, was discussed within his circle of acquaintances, some of whom are retired military personnel and police officers, who frequently engage in discussions about Vietnamese politics.

People are clearly aware of the corruption taking place around them but usually take it for granted. The compulsory military service system in Vietnam is another example. Male citizens between the ages of eighteen and twenty-seven are required to serve two years of compulsory military service. Since serving for two years may cost a conscript his career and there is a risk of hazing, many people actively avoid it. On the other hand, conscripted personnel receive a monthly allowance and are supported with job training and employment upon discharge, so many poor families want to enlist their children. Recruiters can choose who to enlist and have actively abused their power by taking bribes from families with male children suitable for compulsory military service either to exempt or conscript them. Most people put up with this practice and pay the requested bribe because they are both victims and culprits in this situation. This is rather ironic because many of those who pay the bribery to avoid conscription are also the people who glorify military service on social media networks. The same scenario can be observed in many public sectors, only in different scenarios.

Many family members of the author's mother have fought in service to the CPV, with some currently holding party membership and working in the government, who frequently discuss politics in private. Despite benefitting from the system, each has eventually grown disillusioned with it. However, while acknowledging the system's shortcomings, they advocate for its preservation. Anecdotes and critiques of high-ranking officials are deemed taboo, often only shared amusingly yet discreetly among family members. Uncertain of the extent of their freedom of speech, they often opt for silence in public to ensure safety. The author vividly recalls a summer day in first grade when, while walking home and singing the national anthem he had just learnt at school, he was abruptly silenced by his First Indochina War veteran grandfather, who warned of potential police scrutiny for perceived mockery or provocation.

The author's father, who was born in 1961 into a South Vietnamese family with many members who had worked for the Republic of Vietnam and migrated to the United States, holds a different perspective. He harbours a negative view towards the CPV and northerners in general. Although he usually refrains from expressing his political opinions openly to avoid potential trouble, he can often be heard loudly criticizing the government when intoxicated. One might be inclined to assume that individuals from the South vehemently oppose communism and the CPV, while those from the North favour it. However, such sentiments are more nuanced. Despite his regret over the collapse of South Vietnam and his negative perception of the CPV, the author's father takes great pride in being born on the Unification Day, viewing this day as a significant victory for the Vietnamese people in their struggle to unify the country against overwhelming odds.

When discussing their past, the author's family members in the South often say that they enlisted[3] or drafted[4] to fight for the United States, emphasizing that "if you did not work for the Americans, there was nothing we could do then". While many Vietnamese describe the Vietnam War as a conflict to liberate the South from American imperialism, others emphasize the aspect of national unification, arguing that there was no liberation without occupation. For many Southerners, the Vietnam War was not their conflict; a conflict in which they were merely bystanders. Conversely, many overseas Vietnamese, particularly refugees and their descendants, see the Vietnam War as their struggle against communism, blaming American betrayal for their defeat and exile.

Like many other children born in a unified Vietnam, the author was exposed to state propaganda from a young age. However, the author also encountered criticisms of communism, the ruling party and various perspectives on the Vietnam War from individuals who fought on both sides. This exposure prompted the author to undertake a personal quest to understand how Vietnamese truly view their rulers as for better or worse, the CPV has been playing a central role in shaping Vietnam's past, present and future.

Throughout its history, the CPV has weathered military conflicts with some of the most powerful armies of its time and collapse of communism. Scholars have attributed the CPV's resilience to several factors, including strong organizational structures, adaptability, competent leadership, divided opposition and external support. One of the most prominent characteristics that has helped the CPV survive is its adaptability. Although the Party has made its fair share of military, economic and diplomatic mistakes, it has consistently rectified them before they became irreversible. Both during wartime and peacetime the CPV has been afforded the opportunity to rectify its mistakes, thanks in no small part to its perceived legitimacy.

CPV has based its legitimacy on the following pillars: achievements rooted in traditional values, Ho Chi Minh's charismatic leadership and socioeconomic performance with the promise of a socialist future. However, past achievements and charismatic leadership will not last forever, socialism lacks substantial achievements, and economic growth is accompanied by a widening rich-poor gap, staggering inequality and widespread corruption. As such, the CPV has been turning to democratic legitimacy, particularly through the election and operation of the National Assembly, to bolster its authority.

The most notable improvements to the National Assembly elections occurred with the ratification of the 1992 Election Law. This law introduced several changes aimed at making the National Assembly elections more substantive and less nominal. Most importantly, the minimum number of candidates had to exceed that of elected officials, and self-nominated candidates were allowed to run for elections.

Subsequent election laws and revisions added further changes to make the National Assembly elections appear more genuine.

However, the scrutiny of candidates through consultative conferences have also become more sophisticated, and the role of the CPV-controlled Fatherland Front had become increasingly dominant. On the surface it might seem that the CPV is making a gambit by sacrificing current materials for long-term gains, here by granting the National Assembly more autonomy in exchange for democracy authority. While improvements to National Assembly elections and functions are undeniable, ultimately these changes are unlikely to result in a transition to a more democratic system or challenge the monopoly of power held by the CPV.

Most seats in the National Assembly are occupied by CPV members, with the remainder held by non-members nominated by the CPV and its umbrella organizations. Self-nominated candidates have little chance to pass all the consultative conferences and even slimmer chances of being elected at all. While upsets do occur, such as when centrally nominated candidates fail to secure seats, these are manageable risks for the CPV, as the failure of these candidates can be used for propaganda purposes, and nominally independent candidates who win their seats are also nominated by the Party. In reality, there is little risk in this game between red pawns and blue pawns.

This reality is masked using terms such as "democratic centralism" or "socialist democracy", which are indoctrinated to the masses via a multi-levelled propaganda mechanism, from school textbooks for children to advanced political classes for high-ranking government officials. Nevertheless, although Ho Chi Minh's adherents claim that the government of Vietnam is "of the people, by the people, and for the people", not all Vietnamese believe in this claim. Most Vietnamese voters acknowledge the fact that they have little choice during legislative elections. However, they are tolerant of the CPV's rule because their perception of democracy differs from that of their counterparts in the West. They sometimes confuse improvements in the standard of living with advancements in political freedom and can be placated with "bread and circuses".

Nevertheless, it is not inconceivable for the CPV to genuinely claim democratic legitimacy. Opposition to the CPV focuses on criticism of the regime's human rights record, corruption, governance, socialist ideology and dependence on China. However, these opposition groups are fragmented and lack actual achievements, with many based overseas and receiving foreign support. Many among these groups also base their legitimacy on the Republic of Vietnam and its legacy, which was in fact scarcely democratic or liberal and is regarded by many Vietnamese as an American puppet.

Even if multiparty elections were held in Vietnam, the CPV, playing its cards right, could stand a considerable chance of winning a free and fair election. It is not uncommon for a party to retain power for an extended period following a transition to a more democratic political system, particularly in Asia, as exemplified by the experiences of the Liberal Democratic Party of Japan, the Indian National Congress in India and the People's Action Party in Singapore. The CPV could undoubtedly draw lessons from these instances if it opts to liberalize the political system, an idea that has been vehemently opposed until now.

As the author writes the last chapter of this book, more and more high-ranking officials are being prosecuted. As of May 2024, out of the two hundred members of the elite Thirteenth Central Committee of the CPV, who were intended to serve until 2026, twenty-one have been dismissed, with eleven of them facing criminal prosecution. Six of the dismissed officials were members of the Politburo, the highest echelon of the CPV's power hierarchy.[5] While top leaders such as former State President Vo Van Thuong and former Chairman of the National Assembly Vuong Dinh Hue were spared prosecution, their dismissal and the extensive coverage by state-sanctioned domestic media were unprecedented and signify efforts to combat corruption and improve governance to restore the CPV's reputation.

While efforts to shake up the system were spearheaded from within the Party as always, pressure from the population also plays a significant role. Some scholars point out that the CPV can respond positively to constructive criticism from its subjects. This demonstrates that, in its own manner, even if it does not entirely conform to Western democratic criteria, the CPV is not completely averse to listening to those under its rule. Nevertheless, while anti-corruption efforts are well-received by many Vietnamese, criticism of the ruling regime remains taboo for the majority. During the final period of writing this book, requests for interviews and endorsements were almost always turned down, despite the author's status as a "family member",[6] as described by a CPV member: "The situation in Vietnam is very chaotic now, and we cannot help you because we do not know if we could get into trouble for that or not." While some have become increasingly outspoken, the majority remain fearful of expressing their opinions despite their dissatisfaction with the system.

He who is silent is taken to agree.

Latin proverb

While a democratic government derives its authority from its citizens through free and fair elections, the survival of a dictatorship depends on the tacit silence of the majority. In a democracy, citizens have various legal means to express their disapproval, with voting being the most powerful. In non-democratic systems where free and fair elections are rare, and acts of dissent are limited or prohibited, the options become more constrained: either take risks to voice your dissent or remain silent. For most people, this is a simple choice.

Nevertheless, while it appears unlikely in the foreseeable future, a peaceful and orderly transition to a more democratic system would be beneficial not only to Vietnam as a country but also to the CPV in the long term. People protesting corruption and unjust land confiscation usually carry the red flag with a golden star and Ho Chi Minh's portrait, showing that they still have trust in the CPV to support their rightful resistance and that they still acknowledge the CPV's authority. With the right moves, the CPV is well-positioned to win the gambit to gain democratic legitimacy through free and fair elections and fulfilling Ho Chi Minh's claim that the government is "of the people, by the people, and for the people", instead of relying on a rigged game of blue pawns and red pawns. This transition, however, necessitates not only determination from within the Party but also the voice of the silent majority.

Notes

1. BBC Vietnamese, "Vua và Hoàng hậu Hà Lan hủy thăm vào phút chót 'vì chuyện nội bộ của Việt Nam'" [King and Queen of the Netherlands cancel visit at the last minute 'due to internal matters of Vietnam'], 15 March 2024, https://www.bbc.com/vietnamese/articles/c3ge9v4n91qo (accessed 17 July 2024).
2. VOA Tiếng Việt, "Ông Võ Văn Thưởng bị bãi miễn các chức vụ: Liệu có thỏa đáng?" [Vo Van Thuong dismissed from positions: is it justified?], 21 March 2024, https://www.voatiengviet.com/a/ong-vo-van-thuong-bi-bai-mien-cac-chuc-vu-lieu-co-thoa-dang-/7536806.html (accessed 17 July 2024).
3. *Đi lính cho Mỹ* [in Vietnamese].
4. *Bị bắt đi lính* [in Vietnamese].
5. *VnExpress*, "26 ủy viên, nguyên ủy viên Trung ương bị kỷ luật 3 năm qua" [26 incumbent and former central committee members disciplined in the past 3 years], 13 June 2024, https://VnExpress.net/26-uy-vien-nguyen-uy-vien-trung-uong-bi-ky-luat-3-nam-qua-4758062.html (accessed 17 July 2024).
6. *Người nhà* is a Vietnamese term that indicates the status of a trustworthy insider and does not necessarily denote an actual family member.

Index

E

Early Le dynasty, 27
Eastern Bloc, 56, 86, 89–91
economic collectivism, 176n27
economic development
  vs. democracy, 257–59
  GDP, 63, 181, 302
  and living standards, 8–9, 11, 59, 62
  as performance legitimacy, 10–11, 20, 49–50, 84
economic mismanagement, 141–43n81
economic plans, 55–56
economic sector, 56, 60, 61, 63, 79n134
Economist Intelligence Unit, 254, 301
education, 34, 40–41, 88, 91–92, 160, 261
Eisenhower, 44
elected representatives, 186, 191, 240n52
election law
  on administrative unit, 239n48
  on candidates, 194–97, 314
  on election organizing groups, 207–8
  for National Assembly elections, 185–90, 239n44, 239n45
  on photo taking, 204–5
elections
  in authoritarian regimes, 181–85
  campaigning for, 195–96, 240n55, 268, 291–92
  free and fair, 85, 251–52, 261
  law on (see election law)
  organizing groups for, 207–8

process of, 189–92
results of, 274–75, 279–83
  See also democracy; voting
elites, 6, 23, 25, 68n8, 78n113, 88, 92
Ellsberg, Daniel, 36
embezzlement, 102, 139n68, 141–42n81, 224, 246n114
emperor, 43, 71n45
enlistment, oaths of, 30
Epco-Minh Phung case, 224
equality, 188–90, 253, 262. See also inequality
ethnicity, 26, 112, 136n37, 171, 189
European Union, 85, 90, 91, 98
exile, 88
expatriates, 202–3, 264–65, 305–6.
  See also overseas citizens
exports, 63
external pressure, 68n8. See also Western influence

F

Facebook, 128, 131–32, 170
fact-checking, 129
family connections, 113–19
farmers, 53–55, 77–78n113, 164–65, 269–70. See also peasants; proletariats; workers
father-son relationship (*cha-con*), 71n41
feudalism, 21–26, 50, 54
fidelity (*tín*), 24–26
filial piety, 30
financial damage, 108, 141–43n81
Finland, 158
firewall, 128, 131

About the Author

Nguyen Hoang Thanh Danh was born to a mother who is a member of the Communist Party of Vietnam and a father from the South. Domestic quarrels sometimes escalated into ideological name-calling, leaving many questions in the mind of an innocent child about his country, his people and the Party. Danh began his doctoral studies at Waseda University in 2015 to answer the questions he had as a child, and after completing them in 2020, he continued his journey. This book is the result of his eight-year effort. Danh currently teaches Politics of Southeast Asia at Hosei University and Vietnamese at Showa Women's University, both located in Tokyo, Japan.